State and Society in Transition
The Politics of Institutional Ref[
1838–1852

Examining the process of state formation as it occurred in the Eastern Townships of Quebec following the unification of Upper and Lower Canada, J.I. Little argues that institutional reform was not simply imposed by the government but was the result of a complex process of interaction between the state and the local community. While past studies look at the reform process in the post-Rebellion period largely from the perspective of the central government, *State and Society in Transition* focuses on the significant role the local population played in the establishment of new public institutions.

Using a variety of documentary sources, including hundreds of petitions, letters, and reports to the government, Little traces the complex relationship between community life and government regulation. He reveals that at the same time that development of responsible government was leading to increasingly centralized authority at the provincial government level, a persistent sense of localism was forcing the state to decentralize its key institutions at the community level. The local population of this American, British, and French-Canadian settled corner of Quebec, Little shows, clearly helped to exert an important influence on the evolution of the educational, legal, social welfare, and municipal systems.

State and Society in Transition makes a major contribution to our understanding of the transitional era in Canada by taking into account not only the dialectical process between the centre and periphery but also the impact of institutional reform on the development of a little-known area of the country.

J.I. LITTLE is professor of history, Simon Fraser University.

STUDIES ON THE HISTORY OF QUEBEC/
ÉTUDES D'HISTOIRE DU QUÉBEC

John Dickinson and Brian Young
Series Editors/Directeurs de la collection

Habitants and Merchants in Seventeenth-Century Montreal
Louise Dechêne

Crofters and Habitants
Settler Society, Economy, and Culture in a Quebec Township,
1848–1881
J.I. Little

The Christie Seigneuries
Estate Management and Settlement in the Upper Richelieu Valley,
1760–1859
Françoise Noël

La Prairie en Nouvelle-France, 1647–1760
Louis Lavallée

The Politics of Codification
The Lower Canadian Civil Code of 1866
Brian Young

Arvida au Saguenay
Naissance d'une ville industrielle
José E. Igartua

State and Society in Transition
The Politics of Institutional Reform in the Eastern Townships,
1838–1852
J.I. Little

State and Society in Transition

*The Politics
of Institutional Reform
in the Eastern Townships,
1838–1852*

J.I. LITTLE

McGill-Queen's University Press
Montreal & Kingston · London · Buffalo

© McGill-Queen's University Press 1997
ISBN 0-7735-1544-5 (cloth)
ISBN 0-7735-1545-3 (paper)

Legal deposit second quarter 1997
Bibliothèque nationale du Québec

Printed in Canada on acid-free paper

This book has been published with the help of a grant from the Humanities
and Social Sciences Federation of Canada, using funds provided by the
Social Sciences and Humanities Research Council of Canada. Funds have
also been received from the University Publications Fund, Simon Fraser
University.

McGill-Queen's University Press acknowledges the support received for its
publishing program from the Canada Council's Block Grants program.

Canadian Cataloguing in Publication Data

Little, J.I. (John Irvine), 1947-
    State and society in transition: the politics of institutional reform in the
    Eastern Townships, 1838-1852
    (Studies on the history of Quebec - Études d'histoires du Québec)
    ISBN 0-7735-1544-5 (bound).–
    ISBN 0-7735-1545-3 (pbk.)
    1. Eastern Townships (Quebec) – History. 2. Eastern Townships (Québec) –
    Politics and government. 3. Eastern Townships (Quebec) – Social
    conditions. I. Title. II. Series: Studies on the history of Quebec.
    FC2943.5.L55 1997   971.4'602   C96-901051-6
    F1054.E13L55 1977

This book was typeset by Typo Litho Composition Inc.
in 10/12 Baskerville.

To the memory of Edith (Taylor) McCrea and Margaret (Marshall) Little

Contents

Tables

Acknowledgments

I would like to thank the Social Sciences Research Council for providing a research grant as well as a publication grant through the Social Sciences Federation. My thanks also to Simon Fraser University for the various grants over the years, including one to help subsidize this publication, and the sabbatical leave that enabled me to complete this project.

I also wish to express my appreciation to all the archives staff members who made the time I spent in their institutions so enjoyable. Pat Kennedy of the National Archives has been especially helpful in guiding me through the Byzantine complexities of the government records. I would also particularly like to thank Pamela Miller, formerly of the McCord Museum, for granting me access to the Hale Papers while the museum was undergoing renovation, Pierre Jean of the Musée Beaulne in Coaticook for placing the Child letters at my disposal, Helen Colby of Stanstead for kindly opening the Colby Papers to me, Marion Phelps for patiently guiding me through the wonderful archives of the Brome County Historical Society, and the staff at the Ascot Township town hall for providing me with the local township records. In addition, I have received invaluable assistance at the Archives nationales branches in Montreal and Sherbrooke, the Sherbrooke Historical Society Archives, and the Eastern Townships Research Centre at Bishop's University.

I wish to thank Steven Moore for his research assistance in the education records at Quebec, and Wendie Nelson, Tina Loo, René Hardy, Brian Young, and the anonymous reviewers for their many helpful comments. I greatly appreciate their advice, and take full responsibility for all the shortcomings of this study. To this list must be added Philip Cercone and Joan McGilvray for cheerfully supporting me through another publication with McGill-Queen's University Press, and for assigning this manuscript to such an excellent editor as Diane Mew.

Finally, my heartfelt appreciation once again to my extended Eastern Townships family for their kind hospitality, and to Andrea, Mark, and Brett for their love and support.

The counterfeiters of Brome and Missisquoi counties were known as cogniacers because an early centre of operations had been at Farnham's Corner on the road known as Cogniac Street. The plate from which this $3 American note was printed appears to have been recovered from a stream in Brome Township where it was hidden during a raid in 1853 on the counterfeiters operating in a local sawmill. According to one local historian, the business was largely master-minded by Seneca Paige of Dunham, who was Missisquoi's MLA from 1851 to 1853. (Brome County Historical Association)

Edward Hale. This photograph by Notman, embellished by the painter Henry Sandham, was taken after the aging Hale became chancellor of the University of Bishop's College in 1866. As member of Sydenham's Special Council, warden of the Sherbrooke District Council, and Sherbrooke's first MLA after the Act of Union, Hale was the most powerful political figure in the region during the early post-Rebellion era. However, he was too much the patrician to play an effective role in exerting political pressure for economic development or establishing a party machine. (Bishop's University Art Collection, Lennoxville)

The Hale family residence, Sleepy Hollow, approximately seven years before Edward Hale's death in 1875. Despite his wealth and social prominence, Hale and his wife remained in the same rather modest farmhouse they had built after moving to Orford Township, near Sherbrooke, in 1834. (NA, PA119326)

Alexander Tilloch Galt. As local commissioner of the British American Land Company, Alexander Galt's chief concern during the 1840s and early 1850s was regional economic development. He played a key role in establishing industries in the town of Sherbrooke and promoting construction of the province's first trunk railway line from Montreal to Portland, Maine, through Sherbrooke. On the other hand, he was able to exert enough political pressure to prevent the Sherbrooke District Council from collecting taxes on the company's vast land holdings.

Marcus Child, artist and date unknown. Marcus Child of Stanstead was the longest
serving MLA from the Eastern Townships by the time of his defeat in the 1844 election, when he finally succumbed to the conservative trend in the region. However,
he continued to play an important local role as the county's senior justice of the
peace, and he became the St Francis District's first schools inspector in 1851 despite his earlier criticism of compulsory school taxes. (Stanstead Historical
Society)

Sherbrooke's second court house, begun in 1839, sixteen years after the establishment of the St Francis Judicial district. The imposing Greek Revival architecture presents a striking contrast to the rather untidy scene in the foreground. (NA, PA51827)

The Old Church Tavern on the Magog Road, halfway between Stanstead and Montreal. Given its location on the busiest thoroughfare in the Eastern Townships, this must have been a popular establishment for tired and thirsty travellers. Gray's map of 1863 suggests that nearly all roadside taverns had become "temperance houses" by that time. (Eastern Townships Research Centre, Eastern Townships Heritage Foundation Collection, PO20, 79-31-4A)

Stanstead North Meeting House, built in 1817. Even before the municipal system was introduced, residents gathered in buildings such as this to discuss local issues, hear political speeches, and elect township officers such as road overseers and fence viewers. This building also no doubt hosted itinerant preachers and a wide variety of social events. (Photo: J.I. Little, June 1996)

Melbourne Town Hall. Once the municipal system was established, substantial buildings such as this one were erected to serve the local government, a purpose it still fulfills today. (Photo: J.I. Little, June 1996)

Bolton Pass, William James Topley, 1912. When this photograph was taken the means of local transportation had not changed much in the previous century. However, the introduction of the municipal system in the 1840s resulted in improved road conditions, particularly in thinly settled, mountainous areas such as Bolton Township. (NA, PA 10707)

This undated photograph of a covered bridge at Sherbrooke illustrates the challenge presented to municipal authorities by the St Francis River. (NA, PA 51823)

Melbourne Township school, built *c.* 1826 by eight local families whose names are recorded on a plaque by the front door. Most rural schools were built of wood, even after government assistance for construction became available during the 1840s. School inspector Parmelee notes that this school also served as a meeting place for worship long before any church building was erected. (Photo: J.I. Little, June 1996)

The Old South School on Tibbits Hill, Brome Township, commenced in 1844. One of several stone schools built in Brome and Missisquoi counties during the 1840s, this building replaced a squared-log school erected on the same site in 1827. Two sisters who were students on opening day in 1846 recalled that "the teacher was an Irishman who wore a paper hat, and had a long cane or whip with which he could reach the pupils from his desk." This school did not close its doors until 1928. (Brome County Historical Society)

Knowlton Academy was built in 1854 with a donation from the prominent local entre-preneur and tory politician, Paul Holland Knowlton, and held in trust by the Church of England. By this time the region's newly appointed school inspectors were questioning the value of such government-subsidized but independent institutions. Conflict between the trustees and the local school board resulted in the academy closing and becoming a museum early this century. (NA, PA21409)

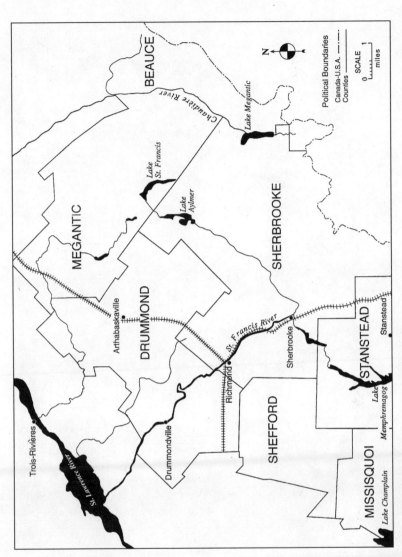

Map 1   Counties in the Eastern Townships, 1829-53

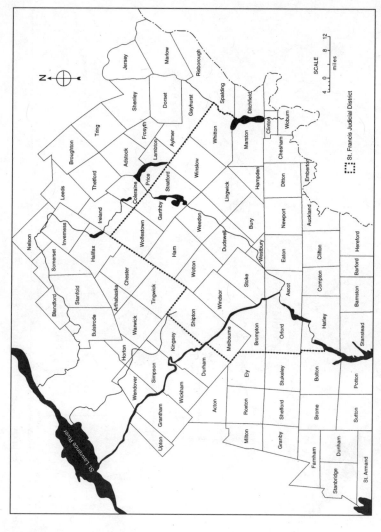

Map 2   Townships of the Eastern Townships
Source: Map of Montreal and the Eastern Townships (St Johns, Quebec: E.R. Smith & Son, 1897)

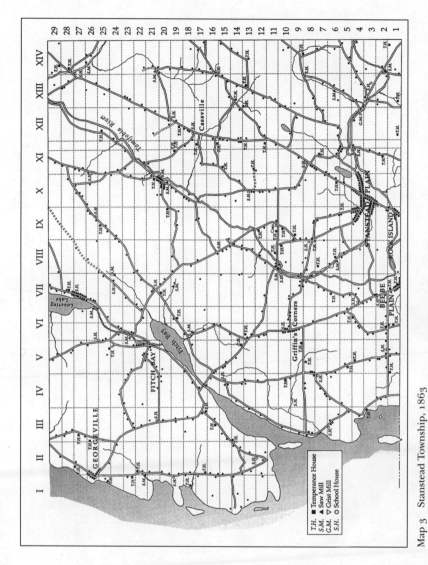

Map 3   Stanstead Township, 1863

Source: Map of the District of St. Francis, Canada East, from surveys... under the direction of O.W. Gray, Topographical Engr. Putnam and Gray, 1863, NA, NMC, 13807, no. 5/16.

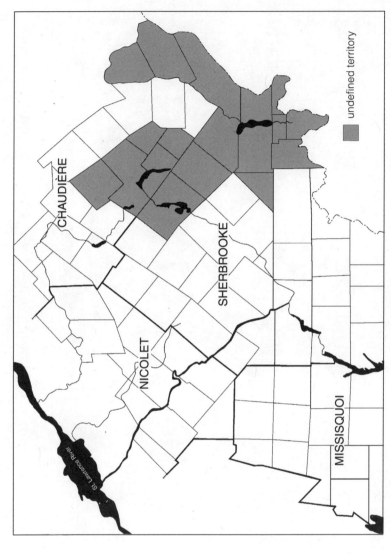

Map 4   Municipal Districts in the Eastern Townships, 1841–45
Source: Journals, Legislative Assembly, Canada, vol. 1 (1841), Appendix X, no. 8. (Durham and Kingsey were originally in the Sherbrooke District).

State and Society in Transition

Introduction

Political history becomes history in depth by becoming the history of power.

Jacques LeGoff[1]

The 1840s were a decade of transition in the newly formed Province of Canada, not only because they ushered in the railway and responsible government, but also because of fundamental reforms at the local level of society. The defeat of the Rebellions of 1837–38 brought an end to the constitutional and political impasse which in Lower Canada had pitted the elected Legislative Assembly against the governor and his appointed councillors – that is, the French-Canadian majority against the English-speaking merchant and official elite. While important initiatives had been taken towards establishing a more decentralized court system and a publicly funded school system, the state otherwise played no greater social role outside the main urban centres in 1837 than it had when the Legislative Assembly was first established in 1791. There were no municipal councils or school commissions to raise and administer taxes, no poor houses or asylums for the insane, no penitentiary, and only a few district jails.[2] Only in the vital realm of local communications had a hesitant step been taken in 1796 when legislation provided for the election of road overseers who would supervise the corvée (statute labour) system in each parish or township. In addition, a parish road surveyor would be appointed by the district's grand-voyer or his deputy, both officials with roots in the French regime.[3] Otherwise, the formal regulation of local public affairs remained largely in the hands of the centrally appointed justices of the peace whose administrative authority was strictly limited in scope.

Despite the fact that the radical Patriote MLAs attempted to pass legislation that would provide for the election of more parish officers, their failure to promote the municipal system suggests that the status quo generally suited the liberal-professional elites whose only rivals for prestige and influence at the local level thereby remained the parish priests. As long as French-Canadian settlement remained largely confined to the shores of the St Lawrence River and its major southern tributaries, there was little pressure to change fundamentally the traditional corvée system for the construction and maintenance of local roads.[4] As for the tories who controlled the Executive and Legislative Councils, they instinctively resisted any moves towards local democracy or state-supported social welfare. Even after the massive influx of Irish immigrants fleeing the potato famine in the mid to late 1840s, Lower Canada's poor remained largely at the mercy of ad hoc community support or charitable institutions organized by the various churches. And, since the colonial government's main economic role was to build canals to enhance Montreal's competitive position as a port for Upper Canadian and American wheat, the councillors found little reason to improve the transportation infrastructure within most of Lower Canada.

But when the population of the overcrowded seigneuries began to emigrate to the United States after the Rebellion, French-Canadian nationalists insisted that a network of colonization roads be extended into the rugged back country, a network which could only be maintained by an effective system of municipal government. And when railways began to replace canals as the key to commercial and industrial growth, the province's entrepreneurial elite turned to local ratepayers as a lucrative source of investment capital. Thus, keeping in mind that an unpopular and ineffective form of municipal government was introduced to the new Province of Canada by Governor Thomson (later Lord Sydenham) before such political pressures were exerted, one might state that the municipal system of Canada East developed as a product of both nationalist and capitalist impulses.

In addition, social-control theory argues that urbanization and industrialization heightened the elite's concerns about social disintegration and increased its need for a passive, regimented workforce. To achieve this, the elite instituted a modern, state-controlled school system. The problem with this hypothesis is that the basic school reforms were instituted while Canada was still largely a pre-industrial rural society.[5] Admitting that this was also true of the northern United States, Michael Katz has argued that the focus should be on the spread of wage-labour and the values associated with capitalism rather than on urbanization and industrialization. Katz's emphasis on the rise of institutions to deal with "crime, poverty, disease, mental illness, juvenile delinquency, the blind, the deaf and dumb, and the ignorant,"[6] nevertheless remains much more pertinent to an urban than a largely rural society.

One could still argue that the Canadian bourgeoisie, including those concerned about social control, benefited from the earlier experience of the United States and England. After all, the first two governors of the post-Rebellion period, Lords Durham and Sydenham, were Philosophic Radicals whose ideas were shaped by conditions in the mother country. As Ian Radforth has demonstrated, the reforms Sydenham introduced were stimulated by Bentham's Utilitarian political philosophy which "shared much with the outlook of the rising industrialists whose preoccupations were efficiency, simplicity, and organization." Indeed, Sydenham saw Canada as an ideal field for instituting the Benthamite program which vested aristocratic interests were resisting in Britain.[7] From this perspective, then, the administrative reform process of the post-Rebellion era was launched by two modern bourgeois-minded governors and carried forward by reform-oriented Canadian politicians with close ties to the rising capitalist class in Britain.

The British inspiration of the Canadian "state-formation" process is also stressed by Bruce Curtis, who claims that "to English Radicals and Whigs, French Canadians and republican farmers were at least as alien as English proletarians."[8] Inspired by Foucault, Curtis is less concerned with the link between administrative reform and the socio-economic transition than he is with the exercise of power. He is primarily interested in how the governing classes achieved their hegemony by "the practical habituation of the population to the operation of parliamentary and narrowly representative forms of rule." From Curtis's perspective, the creation of municipal councils and school commissions was essentially an exercise in popular *dis*empowerment. In his words, such representative institutions "were to stand between 'the people' and the 'Government,' disciplining the former, habituating them to the limitation of their political power, to the containment of their 'talents' in a narrow circle, situating the source of their potential complaints in their own activity."[9]

While there is obviously some value to this interpretation, and to the closely related social-control thesis, it ignores the fact that the locally elected bodies were not simply institutions of the central state or of some narrowly defined dominant state class. Foucault's own later work places less emphasis on power as repression, and acknowledges that it is not simply "the product of a vertical initiative coming from above." Not only are individuals "always in the position of simultaneously undergoing and exercising this power," but there are "no relations of power without resistance." In other words, power is a dynamic process which must be examined at all levels of society.[10]

Admittedly, Foucault continues to emphasize how the power struggle inevitably results in the circumscribing of popular freedom, but his later perspective nevertheless encourages us to pay more attention to local communities not only in terms of their reaction to state-initiated reforms, but also in terms of their own demands. To take municipal government as one example, many in the Eastern Townships had been demanding such institutions long before Sydenham's district councils were introduced in 1841, and the people of Canada East forced the government to decentralize the municipal system so that they could exercise more control over its activities. Also, public education may have been "at the heart of projects for the stabilization of bourgeois hegemony in the mid-nineteenth century,"[11] to use Curtis's phrase, but it had strong roots in the pre-Rebellion era and it was supported at the local level throughout the Province of Canada.

The imposition of taxation at the local level was doubtless the most dramatic innovation of the 1840s, and it was not accepted without a good deal of resistance throughout Canada East. Just as municipal and school reform required popular consent, however, so taxation could never have been imposed by force against the will of the general population. The state's only effective weapon in terms of instituting municipal reforms was the popular desire for an efficient transportation system. Even in the Eastern Townships, where the largely English-speaking population was completely unaccustomed to taxation, having never paid seigneurial dues, church tithes, or road levies, the chief objection to municipal assessment during the early 1840s was simply that the tax base was not broad enough in scope.

As far as public schools were concerned, the government employed the added incentive of matching grants for locally raised funds. In the Eastern Townships, the popular resistance to school taxes arose largely from a concern that some of the money would be diverted to neighbouring communities. This concern was soon allayed, but the state came close to surrendering the school-taxation principle after the outbreak of popular violence in the French-speaking parishes in 1849–50. In short, the 1840s and early 1850s were years of trial and error for the municipal and school systems, with the provincial government forced to pass a series of reform bills before the local population was satisfied with the results. Clearly, administrative reform was a two-way process, the result of protracted negotiations and conflicts between the government and the governed.

There nevertheless remains the thorny question of who represented the state and who spoke for the local communities. If, as state-formation theory suggests, the state incorporated not only all the centrally appointed officials, such as the justices of the peace, captains of militia, school inspectors, and customs collectors, but the locally elected councillors and commissioners as well, then obviously the local communities must have been essentially voiceless and defenceless. But the fact is that even the members of the Legislative Assembly had to articulate local concerns if they wished to be re-elected, and the full-time salaried officials had to demonstrate their usefulness if they were to gain any measure of co-operation from the public at a time when the state's repressive apparatus was rudimentary at best.

One of the main objects of this study is to examine where on the state-community spectrum the public figures and public institutions of the Eastern Townships tended to fall during the crucial decade of the 1840s. Like the concept of state, that of community is a rather fluid one. Even the borders of the region we are studying have been defined somewhat arbitrarily, since there has never been an official political or administrative jurisdiction known as the Eastern Townships. For our purposes, the term will apply to the seven electoral constituencies (the Town of Sherbrooke was separate from the county for electoral purposes) established in 1829 to include virtually all the freehold territory surrounded by seigneurial zones to the west, north and east, and the American border to the south (see Map 1).

This upper Appalachian area of roughly one hundred miles from east to west and eighty miles from north to south (at its widest points) was not surveyed into townships (see Map 2) until the 1790s, and the settlement process remained slow thereafter because of the difficult access to the St Lawrence River and external markets. Its physical geography, land tenure system, and predominantly English-language population distinguished the Eastern Townships from the rest of Lower Canada. Internally, however, the southern, American-settled townships remained quite separate from the less prosperous northern section, which was settled somewhat later by British immigrants and French Canadians. A rough dividing line would fall between the counties of Missisquoi, Stanstead, southern Shefford, and southwestern Sherbrooke, on the one hand, and Drummond, Megantic, northern Shefford, and northeastern Sherbrooke on the other. From the perspective of local metropolitan influence, however, the strategically located town of Sherbrooke would strengthen its dominance over the central part of the region drained by the St Francis River, while the peripheral areas (moving from west to north to east) would remain more oriented towards Montreal, Trois-Rivières, and Quebec City, respectively.[12]

But the degree to which the Eastern Townships was or was not a region is not a crucial issue for the purposes of this study. Since the focus is on local response to state formation, the broad definition of the study area offers the advantage of including townships at different stages of development and of different ethnic composition, including those with a combination of American, British, and/or French-Canadian inhabitants.

Each township itself was a somewhat arbitrary and artificial creation whose name and boundaries of roughly ten miles by ten miles was assigned by distant government officials before the first settlers had arrived. Yet the township did come to represent the basic unit of social organization and governance.

When first opening the region to colonization, the government informally accepted that each township would be granted and developed according to the New England model of township leader and associates.[13] The British officials clearly did not approve of authority being assumed by town meetings, though road overseers and, after 1829, school trustees (syndics) were elected on a township basis. In addition, Catholic parishes in the French-Canadian settlement zone formally assumed the township boundaries. Finally, the very fact that people outside the major towns identified their home addresses as in a particular township must have contributed to a sense of identification with that space.

More significant on a daily basis, however, were the localized neighbourhoods within which families socialized and intermarried.[14] While families in the seigneurial zones and more recently opened townships were settled along "rangs" or straight concession lines which essentially became the local communities, Map 3 reveals how roads in the southern townships followed the lay of the land in a winding irregular fashion. No study has yet examined the question of what impact this settlement pattern had on how local communities were identified in the older American-settled district, but there was a widespread network of small villages and hamlets, and schools were commonly located at forks and crossroads.[15] Furthermore, funds for each school appear to have been exclusively raised in the immediate neighbourhood serving that school, local meetings and religious services were generally held in the local schoolhouse, and those elected as road overseers, fence viewers, and so on represented local sub-divisions within each township.

No matter what the settlement pattern, then, there were clearly local communities of regular human interaction but with little if any official identification throughout the Eastern Townships. While he overlooked the degree to which segments of the population were geographically mobile, Lord Durham's comment about localism in Upper Canada was even more fitting for the Eastern Townships:

The province has no great centre with which all the separate parts are connected, and which they are accustomed to follow in sentiment and action; nor is there that habitual intercourse between the inhabitants of different parts of the country, which ... makes a people one and united, in spite of extent of territory and dispersion of population. Instead of this there are many petty local centres, the sentiments and interests ... of which are distinct, and perhaps opposed.[16]

Noting that the basic proposition of localism was that the interests of the people were best served by government that was closest to the people, Elwood Jones claims that the roots of this concept in Upper Canada can be traced back to the radical Whigs of mid-eighteenth-century America. Transferred by the American settlers, this legacy was later reinforced by immigration from Britain as reflected particularly in the popularity of the Orange Lodge.[17] Bruce Hodgins adds that the persistence of localism "owes quite a bit to the practice and theory of self-government in various Presbyterian, Congregational, Baptist and Methodist denominations and to the pragmatically successful operation of Baldwin's Municipal Government Act of 1849 in the organic structure of small town and rural Upper Canada."[18] Useful as such insights are, it should be noted that these institutions had adapted to the social conditions of the time, rather than vice versa, and that these conditions were largely a product of the rural pre-industrial environment. Certainly the standard view of rural French-Canadian society, which would have directly experienced none of the influences mentioned by Jones and Hodgins, is that it was at least as localized as that of English Canada.[19] Identity was also defined by ethnic or national origin and religion, and there existed a sharp distinction not only between French-speaking Catholics and English-speaking Protestants in the region, but also between those of American origin on the one hand, and British origin on the other. Furthermore, many of the Irish, Scots, and even the English (in the British American Land Company's St Francis Tract), settled in distinct pockets where they maintained their separate ethno-cultural identities for some time. Ethnicity and national origin may have weakened the development of regional identity, but such a settlement pattern would only strengthen the sense of local community, particularly outside the larger villages where a greater mixing of people occurred.

The question of religious affiliation is a more complex and largely unexplored one, for within the Protestant population there was a variety of denominations, and the Anglican Church had established a surprisingly strong presence in the older American-settled communities. Indeed, the Methodists had yet to dislodge the Church of England as the main Protestant denomination in the region at mid-century.[20] One of the most striking images in the Eastern Townships today is the number of small (seldom used) Protestant church buildings in each village, and it is clear that sectarian heterogeneity served to weaken these communities and further hasten the English-speaking exodus once local populations had declined to the point where individual churches began to close.

But it is likely that for much of the nineteenth century separate denominational affiliation actually created another web of local loyalties which generally did not conflict with, indeed probably strengthened, the sense of community identification. Anglican and Methodist proselytization was declining by the 1840s, and mutual toleration was encouraged by intermarriage, the shared sense of anti-Catholicism, and the very fact that no single denomination held a dominant position in the region. Certainly, as far as community response to state formation is concerned, religious affiliation beyond the basic Catholic-Protestant division was of little consequence.

Finally, a crucial issue related to the conception of community is that of class identity based on occupation and wealth (or lack of it). Farmers clearly distinguished themselves from townspeople, merchants from manual labourers, and so on, but for our purposes the central class-related issue is whether there was a community voice in the democratic sense, or whether the public resolutions and petitions speak only for the local elites who drafted them in most cases. This is a difficult question to answer categorically. A dominant elite of mostly American-born merchants and entrepreneurs had emerged in Sherbrooke and its environs by the early 1840s – an elite which was adept at exploiting the advantages of the town's location between Montreal and Boston.[21] While the regional economic-development agenda may have been largely set and controlled by this group of men, however, the outlying areas were not slow to protest when their self-perceived interests were threatened by Sherbrooke. Thus strong objections were voiced in petitions from Stanstead when the railway promoted by Alexander T. Galt touched only the western edge of that county.

Nor, given the relatively broad base of the franchise and the large rural majorities, were the village notables completely able to dominate the local political agenda. Tenants, who were eligible to vote provincially only in villages and towns, represented a sizeable proportion of the population according to the 1844 census (from 31 percent in Sherbrooke County to 53 percent in Drummond), but the early Stanstead elections reveal that they were not entirely excluded from the electoral process. In 1829 it was tacitly agreed that "persons settled in the Country from twenty to thirty years, and in possession of Lands without having their Title Deeds, many of whom held bonds for them, should not be objected to; and also, their sons being of age and cultivating Lands originally occupied by their fathers, but now set off for them as theirs."[22] Only one person was refused the vote in this contest, and the returning officer accepted all votes in the 1833 by-election, though he then denied Marcus Child the seat on the grounds that many of his supporters were squatters. The Assembly eventually overturned this decision but, with the 1834 general election, objections were registered against fifty-three voters in Stanstead.[23]

The increasingly rigorous enforcement of property qualifications contributed for a time to a steady decline in the number of votes cast in

Stanstead. There were 750 voters in 1829, 691 in the contested 1833 by-election, 616 in 1834, and only 464 in the 1837 by-election which, not coincidentally, brought a conservative victory. In 1844, however, the number of votes increased dramatically to 852, and they grew again to 1,101 in 1851, with conservatives winning in both cases.[24] Stanstead County included only 1,028 proprietors in 1844, and there is nothing to suggest that this number had changed substantially by 1851 when the number of occupiers (owners and tenants) remained almost the same as in 1844. Given the relatively small number of votes that could have been cast by villagers (85 percent of the voters were identified as farmers in 1829 and 1834),[25] it follows that either the great majority of rural proprietors must have exercised their franchise in 1845 and 1851, or a relatively large number of rural tenants and squatters did so illegally.

The frequent protests on the part of defeated candidates do suggest that restrictive voting regulations were commonly subverted. When the reformer Marcus Child won the 1841 election in Stanstead, the conservatives claimed that 135 of his supporters were not genuine landowners. They were said to include "men who have brought forward their aged parents to swear they were owning land of which they were themselves the lawful owners – Fathers giving deeds to their youthful sons, and urging them to swear and vote for Mr Child." The conservatives boasted that their candidate, on the other hand, had been supported by all the county magistrates and most of the militia officers, as well as "a large number of respectable female voters, and a number of persons in the Counties of Sherbrooke, Shefford, and Missisquoi, and one from the County of St Hyacinthe, all willing to record their votes in favour of a loyal candidate."[26] Despite this claim, it is doubtful if non-residents generally took the trouble to vote, and almost all married women were ineligible to do so since family property was invariably held in their husbands' names.

If it was difficult to enforce the regulations in provincial elections, it must have been still more so for municipal contests, though those eligible to vote did include all tenants who paid £5 per year in rent.[27] Likewise, there is no suggestion in the local petitions that anyone who paid school taxes was barred from voting. In fact, petitions make it clear that the property qualifications for local offices were commonly disregarded in the poorer townships. We must also remember that for many household heads the status of tenant, location-ticket holder for a crown lot, or squatter was not a permanent one. In addition, the electoral arrangements made in Stanstead in 1829, and the protest against Child's victory in 1841, suggest that some aging fathers held titles to farms occupied by several sons who were therefore landowners in all but name. Finally, the joint petitioners to the governor were much more likely to identify themselves as "inhabitants" than as "ratepayers" or "householders." In short, we cannot simply assume that the substantial number of non-proprietors in the region fell entirely outside the broader political community.

The degree to which local communities in the Eastern Townships were divided by classes with fundamentally opposed interests requires further detailed analysis, but the following chapters will reveal that the local elites were not always able to impose their wishes on the majority. In the case of municipal government, for example, the Sherbrooke bourgeoisie's hostility to increased decentralization was probably shared by its counterparts elsewhere in Canada East, but popular pressure ensured that the decentralization took place in any case. We shall see that the overriding concern in the Eastern Townships was that local tax dollars be directed to local projects and institutions rather than being administered by distant officials over whom ratepayers could exercise little control.

The dynamic of the state-formation process was therefore played out not only between the centre and the periphery of the province, but also within each community, whether it be defined at the regional, the county, the township, or the strictly local level. The state, in Michael Braddick's words, "is distinct from the locality not by being central but by being more extensive than the locality – it is one of the things common to a number of localities rather than an alien and hostile body."[28] By focusing on politics, reform of the legal system, and the establishment of modern tax-supported municipal and school systems, this study will attempt to assess the impact that local communities had in determining what form the modern state would take. And even while acknowledging that local leaders by definition articulated the local initiatives and responses, it will be assumed that the rest of the community could generally decide how or whether to follow.[29]

Chapter 1 will examine briefly the social and economic characteristics of the region. It will also survey the political developments in the Eastern Townships in order to establish the broader context of state formation during the post-Rebellion era. Technically, the Eastern Townships was represented in the Legislative Assembly ever since that body's inception in 1791, since the counties of Bedford, Richelieu, and Buckinghamshire extended all the way from the St Lawrence River to the American border. But with no polling stations in the region, its people were effectively disfranchised prior to the erection of the six new counties of Sherbrooke, Stanstead, Missisquoi, Shefford, Drummond, and Megantic in 1829. As a result, there emerged a strong tradition of addressing the provincial government by petition or memorial, and after 1823 Stanstead's *British Colonist and Saint Francis Gazette*, the region's only newspaper for a number of years, served as a kind of public forum. The people of the Eastern Townships had therefore adopted their own public voice before being granted political representation, and this tradition of local democracy persisted into the 1840s. The region's primary concern remained its economic isolation, an isolation which clearly reinforced the strong sense of community localism even while it fostered a regional identity based on common grievance. As a result, the modernizing reforms of the 1840s were welcomed and even demanded in much of the Eastern Townships as a means of promoting social and economic development.

Turning to the process of law in chapter 2, we shall see that in the Eastern Townships of the 1840s there was a persistent and widespread demand for ready access to the law courts, especially those that would facilitate collection of overdue debts. But this was more a reflection of a cash-poor society than the weakening of informal community sanctions, and social institutionalization did not prevent informal social codes from commonly taking precedence over formal law. Because the moral reform movement is generally seen as another weapon in the bourgeoisie's struggle to regulate the masses, or at least to combat what in their view was social disintegration, the following chapter will begin with a brief discussion of the temperance movement and perceptions towards poverty and madness in the region. Then, to gain some appreciation of how popular mechanisms of social regulation still operated, we will examine the role of the charivari. Closely tied to this theme is the question of how the local definition of crime might differ from that of the state. We will therefore continue our examination of what Keith Wrightson has called the "two concepts of order" by turning to smuggling and the attempts at its repression alongside the American border.[30] The resulting picture is complex because it was not simply a question of imposing state institutions on a reluctant community, or of class repression during an era when the proletariat was only a small fraction of the population. The evidence suggests that social regulation was still largely a product of community pressure, pressure which in extreme cases took the semi-ritualized form of the charivari, which still cut across class lines.[31]

It is somewhat ironic that Canadian historians interested in the various social reform movements during the transition era have largely ignored the development of municipal government. After all, this was the institution that most clearly represented the state at the local community level, as well as the one that would make the most direct impact on the growth of capitalism through the facilitation and encouragement of economic development. One could therefore simply interpret the creation of municipal councils as a centralizing measure designed to serve the interests of the bourgeoisie. This it was to a considerable degree, but in chapters 4 and 5 we shall see that to the people of the Eastern Townships it was also a means of breaking out of their economic isolation and exercising some control over their own local affairs. Rather than being imposed on the region, town councils had long been suppressed because of their association with American republicanism. Governor Sydenham did his best to ensure that democratic elements were minimized when he finally introduced municipal government, but community pressure would force the province to cede to a considerable degree of decentralization by mid-century.

The pioneer superintendent of education, Jean-Baptiste Meilleur, has received only a fraction of the attention accorded to his Upper Canadian counterpart, Egerton Ryerson, but, as with the municipal system, there were important differences between the way the educational administrative framework evolved in the two sections of the province. These differences made a profound impact on the response to school reform at the local level, though they had little to do with the competing role of the Catholic Church, since the public schools system was actually more bureaucratically centralized in Canada East than in Canada West. Chapter 6 traces how the voluntarist principle of school support was reluctantly surrendered by the inhabitants of the Eastern Townships, though the government and its educational bureaucracy were forced to make significant concessions to localism as the decade of the 1840s progressed. Chapter 7 shifts to the British and French-Canadian communities which began to develop in the peripheral northern townships during the later 1820s, examining how their poverty and isolation caused greater resistance to the taxation system than in the southern part of the region.

The local perspective presented in this study has been made possible primarily by analysis of the petitions which, in the Stanstead MLA's words, descended on the provincial capital "like swollen mountain streams."[32] The letters and petitions concerning schooling and customs offices were, for the most part, directed to the superintendent of education and the commissioner of customs and excise, respectively. Despite the rapid transition to responsible government during the 1840s, however, most of the other incoming petitions and letters continued to be addressed to the provincial/civil secretary. Separate files were subsequently created for such subjects as stipendiary magistrates, district councils, and annexation addresses, but the bulk of the documents are simply catalogued as RG4 A1 prior to 1839 and RG4 C1 thereafter.

This collection is considerably larger for the 1840s than for previous decades. Not only was the public responding to the initiation of widespread institutional reform, but the basic idea that the provincial government should be responsible to public opinion was new to the early

1840s.[33] Historians have paid some attention to the equivalent collection of petitions for Upper Canada/Canada West but, aside from a recent study on the schools, another on the stipendiary magistrates, and a third on the popular resistance movement known as the Guerre des Éteignoirs, these government records have been virtually ignored as far as Lower Canada/Canada East is concerned.[34] One reason, clearly, is the intimidating volume of records which makes research on a provincial scale a daunting task, while for a local community or a specific institution it would be somewhat akin to searching for a needle in a haystack. The incoming correspondence of the civil secretary is most amenable to the study of a geographical area which falls between the extremes of province and local community simply because it is quite feasible, if time-consuming, to research the documents which are addressed from a mid-sized region over a limited number of years. The institutional reform process was far from being completed by 1852, but this study ends at that date because enough major reform initiatives had been taken to allow for a detailed study of state-community interaction over a reasonably extended period of time, and because the first comprehensive provincial census enumeration was taken in the spring of that same year. This census provides a convenient social and economic anchor for what is basically a political study.

Another complement to the manuscript government records was the appendices to the *Journals of the Legislative Assembly,* which include the detailed annual reports of the superintendent of education, among many other items. To avoid an exclusive focus on the centre-periphery dynamic, and thereby escape a purely institutional view of the state, research was also conducted in the limited local sources that are available. Very few local institutional records have survived for our study period, but I did examine the private correspondence of four prominent figures in the region: Edward Hale, Marcus Child, Moses Colby, and Robert Hoyle. Finally, I researched the region's press, though only the *Stanstead Journal* survives as more than a few fragments for this period, and it did not begin publication until 1845. Fortunately, Michael McCulloch's doctoral dissertation includes an excellent survey of politics in the Eastern Townships during the early Union period based largely on research in the Montreal and Quebec press.

A final word on methodology is in order. This volume tells a considerable number of stories in some detail. Such an approach, I believe, is necessary in order to unravel the complex dynamics of local community relations as well as the community responses to outside pressures. Furthermore, I happen to believe as a historian that social theory is useful for what it tells us about the lives of flesh-and-blood people, rather than vice versa. Such notable political figures as William Bowman Felton,

Edward Hale, and Alexander Tilloch Galt have been studied in detail elsewhere, but much can also be learned about community dynamics and the state, broadly defined, from the experiences of such little-known individuals as William Vondenvelden, the unpopular tory target of an extended charivari; Aaron Workman, the much-abused but hard-headed customs officer; and Philip Adolphus Barker, the victim of a grave miscarriage of justice. Finally, please note that the quotations in French have been reproduced as I found them, except to add missing accents.

1 The Politics of Patronage and Economic Development

REGIONAL DEVELOPMENT

The first permanent settlers in the region which had been reserved as an Abenaki hunting and fishing territory during the French regime were a small number of Loyalists in the vicinity of Lake Champlain's Missisquoi Bay.[1] However, this extensive territory was not officially opened to colonists until 1792 when it began to be surveyed into townships. Though welcomed by government proclamation, American settlers were effectively discouraged by British officials in Quebec, who managed to acquire much of the region for themselves and their merchant allies in Montreal.[2] The failure of these absentee proprietors to develop their holdings retarded the region's population growth for many years, but it did not entirely prevent the New England settlement frontier from expanding northward in search of cheaper lands and lower taxes. One can estimate from an informal census taken in 1803 that there were about eight thousand inhabitants in the Eastern Townships that year, and a survey taken by Surveyor-General Bouchette suggests that this number had increased to approximately twenty thousand by 1815.[3]

In contrast to Upper Canada, the Eastern Townships had no military garrisons to serve as an important early market, and the region's settlers were heavily dependent on snow-packed trails to haul their produce to the distant markets of Montreal and Quebec. But soil and growing conditions were quite favourable in the southern part of the region, and its economy may have been stimulated by the military market created by

Table 1.1
Population of the Eastern Townships by County

County	1825	1827	1831	1844	1852
Missisquoi	6,951	7,766	8,801	10,797	13,471
Shefford	2,294	4,467	5,081	10,063	19,992
Stanstead	7,088	8,272	10,248	11,913	13,884
Megantic	249	626	2,282	6,745	13,497
Drummond	1,325	1,907	3,543	9,159	16,537
Sherbrooke	4,703	5,471	7,085	13,391	16,470
Totals	22,610	28,509	37,040	62,068	93,851

Sources: Joseph Bouchette, *The British Dominions in North America* (1831; reprinted New York, 1968), 350–3; *JLA Lower Canada*, vol. 41 (1831–32), appendix oo; *JLAC*, vol. 5 (1846), appendix d; Canada, *Census Reports*, 1851–52. Higher population figures for 1831 are recorded for most of the Eastern Townships counties in the 1870–71 *Census Reports*, vol. 4. The 1830–31 census mistakenly totals Stanstead's 1825 population as 6,088. This table does not include reported absentees.

the War of 1812. Certainly, there was much smuggling to the British garrisons in Lower Canada from across the border in Vermont, and Bouchette reported in 1815 that the farms in Compton Township were "in a thriving and excellent condition, generally producing crops of wheat of excellent quality, and in quantity far beyond the home consumption."[4] But widespread summer frosts destroyed much of the harvests throughout Lower Canada between 1816 and 1820, leading to a period of economic and demographic stagnation.[5] As Table 1.1 reveals, the years following 1815 were disastrous ones for the development of the Eastern Townships. With the surplus population in neighbouring New England turning its attention more and more exclusively westward after the opening of the Erie Canal in 1825, and the French Canadians still able to find land in the seigneuries, the Eastern Townships would become increasingly dependent on British immigration.

Although the Legislative Assembly began investigating the potential for French-Canadian settlement in the Eastern Townships as early as 1820, the French-speaking deputies hesitated to encourage economic development of the region when the chief beneficiaries would be the province's land-holding merchant-official elite, and where the majority of settlers would for some time be English-speaking Protestants. In 1818 the Assembly's chief spokesman, Pierre Bédard, had asked rhetorically: "Is it possible that the assembly will not see the absurdity and cowardice of using the funds of the province in having roads made for these Yankees and afterwards in having the roads kept in repair for large sums of money?"[6] On the grounds that such institutions were alien to French civil law, the Assembly also opposed the opening of registry offices, which would have made it much easier to keep track of sales and encumbrances on freehold property.[7] Finally, after 1829, when the Townships region was granted its own electoral constituencies, it benefited briefly from the attention of the province's two rival political forces. During the following two years the *Parti canadien* MLAs wooed Townships voters by providing considerable sums for roads and bridges, and the Colonial Office made a concerted effort to direct British emigration into the region by sponsoring a settlement project alongside the Craig Road in the northeastern county of Megantic.[8]

The region responded dramatically to the much-needed official attention, for according to the 1831 census the population had expanded to 37,000, an annual increase of 11 percent during the previous six years. In spite of the major influx of Irish settlers to the port of Quebec during the following years, however, the growth rate of the Eastern Townships slowed considerably after 1831, so that the total population was only 62,000 in 1844 (see Table 1.1). One reason was that the British government had continued to regard the region's crown lands as a convenient and cost-free reserve to draw upon for the compensation of redundant military officers and other claimants to the crown's patronage. Between 1826 and 1839, 641,000 acres of Lower Canadian crown land, much of it in the Eastern Townships, was alienated by free grant directly from London. One of the chief beneficiaries of the government's largesse was the retired English naval officer, William Bowman Felton of Sherbrooke. Furthermore, in his role as commissioner of crown lands, Felton sold an additional 400,000 acres during the 1828–36 period, mostly in blocks of over 200 acres. Thus, even the land sales policy was drafted with revenue rather than settlement as its primary consideration.

The same order of priorities led in 1833 to the massive sale of 850,000 acres of crown land to the British American Land Company, including all the crown reserves and surveyed crown lots in Sherbrooke, Shefford, and Stanstead counties as well as the unsurveyed St Francis Tract in northeastern Sherbrooke County. By 1835 the London-based company had solidified its hold over much of the region by acquiring at auctions another 60,000 acres in clergy reserves as well as some 32,000 acres in privately held land. Aside from building an ill-fated road from Sherbrooke to Port St Francis, at the mouth of the St Francis River, the land company squandered much of its remaining capital on the isolated and mountainous St Francis Tract.[9]

The British American Land Company's hopes of recuperating capital expenditures from the immediate sale of the former reserve lots were destroyed in 1837 when the outbreak of rebellion brought British immigration to a halt. In addition, many of the English and German families located at the company's expense in the St Francis Tract fled the region. Unable to meet its payments to the government, in 1841 the company rescinded over 500,000 acres of the St Francis Tract in exchange for cancellation of its remaining debt to the crown. Although the seeds of a growing colony of Hebridean Scots had been sown in the upper St Francis district, the land company would henceforth turn its attention to the sale of its more centrally located land and to the development of its mill sites in the town of Sherbrooke.[10]

While the Irish influx to the port of Quebec became greater than ever during the mid-to-late forties, only a relative handful trickled into the Eastern Townships where the number of British-born residents increased by only three thousand between 1844 and 1852, and many of these were transient navvies working on the St Lawrence and Atlantic Railway.[11] The major expansion in the region during these years was French-Canadian. While it was encouraged by the establishment in 1848 of colonization societies sponsored by the Catholic Church and the radical Institut Canadien, and by the government's offer of free grants alongside the newly constructed colonization roads in the former St Francis Tract, the largest part of the French-Canadian influx was simply an expansion from the nearby seigneuries into eastern Shefford and northern Drummond and Megantic counties (see Table 1.1). By 1852, 36 percent of the region's population was French-speaking (see Table 1.2), a substantial increase from the 23 percent of 1844.

Much of the population growth by mid-century therefore represented an expansion of the subsistence-oriented settlement frontier rather than a profound transition towards a market-oriented economy. Ever since the pioneer era, however, local farmers had concentrated largely on livestock production, largely because it was more profitable to walk cattle long distances to market than to transport grain. As early as 1821 the farm of Stanstead Township's Charles Kilborn was 400 acres in size, with 100 acres cleared and 200 head of livestock. In 1830 the township's six largest farmers shipped 115 cattle and twenty-five horses to Montreal and Quebec, and in 1835 the future MLA, John Moore of Eaton, claimed to be marketing one hundred head of cattle per year in the same two cities. Near the town of Sherbrooke in 1831 W.B. Felton owned 500 cleared acres as well as sixty cattle, thirty-four horses, and twenty-one pigs. Felton employed six farm labourers that year, while a single farmer in Stanstead advertised in the Montreal press for one hundred hands to work on the harvest.[13]

Table 1.2
Population in Eastern Townships Counties by Country of Origin 1852

County	U.S.	England/ Wales	Scotland	Ireland	Canada (English)	Canada (French)
Missisquoi	2,171	371	110	643	7,548	2,628
Shefford	1,839	1,279	1,867	2,766	9,224	3,017
Stanstead	3,127	329	141	342	8,653	1,292
Megantic	49	265	447	1,664	2,949	8,123
Drummond	237	267	174	1,150	3,293	11,416
Sherbrooke	1,332	320	301	1,151	6,076	7,290
Totals	8,755	2,831	3,040	7,716	37,743	33,766

Source: Canada, Census Reports, 1851–52. Excluded are the few born in other British colonies and non-American foreign countries.

These agricultural capitalists were obviously exceptional, but Jean-Pierre Kesteman has calculated from the surviving manuscript census schedules of seven older townships in 1831 that of the nearly seven hundred farmers, forty-five had more than 100 cleared acres each, averaging twenty-seven cattle, five horses, and thirty-one sheep.[13] Beginning in the 1830s, however, competition from the mid-western states and Upper Canada damaged the meat market, so that the ratio of townships farmers with ten or more cattle declined from 36 percent in 1831 to 27 percent in 1844. Some relief for the Eastern Townships farmers came after 1843 with the levying of duties on foreign agricultural goods, but only in 1848 did the Montreal market cease to be glutted with American produce. Western expansion, and the construction of railways to cities on the eastern seaboard ensured that cattle, horses, sheep, meat, coarse grains, butter, and wool all commanded high prices, inaugurating a period of unprecedented prosperity throughout the province of Canada.[14]

Between 1844 and 1851 the one-third expansion in the Eastern Townships' cattle and horses at least kept pace with the population increase. The fodder crops of oats, buckwheat, and corn increased by 44 percent during the same period, and the approaching railway links to Boston and Portland, Maine, ensured that a substantial proportion of the two million pounds of Eastern Townships butter and half million pounds of cheese produced in 1851–52 would be absorbed by the American market. While the District of St Francis had only 4 percent of the cows in Canada East, it produced 8 percent of the butter and 26 percent of the cheese.[15]

As of mid-century, then, the Eastern Townships remained largely a rural region with agricultural production just beginning to become integrated into a broader capitalist market. The many villages dotting the countryside basically served the needs of local farmers. By 1852 there were over six hundred industrial establishments in the region, but only a small number of hands were employed in each of the village sawmills, grist-mills, wool-carding mills, foundries, tanneries, potash and pearlash works, whiskey distilleries, and so on.[16] Furthermore, these industries generally remained closed for part of the year. In the Sherbrooke area, however, an aggressively entrepreneurial elite had begun in 1844 to erect substantial factories in anticipation of the railway's arrival. These included the province's first cotton factory, and establishments which produced nearly half the woollen cloth and 20 percent of the paper in Canada East.[17] Jean-Pierre Kesteman has calculated that during the two decades from 1823 to 1843 accumulated investment in the capitalist enterprises of the St Francis District was only $14,000, while during the following ten years this figure increased fifteen-fold to $218,000. Textile factories alone accounted for $45,000 of this amount.[18]

The town of Sherbrooke's population may have been under three thousand in 1852, but this represented a substantial increase from the six hundred of eight years earlier.[19] Even before its arrival, therefore, the railway was ushering in a new era of capitalist development in the older southernmost townships where it would eventually spawn a number of manufacturing centres. In the meantime, the main political aim of the local merchants and producers was to pressure the government to help the region break out of its economic isolation.

THE FELTON ERA

It would not be much of an exaggeration to state that during the 1820s the state's power in the Eastern Townships was largely controlled by one man, William Bowman Felton.[20] After serving as an "agent victualler" in the British Navy during the Napoleonic Wars, Felton brought his extended family to the Eastern Townships where they settled near the small mill centre that would become known as the town of Sherbrooke. By 1826, in return for the promise to invest £5,000 in local development, Felton had been granted 15,000 acres by the crown, while his two brothers and two brothers-in-law had each been favoured with 1,200 acres. Felton was obviously meant to represent the equivalent of the English squire in the southern part of the Eastern Townships. But the decentralized English system of social and economic subordination to a local squirarchy failed to function effectively in the Eastern Townships.

Once he had acquired all of Sherbrooke's mills and water-power sites, in addition to building an impressive landed estate, Felton ensured that he and his family received most of the key patronage positions in the region. He asked that he, his brother, and his brother-in-law be appointed justices of the peace in 1816. He then became lieutenant-colonel of the 5th Battalion of the Eastern Townships militia in 1821, followed the next year by an appointment as the region's only member of the Legislative Council. Soon afterwards, the legislature ratified Felton's bill to establish the Inferior Judicial District of Saint Francis, thereby ensuring Sherbrooke's position as the chef-lieu of the region. This enabled Felton to win the appointment of his brother, Charles, as prothonotary (court clerk), and his brother-in-law, Charles Whitcher, as sheriff.

Referring to the local American-born residents as "a horde of disaffected and disloyal squatters," Felton did his best to strengthen British influence in the region, but he could do little to stimulate economic development or attract British immigrants without effective all-season transportation links to external markets. Furthermore, because of the relatively small influx of British immigrants, the deliberate establishment of an English-born official elite in the region simply served to alienate the local population. Thus, in 1826, a correspondent to Stanstead's *British Colonist* complained that the government, after having invited Americans to settle in the Eastern Townships, had treated them "with distrust; with a cold reserve, and a freezing indifference bordering on contempt." Once they had cleared the forests and surmounted "all embarrassments, both natural and artificial, so as to compose a population of forty thousand souls," the settlers needed "internal regulations by which to conduct and manage our little concerns. – To carry such a purpose into effect, there have uniformly been sent among us foreigners, unacquainted with our habits, manners and customs, to fill and execute every official function, thereby declaring, in language too unequivocal to be misunderstood, that no confidence was to be placed in a native born American."[21]

This feeling of resentment explains why, despite his considerable powers, Felton exercised so little of the political influence that S.J.R. Noel attributes to the "grand patrons" of early nineteenth-century Upper Canada.[22] As a result, he could not prevent the region from going solidly reform when it was finally granted its own constituencies in 1829. The election of eight Townships deputies meant that Felton was no longer the region's only voice in government, and during the following two years the Patriote-controlled Assembly rewarded the region with £3,000 in subsidies for the St Francis River road artery. The region's pro-Papineau sentiment nevertheless cooled as the political situation became more polarized. The American-born Marcus Child of Stanstead was the only MLA from the Eastern Townships to support the radical Ninety-Two Resolutions in 1834, and was careful to present himself to his constituents as a supporter of British rights and liberties rather than as an American-style republican.[23]

Child's published speech to the electors of Stanstead North in 1834 must nevertheless have given the governor and his councillors some cause for concern. Without referring directly to the governing elite's mistrust of the Americans in the Eastern Townships, Child declared that "this is the land of our adoption and choice, and as properly ours as though it were the land of our birth; its chartered rights are ours, and it is our political happiness and prosperity to join its ancient inhabitants in supporting and improving what they have obtained by their birth and blood, 'civil and religious liberty'."[24] As in the seigneurial zone, the Stanstead meeting established a solid organizational base by electing corresponding committees of six members for each of the three townships represented.[25]

Two weeks later a similar meeting was held by the reformers from the county's remaining two townships, which lay west of Lake Memphremagog. Among their resolutions was one vowing their support for Papineau and the Assembly in the struggle against "self-interested individuals, high-minded Tories, cringing sycophants, and overbearing aristocrats, bent upon despoiling the people and aggrandizing themselves."[26] Stanstead was the only constituency in the region to have candidates in the fall election who supported the Ninety-Two Resolutions, but Child and his running mate soundly defeated their opponents.

Child continued to lead the attack in the Townships against the government's massive alienation of crown land to the London-based British American Land Company. He also headed the Assembly's inquiry in 1836 into the conduct of Sherbrooke's sheriff, Charles Whitcher. Indeed, the Felton family oligarchy had begun to crumble under the force of a concerted attack by the Assembly's grievance committees. Not only did Child's committee begin impeachment proceedings against Whitcher, but a second committee inquired into the character and conduct of Charles Felton as prothonotary, and Sherbrooke's staunchly anti-Patriote MLA, the Swiss-born B.C.A. Gugy, chaired a third one to investigate charges against W.B. Felton himself as commissioner of crown lands.

Felton was dismissed the following year, after the inquiry had uncovered relatively minor improprieties, for he and his family had become political liabilities to the administration during this tumultuous pre-Rebellion era. The British authorities clearly wished to maintain the region's support should the French Canadians resort to arms, and even in Stanstead there were grumblings against the Assembly when it refused to consider a petition for a vital economic project which Child himself had been promoting – a railway from Boston through the Eastern Townships to Montreal.[27] With Papineau calling for the extension of the seigneurial system into the Eastern Townships, the Land Registry Offices Act about to expire due to a balky Assembly, and the tory press constantly appealing to ethnic prejudices and fears, people throughout the region were becoming increasingly uneasy about the prospect of increased dependency upon the French-speaking, Catholic majority. Upon abandoning the Patriote party, the *Sherbrooke Gazette* was nevertheless careful to declare (23 September 1837) that "every reflecting man must ... call himself a Constitutional Reformer or a Radical ... The ultra Tory school is too limited in its numbers to call for much notice at our hands." The newspaper began its new life with a long list of demands: a modified Executive Council, new members for the Legislative Council "drawn from various sections of the Province," less expense and delay in the judicial system, the abolition of feudal "burthens," "greater facilities in the granting of the waste Lands of the Crown to actual settlers," amelioration of the road laws, taxation of non-resident proprietors, improved educational facilities, and internal improvements.

Lord Gosford was clearly making an astute observation when he stated that the "radical" representatives of Stanstead and Missisquoi were not elected to defend the "feudal system" and the French language or to object to the establishment of registry offices, but to punish a government "which neglects or regards with disfavour" settlers from the United States.[28] One of Gosford's informants was doubtless Edward Hale, a member of a distinguished Quebec family who had recently settled in Sherbrooke. Hale was acutely aware of the link between patronage and government subsidies on the one hand, and political loyalty on the other. In 1836 he wrote to the tory Montreal merchant and legislative councillor, Peter McGill, concerning a Sherbrooke petition to open a local branch of the Bank of Montreal. Hale admitted that he was unable to judge whether or not the venture would be profitable, but he was confident that it would benefit the region by introducing cash payments, thereby "remedying one of the greatest wants they have yet felt." Referring to the political state of the country, Hale appealed to the public spirit of the bank directors, adding that a Sherbrooke branch "would also facilitate the emigration which we hope to see directed to these Townships, and encourage the advancement of this village & neighbourhood which you must know is the only District Town in the Province in which the Constitutional party has a majority & as such deserves encouragement."[29]

The Bank of Montreal was not forthcoming at that time, but the less conservative City Bank of Montreal did take the risk of opening a

Sherbrooke branch in 1836, and a political contest the following year in Stanstead would confirm the regional trend away from the Patriotes. In January 1837 the conservative Stanstead physician, Moses French Colby, won the by-election held to replace Child's deceased running mate. A recently arrived American who was an enthusiastic promoter of economic progress, Dr Colby assured the electors that by sustaining the constitution they would

find in the concentration of foreign capital among us increased means for accomplishing those projects of internal improvement we so ardently desire. Our lakes and rivers will soon be chained together by Railways, and our vallies intersected by Canals. The invincible power of steam will impart new life and vigor to every department of labor and every enterprise of trade, and thus an incalculable benefit will accrue to the agricultural, commercial and mechanical interests of the community.[30]

Child took pains to disassociate himself from the Patriotes once the Rebellion broke out. Nevertheless, he was immediately dismissed as village postmaster and, at the outset of the second uprising a year later, the local oaths commissioner, William Ritchie, accused him of being an active promoter "of the troubles that this County is now involved in."[31] After being summarily dismissed as commissioner of the peace, Child took the precaution of fleeing across the border to Vermont, but it is highly unlikely that he associated with the rebel exiles. Despite a number of border skirmishes, the presence of both a cavalry and an infantry company in the village of Stanstead, coupled with the arrest of a number of potential leaders, was enough to discourage any local outbreaks of organized violence.[32]

THE HALE ERA

The Rebellion may have been a minor affair in the Eastern Townships, but it did mark a change in political and economic development there, as in the rest of the province. Felton's death in disgrace in 1837, and Child's temporary exile in 1838, marked the end of the local tory-Patriote struggle even before Lord Durham's *Report* introduced a new political era at the provincial level. The leading figure in this new era was Edward Hale, the grandson of both General John Hale, who had served as a colonel with Wolfe at Quebec, and General William Amherst. Edward Hale's father, John, was receiver-general for Lower Canada from 1824 to 1838, and he himself had served as secretary to his uncle, Lord William Pitt Amherst, while the latter was the governor-general of India from 1823 to 1828. Hale and his wife, the daughter of Chief Justice

Edward Bowen of the Superior Court of Lower Canada, had moved to a farm near Sherbrooke in 1834.[33] From here, Hale managed his widespread property investments, as well as promoting local industries, acting as a broker for land speculators, and lending money to local capitalists.

While Edward Hale was cut from much the same gentrified tory cloth as Felton, he proved to be much more accommodating to the local American population, whose leading figures were in turn becoming more conservative and pro-British. Hale demonstrated this attitude in January 1838, when he wrote to Colonel F.G. Heriot concerning a rifle company that Sherbrooke inhabitants "principally of American origin," had organized at their own expense. After purchasing arms, ammunition, and uniforms, as well as drilling regularly, they had been chastised by the military authorities for choosing their own name for the corps (the Royal American Rifle Company), and for recommending certain individuals as officers. Claiming that "I for one thought that in time of emergency such irregularities would be overlooked," Hale informed Heriot that "our people have certainly shewn very praiseworthy spirit since the disturbances broke out and I humbly conceive that any measure which would check the zeal they have displayed would not only be grating to their feelings but might in the end tend to damp their Constitutional principles." Clearly confident that the Eastern Townships would not become a centre of armed conflict, Hale added that he did not "look upon this affair as important in a military view, but as likely to secure the tory feelings of the Individuals in civil matters, and future Elections." At Heriot's suggestion, Governor Colborne complied with Hale's wishes.[34]

Hale's experience serving in Stanstead during the Rebellion, with the lowly rank of private, only reinforced his sympathies for the American-descended inhabitants of the region. After marching to Potton Township to help repel an attack from Troy, Vermont, in February 1838, he wrote to his wife that 220 volunteers had flocked in during the night, "fine fellows from Brome and Potton and Shefford – I never saw such loyalty it beats the British hollow." Anxious to return home after his "frolic," Hale's only complaint was that the Stanstead people "are very croaky & don't like to do without us."[35] Because the volunteer units were considered to be such important instruments for fostering British loyalty, the conservative Sherbrooke attorney, Joseph Gibb Robertson, would protest in 1846 when the militia bill failed to provide any funds for such companies. Reflecting the deep attachment in the Eastern Townships to voluntarism, Robertson argued that two or three such companies for local defence would be more effective than three times that number of militia under direct state control.[36]

Once the Rebellion was over, Hale was inclined, in his capacity of justice of the peace, to be lenient with those individuals in his area who had been politically disaffected. In August 1839 he reported to the attorney-general that three radical farmers from Ascot, who had felt it prudent to leave the province during the hostilities, now wished to return. They were willing to stand trial if necessary, but Hale questioned "whether it would be expedient to resort to strict measures" against these men, who were "in a respectable walk in life." Several weeks later he informed the civil secretary that even though proof could likely be obtained "of their having committed themselves in language or threats – at the same time nothing I believe of the nature of participating in open rebellion can be charged against them." In reply, the attorney-general simply ordered that the returned exiles should be kept in suspense by informing them that the "safety and tranquillity which they appear to desire must depend on the tenor of their conduct while they continue to reside within the Province."[37]

Soon afterwards, with the Lower Canadian constitution under suspension, Hale became the leading Eastern Townships member of Colborne's Special Council. One of his first tasks was to recommend six names to become commissioners of the peace; all his choices appear to have been American-born.[38] Hale was also careful to solicit the opinion of leading residents in the townships concerning local affairs,[39] and in the spring of 1840 he strongly recommended that one or more of the district's "gentlemen of American origin" be added to the Special Council. At the moment there was only one American-born member, even though "of the three Races which compose the Population of this Province, from British French and American origin the latter had conspicuously & practically manifested their attachment to the British Government during the troubles of the past Years."[40]

As the life of the Special Council drew to a close in 1840, the patrician Hale somewhat reluctantly contemplated offering himself as a candidate for the Legislative Assembly in the newly united Province of Canada. He was not motivated by the desire to prevent a reform victory, for he was confident that there was no chance of a local division on party principles. Rather, he wished to prevent the return of Sherbrooke's former MLA, Colonel B.C.A. Gugy, who had demonstrated considerable zeal in battling the Patriotes at Saint-Charles and Saint-Eustache, and was now serving as chief officer of the province's stipendiary magistracy.[41] Hale's letters do not explain the reasons for his opposition to Gugy, but the latter's moral character may have been a key factor. An undated anonymous broadside refers, among other charges, to Gugy's mistress, their several illegitimate children, and his being "mobbed in Toronto for horse-whipping his daughters 'till their cries alarmed the neighbourhood!"[42] Whatever the reason, Hale certainly had a strong antipathy towards the ebullient colonel, for he confided to his wife that more disagreeable than a personal defeat in the election would be the disgrace of having Gugy as their member.[43]

Under the assumption that Hale would be appointed to the Legislative Council, Sherbrooke's power-brokers eventually chose the American-born merchant Samuel Brooks to run in the town constituency. John Moore, who was Brooks's assistant as the local secretary for the British American Land Company, would represent the county. Hale was confident that both candidates were unbeatable, but Brooks stepped down long before the election was finally held, in March 1841. Hale took his place in October 1840 on the assurance that a contest could be avoided.[44]

But solid as the local support for Lord Sydenham may have been, J.S. Walton of the tory *Sherbrooke Gazette* complained in December of the lack of funds provided for public improvements in the Eastern Townships "while thousands are lavished in the vicinity of Montreal & Upper Canada." The discouraged editor asked Hale whether he could not at least make an effort as a member of the Special Council to have the province assume part of the cost for the railway projected to run from Montreal through the Townships to Boston. Hale's heart was clearly not in the project, however, for he complained to his wife about being kept in Montreal by "this humbug," the railway ordinance: "Oh how I rue the day when I consented to become a Candidate!"[45] Hale dutifully stayed in Montreal until late January, when the railway bill was finally passed, but he overlooked one rather crucial detail. His well-intentioned requirement that construction should begin in Sherbrooke meant that the heavy rails would have to be transported sixty to seventy miles by road![46]

In the meantime, Brooks attacked Gugy's character in the local press, while Hale remained in Montreal above the fray. The government obligingly weakened Gugy's chances by extending the town of Sherbrooke's boundaries to include Lennoxville as a constituency, and, after the life of the Special Council finally expired in early February, the reluctant Hale was advised that he might "take a drive round amongst the constituency of the Town and ask them for their votes." Hale may not have been particularly committed to the campaign, but he opposed Sydenham's suggestion that the Quebec-based government official, John Davidson, run in place of both himself and Gugy. Hale argued that his withdrawal at this stage would cause him to lose caste among his friends in Sherbrooke, and he made it clear that the local voters would not tolerate being used for the governor's convenience: "our township constituencies are composed of intelligent and thinking people, far less easily led than other Constituencies of the Lower part of the United Province." Sydenham was reluctant to take no for an answer, but Hale persisted, and he went on to defeat Gugy quite handily.[47]

The 1841 election produced the highest number of resident candidates in the Townships of any election after the Union.[48] Sydenham's pet project of provincial union was popular for obvious reasons among the English-speaking minority of Lower Canada, but the Sherbrooke notables had rejected Sydenham's attempt to impose a non-resident on their constituency, and a survey of the other six ridings in the region reveals that not all the victors were Sydenham's choices.[49]

In Shefford the tory, Alphonso Wells, retired early from the contest, protesting that opponent Dr S. Sewell Foster's party had administered the qualification oath to a large number of men who owned no property.[50] One of Sydenham's Montreal officials, Andrew Robertson, complained that if Wells had taken his advice and minded his own affairs rather than supporting – or appearing to support – Colonel Gugy, "why he might have been an MLA at this moment." As it was, Shefford was now represented by "another Radical, a thousand fold more ignorant than Child."[51]

Child's own narrow victory in Stanstead over the talented Dr Colby, who had easily won the 1837 by-election, came as a particular shock to the government party. Child's old nemesis, William Ritchie, was now in a position as county registrar to know which individuals held land titles, and he protested that 135 of those who had voted for the reformer were not genuine landowners. Ritchie further alleged that Child's supporters had included counterfeiters and men "notorious for their disaffection towards the Government, men who refused once to take to oath of allegiance, and afterwards took it through fear – men who have been deprived of their commissions for their seditious practices." Supporting Colby, on the other hand, were the most respectable members of society, including all the county's magistrates and most of the militia officers.[52]

Stanstead's ideological split was not reflected in neighbouring Missisquoi County, which had borne the brunt of cross-border raids by the Patriote exiles and their American supporters, as we shall see. Robert Jones was a former member of the Legislative Council, and his victory over Philip Moore appears to have simply reflected local sectional rivalries. While Jones was presumably a tory, Sydenham may have favoured Moore, for he named him to the Legislative Council soon after his defeat.[53]

Sydenham presumably had no objection to the remaining four candidates returned in the Townships. John Moore of Sherbrooke County had been critical of Hale, but we have already noted his ties to the

Sherbrooke elite, and the governor allowed him to win his seat without a contest. Likewise, in Drummond County no candidate opposed R.N. Watts, a government official who had been a member of the Special Council. But Watts also happened to be the nephew and presumed heir of Drummondville patriarch Colonel Heriot, and, once in the Assembly, both he and Moore would demonstrate alarming independence from the governor. Only in Megantic County, on the northeastern periphery of the region, was an absentee returned. Here the recently arrived settlers were still too dependent on the governor's good will to mount any opposition to his civil secretary, Dominick Daly of Quebec, even though the Irish Protestant majority was less than happy with Daly's affiliation to the Catholic Church.[54]

THE PATRONAGE ISSUE

If patronage distribution served as a tool in the government's attempt to impose a British elite on the Eastern Townships during the pre-Rebellion era, and to pacify the disgruntled population during the transition to the Union era, it had essentially become an instrument to soldify party loyalty by the time responsible government was fully recognized in 1848. In this respect, the patronage system also served to establish the popular legitimacy of the state, and is therefore relevant to our examination of local response to state formation during the 1840s. But the government only had a limited number of lucrative positions at its disposal, and the justices of the peace and militia officers who signed the annexation manifesto in 1850 revealed the limitations of such appointments as instruments of party and even state loyalty. While patronage distribution could become a potent source of political discontent, it appears to have been less effective in forging political loyalties during this transition era.

As a member of Sydenham's Special Council after the Rebellion, Edward Hale had ensured the expansion of government appointments to the region's American-descended majority, but during the Union era he became only one of several MLAs. Furthermore, not only would much of his energy be absorbed by his role as a warden of one of Sydenham's abortive district councils, but he was too much the aristocrat to be comfortable with the rough and tumble of party politics. Soon after the first Assembly went into session, Hale complained to his wife: "I am already receiving numerous letters from the Townships about Patronage & Place, all of which would bring me more odium than good will." Ironically, in light of the decline and fall of the Felton family, Hale now claimed that his chief concern was to find a place for his brother-in-law and business partner, George Frederick Bowen: "If I can get Fred a good berth that is all I shall care for."[55]

As warden of the Sherbrooke municipal district, Hale was in a particularly good position to distribute favours, and Bowen was far from the only relative seeking them. A month later, Hale confided that "I have at present a great many suitors for office for whom I am anxious to provide – Jeff [presumably his brother Jeffrey], Bill, one or two Ancaster [Upper Canada] Hales, Webster, Elkins, C. Whitcher, Richardson – E.L.M. – but first on my list is poor old Fred – for whom as well as for E. Short I should like to get a District Judgeship." Still later Hale wrote: "All the good I shall get by being in Parliament will be the possibility of serving some of my friends and this may be assisted by my being kept here a little longer, and this may be the case in particular with regard to Fred."[56]

Bowen initially had to be satisfied with an appointment as clerk of the newly established district court, a position he had not applied for. The problem was that he thereby displaced another of Hale's relatives, the alcoholic William Bell, who had been clerk of the defunct Provincial Court. However, Bell eventually became the clerk of the local Superior Court of Queen's Bench, while Bowen was named the district's bankruptcy commissioner.[57] In 1846 Hale entered into a business arrangement to benefit Bowen once again. In order to have the radical George Brooks (whose brother Samuel was now the conservative MLA for Sherbrooke County) withdraw his application to become sheriff, Hale rather reluctantly agreed to accept him in place of Bowen as a partner in operating a new grist-mill.[58] Soon afterwards, Bowen was appointed sheriff. In 1845 Lennoxville's Lieutenant-Colonel Morris wrote to his office-seeking son, "as for Hale little is to be expected from him. If you were a Yankee you would have a better chance."[59] Otherwise, however, the patronage script in the town of Sherbrooke remained much the same, with only a change in the cast of main characters.

More representative of the region as a whole than Hale's nepotism was Marcus Child's careful attention to the role of patronage distribution in building and maintaining party loyalty in Stanstead County, though this did not preclude the personal motive of seeking revenge against those who had humbled him during the Rebellion. Presumably because he had won Sydenham's favour by voting with the government on some key issues, Child was even able to block the attempt of his defeated rival, Dr Colby, to succeed Robert Hoyle as the local customs collector. Child wrote to the civil secretary that Colby's "education and habits" were professional rather than business-related, he was a relatively recent newcomer from the United States, and he was "not acceptable to the great body of the people."[60]

Likewise, when William Ritchie arrived in Kingston during the summer of 1841, Child did his best to ensure that no additional appointments would be offered to the man who had kept him from his seat for several months after the 1833 by-election, and who had hounded him into exile in his capacity as the local oaths commissioner during the Rebellion. Child warned the civil secretary that any favours bestowed upon Ritchie "would weaken instead of strengthening [the Crown] in the opinions of people I have the honor to represent." The Stanstead MLA later confided to his wife: "I am willing to make peace with my Opponents but they must honorably lay down their weapons of warfare and acknowledge me the victor else they cannot even expect honorable notice from me much less favors which my friends only have a right to expect."[61]

But even if there was more than a touch of vindictiveness in Child's observation of his old rivals' movements, his main governing principle was the establishment of a power base in a county which was shifting to the right politically. While Hale continued to embody the somewhat independent and personal characteristics of the grand patron (even while he lacked the political ambition to exert as much influence as a man in his position might have), Child had assumed the role of political broker by instituting the extensive and complex clientele networks which became characteristic of the union era.[62] Much to the annoyance of the local tories, in 1841 the newly elected Child was quick to set in motion a petition asking for the appointment of a number of his partisans as magistrates.[63] The tories expressed outrage that a candidate who had been elected against the expressed will of the government now laid claim to local patronage distribution, and the fact that Child's supporters could be associated with the losing side in an armed rebellion only added to the level of their indignation.[64]

Again the following year Wright Chamberlin, Dr Colby, and several other tory notables objected to the four names being circulated in a petition for appointment as commissioners of small causes. Crossed out of their second letter to Hale on the subject, but still legible, were references to Elias Lee and Asa L. Harvey as "men of rebellious notoriety in the winter of 38 & 39, Mr Lee having been actively employed in promoting disaffection until lodged in safe winter quarters at Sherbrooke and Mr Harvey having found it convenient to spend an equal portion of time on the other side of the line watched by us at great inconvenience." Finally, while the organizers of the counter-petition claimed that there was "no desire on our part to be exclusive," they argued that Child's nominees "will immediately make every vestige of power which they may wield subservient to party or political purposes."[65]

Metcalfe himself was hesitant to surrender control of local patronage to the MLAs. In 1844 he rejected Hale's recommendations that Robert Vincent, the senior magistrate and former registrar of Sherbrooke, be appointed customs collector at Stanstead. Hale had argued that it would be "equitable and expedient that the Patronage of Government should be extended to some considerable extent to the Class of British Subjects viz of American origin of which Mr Vincent is one," but Metcalfe instead appointed James Thompson, a British naval veteran. This led the Sherbrooke MLA to complain that Child was making political capital out of the matter, and he reminded the new governor that "A large number of Americans at Stanstead are as thorough Tories & as warm Const[ts] as any in the Province, and it is my opinion that they deserve and that it would be wise to confer upon them some notice."[66]

As for Child, Metcalfe certainly did not feel obliged to accept the recommendations of one who had supported the executive councillors, Baldwin and LaFontaine, when they resigned over the patronage issue in 1843. Thus, he simply ignored the Stanstead MLA's wishes in 1844 by appointing the Lennoxville notary, C.A. Richardson, as county registrar. Child's response was bitter: "If His Excellency and his present cabinet place no weight to our wishes and interests, when expressed, it is a matter of the deepest regret to me and those who have sent me to Parliament so many years." In July, when the chastened veteran politician was claiming to have become a Metcalfe supporter, he was invited to nominate two local postmasters.[68] However, the governor then threw his support behind the candidacy of John McConnell in the fall election, thereby ensuring Child's defeat.

Neither Child nor any other Stanstead liberal contested the following election three years later, but with the reform victory and the official recognition of party-based responsible government, the old warhorse was once again in a position to dispense patronage. Conveniently ignoring his earlier claim that the local MLA should be consulted even when on the opposition benches, Child expressed his gratitude for "the respect thus shown to me by my esteemed and confidential friends" when he was invited to nominate the new postmaster for Georgeville.[68] The dismissal during the annexation crisis of a number of Stanstead's leading magistrates and militia officers, including deputy McConnell himself, gave Child the opportunity to nominate seven new JPs for the western part of the county shortly before the 1851 election. As local MLA, the disillusioned McConnell could only lament that the chief concern of both parties, once in power, was to increase "the number of offices in the Government," so that they could divide "the public revenues as party spoils among their friends and supporters."[69]

Child himself had become a seeker of a patronage appointment in 1850 when he asked for a position in the customs service, fallaciously claiming to have lost his seat in 1844 while "contending for the principle of Responsible Government." Child spelled out his conception of the link between patronage and politics when he added:

It is a matter of importance to me as well as the restoration of this county to its former political character & standing in the country to have some mark of favor & confidence bestowed by a liberal Government on an old and faithful supporter as I may lay claim to be, and I beg leave to observe had it have been done on the regaining of power by the present Ministry my feelings would have been gratified instead of being mortified and my supporters in this county encouraged to arouse from their defeat and ere this have replaced the county of Stanstead where myself and friends [illegible] for fifteen years maintained it – among the Reformers – represented by a supporter of the present Ministry instead of being disgraced as it now is by Toryism & Leaguism and the Annexation mania.[70]

Child's application was rejected, and his role in the distribution of local patronage failed to regain him the Stanstead riding in 1851, but at least he was rewarded with an appointment as the district's first schools inspector.

The degree to which the patronage system had changed in the Eastern Townships since the pre-Rebellion era is illustrated by the appointment in 1850 of John Carty Tuck as customs officer aboard the Lake Memphremagog steamer, the *Mountain Maid*. Where such positions had once been reserved for British-born officers, Tuck had been imprisoned in Sherbrooke as a Patriote sympathizer during the Rebellion. W.F. Parker, the British-born father of the man whom Tuck had replaced, could not contain his anger: "That an officer who has been tried & proved efficient, who has faithfully & with honor performed his duty for some years past and been twice wounded in the service; to be displaced by a *Rebel Dog Rascal* and noted smuggler, who for months past has been boasting that the whole of the d—d Tory *click* will shortly be displaced is so unaccountable in a Colony under Her Majesty's control, that I must beg to demand an explanation." Parker added:

[the] few Gentlemen who reside as British Subjects in these Townships ... are tried Men and Loyal, and some of us descended from those Heroes who have assisted to place England in the high station in which she is placed among nations: and we will no longer submit to be trampled upon and insulted by the offspring of Convicts, who by fraud and extortion, have acquired a position in society, which has enabled them to become traitors to their sovereign & adopted Country.[71]

Bluster as Parker would, though, the day of British favouritism had come to an end in the Eastern Townships, and the business of establishing family oligarchies was also giving way to that of forging party ties. But patronage distributed on a petty local level failed to satisfy the region's elites, making party loyalties somewhat uncertain during the 1840s. They demanded patronage on a grand scale – that is, generous government grants to improve the transportation network and end the region's economic isolation. All other considerations were secondary as far as the political history of this decade is concerned.

THE POLITICS OF ECONOMIC DEVELOPMENT

At the outset of the first parliamentary session after the provincial union, Edward Hale happily informed his wife that Dr Foster of Shefford "is no radical at all," but "a quiet, sensible man." The Sherbrooke MLA added that he, Foster, Moore, and Watts were "inclined upon all occasions to consult each other and to endeavour to act together."[72] Since Jones of Missisquoi and Child of Stanstead were also eager to co-operate in the interests of Townships development, the only outsider was Megantic County's Daly who was excluded by virtue of his position as civil secretary. Such unity was fostered by the common feeling that the region's loyalty entitled it to a fair share of the £1.5 million guaranteed loan provided by Britain to facilitate Canadian economic development. Unfortunately Sydenham did not agree, for he dismissed Sherbrooke as "a village in the woods," and stated that the "want of Water Communications & the rigour of the climate" would, for the forseeable future, retard growth in the Townships "and set limits to their improvement."[73] In short, Sydenham was quite prepared to see the isolated region remain a backwater in the flow of wheat and timber from Upper Canada.

Soon after the Assembly went into session, Sherbrooke's Hale and Moore approached Sydenham concerning the projected railway, only to be told that grants would henceforth be limited to leading public works which were exclusively government concerns. Hale confided to his wife: "It will be a sad bone of discontent to Rea and Pomroy etc etc and will almost make them radicals." The following month a discouraged Hale reported that the government had targeted £800,000 for public works in Canada West (largely for the St Lawrence canals) and only £90,000 for Canada East: "I complained of this in the House [...] but no one seemed to follow me in the same strain."[74]

After Sydenham's death, Hale was initially shocked by the decision of Sir Charles Bagot to include LaFontaine and four other reformers in the Executive Council. However, he adopted a pragmatic approach, stating that "we must try the thing and see how it works and perhaps we shall have many abuses corrected."[75] Consequently, all the Townships MLAs supported the new administration. Bagot was not in office long enough for the question of a railway subsidy to be settled, but this was not the only economic issue uniting the Townships deputies. One of the local grievances against the Patriotes had been their rejection of bills to impose a reciprocal tariff on the import of American agricultural produce.[76] In 1838 a petition from Philipsburgh and vicinity also complained that, because there was no local customs office, lake schooners were carrying away large shipments of wood and marble to the United States, leaving "the merchant and the Artisan deprived of a great portion of the natural support of the country, by its being diverted into a Foreign Channel."[77]

But protection of the local markets was not a major issue for the region's constitutional associations during the pre-Rebellion era. It was only in 1842, when the United States imposed a still higher duty against foreign agricultural products, that an organized protective tariff campaign was launched in the Eastern Townships. As the session drew to a close in October, however, Hale conceded that "we shall have to return home with all the disagreeable reflection that we have not been able to accomplish the great object of agricultural Protection – but we nevertheless have made a good fight about it upon which occasion Moore managed to make a very good Speech for the first time in Parliament – and I shall have another rap [?] at them, perhaps this Evening."[78]

That same year Hale reported that he, Child, and Moore had "put contested points to the vote" relating to Hincks's agricultural tariff bill, "but lost them all."[79] A week later, however, Child convinced the Assembly to raise the proposed duty on steers from $3.65 to $5.00 a head, and still later to extend the charge "to the femenines [sic] of the horned race as well." The bill also included duties on meat, cheese, butter, and coarse grains, and Child predicted that "Stanstead will be for roasting an ox on the occasion" of its enactment.[80] The *Sherbrooke Gazette* still complained, however, that the bill fell far "short of what the agriculturist had a right to expect." In reply, Child could only note that the American tariff was *ad valorem* and therefore effectively imposed at a much lower rate than the Canadian one, at least by the customs collector at Derby, Vermont.[81]

Child's information appears to have been correct, for a Sherbrooke resident informed Hale in October 1843 that, the American tariff notwithstanding, Samuel Brooks had shipped 130 head of two-year-old cattle to the United States, and two hundred more were to follow. Exemptions from the tariff nevertheless remained very unpopular in the Eastern Townships, and Hale reported in November that "Poor Moore made a sad mistake in his vote about the Army Contractors being exempt from Agricult. Protection after his violent speech against it. It was a memorable speech moreover, & he roared it out as loudly as if he had been talking to the main top – and Dunlop has called him the Sea Monster ever since."[82]

Yet there was no denying that Metcalfe was considerably more sympathetic to the region's interests than Sydenham had been. In his first speech from the throne the new governor-general referred to "the cry for improved roads for the conveyance of produce to markets," adding that "nowhere was this anxiety more strongly expressed than in the Eastern Townships" where high US tariffs had closed "the market to which they had formerly recourse."[83] Not surprisingly, then, when LaFontaine, Baldwin, and their allies resigned from the Executive Council over the patronage issue, the only Townships MLAs to vote in their favour were Child and Moore.[84] In return, Metcalfe's administration responded liberally to petitions from the region for roads and schools.

The local secretary of the British American Land Company, Alexander T. Galt, also exacted a promise of assistance for the beleaguered operation in return for ensuring the election of three or four government supporters in the Townships.[85] But Metcalfe would have few financial resources at his disposal for the region as a whole as long as he governed without the Assembly, and neither Galt nor the other members of Sherbrooke's entrepreneurial elite would be satisfied with local public works, or with the offer of a plank road from Chambly to Granby in place of a railway subsidy.[86] Prior to the 1844 election Alexander Galt, who had now become the local commissioner of the land company, extracted a pledge from the two conservative Sherbrooke candidates that "so intimately did they consider the railway to be [tied] with the prosperity of the Eastern Townships that they should look upon the refusal of efficient assistance by the Executive as a denial of that just share of the notice of government to which the Townships were entitled, and that they should, except upon important constitutional questions, hesitate to afford their support to any administration which would not enter into their desires on that head."[87]

Hale had little fear of opposition in the urban riding of Sherbrooke, but county representative Moore had alienated the Sherbrooke elite when he supported the reformers in the previous Executive Council. Moore therefore reluctantly had to make way for his former business associate, Samuel Brooks, who enjoyed the added advantage of being the local agent for the only bank in the region.[88] Likewise, as we have seen, Child was challenged by John McConnell who, according to Hale, had been "Child's main stay at the last Elect. but who condemns his vote on the Minist. Crisis."[89] As Hale had hoped, Brooks was too powerful a figure to be opposed in the 1844 election, and McConnell defeated Child by 496 votes to 356.

In Shefford, Dr Parmelee would, like Child, be forced during the election to recant his support for the ex-ministers, but again to no avail since Dr Foster retained his seat. In Drummond County Metcalfe demonstrated his disapproval of R.N. Watts by opposing him with his bright young assistant provincial secretary, Christopher Dunkin, but Watts won the election by the narrow margin of 495 to 456 votes. Largely because of the support he received in Megantic's French-speaking townships, Daly was again returned by a comfortable majority in that unwieldy county. Finally, in Missisquoi, the tory Loyalist stronghold of Frelighsburg and nearby Philipsburg ensured that Attorney-General James Smith of Montreal defeated the "ultra-radical" Dr Leonard Brown by over 200 votes.[90]

The Eastern Townships had therefore gone solidly conservative in 1844, even if Watts would for a time support the reformers. Buoyed by the election results, by Metcalfe's sympathetic attitude, and by the promotional zeal of the land company's new commissioner, the Sherbrooke entrepreneurs proceeded to build a cotton factory and to plan for "a sewing-Silk factory, a Knitting Factory, a Pail Factory, a Paper Factory etc etc."[91] Galt wasted no time in circulating a petition demanding a government railway subsidy, and enclosed with the list of signatures was his somewhat intimidating note to Hale: "I have every confidence in your success in obtaining the required vote of money – The very difficulty which you say the Government has in maintaining itself must render the support of the Eastern Townships worth their straining a point to secure – The attainment of this important work is, I believe, now in the hands of the Townships members and I therefore have little dread of the result." Likewise, Benjamin Pomroy of Compton wrote: "There was never a house of Representatives in which I have so much confidence of doing good for the Country as the present and I think should you succeed in obtaining a charter & the grant for our Rail Road that we are allmost [sic] sure of it going into operation."[92]

Following a series of mass meetings in the southern townships, the legislature finally incorporated the St Lawrence and Atlantic Railroad Company in March 1845, with power to build to the New Hampshire border where it would connect with the Atlantic and St Lawrence running from Portland, Maine. Portland had replaced Boston as terminus because it was closer to a direct line through Sherbrooke, and because it represented less of a threat to Montreal as a transatlantic port. Capital was set at $2,400,000, all to come from private sources, and by the summer of 1846 enough money was finally raised to begin construction. But state assistance was needed to proceed beyond the first thirty-mile section of track from Montreal, assistance which was not forthcoming.[93] With work on the railway at a standstill, and the Sherbrooke Cotton Factory facing bankruptcy in April 1847, Galt informed Hale that "a strong feeling of discontent is arising against the present administration – who

– it is asserted – have been merely humbugging the Townships – by the vote for the Maine Road – without any intention of doing the work. I confess I share this feeling myself – as it seems as if everything were tending westward – to the exclusion of Lower Canadian interests." Galt now looked forward to a change in government. In his opinion, "no practical benefit to the country will arise while these constant squabbles occur, and when the ministry are obliged from their weakness to defer to the opinions of every one of their supporters in every respect to the measures they introduce."[94]

The pro-railway policy of the opposition party was helping to establish liberal credibility in the Eastern Townships, and on 19 August 1847 the *Stanstead Journal* suggested that the region's representatives should have joined the opposition, after all, since they were "looked upon with cold apathy and indifference" by the ministry. The administration did win a by-election in Missisquoi when William Badgley was attracted from the bench in Montreal to replace James Smith as attorney-general, but Watts had crossed the floor to the liberal opposition,[95] and Hale had by now lost his enthusiasm for public life. The Sherbrooke deputy's letters to his wife reveal an increasingly obsessive concern with the health of himself and his family during this decade of epidemics, and he privately expressed his delight not to have been chosen as one of the new directors for the railway company in 1846.[96] In November 1847 Hale informed the attorney-general that even though his support for the governor remained unchanged, he would not be running in the next election.

Hale's imminent departure and the political transition taking place in the province created a vacuum in the town of Sherbrooke when John Moore refused to stand in that constituency rather than running against Brooks in the county seat. The perennial candidate, Colonel Gugy, was thereby able to take the town seat without a contest even though neither party wanted him. The Sherbrooke conservatives had their revenge against Moore when Brooks defeated him by a majority of 301 votes.[97] In Stanstead, John McConnell was re-elected by acclamation after Marcus Child decided that he did not have enough support to make a come-back. Despite these victories of three erstwhile conservatives, Gugy promised his backing to the new liberal regime, McConnell had actually run as an independent in favour of changes to the new school and municipal acts, and even Brooks was now said to be an independent whom some of the liberals claimed as their own.[98]

The clearest conservative victories were in the two ridings represented by executive councillors, for Attorney-General Badgley retained his Missisquoi seat, as did Civil Secretary Daly in Megantic. Situated at opposite corners of the region, these two counties were clearly pulled towards the metropolitan centres of Montreal and Quebec where their respective representatives lived. An absentee also won the Shefford riding when Dr Foster felt obliged to drop out of the race after being challenged by the Montreal lawyer and leading liberal politician, Lewis Thomas Drummond. The old tory, P.H. Knowlton, lamented that Shefford's new representative "has been foisted upon us by a combination of circumstances and combination of persons for local purposes more base and more unmitigatedly wicked in Waterloo and Granby Village than it is possible for me to describe ... I solemnly believe that the whole bunch of them care no more for the British Government or British connection than I do which way the wind will blow a year hence."[99] Ironically, when the wind blew briefly towards American annexation the following year, Knowlton would be wafted along with it, and Drummond himself would revoke the venerable colonel's militia commission.

Finally, in Drummond County, Watts reclaimed his seat, but this time as a liberal. The final count in the Eastern Townships was therefore four conservatives of varying commitment to the previous administration, two liberals, and one independent. Because the ruling party had failed to meet the region's demands, Townships voters had begun tentatively to swing towards the liberals in the 1847–48 election despite their fears of French-Canadian domination. That swing would be interrupted in 1849–50 when the apparent realization of those fears helped to foster a strong demand for annexation to the United States.

THE ANNEXATION CRISIS

Under the new Baldwin-LaFontaine administration, the railway promoters would finally receive the support they had been waiting for, and in November 1848 Galt predicted that "the rails will be at Sherbrooke in 1850 – our Cotton Factory stock will soon look up then."[100] The picture painted on 20 September 1848 by the *Stanstead Journal* was a tantalizing one:

We fancy we see the hitherto long and sober faces of the honest yeomanry relaxing into a cheerful smile in anticipation of the "good time coming," when the products of the farmer will bear a cash value; when freight, commission and per cent, will not absorb all the profits of labor beyond a bare subsistence; when our forests and waste lands, shall be changed into fruitful fields; our vast water power employed in driving machinery; and our Townships filled with an industrious, thriving and happy people, who shall have no occasion to look Southward with an envious or longing eye.

But the problem remained the protectionist policy of the American government. The *Journal* added that either "reciprocity of trade ... or if that cannot be had, an obliteration of the boundary line" would be necessary in order to "soon realize the picture we have drawn." The chief concern was to gain greater market access for farm and forest production, but manufactured goods were also becoming a consideration.

Clearly, then, the Canadian government's move in 1849 to increase tariff protection would no longer be enough, even if it had included protection for manufacturing and commerce, as requested by Galt and others from Sherbrooke.[101] Paradoxically, the construction of a railway through the Eastern Townships, made possible by a bond guarantee from the liberal government,[102] had helped to foster a new political threat to the government by increasing the region's desire for closer economic ties with the United States. But the immediate stimulus for the annexation crisis in the Eastern Townships, as in Montreal, was the passage of the Rebellion Losses Bill in the spring of 1849, and Dr Colby of Stanstead was particularly outspoken about what he perceived to be the government's aim of "transferring all legislation in Lower Canada to the French Canadians, to a race of people behind *all* others in enterprise, in agriculture, commerce and the arts, as well as in education."[103]

Colby's rhetoric undoubtedly struck a particular chord with the region's disillusioned tories, for Knowlton, Walton, and McConnell were among the thousands in Sherbrooke and Stanstead counties who signed the annexation manifesto. But other considerations were paramount in the mind of Galt, who himself became an annexationist shortly after replacing Brooks as Sherbrooke County's MLA in 1849. Galt did not directly mention his company's major investments in Eastern Townships land, industries, and the railway, but he argued that Canada would either have to remain a weak dependant of the British Empire or become an integral part of the American Empire:

A Union with the United States will give Canada a place among the nations; the accumulated wisdom of their legislators will become our own; we shall share in the triumph of their unparalleled progress; we shall reap the fruits of the political skill which has thus far shielded their institutions from harm; our interests will be watched over, and our industry protected by their wise commercial policy; and although no longer dependent upon Great Britain we shall feel that we have served her well in ensuring that harmony between the two Empires which is now constantly in peril from conflicting interests.[104]

L.R. Robinson, editor of the non-partisan *Stanstead Journal*, was less rhetorical. He simply argued that because Townships farmers were dependent upon the United States market for disposal of their surplus produce, their profits were minimized by a 20 percent tariff "to help support the American government." And while they were also able to purchase "necessary articles of comfort and luxury" more cheaply in the United States than in Canada, here again they had to pay a 12.5 percent duty "to support their own government."[105]

The dismissals in late 1849 of the Montreal militia officers and justices of the peace who had signed that city's annexation manifesto did nothing to slow down the protest movement in the Eastern Townships. Twelve hundred and thirteen signatures were appended to the manifesto in Sherbrooke County, almost as many as in Montreal. When Galt's business commitments precluded him from attending the legislative session, which had been moved to distant Toronto after the burning of the Montreal Parliament Buildings, a county convention put forward another annexationist as its candidate for the January 1850 by-election. John S. Sanborn was an American-educated teacher of advanced liberal views, but he had also married Samuel Brooks's daughter. Sanborn subsequently became the only MLA in the province to win a seat on the annexation issue, though concerted opposition in the British-settled sections of the county narrowed the margin to only thirty-four votes of 1,448 cast.[106]

Meanwhile, in Stanstead, McConnell had openly declared himself an annexationist as well, and 1,413 residents of the county had signed the manifesto by the end of January 1850. The Stanstead deputy gave as his principal reason the economic stagnation of the region: "Long have we waited and hoped that our resources, particularly those available for lumbering, agricultural and manufacturing purposes would be so encouraged as to lead to their gradual, but healthy developement [sic], thus furnishing employment to our increasing population, and equitable remuneration for the investment of capital and labour." The problem was basically that the Americans would not grant "free and reciprocal intercourse" to Canada as long as it remained a colony of Britain. Canadians therefore had little choice but to dissolve their connection with the parent state and join the United States: "Let tyranny frown and cry treason! but free and enlightened governments cannot deny this inalienable right to the governed."[107]

But Britain did eventually express its displeasure with the annexationist movement, thereby taking the wind out of its sails by late spring. Perhaps, as well, the growing export market made more accessible by the northward advance of Vermont's Passumpsic Railway was enough to reassure local producers. The Stanstead Journal reported in April 1850 that ever since the enactment of the 1846 tariff the American customs collectors had given special consideration to the farmers and breeders of the Eastern Townships: "Such has been the well established reputation of Eastern Townships' cattle, (horses particularly) that quite a thriving business has been done in some seasons with our Southern neighbors."

The newspaper added, however, that the United States government had now passed a prohibitive regulation requiring 20 percent *ad valorem* on cattle and horses, and the treasury department had issued orders to exact the full evaluation on all imports from Canada.[108]

While this development was far from reassuring, the *Journal's* fall report of the annual sales at the Cambridge market near Boston included 1,326 Canadian cattle (2 percent of the total) and 488 Canadian horses (39 percent of the total). Likewise, in 1850 the Eastern Townships customs ports reported the export of 3,900 cattle; 770 horses, 8,610 sheep, 503 hogs, 37,600 pounds of butter, 3,710 bushels of seed, 23,520 bushels of hops, and 1,860 bushels of wheat, for a total value of £23,575. Concurrently, imports of American livestock had obviously declined drastically because the Townships ports reported only ninety-nine horses, sixty-seven sheep, nineteen cattle, and five pigs in 1850. Indeed, imports of all farm produce were negligible, with the only significant specified items being cotton goods, iron and hardware, tea, tobacco, tanned leather and leather goods, cotton wool, machinery, woollen goods, and wood manufactures, a total value of £14,031.[109]

An elated *Stanstead Journal* would report in January 1851 that a local merchant was paying cash for oats to be sent to Boston despite the customs duty and the forty-seven mile haul required to the northern rail terminus at St Johnsbury: "Bring about the connection of roads which we have been advocating, and every bushel of grain, every pound of beef, pork, butter, cheese, lard, etc., etc., which this country produces, could be sold for cash here." Finally, in March, the newspaper announced that one local "teaming concern" alone was delivering five hundred tons of merchandise a year to the local border crossing, and that the export trade of Stanstead and Sherbrooke counties was worth at least one million dollars.[110]

The outburst of annexationist sentiment in much of the Eastern Townships had certainly reflected a deep concern about the political future of the local English-speaking population under responsible government, but for pragmatic spokesmen such as A.T. Galt and L.R. Robinson the economic issue had been paramount. This sentiment was nicely expressed in one segment of Robinson's lengthy New Year's address to his newspaper customers in 1850:

And we (like every man of sense)
Will make the question one of pence.
If better off with Uncle Sam,
No man of sense will care a d—
For Lords or Commons long I ween
If worse, why then, "God Save the Queen!"[111]

With the American demand for Canadian products growing even before the passing of the Reciprocity Treaty in 1854, no more annexation rhetoric was heard from the Eastern Townships after 1850.

The annexation crisis did not prevent the region from swinging toward the liberal government in the 1851 election, for only Megantic and Stanstead returned clearly defined conservatives. Megantic's scattered settlement pattern, ethnocultural diversity, and marginal economic status would ensure repetition of the pattern whereby a large number of candidates, most of whom were non-residents, would campaign without a major issue, and produce a geographically polarized vote. Largely as a result of local community rivalries over the choice of municipal seats, the Quebec liberal, Dunbar Ross, was defeated by the Quebec conservative, John Greaves Clapham, in 1851.

As for Stanstead, the main reason it failed to return a liberal was clearly the sense of betrayal felt over the decision by the St Lawrence and Atlantic directors to have the line pass through what the *Stanstead Journal* called a "howling wilderness" ten miles to the east of Stanstead village.[112] With the politically disillusioned McConnell standing aside, he was replaced by a young Stanstead lawyer named Hazard Bailey Terrill who had been represented the local stockholders in their dealings with the railway company. Terrill did not pledge himself to any party, but he criticized the municipal, school, and road laws, as well as the government's projected intercolonial railway and Dr Fortier's plan for the French-Canadian colonization of the Townships. Running against him was the aging Marcus Child, who admitted that the "road, school, and municipal laws need careful revision," and who also declared himself in favour of government retrenchment, but Terrill won the election with an overwhelming majority of 743 votes to 358.[113] Liberal fortunes soon rose in Stanstead, however, with the promise of a new rail line, the Stanstead, Shefford, and Chambly Railway.[114] For this reason, when the Stanstead MLA died of cholera in 1852, he was replaced without a contest by his formerly annexationist brother, Timothy Lee Terrill, who soon joined the governing party's ranks.[115]

In the town of Sherbrooke, which was the region's main beneficiary of the Montreal to Portland railway, the anti-annexationist Gugy had become so unpopular that he was forced to retire. As a result, the well-connected local lawyer, Edward Short, defeated a virtual unknown, John Griffiths, by a ratio of two to one. Short, whom Hale had identified as liberal in his political orientation, ran as an independent.[116] As for Sherbrooke's rural riding, John Sanborn faced John Henry Pope, a young conservative farmer and entrepreneur from Eaton Township. Pope would dominate politics in the future county of Compton for close to half a century, but in 1851 Sanborn outpolled him by a vote of 1,041 to

717. Again, even if the formerly annexationist MLA was not yet a liberal partisan, he promised to support the ministry "in all measures which I conceive calculated to promote the prosperity of the Province."[117]

The liberals also gained Missisquoi, where the centre of population had shifted sufficiently away from the Loyalist tory community around Frelighsburg in the south to end the possibility of further representation by non-resident conservatives such as William Badgley. A.L. Taylor of Pike River, who was a strong supporter of a railway to serve the Missisquoi Valley and a self-described "*Reformer* in the most comprehensive sense," won the October election.[118]

In addition, the liberals retained the counties of Shefford and Drummond. In the former, the Irish Catholic Solicitor-General Drummond defeated the Irish-born Freemason and lawyer, James O'Halloran, by 1,146 votes to only 652. Predictably, Drummond took nearly all the votes in the French-Canadian townships, but he also won a slight majority in strongly English-speaking Shefford Township.[119] In neighbouring Drummond County the sitting member retired, for the independent-minded Watts had been reprimanded by the local freeholders for the irregularity of his attendance at the legislature. A liberal merchant, John MacDougall of Trois-Rivières, subsequently defeated the Drummondville merchant, George Marler, by the wide margin of 1,497 votes to 504.[120]

Despite the political confusion created in the southern part of the region by the annexation issue, the liberal government was finally able to reap the rewards of its railway promotion policy in the Eastern Townships when the American market began to grow for local products. Annexationism had only briefly interrupted the shift in allegiance on the part of the capitalist entrepreneurs (as well as the farmer majority) from the moderate conservatives of the early 1840s to the increasingly conservative liberals in the 1850s. In making this shift, they were following the provincial trend for pragmatic reasons. As late as 1851, Terrill, Sanborn, and Short had declared themselves independents who would place regional interests ahead of party. In H.B. Terrill's victory address, he declared: "If there may be, as there ought to be, a union of Township action, as there evidently is of Township interests, the influence which the six or seven Township constituencies may exert in the legislation of the Province, and in the welfare of this portion of the Province, will be an influence which has not yet been felt in its force."[121]

While it would obviously be simplistic to reduce Eastern Townships politics during the decade to a single issue, the demand for a railway certainly defined the major trend. And even in constituencies where the prospect of a railway was too distant to be a decisive factor, local self-interest was the main driving force in the provincial elections. This

motivation naturally resulted in a tendency to follow the provincial tra-
jectory in politics, but the governing party could not take Townships
support for granted. After years of government neglect and economic
stagnation, even a judicious distribution of patronage would not buy loyalty. As we shall see in the following chapters, the same sense of local independence and economic self-interest would characterize the response
in the Eastern Townships to state reforms of the judicial, municipal, and
school systems.

2 The Legal System

Referring to the law-enforcement system in Lower Canada, Lord Durham's *Report* simply stated that there was "not the slightest provision for criminal justice" outside the five district court towns, "and to these places all prisoners must be brought for trial from the most remote parts." In addition, there was only one sheriff per judicial district, and these lucrative offices "are said to have been frequently disposed of from personal or political favouritism."[1] This was certainly the case for the St Francis District, where W.B. Felton's brother-in-law, Charles Whitcher, had faced impeachment charges by the Legislative Assembly prior to the outbreak of the Rebellion.

Furthermore, the sheriff's duties were confined to administration and enforcement, such as the serving of warrants and the seizure of property for unpaid debts.[2] A more direct agent of law and order was High Constable Joseph Hazard Terrill, first appointed for the St Francis District in 1824. We still know little of his activities, but he outlined his duties in some detail to Edward Hale in 1840. In addition to executing magistrates' warrants, Terrill was expected "to use every exertion in cases of tumult riot rebellion and felony to suppress every thing of the kind and try to preserve the peace in cases and give information of all misdemeanors that come within his knowledge, and always to be in attendance at the general sessions of the peace to execute all orders from the Court he being their immediate servant and the link between the Court and the petty Constables." He was also to serve subpoenas obtained from the clerk of the peace, compel the attendance of witnesses to sub-stantiate felonies, notify all the local magistrates whenever one of them wished to hold a special session, and summon the petty constables to at-tend such sessions.[3] In other words, though he received no salary and his fees for service amounted to only about £40 annually,[4] the high con-stable was effectively the only professional police officer in the district. As the experience of Terrill's successor in 1844 would demonstrate, one such officer could not make much of an impact upon an entire judicial district.

While Durham did not mention the high constables, he did complain that juries were perverted by the political and national prejudices of their members, with the result that the people had no confidence in the administration of criminal justice. In addition, he claimed that the jus-tice of the peace as an institution was unsuitable for the colonies be-cause of the absence of a social class with the education, sense of moral responsibility, and public experience needed for popular legitimacy.[5] These unpaid magistrates nevertheless played an important role in local communities, including the fulfilment of low-level legislative and administrative functions such as the regulation of markets. But, prin-cipally, all justices of the peace performed such preliminary judicial functions as issuing warrants and interrogating witnesses, as well as as-signing summary punishments for minor offences in informal hearings known as petty sessions. In addition, three or more JPs constituted the district Quarter Sessions of the Peace whose jurisdiction extended to crimes with punishments not involving the loss of life or limb. Its judg-ments could not in general be appealed, but a superior criminal court could order a case removed to itself before the quarter sessions had reached a decision. Finally, in certain townships and parishes, those JPs who were appointed commissioners for the trial of small causes had ju-risdiction over civil suits involving sums up to £6 5s.[6]

Based on his detailed examination of the Judicial District of Montreal prior to 1830, Donald Fyson argues that, contrary to the common wis-dom, the JPs were generally neither inefficient, corrupt, nor ineffectual. He also suggests, however, that for the rural population in particular "the criminal justice was clearly a tool, to be used as necessary and dis-carded when no longer needed."[7] Durham's only recommended solu-tion to what he considered an untenable situation was the appointment of a small number of stipendiary magistrates.[8] We shall see that this sug-gestion, which echoed that of William Kennedy and Adam Thom, his as-sistant commissioners on municipal reform, would be repeated with little effect throughout the decade. There was also the matter of police enforcement in rural areas, which had effectively ended once the militia had been discharged. But Kennedy and Thom warned that, given the current political climate, municipal bodies should not possess "the power of organizing or controlling a constabulary force."[9] Durham again agreed with them, stating that there was little that could be done in this respect for the time being.

No fundamental changes were made to the law enforcement system during the 1840s, except that in 1843 the government restored the district circuit courts with jurisdiction over civil matters involving sums not over £20. Brian Young claims, nevertheless, that the 1840s and 1850s were decades when rural communities in the Eastern Townships "were forced to cede their particular judicial traditions in favour of a centralized and uniform system of Quebec law." These traditions, which included laws concerning "marriage, debt, and other contractual arrangements," were based on the assumption prior to 1857 that English common law applied to freehold areas within Canada East.[10]

But no matter which of the two legal codes, French or English, was in force in the Eastern Townships, it would be misleading to assume that courts of law were imposed on the region. During the pre-Rebellion era residents of Missisquoi County submitted petitions demanding local courts and, to take one example from our study period, in 1846 the Missisquoi circuit court was restored after 645 petitioners protested that it had been terminated "without our consent or knowledge."[11] Two years later, 497 inhabitants of Shefford County were less successful in requesting that a new judicial district of civil and criminal jurisprudence be established between Lake Memphramagog and Missisquoi Bay. The same request was made in 1851. This submission complained that minor offences were seldom prosecuted because of the distance to the Montreal courts, especially since the sums paid to witnesses were never adequate to cover their expenses.[12] Dissatisfaction with access to the court system was even expressed from within the Judicial District of St Francis, as we shall see. The persistent demand throughout the Eastern Townships was that justice be made readily accessible and affordable to all. The justice in question primarily concerned civil matters, for violent crime was not a serious concern and other forms of social disorder could largely be managed within the local communities.

THE PRE-REBELLION TO EARLY POST-REBELLION YEARS

During the early nineteenth century, a significant source of income for some of the more isolated border communities was the printing of bogus American bank notes which were exchanged for cattle and horses stolen in the neighbouring states. The district customs officer reported in 1822 that because there were no criminal courts or jails in the Eastern

Townships, and no secure method of transporting criminals to the Montreal jail, magistrates were often deterred from prosecuting criminals. W.
B. Felton complained the same year that "every facility is afforded to ill-
disposed persons to plunder and to escape from the Townships."[13] As a
member of the Legislative Council, he was instrumental in the establishment of the Judicial District of St Francis (see Map 2), with its own Court
of King's Bench (though without criminal jurisdiction) in 1823.

A circuit court had been introduced only the previous year, shortly
after the Sherbrooke home of the newly appointed customs collector,
William Hamilton, was burned to the ground. While this court, like the
King's Bench, was restricted to civil cases, Felton and seven others formally reported that "the more remote but not less important effects of
this measure will be the improved tone of public opinion, political and
moral." Referring to the detachment of troops sent to the town following the arson attack on Hamilton's house, Felton added that if they
were withdrawn too hastily people might conclude that their role had
been to protect the judges on circuit.[14] This, presumably, would be a
sign of weakness that the state should carefully avoid, but there is no
evidence to suggest that the local populace resented the new court
system.

As a matter of fact, thirty prominent residents of Stanstead also complained in 1823 about the "contagious influence" of the criminal element in that township, and they volunteered to raise half the estimated
£1,200 required to build a jail and court house in the village of Stanstead.[15] But their offer was not accepted, which may explain why that
year the residents of neighbouring Hatley organized a society "for the
suppression of Felonies, Vice and Misdemeanors," with the power to assess the property of subscribing members and pay "pursuers" to apprehend offenders.[17] This organization was particularly concerned about
horse-stealing, burglaries, and counterfeiting. But most of the criminal
cases tried before the St Francis District's General Sessions of the Peace
were for violent assaults, which the grand jury of 1826 attributed to "the
facility with which ardent spirits were to be procured at several unlicensed Stores and Taverns in each of the Townships."[16] Much the same
refrain would be heard during the 1840s, but the government had already given Felton and two others permission to construct a substantial
jail in Sherbrooke. They were to finance the building by a loan which
would be paid off by taxing district law processes. By 1828 Felton and
his colleagues had completed a two-storey structure, with brick walls
three feet thick and hewn granite sills for the door and windows. The
new jail was said to be capable of holding ninety-six inmates, although
there was seldom more than a small fraction of this number incarcerated during the post-Rebellion period.

Unfortunately for the builders, they were left holding a £1,200 debt which the court tax was slow to reduce and the government refused to assume. Felton could at least console himself that within two years the centre of counterfeiting operations had reportedly moved westward from Stanstead to the Dunham and St Armand area, which lay outside the St Francis District. But the main reason for this development, according to the *Montreal Gazette*, was that local innkeepers and merchants had simply resolved not to deal with suspicious characters.[18]

The village merchants of the Eastern Townships were less concerned with the suppression of counterfeiting than with the reduction of expenses to recover small debts. The region had a largely cashless economy in which long-term credit was unavoidable, and the commissioners' courts established in 1821 gave any JP who had been appointed as commissioner for the trial of small causes the authority to hear cases concerning goods, wages, loans, rents, and non-endorsed notes of hand in any parish or township outside Quebec, Montreal, and Trois-Rivières. But the jurisdiction of the commissioners' courts was limited to sums not over £4 3s. 4d. Furthermore, they were abolished in 1829, requiring a petition of one hundred proprietors to be re-established in any parish, seigneury or township.[19]

Not satisfied with the commissioners' courts, inhabitants of Stanstead Township complained in 1822 that it was so expensive to take witnesses to Montreal that it was less costly to relinquish the debt than to prosecute. They also held grievance meetings during the winter of 1824–25 demanding county courts with jurisdiction to £10, and the extension of the district Provincial Court's ceiling from £20 to £100.[20] But Sherbrooke's British officialdom had little sympathy for the problems of the local American-born merchants, and Judge John Fletcher of the King's Bench was particularly hostile. In 1825 he declared that in order to eliminate "unnecessary" actions for small and trivial causes, a plaintiff would henceforth have to prove that three days' notice had been given the defendant in any case involving debts. Furthermore, the cost of the suit was not to exceed the debt and charges owed. The result, according to Stanstead's *British Colonist*, was that the recovery of sums under five or six dollars would become unenforceable. In March 1826 a published letter from "Philo Junius" claimed that Fletcher's regulation had practically eliminated suits in the Provincial Court, and that property values were declining as a result. These criticisms ultimately led to contempt charges by Fletcher against editor Silas Dickerson and his correspondents, with Dickerson being fined and jailed repeatedly until he was forced to sell his newspaper.[21]

The people of the Eastern Townships may have failed to join the Rebellion, despite their resentment of the British government and its appointees, but the armed conflict brought the repressive arm of the state closer to their daily lives. For example, many of those whose loyalty was suspect were required to take an oath of allegiance to the Queen. Dr J. Chamberlain of Frelighsburg in St Armand proved to be particularly enthusiastic about his duties as oaths commissioner, keeping a register of all those to whom he had administered the oath. Chamberlain claimed that the register "will have the very best effect in the country, more especially over the lukewarm and disaffected, and the granting of certificates will give an idea of importance which otherwise would not be created." He even asked the civil secretary for an assistant to handle the clerical duties, but the government had more pressing matters to deal with, and Chamberlain and his fellow commissioners were left in the dark as to procedures to be taken against those who refused to comply.[22] As late as April 1838 one correspondent to the government complained that no oaths had been administered in Compton Township, "although a considerable number of People of American origin here are represented, I believe upon good Authority as disaffected to the Government of the Queen."[23]

Political tensions were greater in Stanstead Township, from where commissioner William Ritchie reported in January 1838 that "I meet with a good deal of opposition and many refusals." As a way of saving time and expense, Ritchie suggested that the various militia units should be mustered for the purpose of administering the oath. He also recommended that more magistrates be appointed to each township in the county.[24] Indeed, there were none at all in Hatley, Barnston, and Bolton, while in Stanstead Township Marcus Child had been deprived of his magistrate's commission after refusing to take the oath. As for the Compton area, the Irish-born J.S. Jones had complained in October 1837 that there was no magistrate within ten miles of the village, where many criminal acts had recently been committed.[25] The section of the Eastern Townships which lay within the Judicial District of Montreal was better served in this regard, for in December 1837 there were thirty magistrates living in ten of these townships. Their effectiveness was obviously somewhat limited, however, since the county also boasted an association for "the detection and bringing to justice of HORSE THIEVES."[26]

Despite the incarceration of a number of those suspected to be leaders of the politically disaffected,[27] the hand of the state did not weigh particularly heavy on the Eastern Townships during the Rebellion years. Indeed, the demands for a more effective judicial system simply intensified in 1838. Taking advantage of the appointment of the Durham Commission, delegates from several townships in the St Francis District met in the fall of 1838 to draft and submit a detailed list of demands. The meeting was chaired by Lieutenant-Colonel William Morris, the retired

British army officer who had become the commanding officer of Sherbrooke's unattached militia.[28] The first motion was for "Courts of Judicature of equal authority and with equal privileges as the other Districts of the Province, with all the powers of the Courts of King's Bench of civil and criminal jurisdiction and of Courts of Quarter Sessions." This resolution was at least partially heeded, for in 1841 the St Francis Queen's Bench was finally given jurisdiction over criminal cases.[29]

The 1838 meeting's second demand was that the governing laws be "equally accessible to all classes of the community, and as little burthensome to the people as may be consistent with the due administration of justice." Included in this motion was the request for jury trials in civil cases, as in England. Thirdly, the delegates asked that the government place their district on an equal footing with other districts by granting an annual sum towards defraying the expenses of public and criminal prosecutions, the payment of witnesses to attend courts, the reimbursement of expenses incurred by grand and petty jurors during the criminal terms, "and generally for all other expences [sic] of the administration of public justice throughout the District." The fourth motion noted that the district "labours under the want of municipal regulations for the maintenance of good order and the due observance of the laws in each and every Township," and asked that a stipendiary magistrate be appointed "to attend to the ready and constant discharge of all the duties required to maintain the peace and tranquillity of the District." Finally, the delegates complained that the district court house was "perfectly insecure and insufficient for the preservation of the records of the Country, and the accommodation of the Court, the Jurors or the public."

These were the delegates' only requests as far as the judicial system was concerned, but they also complained that the revenue laws were "totally insufficient to prevent the illicit introduction of prohibited goods, and goods paying high duties, from the United States, at once discouraging the honest, and affording reward to the illicit, trader." What was needed was a reduction of the duties and a stricter enforcement of the law by the appointment of more customs officers. Resolutions were also passed protesting the inefficient execution of the road laws and the disorganized state of the militia, which was "incapable of fulfilling the various duties appointed by the laws, in civil as well as criminal matters." Indeed, the Sherbrooke meeting laid the blame for both problems at the door of Sheriff Charles Whitcher, for he was deputy grand-voyer in charge of all public roads in the district, as well as being lieutenant-colonel of the Fifth Battalion of the Eastern Townships Militia. It is quite possible that Chairman Morris saw Whitcher as a rival, but the motion clearly also reflected the widespread animosity in the district towards the discredited Felton clan.[30]

The 1838 petition illustrates how the region hoped to take advantage of its loyalty during the Rebellion to gain more attention from the government. The campaign was clearly supported by both British and American-born notables, for five months later, in January 1839, another meeting chaired by Morris recommended several men of each origin for the position of stipendiary magistrate. The resolution disclaimed "all intention of improperly interfering with the patronage of prerogative of the Governor General," but declared that these appointments "would tend to strengthen the hand of the friends of British Institutions in their efforts to sustain the Government."[31]

Lord Durham may have made it known that he planned in his *Report* to recommend a stipendiary magistracy, for a number of inquiries concerning the position were sent to the civil secretary during the latter half of 1838. To take one example, C.P. Elkins, a British-born Sherbrooke lawyer whose daughter had married Sheriff Whitcher's only son, submitted his application in August. Elkins noted that the nearest magistrate, Edward Hale, lived two miles outside the town, and he complained that "the peaceable part of the Inhabitants are much annoyed by the firing of arms at all hours *after dark*, not merely small arms but *Cannon*." He also complained about the prevalence of charivaris, and added that "the Magistracy here are not (for the kind of people we have here) energetic enough – they take Bail for any offense be it what it may, consequently when the Sessions come on the principal is not forthcoming. He goes over the line."[32]

Other applicants were P.H. Moore of St Armand and Alexander Kilborn of Stanstead, both American-born,[33] but the government chose to focus instead on the districts where armed conflict had occurred. It established a special mounted police force of two to three hundred constables acting under the orders of fourteen stipendiary magistrates in the rural communities of the Montreal District. The commanding officer (with the official title of Inspecting Stipendiary Magistrate) was none other than Colonel Gugy, Sherbrooke's tenacious former and future MLA.

"Political surveillance and pacification" may have been the police force's main mandate,[34] but Gugy was anxious to move against the smugglers and counterfeiters based in the Eastern Townships. He clearly depended on knowledgeable informants, for a trader from Boston named Edward Thomas identified three Dunham Township labourers as forgers of bank bills and promissory notes from four New York banks. According to Thomas, they were assisted by a local mason and a carpenter, as well as their own wives and grown offspring. "Certain thieves and other profligate characters of and about the City and State of New York" supplied the counterfeiters with "divers goods, wares and merchandise, wearing apparel and household articles evidently stolen."[35]

Gugy realized that the governor and Special Council would be more inclined to take action when Americans were not the only victims. Thomas's affidavit therefore added that the counterfeit ring planned to extend its activities to Canadian bank notes and "current coin of the Realm." But the governor maintained his equanimity, informing Gugy that the interested American parties would have to meet all expenses, aside from subsistence costs for the police.[36] E. Derby, the Boston-based agent for the Bank Association of Massachusetts and other New England states, subsequently paid Gugy £50 towards expenses on condition that all the offenders be arrested and punished "without any further pecuniary claim on him." When Gugy informed the Canadian government that this sum would not cover a third of the costs involved, it agreed to cover up to £100 in expenses for the operation. After contacting the local magistrate already involved in the affair, Gugy sent to the area small groups of police officers disguised as civilians.[37] He suggested that, in addition to moving against the thirty to fifty individuals directly engaged in the activities over a seventy-mile area, it might be necessary to arrest their many confederates in order to prevent them from "bearing intelligence or destroying the implements & tools." A few days later Gugy reported that after having visited Dunham Township in person, he had found "the numbers of the more notorious counterfeiters to be not only greater than I had anticipated but that they were extensively connected by marriage and interests."[38]

With the aid of two stipendiary magistrates and thirty to forty members of his police force, Gugy was able to report that the mission was successful. Fourteen individuals were arrested, even though all were armed and the "most resolute … had declared they would never be taken alive." Missing no angle that would accentuate the importance of his accomplishment, Gugy added: "With one exception the counterfeiters were avowedly opposed to the British government and though hourly engaged in defrauding the citizens of the United States, they did not hesitate to declare their desire to become connected with that republic." But "the worst feature of the case was the frequent intercourse they had with thieves, Burglars, horse stealers, and other profligate characters from different parts of the Union."[39]

Not content with the arrest of only one group of counterfeiters, Gugy extended his operation eastward, where he placed W.F. Coffin, stipendiary magistrate for Ste-Marie-de-Monnoir, in charge of the operation. Coffin obviously cast a wide net, for he arrested two men from Compton Township, two from Barford, six from Barnston, and two from Stanstead.[40] Of the twenty-nine individuals who were apprehended in the region as a whole, fifteen were committed to the Sherbrooke jail and charged with counterfeiting "the silver coin by law current in this Province." Seven were sent to Montreal on charges of forging New York bank bills, promissory notes, orders, and draughts; and the remaining seven were released.[41]

Drawing the attention of the governor to the state of the jails in Montreal and Sherbrooke, Attorney-General Ogden recommended that rather than waiting for the regular session of the King's Bench in Montreal and Trois-Rivières (St Francis still did not have criminal jurisdiction), a Commissions of Oyez and Terminer and Gaol Delivery be held in the Eastern Townships. Not only would this save the expense of transporting the prisoners, but "the example of a trial in the immediate vicinity of these misdeeds, would increase the general feeling throughout the population of the Townships which I am informed is that of sincere gratification at the breaking up of a Gang who have been a pest and a disgrace to the Country." Furthermore, the privilege of participating in the administration of justice as jurors would "go far, to remove the too long standing impression amongst them of their being, as it were, a proscribed people."[42]

But subsequent events would tend to undermine the image of a forceful and efficient state apparatus. The governor agreed to hold the trial in Sherbrooke,[43] but action had not yet been taken at the end of January, more than two months after the arrests. Citing the deplorable condition of the jail, a local magistrate requested that either the trial be held as speedily as possible or the inmates be allowed to post bail.[44] The prisoners themselves complained that, as British subjects and long-time local residents with families to support, they were entitled to bail, especially since the testimony against them had been given by a person sentenced twice to the New York State Prison for burglary and once for perjury.[45]

The attorney-general was finally compelled to release the prisoners on bail in March, after the trial had been delayed by the failure of the American banks to produce the evidence necessary to prove that the notes in question had been forged. According to the governor of Massachusetts, whose predecessor had helped launch the operation, only one bill from his state had been seized and the bankers' association had no further funds with which to send an agent to Canada. Nor, apparently, was there any case pending against those arrested for counterfeiting Canadian coin.[46] Gugy's grand demonstration of the state's coercive powers was ending in embarrassment, if not public ridicule.

Nor was there any discernable public support for the recommendation by both Gugy and Colonel Robert Nickle, the commanding officer of the border military force, that a police force be established in the Townships region to prevent counterfeiting and smuggling.[47] Edward Hale himself was less than enthusiastic, and the government simply extended the police ordinances to the St Francis District in December 1839, while maintaining Nickle's military presence there until the spring of 1840.[48] Even though no stipendiary magistrates were sent to the region, a Sherbrooke meeting with such influential figures as future MLAs John Moore and Samuel Brooks in attendance condemned the rural police as an attack on local autonomy.[49]

Despite the conservative political shift in the Eastern Townships, then, definite limits persisted as far as imposition of the state's repressive apparatus was concerned. And whatever short-term impact Gugy's campaign may have had on the region, the jail calendars and the grand jury reports reveal that local residents continued to be arrested for forging and passing counterfeit notes up to the end of our study period. Still, there would be no more major police campaigns, and no indications that the people of the Eastern Townships considered these outlaws to be a serious threat to their communities. Of much more concern than counterfeiting to the residents of the border townships in the post-Rebellion era were the gangs of rebel exiles and their sympathizers living in northern Vermont, though the situation west of Missisquoi Bay on the New York border appears to have been worse.[50] Aside from a few isolated incidents, the Eastern Townships had been generally peaceful during the Rebellion. There was more shooting and destruction of property after the hostilities had ended than before, though it is doubtful that any further aggressive role was played by such leading Vermont figures as Captain Ira A. Bailey, who was Troy's first constable and a justice of the peace.

Bailey had been involved in organizing a raid on South Potton by fifty to sixty men in February 1838. When they attempted to seize the arms of the local volunteers from a house guarded by three men of the Elkins family, one of their band was fired upon and killed. The attackers subsequently took the guns and retreated, but threatened to return and burn down "every building occupied by a government man." Although the anticipated attack never materialized, Harvey Elkins later complained to the government that during the ensuing month he had been shot at and repeatedly threatened with death. He therefore asked for a public position somewhere outside the neighbourhood.[51]

According to the *Missisquoi Standard* in December 1838, sedentary companies of militia volunteers were being organized to drill for one day a week: "The honor of this part of the country being in their hands, they will consider themselves as the main stay of the country, ready at a moment's warning to throw themselves into the breach, whenever and wherever it may be made."[52] Two and a half years later, however, David Kennedy and other Canadian fugitives living in Troy attacked the farm of Captain Moses Elkins of Potton. They succeeded in burning the house, four barns, and two sheds, as well as livestock and other contents to a value of £765. As of 1846, the government had still given Elkins's widow no compensation on the grounds that the attack had taken place too long after the Rebellion had ended.[53]

Meanwhile, though many issues of the *Missisquoi Standard* are missing for this period, those that survive suggest that incendiarism was a regular occurrence in the area. On 2 April 1839 the *Standard* announced the destruction of Captain Charles Miller's barn and shed with all contents – eight horses, ten cows, five calves, and a large amount of hay. Noting that the perpetrators had retreated to Swanton, Vermont, the newspaper asked: "How long are the quiet & peaceable inhabitants on this frontier to be burned and plundered with impunity? If the American government will not take care of these villains, how long can it be supposed that our fellow-subjects will submit to be robbed of their property & their lives, by gangs of pirates and freebooters, without visiting them, with that retribution which they so justly merit?" The arson attacks were not limited to the Canadian side of the border, however, for the *Standard* also announced that two barns were subsequently burned in Highgate, Vermont. Rather than suggesting these were acts of reprisal, it claimed that the same gang was responsible.[54]

Further east, in June 1839, approximately a dozen men from Holland, Vermont, went to the Barnston home of Captain William Burroughs during the night and demanded his militia unit's guns. When Burroughs and his son resisted, the gang fled, but not before setting his barn on fire.[55] By this time the raiders were probably border outlaws more than they were political rebels, which may explain why the government felt it unnecessary to station any rural police detachments or stipendiary magistrates in the region. Whatever their motivation, nothing more is heard of such raids in the Union period. Policing the border became essentially a matter of attempting to regulate trade and raise state revenue by collecting duties on goods and chattels coming into Canada from the United States. Despite the Rebellion, then, there was little fundamental change in the law enforcement system of the Eastern Townships from the early 1820s until the dawn of the Union era. Nor, as we shall see in the next section, was there much pressure for criminal law reform during the 1840s in contrast to the other major institutional changes taking place during this decade.

CRIMINAL LAW

Recent studies have argued that the justices of the peace shouldered the burden of enforcing the criminal justice system,[56] but throughout much of the Eastern Townships the problem continued to be a shortage of individuals to fulfill this role. After submitting the names of four men eligible to act as JPs in Drummond County in early 1842, the district warden, James Brady, reported that the "want of magistrates and of a few efficient and active Police in this & other sections of the District, renders the Sleigh, road, & many other acts, wholly inoperative."[57] The same year, retired Major Alexander Mackenzie reported that he was the only magistrate serving the townships of Shipton, Tingwick, Warwick, Wotton, and part of Kingsey.[58] Referring more specifically to the Drummondville area in 1843, deputy R.N. Watts reported that one of the men appointed commissioner of the peace had no property and therefore did not qualify, one had died before his commission was issued, one had returned to Europe several years earlier, and two refused to serve. The only acting magistrate in the area resided twelve miles off a through road which was itself impassable in wet weather; his nearest colleague was thirty miles distant.[59]

The situation was somewhat improved in the St Francis District by 1845, when fifty-two magistrates were listed for fourteen townships. However, settlers in the more remote areas still remained far removed from the closest resident JP, and a number of those named in the 1845 list would have died, moved, or otherwise become inactive. Only twenty-seven resident magistrates had qualified in the district as of 1 March 1846, and seven of them were from the single township of Stanstead.[60]

Allan Greer has argued that the JPs were not simply state agents, because they were unsalaried officials who were free of any sort of routine supervision or administrative control, and Greg Marquis has suggested that the lower courts also served to engender "a degree of popular legitimacy in the legal system."[61] It should be noted as well that the higher courts were not without their own instrument of popular legitimation, namely the jury. Paul Romney claims that the criminal trial jury traditionally represented the "partial, and tacitly tolerated sovereignty of the local community" because of the jury's ability to censor unjust law "by acquitting a defendant in defiance of the law and the evidence."[62] He might have added that the jury system at one time also provided a voice for the community on a wide variety of issues. The criminal courts actually had two juries, the grand jury and the petty jury. The primary role of the grand jury, which was presumably composed of the more elite members of society as in England, was to decide which cases on the court calendar would go to trial. These would then be heard by a body of lesser social standing known as the petty jury. But, again as in England, the "presentment" drafted by the grand jury foreman and approved by his fellows was not confined to judicial matters. Even after the introduction of elected municipal councils and school commissions in the early 1840s, the grand jury's report continued to express the public needs and desires of the St Francis District.[63]

Thus, the report submitted by the grand jury of the General Sessions of the Peace in February 1842 expressed the hope that the district councillors "will direct their undivided energies to the establishing of a good and efficient Road system, and the construction of new and leading routes of communication, for which the increasing population and settlement of the Country imperatively call." Specifying that Sherbrooke's public bridge "should have proper approaches to prevent accidents, and that the edge of the Hill, commonly called King's Hill, should be fenced for a similar purpose," the grand jurors added that road officers should enforce the provisions against the "too common occurrence" of trotting over the bridges. The report also claimed to speak for "this Section of the province" when it expressed confidence that the municipal representatives would impose as moderate a tax burden as possible, one which "will be applied upon those only, whose means will afford such demands." Moving to the sphere of the provincial government, the 1842 report deplored the inequitable tariff system whereby the United States government exacted a heavy tax on Canadian agricultural imports while American products "may be introduced into this Province without duty, to compete with our own Farmer on his own soil." The legislators were asked to ensure that Canadian produce entered the Mother country duty free, and to protect Canadian farmers against American imports "without interfering with the commercial and other interests of the Province."[64]

If the barrier between popular justice and official justice was not always visible, clearly neither was that between the courts and other state institutions. For the purposes of this chapter, however, the grand jury reports are most useful for the overview they provide of the evolving criminal law system in the St Francis District. As was the custom, the grand jury presentment for February 1842 began with a report on the Sherbrooke jail conditions, which had apparently improved somewhat since the counterfeiters arrested by Gugy's police force had been incarcerated there in 1839. The only complaint was from a man arrested for assault who had been waiting five months for a trial. The report also recommended that the jail's stable be moved farther from the powder magazine, around which an additional safety wall was required. The jail apparently guarded both prisoners and the militia's gunpowder without much consideration for the volatility of this combination.

The grand jury's reports during the following years reveal that the jail's security was not a high priority for the government. In October 1843 the grand jury noted that because of the need for a new outer wall, inmates were given no exercise. Two or three awaiting trial were actually kept in irons, leading the jurors to observe that "the deprivation of personal liberty is a sufficient hardship on an unconvicted prisoner without the aggravation natural to what they can only consider as a punishment."[65] And while the following year the grand jury complimented the district on the improvements to its jail, its report for 1848 noted that a military guard had been necessary to prevent escapes. The jury members again recommended that a portion of the yard be walled off so that the prisoners could exercise. In 1850 the jail's physician complained that the prisoners were unable to take the open-air exercise essential to their health. Sheriff Bowen claimed that his charges were generally so few in number that they could be moved from one floor to another for a change of air, but he added that the building was not secure enough, since the removal of one brick could result in an escape within an hour.[66]

Wolfred Nelson's official inquiry into prisons the following year painted a rosier picture, noting that the jail "bore all the appearance of being clean and neat, the walls were white-washed, and the floors as a tidy housewife would express it, '*bright*;' order was everywhere apparent." As a social reformer, Nelson was less concerned with the prisoners' physical condition than with the fact that nothing was being done to make them productive members of society. Even though the ex-rebel leader had himself spent some time in prison, he wrote that "if it is in contemplation to make the Gaols of Canada not only penal, but, as they certainly should be, reformatory institutions, exercising a detering [*sic*] influence over the vicious and abandoned, it would be proper to make the sojourn there a little less inviting." He recommended that each of the eight large cells in the Sherbrooke jail be divided by a brick wall, reducing them to four feet in width. This would still provide ample room even "to admit of picking wool or cotton" which could be obtained from the two town factories. Finally, Nelson recommended that the prison yard be expanded so that outdoor work could be accomplished both for the health of the prisoners and for the interests of the institution.[67]

If the penal reform movement had failed to reach the Eastern Townships by mid-century, it was doubtless largely because of the infrequency of serious crime in the region. Thus the grand jury reported that there had been an "almost total absence of crime" within the district in 1842. It added that those offences which the courts usually dealt with were of such a minor nature that, under the new acts for the administration of criminal justice, most would in future be determined before local magistrates without ever going to the Court of Quarter Sessions. This prediction appears to have come true, at least for the short term, because there was only one prisoner in the Sherbrooke jail at the end of 1842, and successive reports throughout the decade commented consistently on the lack of crime in the district. Of the 213 Lower Canadians committed to the provincial penitentiary between 1842 and 1847, only four were from the St Francis District.[68]

The grand jury frequently suggested that more of the cases should have been settled by the magistrates in petty sessions. Thus, the report submitted in October 1843 complained that the cases under review were of such a trifling nature that the farmers on the jury should not have been called away from their crops. Even more inconvenient for the local residents was the fact that the Queen's Bench for the St Francis District did not have criminal jurisdiction prior to 1843, with the result that those called for jury duty in the more serious criminal cases had to travel as far as 120 miles to attend the court at Trois-Rivières.[69] The counter-vailing argument (though it was put by an outsider, W.F. Coffin) was that if criminal courts were introduced locally, people would have to serve on juries more frequently, only to "decide a couple of cases" and "receive the congratulations of the Judge on the lightness of the calendar."[70]

The case of Compton Township's Philip Adolphus Barker suggests that the greatest losers under the existing system were the accused.[71] After his arrest in 1839 on the charge of stealing $600 from his elderly neighbour two years earlier, Barker was held in the Trois-Rivières jail for fifteen months awaiting trial. There was no witness to the crime, but none of the ten defence witnesses Barker subpoenaed were on hand when the trial finally took place. As a result, he was sentenced to death (though the sentence was later commuted to fourteen years in the penitentiary), largely on the testimony of two men of dubious character. Barker was not a marginal character in the community, for his father had served as magistrate as well as captain of militia during the War of 1812, and in December 1844 he and two local relatives with distinctly genteel names, Antoinette Cornelia Barker and Theodesa Adelaide Barker, laid claim to his grandfather's extensive estate in Virginia.[72] Indeed, a former French-Canadian resident of Sherbrooke stated in 1846 that Barker was the victim of a plot by former friends who had become jealous of his prosperity. This claim has the ring of truth, for at the trial one neighbour claimed that "Barker did little at farming," while others testified to seeing him with money, and an innkeeper reported that a few days after the robbery Barker had paid his bill even though it was "rare to see any specie in circulation." Among Barker's enemies was the local MLA John Moore, who objected to a possible pardon in 1842. The following year Solicitor-General Aylwin claimed that Barker's neighbours feared revenge through violence or fraud. Yet 162 residents of Compton and vicinity submitted a petition in 1844 asking that Barker be pardoned on the grounds that his conduct in jail had been good, this was his first offence, and he had a wife and six children "in extreme indigence" who depended upon their neighbours for subsistence.

Somewhat embarrassingly for the government, Barker was still in the Trois-Rivières jail three years after his sentencing, apparently because an oversight in the Act of Union allowed him to refuse to be sent to the Kingston penitentiary.[73] He was finally offered a release in 1844, but only on condition that he leave the province, which he refused to do on the grounds that he had already served a longer sentence than normal for a common robbery. The judicial authorities would not tolerate such a challenge to their authority, and Barker languished an additional four years in the distant town's common jail. Finally, in September 1848, the fifty-four-year-old prisoner expressed his "deepest contrition" at not having accepted the state's terms, and a month later he was discharged on condition that he be exiled from British North America.

The Barker case was clearly a miscarriage of justice. Whether or not he was the victim of neighbourhood jealousy is impossible to judge, but the distance of the court hearing from Barker's home appears to have been a major factor in the verdict. Barker was doubtless able to afford to pay for his witnesses' expenses, which defendants were required to do, but the arresting magistrate, Benjamin Pomroy, had apparently told these individuals that there was no need for them to appear at the trial. While it was not unusual for trials to proceed without defence witnesses, positive testimony concerning Barker's character would certainly have played a crucial role in influencing the sentence, if not the verdict.[74]

After the government had finally succumbed to popular pressure by giving the St Francis District full criminal jurisdiction in late 1843,[75] the first grand jury for the Court of Queen's Bench repeated the usual comment about the small number of cases waiting to be examined. Of the five sent to trial in August 1844, only two were heard that term, but Jared F. Blanchard's trial on a charge of arson created at least as great a stir as the Barker case had.[76] Again there was no concrete evidence nor any eyewitnesses, but the sentence was stiff, fourteen years hard labour. Like Barker, Blanchard was a local farmer of longstanding residence, but the circumstantial evidence against him was considerably stronger. Several individuals testified that they had seen him, or someone who looked like him, in the vicinity of Selah Pomroy's house and barns shortly before they were burned to the ground. Still, Blanchard was only one of a number of people who had passed the property in an inebriated state that day on their way home from an agricultural exhibition. More damning was the fact that he had recently threatened Pomroy and the other JPs who had fined him for bootlegging whiskey. Furthermore, there was his record as a political radical who had been imprisoned for five months during the Rebellion, and the fact that memories were still fresh of the cross-border arson attacks by political exiles and their American sympathizers.

As with Barker, a number of local notables (including Marcus Child, four school commissioners, three commissioners of small causes, two ministers, and a militia major) signed a request for Blanchard's release in 1849, long before his sentence had been served, on the grounds that his wife was supporting her aged mother and five children between the ages of six and thirteen. John McConnell intervened against Blanchard, but the conservative MLA probably made less impact on the Baldwin-LaFontaine ministry than did the recent destruction of the Montreal Parliament Buildings by arsonists, not to mention Blanchard's record of insubordination while in prison. Not surprisingly, there is no indication that he was released during our study period.

The third major court case of this decade involved a Brompton farmer named Charles Toussaint who was charged in 1850 with assaulting and raping his sixteen-year-old servant, Melissa Clifford. Toussaint admitted only to the beating, claiming that the girl had stolen his wife's jewelry. Even though no physical examination of Clifford was made until ten days later, Toussaint was sentenced to hang. Within three days, over one hundred individuals had signed a petition asking for a lesser sentence. They included many of Sherbrooke's notables, such as John and W.L. Felton, William Ritchie, Sheriff Bowen, Benjamin Pomroy, Hollis Smith, the local Anglican and Catholic clergymen, and MLAs J.S. Sanborn and John McConnell. The *Sherbrooke Gazette* and the *Stanstead Journal* also opposed the death penalty, the latter newspaper declaring that "although improbable, it is by no means impossible that the crime may have been different in its nature and circumstances from what the evidence of the girl makes it out to have been." Toussaint's conviction was subsequently reduced to life imprisonment.[77]

John Weaver suggests that this ritualized contact between community and crown was aimed at maintaining local deference,[78] but it was the legal arm of the state that was responding to public opinion in such cases, not vice versa. Public outrage probably had a major impact on the severity of the sentences (if not the verdicts as well) in each of the above-mentioned cases in the first place. Certainly there were other rape cases where the results were quite different from the Toussaint case. In one, the accused was acquitted when his fifteen-year-old victim admitted that she had not screamed and that she had subsequently asked him to play cards with her. In yet another case, the guilty party was sentenced to only twelve months in the common jail.[79] Toussaint may have been singled out for special severity because he was a French Canadian and his servant was English-speaking, but it should be recalled that many in the English-speaking community requested modification of his sentence.

Weaver also suggests that increased population mobility was causing a decline in the practice of petitioning for clemency in Upper Canada's Gore District during the 1840s, but it remained both commonplace and effective in the Eastern Townships. Thus, the attorney-general discharged a three-month sentence for "cutting and maiming with intent" against a Bury miller in 1845; he released a Stanstead tailor after four months of a nine-month sentence for theft in 1850; and in 1851 a sixteen-year-old boy who was said to be of unsound mind was freed after serving half of a twelve-month sentence for assault with intent to rape.[80]

As in eighteenth-century England, such requests for clemency may have been motivated sometimes, though clearly not always, by a desire to save the community the expense of supporting the prisoners' families.[81] Nor were such requests always justified, as illustrated by the case of Patrick Ivers and his four sons, who were among seven men from Kingsey convicted of assault during the 1845 election in Drummond County. The Ivers family had supported the victor, R.N. Watts, who joined the local JP, the Anglican minister, and "other influential parties" in asking that the prison sentences be reduced. Watts claimed in October that the Ivers' wives and children "are without the help of any man whatever while all their potatoes are still in the gound ... ruin and starvation awaits them."[82]

Attorney-General Smith recommended the case to Metcalfe's favourable attention, noting that the defendants had been forced to travel to Sherbrooke three times because the case was repeatedly postponed for want of evidence. But a rather different picture emerged from the response of the four convicting magistrates. They reported that they had given the senior Ivers a very lenient sentence of ten days in jail and a £2 10s. fine because of his advanced age, and in order to enable him to look after the households of his sons while they were incarcerated. One had been sentenced to one month in late September, while the other three received two-month sentences. The magistrates also described how, after only three votes had been registered at the Kingsey polling station, the returning officer had sworn in nine special constables, including the elder Ivers, and arranged to admit one voter at a time for each candidate, turn-about. But as soon as the door to the store where the poll was conducted had opened, Ivers signalled to a group of men outside who then proceeded to beat the special constables. One had his ribs broken and another suffered from deafness after being kicked in the face while he lay unconscious on the floor. Given this report, Metcalfe had little choice but to reject the request for leniency.[83]

Election violence was certainly not uncommon, but throughout most of our study period the criminal cases listed by the grand jury and in the jail calendar were quite routine and few in number. There is no indication that imprisonment was used against vagabonds and other disturbers of public order, as in Quebec or the Gore District of Upper Canada, though certainly it was used to punish relatively minor crimes.[84] There were generally no more than five or six charges per biannual term, and these involved assault or larceny for the most part, with sentences from a few days to six months in the Sherbrooke jail. Counterfeiting nevertheless remained a problem, with six individuals being arrested in Granby in 1845, four in Roxton in 1848, and ten on two separate raids in Barnston the same year.[85] The grand jury reported soon afterwards that counterfeiting had been "fearfully and to many fatally on the increase; many families otherwise peaceful and industrious have been broken up and dispensed; many young men and even boys, sons of provident and estimable parents, have been enticed from the paths of virtue and honest industry ... to engage in the making and dealing in bad money." As in the Gugy campaign a decade earlier, however, the Barnston counterfeiters were soon all acquitted, discharged, or admitted to bail.[86] Counterfeiting, like smuggling (as we shall see), was apparently still widely considered to be a victimless crime. Certainly, it was too long-established a practice in the Eastern Townships to raise heightened concerns about social breakdown. Such concerns would arise only at mid-century, when the region's crime rate began to increase, ironically *after* the introduction of most of the state institutions which have been associated with social control.

The grand jury of the Queen's Bench in 1849 forwarded seven cases for trial, but the charges were all relatively minor, and only two were found guilty. The following October and November the Sherbrooke jail was unusually crowded, with ten inmates, but again few of the charges were serious. Indeed, by December, only three of these men remained in jail, charged, respectively, with theft, passing counterfeit money, and violent assault and rape (the Toussaint case, noted above). A fourth man was jailed that month on suspicion of stealing.[87]

The jail calendar for 1849 hardly suggests the outbreak of a crime wave, then, but there were other more troubling signs as far as the authorities were concerned. In September, after impounding some of his neighbour's cattle for trespassing on his farm, a Milton farmer named John Ingram had shot and killed that same neighbour's son when he and some friends threatened to release the livestock.[88] This tragic incident might be dismissed as an isolated and spontaneous act of anger, but there were deeper undercurrents. Ingram was an Irish Catholic, and after he was found guilty by the Montreal court, unknown assailants severely beat two men who were mistakenly assumed to be prosecution witnesses staying at a city hotel. The *Gazette* declared: "We have read of things like these repeatedly in the Irish papers, but always doubted that such brutalism could be found among human beings."[89] But this was only the beginning of a series of apparently random acts of violence which suggested that a disturbing pattern was developing.

In November, High Constable Clark arrested a Hatley labourer named George Badger on suspicion of belonging to a gang which had been stealing goods from local farmers. While Clark was searching for the stolen property the following day, a crowd of some thirty individuals assembled and "threatened his life if he attempted to carry away the prisoner." In a traditional ritual of humiliation, they shaved off all the hair on his horse's head, neck, and tail, and removed two wheels from the wagon as well as cutting up its apron and braces. Clark had little choice but to release the prisoner. Three months later he reported that it would still be unsafe for him to execute warrants alone, given "the present unsettled state of that part of the country in consequence of the *unjustifiable cry* for *Annexation* to the *United States.*"[90]

In contrast to Montreal and Bytown, the reaction in the Eastern Townships to the Rebellion Losses Bill had generally been peaceful, the most serious incident in Sherbrooke being the drowning of Lord Elgin's effigy in the Magog River. But the bill did spark a violent confrontation between opponents and supporters of the government in Durham Township. In January 1850, 112 petitioners asked that the township's senior magistrate, John Bothwell, be dismissed because he had stood by while his brothers and other relatives beat three young men with clubs and stones. Seven men were to stand trial for assault and battery with intent to commit murder. Witnesses swore that Bothwell had spoken in favour of burning the Parliament Buildings, and had actively canvassed for annexation.

But Bothwell denied any involvement in the movement, and claimed that up to seven-eighths of the signatures to the petition against him were forgeries, or the names of common labourers who had gone to work on the advancing St Lawrence and Atlantic Railway line. In addition, a counter-petition with 147 signatures claimed that the original petition had been motivated by malice "arising out of animosities partly Municipal, partly Political and partly religious." It is likely, then, that the beating victims were Irish Catholics who were defending the action of the reform government and their Irish Catholic compatriot, Solicitor-General Drummond, deputy for the neighbouring constituency of Shefford. Whatever the provocation, the grand jury committed Bothwell, his brothers, brother-in-law, and son-in-law to stand trial in April.[91]

The case appears to have been still pending when trouble erupted again in Durham during the summer of 1850, this time because of the high constable's attempt to shut down the unlicensed liquor dealers who were supplying the railway construction workers. Clark laid charges against three individuals with some standing in the community, including a former JP and a shoemaker who had been the secretary of the local annexationist society.[92] When only two witnesses appeared for the state, the case was adjourned until September. Although Clark asked for permission to employ "one or two able bodied men" when he went into "back places and excited neighbourhoods," he had to proceed to Durham on his own when the case was heard. Here he met with the reception he had feared. Several individuals destroyed his wagon and committed "a most disgraceful outrage" on his poor horse, shearing off its mane and tail, cutting off its ears, and slashing one side of its face.[93] And worse was yet to come. On the day of the trial he was served with a warrant signed by Bothwell which charged him with being an accessory to the rape of a woman named Charlotte Findlay.

As the wife of one of the accused liquor traffickers, Findlay had herself been arrested the previous day for ignoring a subpoena to testify against those suspected of damaging Clark's horse and wagon. She claimed that the rape had been committed during the night by the bailiff, J. Cummins, who had been assigned to guard her at the house where Clark was also staying. The accusation was not that Clark was involved with the rape, but that he was instrumental in Cummins's escape the following day. Consequently, the high constable had to face an angry mob in court. After being "very roughly handled," to use his own words, he was rescued by the presiding magistrates who placed several constables at the door of the house where he was taken. The mob dispersed only after the mayor had twice read the riot act, and Clark was then transported to neighbouring Melbourne for his own safety.

A few days later Sheriff Bowen and a JP from Sherbrooke went with a few special constables to Durham where, assisted by twenty-five members of the Melbourne militia, they arrested eight of the principals in the riot. Charges were laid against Bothwell once again, this time as party to a conspiracy to take Clark's life. A militia lieutenant and several other individuals signed affidavits swearing that Clark had not been in danger, but the magistrates investigating the affair declared that "it would materially conduce to the peace and tranquillity of the Township of Durham" if Bothwell's commission were removed. As late as October 1850 Clark was still confined to his office because of his injuries, but he reported that the three accused liquor dealers had pleaded guilty, "and order seems in a measure restored in Durham."[94]

But the trouble was only beginning elsewhere in the district, largely owing, it would seem, to the dual impact of the annexation crisis and railway construction. The situation was complicated by local circumstances in each case, but the dismissal of militia officers and magistrates who had signed the annexation manifesto clearly contributed towards a crisis of authority in the region. The government appears to have withdrawn the commissions of only twenty of approximately sixty-eight magistrates (not all of whom were active) within the St Francis District,[95] but this was a significant number during an era when JPs were increasingly called upon to enforce school and municipal taxes, as well as liquor licences. Eleven of the dismissals were in only three townships – Stanstead, Compton, and Eaton – but other more isolated townships would have had few JPs to begin with.

Solicitor-General Drummond did not find it easy to appoint suitable replacements for those he dismissed, and Sherbrooke's recently elected annexationist deputy accused him of filling up the offices with "men of notoriously bad characters." Referring presumably to his own constituency, J.S. Sanborn complained that "Instead of adopting the constitutional method of consulting the representative of the county in their appointments, they had consulted a gentleman who had been disrobed for fraud, chicanery, and interference with the records of the Courts of Justice." Consequently, the MLA continued, one appointee was a fugitive from debts outside the province, as well as having been bankrupt several times locally, while another had served time in jail in the United States on charges of forgery.[96]

Sanborn's charges reflect a sense of bitterness that would help to explain the sudden outbreak of violence in the region. Furthermore, Solicitor-General Drummond's experience with the largely British-settled Bury Township (where, ironically there had been no dismissals) reveals that there was more than a grain of truth to Sanborn's accusations. Drummond appointed the American-born Hammond McClintock to be a JP in May 1850, only to receive a protest petition signed by the local Free Kirk and Anglican ministers, their elders and churchwardens, the school commissioners, and over one hundred others. They claimed that they were a settlement "exclusively of true and loyal Emmigrants [sic] from England, Scotland and Ireland, under the auspices of the British American Land Company," and that McClintock was "in no way conversant with the habits and Institutions under which it was the happiness of your Petitioners to spend the early part of their lives." Instead, they wanted JPs to be appointed "from among us." Drummond's task of removing McClintock's commission was made easier when High Constable Clark informed him that he was a fugitive from justice in the United States, and that his reputation for "truth and veracity is bad."[97]

Elsewhere in the region, Sanborn reported that as late as July 1851 Shipton Township was without any resident JP, since one had been dismissed, one had resigned, and two had gone to England. The following December, Marcus Child claimed that parts of western Stanstead County were still without magistrates. He recommended two individuals for Hatley, two for Potton, and three for Bolton.[98] The shortage of magistrates to deal with matters in the local courts may largely explain why the Sherbrooke jail calendar recorded more inmates for December 1850 than ever before. The majority had been imprisoned for relatively routine crimes of violence and were released the same day on bail. These arrests were generally in groups; for example, five men were jailed on one day for assault and battery, and three men and a woman for rioting a few days later. But there were also more long-term incarcerations, including one man held since August due to insanity; seven accused of stealing; one counterfeiter; one arsonist; and one man arrested for assault with attempt to murder.[99]

The advancing railway line was still too far away to have been a factor in the arrests of 1850, but by the following June Thomas Christie of Melbourne was claiming that the construction project had attracted "numerous idle & worthless characters who, on holidays & in wet weather, being unemployed, are in the habit of committing depredations on the property & attacking the persons of any one they meet." Christie complained that even though the contractors had warned that this was only a foretaste of what might be expected, there was no police force in the district and the militia was entirely unorganized and unarmed. Having served as a lieutenant in the Montreal Light Infantry during the Rebellion, Christie offered to raise a corps of fifty cavalrymen to be headquartered at Richmond and stationed in small detachments along the railway line.[100]

But the situation was apparently still under control in October when the railway reached Richmond, for the grand jury reported that month that there had been little increase in crime.[101] Somewhat surprisingly, such was not the case in Dudswell Township, even though it lay well beyond the railway terminus. In September a recent arrival from the Niagara district named George Ridgway reported to the civil secretary that a large number of people had asked him to draft a petition for the dismissal of the "aged & feeble" Amos Bishop, the only resident magistrate. Crime had "increased to a fearful extent within the last few months in this hitherto peaceable township." Property had been destroyed, a colt maliciously killed, a farm house attacked, an attempt made to burn a barn and grist-mill, a murder attempted on the queen's highway at noon, and "a most filthy disgraceful outrage committed upon the Communion Table in the only place of Worship in the Township."

Ridgway complained that in none of these cases had Bishop tried to discover the guilty parties, nor had any steps been taken to stop the extensive selling of whiskey in unlicensed houses. In fact, the magistrate simply attempted to hush matters up "being evidently fearful of displeasing his connexions and relatives, it being no less true than strange that Amos Bishop is either connected with, or related to, at least two thirds of the Inhabitants of this Township." Furthermore, Bishop owed money to many of those connected with the outrages, and his "pecuniary embarrassments" made him "capable of doing some curious acts when money is concerned." Ridgway did not explain what had triggered the sudden outburst of crime, but he claimed that he and many others would have to leave if nothing were done "to stem the growing evil." Ridgway was apparently not exaggerating. Two months later, in November 1851, a petition signed by forty-seven residents (including three whose last name was Bishop), made essentially the same charges, adding that the magistrate had used threats to intimidate one individual who had applied for a warrant. In forwarding the document, Sanborn stated that he knew many of those who had signed it to be respectable persons who would not make "a groundless complaint."[102]

Violent crime was also on the increase in other areas within the region by the late fall of 1851. Judge Aylwin's report to the grand jury in October noted that there were two cases which deserved special attention. The first involved the recent discovery of the body of Stanstead's Burdett Sprague in Lake Memphremagog. His apparent robbery and murder had taken place two years earlier, but in the second case, two men had recently entered the Brompton house of the seventy-year old John Sloan and his wife "and committed one of the most horrible outrages ever known in this part of the Province." Sloan, said to be "a remarkably quiet and inoffensive old man," was beaten "almost to a jelly" with heavy clubs, while his wife managed to escape from their bed with relatively minor injuries. No motive was apparent, but Sloan claimed that the attackers' accents were those of "old countrymen."

The reference was clearly to Irish navvies, and Judge Aylwin predicted that the railway's impact would be permanent. As the region became less exclusively agricultural and more commercial, crime would increase and the duties of the grand jury become more arduous. The grand jury certainly took the Sloan and Sprague cases seriously, for it recommended that the government offer a reward for information leading to the arrest of the perpetrators of both crimes, and that the court meanwhile remain adjourned for two months to await the results.[103]

The Sloan case was not the only one to be associated with the Irish railway workers, for the *Sherbrooke Gazette* claimed that a series of outrages had been committed recently in that same neighbourhood, "or in the vicinity of the rail road line below." A week earlier, the McManus family of nearby Melbourne had responded to threats by moving in with neighbours, only to have their house burned down the following night. Also the previous week, railway workmen had attacked four French-Canadian carters as they were returning home from Sherbrooke after having dropped off a load of immigrants. Finally, the battered body of a railway worker had been found in the St Francis River near the Sloans' house. The *Gazette* declared: "These are scenes heretofore entirely unknown to our peaceable population, and have created a good deal of alarm among the inhabitants on the line between this and Melbourne.

The ordinary means of preserving the peace and bringing offenders to justice, are altogether inadequate to the present emergency."[104]

When it reconvened in December 1851, the grand jury again noted that many deeds of a "most atrocious character have been committed." The report blamed the frontier situation of the region (even though this factor was a constant), as well as the influx of labourers who had exposed "the peaceable and quiet Inhabitants of Saint Francis to outrages." But the district's inhabitants were not completely exonerated. Noting that the rewards offered for information during the court's recess had brought no results, the jury report added: "We also fear that there is not among the people generally that respect and subordination to the law, which the friends of good order desire – else why such successful concealment of crime?" It concluded that regular police forces and fire departments were needed for the district's principal towns and villages.[105]

Meanwhile, the railway construction crews were steadily nearing the town of Sherbrooke. Between January and March 1852 the census enumerators recorded the names of more than 1,800 people, including wives and children, living in shanties along the thirty miles of railway line between Richmond and Lennoxville. Mostly Irish Catholics, they represented nearly a fifth of the total population in the five townships they were temporarily inhabiting. The *Sherbrooke Gazette* had begun complaining about drunken brawls in the streets since as early as the previous November.[106] Attributing the incidents to the sale of "ardent spirits" along the railway line, the *Gazette* claimed in late December that "Scarcely a day passes but some peaceable person is ill-treated."[107] As president of the railway company, A.T. Galt made a similar protest in December, but he laid the blame on the district liquor licence inspector, Chauncy Bullock, who had issued a licence to a man who had set up a shanty near the railway works in the Sherbrooke area. The contractor for that section of the line complained that his workmen were disturbed all night by those who became drunk at this "very disorderly house." In reply, the civil secretary informed Galt that the inspector no longer had the discretionary power to refuse liquor licences.[108]

The Sherbrooke jail report for 1851 published by the Wolfred Nelson commission does suggest that a lot of petty crime was being committed by the railway workers. Half of the year's sixty inmates (of whom three were women) were Irish Catholics, a marked over-representation of their population ratio in the region. Only six were Americans, and the remaining twenty-four were said to English Protestants, presumably Canadian-born for the most part. Most of the inmates were identified as labourers, though the report also specified one shoemaker, one schoolmaster and one farmer. There were only seven felonies, leaving fifty-three of the arrests reportedly for "minor misdemeanors and assaults." Sheriff Bowen attributed much of the crime to drunkenness and claimed that there were no repeat offenders in the district.[109]

At the end of 1851, then, the authorities clearly felt that they still had the situation under control, and in February 1852 the grand jury again reported that there had not been any great increase in crime. However, it did add that there were twenty inmates in jail, and it deplored the granting of so many licences to sell spirits "in houses, shops, and shanties."[110] The jurymen expressed particular concern that Daniel Thompson of Sherbrooke had retained his commission of the peace after having been convicted of retailing liquor in small quantities, in contravention of his grocer's licence.[111] On the other hand, it pointed to the deficiency in the number of JPs in the district, especially in the town of Sherbrooke. As a result of the township council's inability to deal with the situation, the town of Sherbrooke became a separate municipality the following June.[112]

Meanwhile, in March, the government had finally appointed a special magistrate to investigate the region's recent "outrages." While R.B. Johnson admitted that a number of serious crimes had been committed, his surprise recommendation was that the ordinance passed the previous session providing for a police force on public works (14 and 15 Vict., cap. 76) not be applied to the St Francis District. The openly disgruntled Johnson complained that instead of being welcomed on his arrival "as the harbinger of protection" urgently requested in reports from Sherbrooke, "a hope was, from the first very earnestly expressed that I should not suggest the presence of any Police Force." Indeed, this hope was reiterated by the very party who had detailed the "nature, number, and proposed location" of such a force.[113] Johnson was probably referring to Alexander Galt, since recent legislation decreed that the police would have to be funded by the railway company.

In any case, Johnson himself played down the seriousness of the crimes caused by the railway navvies. After investigating "the imputed crimes or outrages" inflicted upon the resident population by these transient workers, he concluded that their "irregularities" had been almost entirely among themselves. Yet whenever any of them were seen drunk or loitering about the town, they were thrown into jail without even a warrant of commitment: "In the eyes of too many their offense seems to be that they are Irishmen and Catholics, the study has nevertheless been how much could be abstracted from their hard earned wages."

Johnson admitted that many of the labourers had been hanging about the outskirts of Sherbrooke during the past severe winter "without work, or any possible means of subsistence beyond what they might have saved during the last working season." Yet he claimed that not one act of burglary, larceny, or even assault had been committed by any of them. The still unsolved murder of Burdett Sprague had obviously been committed long before the railway workers were in the district. As for a more recent murder in Compton, a local man was responsible, and another man's death in the streets of Sherbrooke was at the hands of a resident of fifteen years' standing. Finally, Johnson claimed somewhat surprisingly that the "outrage" in Brompton upon the elderly John Sloan and his wife had arisen out of a family dispute, and he strongly suspected that some neighbour was responsible for the destruction of the McManus house. While Johnson's conclusions about some of the unsolved cases may be questionable, and he failed to mention cases in which the railway workers had indeed assaulted residents, he may well have been justified in concluding that the presence of such a force would be "unpopular, nay, *offensive* to the great mass of the permanent population of the Saint Francis District." Certainly, there are no petitions in the civil secretary's files demanding such a force.

Johnson's alternate recommendation was that a stipendiary magistrate and three detectives be stationed at or near Sherbrooke to help compensate for the dismissal of some of the district's more "active and intelligent" JPs as a result of the annexation movement. Sherbrooke itself was poorly served for other reasons: Edward Hale was absent in Boston, the elderly John Felton had ceased to act, and Edward Short was now preoccupied as chairman of the quarter sessions. This left only two active magistrates in the town, Griffith and Thompson, neither of whom had the linguistic ability to serve the growing French-Canadian population. Johnson did not mention Thompson's liquor-vending violations, but he did add that the two men "have quarreled to the extent that they will not meet, even upon Magisterial duty." As a result, any case legally requiring two JPs could not be investigated. This problem had existed for some time, but given that anyone who had signed the annexation manifesto was disqualified, the solicitor-general's difficulty in finding suitable prospects can be appreciated.

While admitting that Sherbrooke's high constable was "a very zealous, active officer," Johnson added that "there is a want of system and discipline in his subordinates which the presence of a Stipendiary Magistrate might correct." Because the part-time constables were engaged only as needed, they lacked expertise and were susceptible to small bribes. Recently, for example, two of them had allowed a handcuffed prisoner to escape. In addition, "many of the Affidavits, Warrants and Commitments, are so badly worded, so misspelled and illegible, that they can scarcely be understood, much less would they bear the test of legal criticism." In the case of a recent murder, Johnson had found that the coroner's document committing one of the accused failed to mention either where or when the crime was committed, and the coroner had also neglected to bind the witnesses under recognizance to appear at the criminal term.[114]

Finally, Johnson mentioned the longstanding problem created by the border, which attracted counterfeiters of American bank notes as well as other criminals wishing to take advantage of a ready escape route to the United States. Since the American authorities were quite co-operative in apprehending fugitives once they were identified, the detectives he recommended would keep themselves informed "of the comings and goings of strangers, and of their character and occupations whilst here." Such a surveillance would become still more necessary when the railway was completed, since it would "so materially facilitate ingress and egress over the frontier line." As to the expense of his recommended solution, Johnson stated that "those competent to know" had assured him that the stipendiary magistrate would actually save money by hearing cases with the country magistrates, thereby preventing "petty difficulties" from being brought to Sherbrooke.[115]

No concrete steps appear to have been taken, however, by the time a riot broke out on the railway line where it crossed the border near Coaticook the following year. The conflict began when two police officers from Sherbrooke were prevented from arresting workers accused of violence in January 1853. Sheriff Bowen and three policemen returned to the site three weeks later, only to be beaten and left for dead. In response, a force of 150 soldiers and militiamen surprised the shanty at dawn on 24 February, arresting thirty-five workers. The following month police officers from Sherbrooke and Vermont apprehended several more workers suspected of the attack on Bowen. The Americans also arrested approximately twenty liquor vendors operating on their side of the line. They then systematically smashed the stocks of alcohol. Decisive as the law enforcement steps were, they came rather late as far as the Eastern Townships was concerned, for the only work remaining on the railway was in Vermont. By July the American and Canadian lines were joined, and trains were running from Montreal to Portland, Maine.[116]

While violent crimes against persons increased with the arrival of the railway construction crews in the Eastern Townships, as elsewhere in the province, the timing was partially coincidental since the Irish workers were not the principal culprits in the more serious cases. Nor do Sherbrooke's surviving jail records indicate a steady increase in imprisonment for drunkenness, prostitution, and vagrancy throughout the 1840s, as in Upper Canada's Gore District. According to John Weaver, these arrests marked not only a changing pattern of social relationships, but also a decreasing tolerance for "the rough pastimes of plebeian culture."[117] Indeed, the adventures of High Constable Clark suggest that law enforcement authorities in the Eastern Townships were rather helpless to act without popular support.

The region certainly was not immune from external forces, but traditional community forms of social control may have been particularly persistent here for three basic reasons: its economic transition was only beginning to gather steam in the later forties; Irish immigration did not pose the same social and cultural problems here as elsewhere in British North America; and the region's rather isolated settlers had been forced to develop stronger habits of social and economic self-sufficiency than the inhabitants of most other regions in the British colonies. But the Eastern Townships clearly differed from other regions in degree rather than kind, for Greg Marquis has noted that even in urban centres Canadian legal authority was "highly personalized, operated on the principle of mutual obligations and combined harshness with benevolence."[118] As we are about to see, however, none of these factors prevented the people of the Eastern Townships from demanding greater local access to civil courts.

CIVIL LAW

Bruce Mann has described how in the eighteenth century the legal system of Connecticut was transformed from one "that allowed litigants to address their grievances in ways that were essentially communal to one that elevated predictability and uniformity of legal relations over responsiveness to individual communities."[119] Law and community therefore diverged as the court system became more formalized, a process that had clearly also taken place in British North America well before the middle of the nineteenth century. Paradoxically, however, local access to the courts was itself an important community issue in the Eastern Townships both before and after the Rebellion.

The new system of civil law courts introduced by the Special Council in 1841 did not find favour in the region largely because of the abolition of the more popular commissioners' courts which had been held in all townships where one hundred petitioners requested that a JP be made a commissioner of small causes. Now the district judge would preside over a smaller number of division courts for each district, again with jurisdiction limited to £6 5s.[120] Consequently, the grand jury of the St Francis District complained that the number of division courts was insufficient, and the Missisquoi District Council demanded the reinstitution of the commissioners' courts, complaining that "the operation of the present division Courts and the Tariff of fees established if continued will prove ruinous and burdensome to the Country."[121] In addition, 134 individuals from Barnston and Barford signed a petition in 1842 complaining that the loss of their commissioners' courts had placed them in a "state of extreme embarrassment in collection of their just dues," especially since they were on the frontier line where fraudulent debtors had easy access to the United States. Not only was the new division court farther away, in the village of Stanstead, but the fees were more onerous. In his capacity as the local MLA, Marcus Child strongly endorsed the petition, claiming that his constituents were effectively deprived of courts for the collection of small debts.[122]

Other such petitions followed from Stanstead County, as well as the townships of Granby (165 signatures) and Compton (147 signatures).[123] The latter petition also asked that the fees for attorneys and officers of the court be "reduced to a scale adopted to the circumstances of an Agricultural community," indicating, along with the number of signatures, that merchants were not the only group interested in access to the courts. As the principal means of exchange in this cash-poor society, promissory notes played an ambiguous role as far as internal community ties were concerned. They created a social-economic web in which virtually every family was tied to others in a fundamental way. But the direct personal link between the original creditor and debtor was weakened as the note was passed from hand to hand, so that a third or fourth party would feel fewer restraint about demanding payment when it became due. Also, the original debtor might feel less personally compelled to hurry to meet the demand of someone outside his or her social circle. Thus, the important role that petty civil courts played in pre-industrial communities.[124]

The Stanstead Division Court was certainly active during its brief life, for its issue book reveals that 470 cases were heard between 21 January 1842 and 31 January 1844.[125] But given their demands for greater access to the court system, the people of the Eastern Townships obviously approved when the commissioners' courts were restored in place of the division courts in 1844.[126] From Kingston, Marcus Child wrote to his wife concerning son George's attempts to collect debts owed by patrons of their Stanstead store, "the little courts will soon go into operation and then – he will have a little *fortiter in re* to back up his exhausted *sanvitu in modo.*"[127] The index to the civil secretary's correspondence reveals that even some of the more peripheral townships were petitioning for commissioners' courts by 1848 and 1849.[128] By 1851 there were 112 commissioners serving twenty-six townships within the region. They were clearly busy for they had issued 2791 summons that year, resulting in 2,177 court cases. Interestingly enough, the township with the highest number of cases, 209, was Arthabaska, one of the smallest and most recently settled, and commissioners in the other Bois-Francs townships were also very active.[129] Unfortunately, we do not know whether it was the agents of the absentee proprietors, the local merchants, or the colonists who were taking most of the initiative.

Also restored in 1844 were the circuit courts, which had the same jurisdiction as the inferior terms of the Queen's Bench – namely, civil suits of £20 and under. There were to be two terms annually in each of three circuits within the St Francis District, held at Eaton, Stanstead, and Richmond.[130] The petitions from the Eastern Townships had been strangely silent about this court, suggesting that the over-riding concern in the region was accessibility for small debts. J.W. Hallowell, an influential lawyer who had practised twenty years in Sherbrooke, informed Edward Hale that circuit courts were unnecessary because the number of inferior terms of the Queen's Bench was sufficient for the district's purposes. Hallowell added that the circuits of the late Provincial Court (with a similar jurisdiction) had been useless, "the Tavern Keepers & their Attachés being the only class of worthies deriving emolument from them."[131]

Perhaps, as well, the people of the St Francis District were not anxious to have the arrogant and arbitrary Judge Fletcher once again dispensing justice in the outlying communities. Fletcher himself was not pleased with the restoration of the circuit courts. He complained in February 1844 that "the supposed utility of Itinerant Courts and the whole of the popular notions respecting the *carrying Justice to every man's door* appear to me to be founded on an erroneous supposition that all the witnesses in a case must of necessity reside in the vicinity of the defendant." Fletcher argued that, to the contrary, in a great proportion of the cases witnesses "are collected from every part of the District." The circuit courts would all be held within thirty miles of Sherbrooke, and their cumulative costs were greater than those of the central court.[132]

The seventy-seven-year-old judge also submitted a court calendar to prove that his duties were "far more unremitting and arduous" than those of any other judge in the province. While there were no public sessions for more than half the weekdays of the year, his "Vacation Business" included taxation of costs, granting of compulsory and special process, appointment of curators and guardians, examination of witnesses, proving of wills, revision of habeas corpus and of jail commitments by the magistrates, and so on. This business required twelve hours per day, and he also had to attend the Queen's Bench in Trois-Rivières for approximately two weeks each February and October. Fletcher claimed that with the circuit courts he would be away from home more than five months a year, leaving insufficient time to deal with the Sherbrooke business. Fletcher also complained that it was difficult to find men with sufficient legal knowledge to act as court clerks in the outlying communities. One clerk he did approve of was Stanstead's Christopher Pferinger Elkins, since he had been educated as a lawyer in London. Elkins had served as clerk of the brief-lived division court, and he complained later in 1844 that as clerk of the reinstated circuit court his annual income had dropped to £15 because the more active commissioners' courts left him with virtually no business.[133]

Meanwhile, having been asked to report on the most economical mode of obtaining the use of buildings for the circuit court sessions, Fletcher noted that inns and churches were obviously unsuitable, which left only schools, though he had used private houses in the past. For example, even though the Stanstead Academy was an excellent building for the purpose, the trustees had complained that the court interrupted the pupils' studies. Since Fletcher felt it was incompatible with the dignity "of my own station, to enter into any *discussion* respecting such matters," he had resorted to the lodgings of the local court clerk, the aforementioned Elkins. Inconvenient as such quarters might be, the judge recommended against erecting or even leasing permanently any special buildings because the "inutility" and "absolute inconvenience" of the circuit courts in his district "would shortly become so manifest as to evince the necessity of some change in the system."[134]

Fletcher would never see such a change, however, for he died shortly after submitting his lengthy report, and the district circuit courts were not abolished until 1849. Furthermore, the change was minimal because they and the inferior terms of the Queen's Bench were simply replaced by a provincial circuit court, which was presided over by a superior court judge or one of the province's nine circuit judges. It is not clear whether the same circuits were maintained in the St Francis District, but it appears that the reform must have made little practical difference to the great majority in the region.[135]

Certainly, as Fletcher had predicted, only a small number of cases were presented to the circuit courts in close proximity to Sherbrooke. For the twelve months ending 26 July 1848 there were only seventeen actions in the Eaton circuit and twenty-six in the Richmond circuit, though there were fifty-nine in the more distant and populous Stanstead circuit. The circuit courts were more useful in the townships outside the St Francis District, which were far removed from their judicial headquarters. Thus, the District of Montreal's Nelsonville circuit reported seventy-seven actions, while in the District of Quebec's remote Leeds circuit there were a remarkable 162.[136]

There was some local support for the circuit courts, even in the areas close to Sherbrooke where the number of cases were relatively few. Thus, in 1851, seventy-five petitioners from Shipton, Melbourne, and vicinity asked that the provincial circuit sit in Richmond four times a year rather than two, even though only fifty-nine cases had been heard in this court during the previous two years.[137] For the most part, however, the circuit courts served the interests of the local merchants. In asking that Ely and Brompton Gore be added to the Richmond circuit, the merchant Thomas Tait stated that their inhabitants were taking advantage of their isolation from the seat of the Shefford court to avoid paying their debts, "and some I am told have moved in there to be out of the reach of the law."[138] Not surprisingly, the plumitif or record book for the appealable cases of the Stanstead circuit court reveals that most were instituted by merchants against farmers, though there were also a number of cases where farmers sued farmers and farmers even sued merchants.[139]

The growing economic ties between the Sherbrooke area and Montreal also meant that some of the latter city's trading firms had a strong interest in the court system of the St Francis District, particularly at a time when difficult economic conditions still prevailed. Twenty-six bankruptcy cases were filed in the district between 1840 and 1846, and though the number had been declining since 1843, the biggest single case had occurred in 1845 when A.G. Woodward of Sherbrooke left a debt of £1,829.[140] Consequently, there were howls of protest from Montreal when the government was slow to replace the St Francis District's commissioner of bankruptcy, G.F. Bowen, after he resigned in order to become sheriff in 1846. In May several Montreal merchants reported that they had sued for a warrant of bankruptcy against a Richmond company, one of whose members was carrying away his estate in order to defraud his creditors. Without a commissioner of bankruptcy, however, the process had lapsed and the plaintiffs were at risk of losing over £1,500. The following September, with still no appointment having been made, a number of Montreal merchants who had "various and considerable claims upon Traders resident in the District of St Francis" protested that they were subject to "inconvenience and loss."[141]

But local patronage considerations were complicating matters, for William Whitcher had been promised the appointment after losing his deceased father's position as sheriff to G.F. Bowen. Whitcher's father-in-law, C.P. Elkins, also applied for the position, but he was passed over even though he was the only lawyer in the running. The government clearly wished to avoid providing the Felton clan with any patronage, yet it had difficulty finding other qualified applicants because the emoluments of the office were said to be low, and the incumbent could not practise law because he was required to serve as chair of the Court of Quarter Sessions, as well as to replace the provincial judge when the latter was absent on circuit.[142] It was not until the summer of 1847 that

Sherbrooke attorney J.W. Hallowell was appointed to the position, but only after he demanded a salary of £200 per annum as well as the right to practice law in cases not before the bankruptcy court or the Quarter Sessions.[143]

While the government was surprisingly unresponsive to the demands of the outside merchants in the case of the bankruptcy court, waiting over a year to fill the position, it had clearly listened to the local protests against the reforms made to the court system in 1841. From 1843 onward, the region appears to have been generally satisfied with the decentralized nature of the civil court system. The circuit courts, with their relatively high level of jurisdiction, may have served the interests of the local merchants more than any other group, but large numbers of names were attached to the petitions demanding the institution of the less-elevated commissioners' courts. In short, the civil court system also served the interests of farmers and other small producers, since they too were inevitably creditors as well as debtors in the largely cashless economy of the 1840s.

Our brief survey reveals how important the civil courts were considered by the property-holders of the Eastern Townships, creating what Tina Loo has referred to as "an arena of economic exchange in which all transactions and the resolutions of any disputes that arose from them would be guided by a set of standardized, rational, and predictable rules."[144] In contrast to the pre-Rebellion era, however, there does not appear to have been much concern in the region about the content of the civil law, whether British or French, as long as affordable and accessible tribunals were made available.[145] Paradoxically, even though criminal law had much less impact on people's daily lives, most of the press reports and law-related petitions to the civil secretary concerned the few serious incidents which did occur in the region. This imbalance presumably reflected the trauma such crimes caused within these generally peaceable communities, and the general lack of confidence in the state's ability to deal with them equitably. But, sensational as the few murder cases may have been, in the following chapter we shall see how during the 1840s the regulation of social norms remained largely an informal community matter.

3 Community Regulation

REGULATING ALCOHOL CONSUMPTION

Many historians have described the great quantities of alcohol consumed in the pre-industrial era,[1] though somewhat less attention has been paid to the social problems that ensued. In the economically isolated Eastern Townships, potato whiskey was particularly plentiful because it was one of the few locally produced commodities that could be transported profitably to outside markets. Writing his local history in 1858, Reverend Edward Cleveland named eight men who had operated distilleries in his home township of Shipton. He claimed that one of them had retailed three thousand gallons in a year, and added: "Those who have witnessed the evening scenes in these distilleries, the gatherings of men and boys from the neighborhood, the songs, jests, and revelry that filled up the time, would not wonder at the worst effects that followed. And when we consider how the same liquid fire was carried into the bar-room, the store, and private dwellings, and was then so common in all departments of society, we shall at once see a prominent cause of all the evils that prevailed." Due to the temperance movement, however, there were no longer any stills in the township in 1858, few of the stores retailed "the poison," and "our private dwellings are generally free from it."[2]

As its name suggests, the temperance movement, which began to make an impact on the Eastern Townships in the early 1830s, originally tolerated the moderate consumption of alcoholic drinks, particularly beer and wine. It adopted a more restrictive policy in the early 1840s, but even in the guise of total abstinence, the onus remained on the individual to "take the pledge." This phase of the anti-alcohol campaign, which was undoubtedly the most important moral reform initiative in British North America during the early nineteenth century, therefore lies outside the realm of our study on state formation.

Suffice to say that Protestant churches and Sherbrooke's entrepreneurs were both involved in different phases of the campaign, which was therefore fuelled by spiritual as well as pragmatic concerns. What seems to have been unique to the Eastern Townships, at least as far as the rest of British North America is concerned, was the emergence late in the 1840s of the American-based Independent Order of the Rechabites. This organization adhered to moral reform and revivalism at a time when support for state prohibition was on the rise elsewhere.[3] The plebeian-oriented Rechabite order was particularly strong in the southern, American-settled townships, reaching close to thirteen hundred members at mid-century.[4]

By this time, the violence and paranoia that accompanied the construction of the St Lawrence and Atlantic Railway was resulting in increased pressure on the government to control the sale of liquor despite the Rechabites' formal opposition to prohibition. As early as 1842 the Sherbrooke Temperance Society had argued in a petition to Governor-General Bagot that were the government to suppress the sale of liquor, it would regain its money "from the increased demand by a better conditioned population for other duty paying articles." The society's members realized that the governor would have to wait "till the advancing light" had further "dissipated the prejudices of custom," but they asked that steps at least be taken against the unlicensed dealers. Of more than twelve liquor outlets in Sherbrooke, only two had permits. The petition added that licences were generally granted to applicants with "comparatively respectable" houses and, being under the surveillance of the law, they were "generally less ensnaring and injurious to the poor labouring people than the reckless illegal receptacles that now waylay them at every turn." Finally, the Sherbrooke society claimed that it was difficult to close these establishments because the people refused to inform against them even for a reward. This was "a new country where each in turn needs the help and sympathy of his fellows," and where the people possessed "in a high degree the chivalrous, honorable feelings that characterize the Saxon Race." The best solution to the problem would therefore be to appoint an officer "to migrate through the entire united province to detect lodges and prosecute informations every where," or to impose this duty on the sheriffs, coroners, or some other public officer of the counties.[5]

The experiences of High Constable Clark revealed the impracticality of the latter recommendation, for when he finally began to prosecute unlicensed liquor sellers in 1845, he met with attempts "to injure him personally,"[6] as well as legal obstructionism. After he served summons on four unlicensed innkeepers and a trader from Hatley and Barnston, the magistrates released all of them at his cost on the grounds that such cases were not within their jurisdiction. The fine for such an offence was £10, half of which was to go to the constable, but the commissioners' court was limited to a ceiling of £6 5s. Under these circumstances, Clark proceeded on his own authority to levy fines of only £5 against three retailers from Stanstead and one from Barnston, thereby foregoing his £5 remittance. The attorney-general's response was that Clark had overstepped his authority, and that he would have to resort to the superior courts in future.[7]

Even though the government soon afterward followed the grand jury's advice by appointing a district inspector of licences, most liquor establishments remained without a permit. The government issued only twenty tavern licences for the entire St Francis District between April 1845 and April 1846, though the number did increase to twenty-nine during the following eight months.[8] The inspector, Chauncey Bullock of Georgeville, also admitted that few of the distilleries in the district were licensed. He reported that most of them were owned by poor men "merely for working Potatoes a few months in the winter season." As a result, the law imposing a tax on stills "has been supposed, by the People Generally in the Townships, to bear heavily on these small concerns." Consequently, Bullock argued that if he had taken action against them, "I should have been frowned down by the People and should not have been sustained by the magistrates."[9]

In 1847 the grand jury claimed that the liquor laws had begun to be strictly enforced, but such enforcement continued to be hampered by the shortage of JPs even in the town of Sherbrooke itself. When Inspector Bullock reported to the high constable in 1848 that two Sherbrooke establishments were retailing spirituous liquors without permits, Clark was frustrated by the fact that the two magistrates legally required to hear the case were not available. John Felton refused to act on account of his age, and Edward Hale was on one of his extended vacations with his family, leaving only the ardent temperance supporter, William Arms.[10]

Furthermore, unlicensed liquor dealers were adept at exploiting legal technicalities. One of the more imaginative, no doubt, was Stanstead's Timothy Taylor. The magistrates had twice dismissed charges against him by 1851, when he appeared before them once again on the charge of dispensing alcohol without a licence. His argument was that he collected money only for a "show," not for drinks. According to a witness, customers went into a back room where there was a decanter of spirits on a table, and the show consisted of "an image of a negro, etc."[11]

When the government did introduce legislation to restrict the sale of alcohol in 1850, there was far from unanimous approval in the Eastern Townships. The *Stanstead Journal* complained that the "injudicious and severe restrictions" of the Bill for the More Effectual Suppression of Intemperance would do more harm than good. The bill's provisions were indeed strict, since they would make innkeepers liable for injury or loss resulting from the actions of those who became drunk on their premises.[12] Claiming that he would be forced to close his Stanstead hotel when these provisions came into force, the outspoken Dr M.F. Colby went before the Stanstead County Council to attack "the advocates for promulgating the principles of moral reform by legislative proscriptive enactments."[13]

While he was himself a Methodist, Colby referred in particular to Stanstead's aggressively evangelical Methodist minister when he charged that "those who would spread and enforce moral and religious tenets by fire and sword" were not "the followers of the great and all-important doctrines which inculcate peace on earth – but the followers of the doctrines of men – those who enforce purification of the heart by outward washings – the Pharisees of modern times – the followers of Mahomet and those whose kingdom is on this earth." A laissez-faire liberal, despite his conservative political affiliation, Colby argued that every attempt to enforce moral precepts, rather than reforming the heart, would inevitably "carry the people to opposite extremes, and encourage infractions of law and morals, the more dangerous for being the more secret." Moving from the moral high ground, Colby complained that "the penal enactments are thrown on that class of vendors where the high charges for spirit, by the glass, would render its sale the least dangerous, while the government itself, by allowing the importation at a reduced duty, and the merchant and distiller who sell cheap and in any quantity from one gallon upward, are exempted from its penalties."[14]

Dr Colby actually appears to have been a Rechabite, for in 1850 a letter from Boston addressing him as Brother Colby informed him that "In this part of the country, a man who keeps a *grog-shop* is rather a disreputable person. A licensed hotel keep [*sic*] or apothecary could not come under this head and if such persons as you mention – creditable and respected in the community where they live, wish to join & you wish to have them, I don't know who there is to object."[15] A committee of the local Rechabite tent nevertheless criticized Colby for attempting to associate its activities with the controversial Reverend Borland, and declared that it was the people who demanded proscriptive legislation." To Colby's complaint that wholesalers would escape unscathed, the committee conceded that "the axe should have been laid at the root of the tree – but there is a step in the right direction when they lop off the branches." The solution was not to repeal the law, but to remove the inequity Colby complained of: "It is a plain case. The public versus the grog seller. The interest of which party, should the Law be made to uphold?"[16]

This hard line was endorsed by the Canada East quarterly session of the Rechabites held in Compton several months later. One resolution declared that "all who are now engaged in the manufacture of, or the traffic in, intoxicating liquor, are *practically* the enemies of our race." However, the delegates remained true to their organization's anti-coercion principles by refusing to support J.S. Walton's motion to the effect that they would be satisfied with nothing short of the Maine prohibition law.[17] They could doubtless take comfort in the awareness that the temperance movement and the restrictive licensing legislation had made a significant impact on the number of taverns in the region. According to the Canada *Census Reports*, the population number per tavern in the six Eastern Townships counties had increased from 576 in 1827 to 2,018 in 1852.

Meanwhile, the hotel owners of Stanstead County collectively took a more moderate stance than Colby had done when they asked that the offending bill be repealed simply on the grounds that merchants and distillers "are not under any restrictions whatsoever." Their petition was supported by Mayor Bigelow, who was a hotel owner himself, but seven councillors spoke forcefully against it at their June 1851 meeting. Consequently, rather than asking the legislature to repeal the act, the Stanstead County Council moved unanimously that it should be "so amended as to apply equally to all persons vending spirituous liquors, both as respects its penal provisions and the obtaining of Licenses."[18]

In Shefford the county council went further, arguing that the act was counterproductive because it would cause respectable houses of public entertainment to close, forcing travellers to resort to establishments "kept by reckless and disreputable characters in violation of the revenue law." The new legislation required the district inspectors to issue liquor licences only to those applicants who presented a requisition signed by the majority of municipal electors, plus a certificate of support from the senior magistrate, senior militia officer, and – inappropriately for Protestant districts – the "marguiller en charge" (translated as the churchwarden in office). The Shefford councillors argued, however, that they were the best judges of how to regulate houses of public entertainment, and that they should therefore be the body to make the relevant laws, control the issuing of licences, and appropriate the fees.[19]

It is somewhat surprising that the demand for greater local control was not more widespread, since this was a dominant theme in the

United States, and it was granted to the municipalities of Canada West in 1848.[20] It also marked the response in the Eastern Townships to municipal and school reform during the 1840s. Perhaps the municipal councils were generally content with receiving the local licence funds from the provincial government without having to enforce the more controversial aspects of the 1851 act. It also appears that a more sympathetic attitude towards state control began to develop after mid-century, for by 1854 there existed an Eastern Townships Prohibitory Liquor Law League whose president was Stanstead's former MLA, John McConnell. As for Dr Colby's business, his "tavern stand" was advertised for sale in January 1852, but his liquor licence was renewed two months later.[21]

THE DESTITUTE AND THE INSANE

Like alcohol, poverty was not only a serious social problem in the pre-industrial era, but it was perceived to represent a threat to social stability. While the indigent were a parish responsibility in England, the English poor laws had been rejected by both Upper and Lower Canada soon after the Constitutional Act was passed in 1791.[22] In Upper Canada, the Court of Quarter Sessions reluctantly subsidized the most desperate cases from district funds, but no taxes were levied by the same body in Lower Canada. Some townships elected overseers of the poor, but it is not clear what their exact function was. Since formal charitable organizations are rarely mentioned,[23] it would appear that the poor of the Eastern Townships were almost entirely dependent upon the voluntary support of their kin, neighbours, and churches. The local elites also played a role, for, as David Murray points out, private charity was considered the public duty of a gentleman (and presumably of his wife, as well).[24] To take one example, it was the members of this class in the Eastern Townships who organized local relief contributions for the Irish famine victims in the spring of 1847.[25]

Private purses might open for those who had fallen on hard times despite their hard work, but sympathy was in much shorter supply for those who transgressed the community's moral standards. After Lydia Child had dismissed a young female servant in October 1843 for stealing a cake of chocolate, she reported to her husband, Marcus, that the absent father "prefers to have the family living upon the neighbors." The neighbours were obviously none too generous, for a month later Lydia wrote that the family "have starved almost for food and fuel. George [the Childs' son] caught the old woman and John carrying wood from our pile ... and George got Andrew Young to go and try frighten them. The old woman said 'if the jail was a warm place she would like to go for she was freezing to death there and the children too'."[26]

Some of the indigent may have resorted to public begging, which was apparently widespread in the St Lawrence Valley,[27] but there is no indication in the grand jury reports, the petitions to the civil secretary, or the surviving municipal records of the 1840s that the poor were considered a serious social threat in the Eastern Townships. An important reason was presumably that few of the many thousands of Irish immigrants who were flooding into the port of Quebec during the potato famine years made their way into the region. Indeed, typhus or ship fever was reported to have claimed only five or six lives here during the 1847 epidemic.[28] In August 1848 Marcus Child, acting as foreman of the grand jury for the St Francis District, concluded his report by thanking Divine Providence for the prospects of an abundant harvest "and the absence of poverty and want and contagious diseases in this District." The following year, the grand jury offered condolences to Sherbrooke's newly appointed judge, T.C. Aylwin, for the loss of his wife (presumably in Quebec) to cholera, while rejoicing "that the District has been delivered from that dreadful scourge."[29]

Conditions were not so promising on the colonization periphery. The British and French-Canadian settlers of Megantic County had been hard hit by three successive years of potato crop failure, and in the harsh environment of the upper St Francis townships the recently arrived French Canadians and Lewis Highlanders were facing difficult years of adjustment.[30] In 1851 a public subscription fund in Sherbrooke raised £30 to assist the three hundred recent arrivals from the Hebridean Isle of Lewis who were said to be "in a starving condition" in the township of Lingwick.[31] But such efforts were rare, and these isolated, hard-working colonists depended heavily on their extended family and neighbourhood ties. They certainly posed little threat to law and order in the region.

Even for those individuals who did run afoul of the law, punishments were applied so as to minimize the burden created by their dependants. As we saw in the previous chapter, JPs were unwilling to impose stiff sentences against those with wives and children to support, and judges granted early pardons to convicted criminals in the same situation. Occasionally, neighbours could be too generous for their own good, as when two Barnston farmers named Kilborn and Hollister guaranteed the £250 bail of accused arsonist Jared Blanchard, so that he could visit his family. When Blanchard fled temporarily to the United States before being arrested and found guilty of the original charge, the Queen's Bench declared the bail to be in default and sued the two guarantors for the full amount. Kilborn and Hollister protested that this would leave them destitute, and that they could not seize Blanchard's property as compensation because he had only enough to support his wife, mother, and five small children. With the urging of two local JPs and a clergy-man, among others, the government finally suspended proceedings against the two men.[32]

The local elites also helped to bring a number of cases of indigence to the civil secretary's attention during the 1840s. In April 1846, for example, a local doctor, a minister, a militia captain, a mayor, four JPs, and four MLAs, among numerous others, supported the petition of a blind man named Silas Perkins who had resided in Hatley for forty-one years. He requested a free peddling licence on the grounds that his house with all its contents had burned down the previous October. One of his five daughters had lost her life in the fire, and the others were too young to support themselves. Perkins's wife, who had partial sight in only one eye, had recently lost the use of her right arm. In spite of the merit of the case and the impressive list of supporters, Governor Cathcart de-clared that it was out of his power to grant the request. The following year the governor gave a similar response to a JP who asked that a free li-cence to sell groceries be granted to a sixty-year-old soldier's widow in Inverness. Her only son had died two years earlier, and she wished to avoid "Begging a mong [sic] her Nabours."[33]

Despite the lack of support from the provincial authorities, there were no demands from the Eastern Townships for formal institutions such as houses of industry, and Eaton appears to have been the only mu-nicipality to request the power to raise an assessment for the poor.[34] The insane were another matter, for they represented a sometimes intolera-ble burden to their families and a possible danger to their communities. Furthermore, even elite families were not immune from this problem. In 1843, for example, Marcus Child wrote of receiving a petition from the Congregational minister of Danville "respecting two poor mad girls – Daughters of Col. Bangs – they are a charge there upon the charitable and have become dangerous, being at large – I am sorry there is no Assy-lum [sic] in this Province."[35]

Sydenham had established a temporary asylum in Montreal in 1839, but there was no room for inmates from the Townships. As a result, Ed-ward Hale was informed in the fall of the same year that "you had better cause the poor woman you mention to be lodged as well as may be in the Sherbrooke Prison." Five years later, in reply to Hale's request about pro-vincial regulations, a government official informed him that no instruc-tions had been issued to sheriffs concerning the admission of insane persons into district jails. He added, however, that in Trois-Rivières they were confined on commitment by a magistrate as vagrants or persons dangerous to the public peace. Sheriffs had the authority, on application, to employ a woman as keeper of such individuals, as well as female prisoners, at a charge of two shillings per day, with the expense being defrayed by an annual grant from the legislature.[36]

A government committee recommended in 1844 that the allowance for the insane in the District of Trois-Rivières be increased by £100 in order to benefit the St Francis District,[37] but the main complaint made by the grand jury about the Sherbrooke jail in January 1845 was that it housed a twenty-five-year-old "female lunatic." The jury report stated optimistically that this evil was expected to end soon with the enactment of legislation for suitable asylums, but the young woman, who was said to be "very violent," remained in the same cell the following September. Emphasizing that "her situation at times is distressing," the grand jury recommended that she be removed to the Beauport asylum.[38] But even though this permanent institution had only recently opened its doors, its facilities were already overcrowded, and a deranged woman was reported to be one of the Sherbrooke jail's inmates the following year. A petition signed by the Catholic curé, as well as by A.T. Galt, John Felton, and 133 others, protested that the Beauport asylum was completely inadequate. "Lunatics" from the St Francis District still had to be confined to jails, which "cuts off all hope of restoring these unfortunate individuals to reason, and outrages all the better feelings of our common humanity." Two years later, in 1848, the grand jury asked that if provision could not be made for the insane in the St Francis District, at least temporary measures be taken.[39]

The request was ignored, even though Beauport was a privately operated institution with limited space for charitable cases. Only in January 1850 were two government-sponsored patients admitted from the Eastern Townships.[40] While these two admissions might have been considered precedents for the region, the following year the government initially rejected a Dunham woman's application to have her husband admitted as a state patient. Elizabeth Beach was also informed that there would be no vacancies in Beauport for some time since the government intended to reduce the number of inmates kept at its expense. However, Beach's husband finally became a state-funded patient six months later, after the local doctor reported that the family was "constantly in danger of being injured by him."[41]

By the end of our study period, little had changed as far as the demands of the Townships were concerned. Dr James Johnson complained to the Wolfred Nelson Commission in 1851 that "accommodation of the Gaol does not allow of a separate ward being devoted to the insane, and thus they become a source of much annoyance to the other prisoners."[42] The grand jury reported in February 1852 that an insane woman had been confined to the Sherbrooke jail for almost a year, and in that year's census the Beauport asylum listed only one of its 153 patients as being from the Eastern Townships. Most of the thirty-six males and forty-four females enumerated as lunatics within the region presumably remained with their families.[43]

The only other group to attract the attention of moral reformers even briefly in the Eastern Townships were those without hearing and speech, recorded as thirty-six males and twenty-three females in the 1852 *Census Reports*. Three years earlier, 140 residents of Stanstead County had signed a petition asking for a provincial institution to teach deaf mutes, "who are compelled to live and die in ignorance and moral darkness – comparatively lost to themselves and lost to the world, or at ruinous expense, go to a foreign country to acquire an Education."[44] This petition was clearly motivated by moral-religious considerations, for the people it expressed concern about could hardly have been considered a threat to social stability.

Likewise, while Foucault argues that the asylum was a response to middle-class fears of social and moral contagion by the mentally deranged, such concerns were evidently still minor in the Eastern Townships at mid-century.[45] The petitions and reports were much more preoccupied with the sad state of those individuals (particularly the women) who languished in the Sherbrooke jail than they were with the much larger numbers whom the *Census Reports* identified as lunatics living in the local communities. The region simply did not have enough impoverished immigrants or urban wage labourers to cause the degree of social dislocation found in Montreal or Quebec where the main impetus for the Lower Canadian asylum movement came from. Furthermore, the initiative for more state regulation and institutionalization of the insane came from the local level, a demand to which the state was quite slow to respond.

THE CHARIVARI

Just as the local communities of the Eastern Townships continued, for the most part, to provide for the indigent and the insane in an informal manner, so did they occasionally resort to a ritualized practice known as the charivari to discourage socially and morally disapproved behaviour. As an institution, the charivari played an ambiguous role between reinforcing conventional morality (commonly being deployed against wife abusers and those engaged in sexual co-habitation outside marriage) and challenging legal authority. Its persistence represents an example of the delicate balance between what Wrightson has called two concepts of order – between power yielded by the state on the one hand and by the local community on the other.[46]

It is impossible to know how common the charivari remained in the Eastern Townships of the 1840s, since documented cases are not numerous due to its informal and clandestine nature.[47] Court records and the press describe only the incidents which resulted in violence, and probably only a small proportion of those,[48] but a petition submitted by C.P. Elkins and T. Turton of Sherbrooke in 1838 suggests that the practice was commonplace in their town: "if there should arise any domestic broil between a man & his wife *Lynch* Law is resorted to by the lower order & they sally out at night just after Dark disguised with Faces blackened (itself a felony) & if they catch the man – they use him dreadfully by Tar[g] & feathering him or drag him to the River and duck him – in fact there will be probably Bloodshed and Murder if this goes on thus."[49] This hyperbolic language reflects the fact that Elkins was petitioning for appointment as a stipendiary magistrate, but it also suggests that the charivari in the Eastern Townships was sometimes aimed at regulating relations within the family. As for other references to "rough justice" in the Eastern Townships, Edward Hale referred in 1841 to a Lennoxville cabinet maker who was "so ill-used in a Charivari some years ago,"[50] and there are several recorded cases in the civil secretary's correspondence.

The first case to be brought to the attention of the government during our study period concerned a Shipton settler named Thomas Gaffney. He complained in 1844 that a crowd of twenty people broke into his house during the night, and forced him and his wife to walk down the road half-dressed. Setting his wife on a fence, they uttered "indecencies to the woman too gross to name." Gaffney's Irish-sounding name, the fact that he was illiterate, and the 11 July date of the incident (on the eve of the annual Protestant commemoration of the Battle of the Boyne) could indicate that traditional Irish religious tensions were involved. But as there was no mention of Orange intimidation, it is possible that Mrs Gaffney was being chastised for immoral behaviour, or more likely a loose tongue given her mature age, since these were traditionally the two principal reasons why a woman would be targeted.

After the grand jury found a true bill against two men who were involved in the incident, they fled to the United States. When they returned, Gaffney refused an offer of money from their friends as compensation, but the local JPs were unable to find witnesses and the Danville magistrate refused to take Mrs Gaffney's deposition on the grounds that the persons she named were not involved. Gaffney's neighbours clearly refused to co-operate with the official court system because they felt that he should have accepted the retribution offered. Furthermore, when Gaffney asked that the case be taken to the Queen's Bench, the solicitor-general replied that it had already been handled by the proper tribunal.[51]

René Hardy's research suggests that charivaris were much more common in the northern part of the region settled by British immigrants and French Canadians than in the American-dominated townships to the south,[52] and there can be no denying that the Irish settlers were particularly prone to violence. But one protracted affair at the "Head of the Bay" (Fitch Bay) in Stanstead Township suggests that popular forms of justice were well known in the American-settled area as well. When George Shurtliff pressed charges shortly after his wedding, the judge declared that "charivaring was 'a serious disturbance of the peace, which must be put down'." After one culprit was sentenced to a £10 fine and fourteen days in jail, and four others to eight days each, Shurtliff was subjected to the wrath of some of his neighbours for transgressing the popular code. Three months later, in May 1850, he was offering a $100 reward for information leading to the conviction of "the Assassin" who had entered his stable and "stabbed one Ox, one Cow, and a Mare."[53] Perhaps because of Shurtliff's stubborn insistence on legal redress, this was only a taste of what was to come.

The following month, a "person or persons" demolished six windows of Shurtliff's house with the rail of a bedstead. In the process, his wife and child were both cut, "so that the blood ran freely." Seventeen days later, the attacks spread to a relative from the same neighbourhood named Ichabod Shurtliff. Expressing shock, a correspondent identified only as "Justice" reported to the *Stanstead Journal* that during the night someone had entered Shurtliff's pasture "and *ripped open the bellies of five of his Cows.*" Two of the cows had to be killed. The correspondent asked: "Have the people of this District, like the gold-seekers of California, no redress against ruffianism but by resorting to *Judge Lynch*?"[54]

The local JP, E. Gustin, replied that he was certainly aware of "the long chain of perpetrated villainy … from the first attack on farming tools to the stabbing of the ox and mare, to the girdling of sugar trees, shearing horses, demolishing the sugar kettle, buckets, sap-holders, and to the recent smashing of windows, down to the late act of inhuman barbarity in dirking the cows." In self defence, however, Gustin reminded the newspaper's readers that magistrates had no legal authority to institute a process without information on oath, unless the breach of the peace was committed in their presence. He promised, nevertheless, that new information would soon lead to arrests, and that "Justice" would not regret having refrained from lynching "those poor, unhappy *specimens of human deficiency.*" As predicted, three or four individuals were arrested in connection with the case the following month, but they were subsequently discharged by the magistrates' court. In September the two Shurtliffs reported to the government that they had "been compelled to keep continuous nightly watch, until at last worn out with fatigue, they have been forced to dispose of all their stock to prevent its falling a prey to these men." They pleaded that unless the state offered them protection, they would be forced to abandon their farms.[55]

We have seen that there was an outburst of violence in the district at this time, apparently connected with the dismissal of pro-annexationist JPs and the construction of the St Lawrence and Atlantic Railway. Unfortunately, it is impossible to say exactly what underlying social tensions the Shurtliff affair reflected; but if it was perpetrated by a half-dozen ruffians, as the Shurtliffs claimed, the victims evidently failed to gain much sympathy or support from their neighbours. This protracted charivari, if that is the proper term for a campaign which included live-stock mutilation, clearly conforms to what René Hardy, following the French example, has labelled a "charivari injure." Commonly aimed to drive its victims out of the community, charivaris in this category con-trast with the more benign variety known as the "charivari plaisanterie," which persisted into the twentieth century.[56]

An even more protracted "charivari injure" took place in Kingsey Township during the early 1840s. The target in this case was the lawyer and landed proprietor, William Vondenvelden. Vondenvelden had in-herited his large and valuable tracts of land in Kingsey and Berthier from his father, who had briefly served as Lower Canada's assistant sur-veyor-general in the late eighteenth century.[57] As an outspoken oppo-nent of the municipal and school reforms which were introducing locally enforced property taxes, the Kingsey lawyer came into conflict with the village notables, and particularly the liberal merchant, François-Benjamin Blanchard.

Vondenvelden made his political ideology known after failing to be elected as a Metcalfe supporter in Berthier in 1844, when he com-plained that the political representatives of Canada East were "men who entertain the opinion that their interest is to make experiments on our social condition, who wish to turn the uses of our territorial resources to their own private behalf." Concerning the schools, he informed Met-calfe that rather than allowing "disaffected school masters" to instill "the poisonous doctrine of rebellion in the school boys' mind," they should be operated by the "Frères Ignorantius" with the support of the local clergy. Though himself the victim of popular justice in Kingsey, Vondenvelden would later play a role in the Nicolet area as a fomenter of the popular revolt known as the Guerre des Éteignoirs.[58]

Blanchard was from the opposing political spectrum. He was said to be the only French-Canadian Unitarian, and he had operated a Mont-real hardware store with the prominent Patriote, Thomas Storrow Brown, before they went bankrupt in 1836. Having moved to the East-ern Townships, Blanchard did not become directly involved in the

Rebellion, but Aegidius Fauteux claims that he helped a number of fugitives escape to the United States. He was briefly arrested in December 1837 for distributing bulletins from General Brown's "Grande armée," and rearrested two months later when Papineau's brother, André-Augustin, was discovered in his house.[59]

Exactly when the conflict between Blanchard and Vondenvelden originated is not known, but in January 1839 the former Patriote informed the civil secretary that the petition submitted by Vondenvelden and James Wadleigh to have a commissioners' court established in Kingsey included the names of children and domestics, while others had made their mark on the paper without knowing what it said. Blanchard objected that none of the recommended commissioners spoke French, even though the majority of the township was French Canadian.[60] The opposition of a merchant to increased local judicial powers was certainly unusual, but Blanchard may have felt that he had more influence over the magistrates' court, as we shall see.

Vondenvelden took the initiative later in 1839, when he drafted petitions by two men whom Blanchard had successfully sued in the local magistrates' court. One case involved a debt allegedly owed Blanchard by a farmer named Jean-Baptiste Cormier who had been working for him during the previous twelve months. Cormier claimed that Blanchard owed him money rather than vice versa, but the court ordered the bailiff to seize Cormier's horses and he was arrested for offering resistance. In the second case, Alexis Noël, who was a mason, complained that a JP named Richard Baird and his assistants had thrown all his family's household belongings into the rain after he had refused to vacate a house owned by Blanchard. The bailiff had then sold the goods at public auction. Noël did not deny owing rent, but he complained that Baird and Blanchard were unofficially partners in trade.

Both petitions claimed that Blanchard and Baird kept the local poor people in constant terror. Because the two aggrieved parties could not afford to sue, they asked that the attorney-general take their cases to either the King's Bench of the Trois-Rivières District, or the Quarter Sessions of the St Francis District.[61] The two petitions were not only signed by Vondenvelden and a notary named J.B. Vincent, they were written in Vondenvelden's hand, and it soon became clear that he was stirring up trouble against Blanchard for his own purposes.

After being sent to Kingsey to arrest Blanchard, who had fled to Montreal, the Nicolet stipendiary magistrate, Lieutenant William Hanson, submitted a report exonerating him from any wrongdoing. Hanson claimed with reference to the Cormier case that it had previously been mediated to the "*perfect* satisfaction" of both parties. When Cormier was arrested for attacking the sheriff who was attempting to seize his horses,

Blanchard had given him £10 above his account, as well as $2 to pay his expenses to Sherbrooke. Here he had been released without having to pay bail. Hanson concluded that Blanchard had acted fairly, and that Cormier, who "bears a very bad character," had been persuaded by Vondenvelden and Vincent to file the protest. The Nicolet magistrate reached essentially the same conclusion in the other case, reporting that Noël was "a troublesome person and well known to myself," who had taken possession of Blanchard's house "with *force and arms.*" Magistrate Baird (whom he identified as Richard Beard) and Blanchard were not partners, as had been charged, and the notary Vincent was "a well known disaffected person" and "a noted drunkard" who had left Nicolet two years earlier "for fear of being apprehended."[62]

Vincent was not involved in the next phase of the Kingsey conflict, which took place in 1841–42. From his second home in Berthier, Vondenvelden complained vaguely in January 1841 that the existing legal authority was of no avail "against a secret combination by individuals whose poverty and wild manner of existing enable them to be mischievous with comparative impunity."[63] Vondenvelden was probably referring to the situation in Kingsey, for the following September he submitted an affidavit to Judge Fletcher of Sherbrooke stating that he had been aroused from his sleep by a mob of twelve or more individuals with their faces blackened. He had attempted to escape when they began to demolish the windows, "vociferating in a fearful manner," but had been dragged nearly naked into a cart where he was driven blindfolded in a falling rain towards the house of magistrate Edmund Cox. On the way he was subjected to continual threats of murder, and "slightly struck at times." When the blindfold was loosened, he recognized Blanchard. Though Vondenvelden did not say so, the group had obviously planned to deposit him at Cox's house. While he was there, his own house was "sacked and made uninhabitable."

It would appear that the aim was to drive Vondenvelden out of the community rather than simply expressing displeasure with his behaviour. He reported that while he was still at Cox's house six days later, a mob of about the same size as the previous one demanded his surrender. When Cox refused to comply, threats were voiced of another visit, and Vondenvelden claimed that he recognized Blanchard's voice perfectly. He also noted that a man named L. Wentworth, "and more principally his wife," had abetted in the outrage by allowing the mob to make all its preparations in their house. Vondenvelden closed by claiming that "there is a general intimidation in the country ... no one apparently is safe from being attacked in the night."[64]

But the aggrieved lawyer was the only individual to submit such a complaint, and Edward Hale refused Judge Fletcher's request to investigate the matter further. Claiming that his life was in danger, Vondenvelden then demanded that a stipendiary magistrate be sent to Kingsey with the power to compel witnesses to testify.[65] After leaving home for a few days "to avoid throwing the whole township into confusion," Vondenvelden reported that he had learned of a secret association formed "to keep people within doors after dark." What the purpose of doing so might be, he failed to say, but he did add that the house of a man named Lyman Young had been broken into, its windows destroyed, bed and bedding carried off, fences let down, and cattle driven into the crops. The reason Young was targeted was never mentioned, but he may have been Vondenvelden's tenant farmer who was later reported to have been driven out of his quarters. It is clear that no harm was intended against Young's person, but Vondenvelden stated that he had armed himself in light of information that a band of thirty men would storm his house the following week: "assassination and accidental death must soon take place."[66]

Finally convinced that the situation was getting out of hand, the government ordered Montreal's commissioner of police to institute an inquiry.[67] Charges were laid against Blanchard, but Vondenvelden then asked that they be dropped on the grounds that John Rolph, who had rescued him from the cart, was too afraid to testify. It is equally likely that Rolph was involved in the charivari, for the excuse he gave to the JP was that his testimony "would accuse himself." Vondenvelden had also named two witnesses to the carousing and feasting which reportedly took place on the public road after the attack on his house, as well as three others who had observed the organization of a charivari against François Blais. Whether Blais was somehow connected to Vondenvelden is unclear, but these individuals were presumably also unwilling to testify, and Vondenvelden closed by stating: "Summary and moderate punishments would be the best means I believe to awaken these deluded people, and exemplary punishment is requisite only against Blanchard who has duped all into the belief of the impotency of the law."[68]

The charivaris achieved their purpose, at least in the short term, for the disputatious lawyer again retreated to Berthier. But he refused to let the matter end there, and in December 1841 he again asked the government to take action against Blanchard in order "to prevent my property from being destroyed and my liberty invaded by accusations of the most atrocious and improbable nature."[69] Vondenvelden's veiled references to accusations against himself actually pointed to a key factor in the charivari, for he had apparently been living with the wife of his farm tenant/servant. Unaware of this situation, the government again ordered the commissioner of police to intervene. He was to inquire into "certain outrages" committed on the premises of Edmund Cox, actions which had presumably been designed to intimidate this local magistrate after

Blanchard's arrest. But rather than showing gratitude, Vondenvelden charged that Cox had illegally dismissed Blanchard who was his intimate friend, and complained about the "strange and wild" behaviour of the police magistrate sent to investigate the matter, adding that the crisis was "above the range of his intellect."[70]

Finally, a month later, the government sent Lieutenant Hanson of Nicolet to Kingsey once again to get to the bottom of the affair. Hanson had supported Blanchard against Vondenvelden in 1839, as we have seen, and it wasn't long before the latter was complaining about the suppression of his right as a private prosecutor to examine witnesses. Hanson did not mince words in his second report, which stated that Vondenvelden was "a bad and troublesome character" who had been driven from Kingsey "in consequence of his having married his — woman to his Farmer and afterwards continued to be intimate with her." The case against Blanchard had been dismissed by Chief Justice Stuart at the last Criminal Court of Queen's Bench at Trois-Rivières after Vondenvelden had asked Hanson "to *Summons & arrest* a number of quiet individuals in order that he might *harangue* and make himself conspicuous."[71]

Governor-General Bagot approved of the course Hanson had taken, but the case did not end there. Vondenvelden reported a few days later that his Kingsey house had once more been attacked while he was in Berthier. A year later, in September 1843, Blanchard again faced trial in Trois-Rivières, but the case was postponed because he was suffering from cholera. Vondenvelden also complained that the "poor ignorant constable" sent to serve bench warrants had simply returned "with a sad story of the fight given him by the Kingsey *devils*." He asked for an efficient officer with the authority to raise a "posse," as well as higher bail for Blanchard. The outcome of the case is unknown, though it apparently prevented the Kingsey merchant from being appointed commissioner of small causes in 1844.[72]

More information would be needed to assign relative weights to the roles played in this protracted affair by social class, ethnic origin, political rivalry, personality, and community mores. Each of these factors clearly played a role, though ethnic conflict appears to have been surprisingly negligible despite the fact that Kingsey's French and English-speaking populations were quite evenly divided in numbers at this time. Vondenvelden himself was not of British origin, having had a German father and a French-Canadian mother. Furthermore, his father, despite the considerable properties he had accumulated and his government appointment, had been a supporter of the French-Canadian reformers during his brief period in the Legislative Assembly. As for William, junior, he had written to Governor Colborne in 1838 that he was leaving

Kingsey for Berthier because he had made himself "equally obnoxious to the *ardent loyalists and* to the Papineau partisans," resulting in the "gratuitous insults of the former and the mysterious threats of the latter."[73]

Vondenvelden's outsider status, in addition to his arrogant and irascible personality, are doubtless the main reasons why he found few supporters in the local English-speaking community, which consisted largely of American-origin farmers. He himself claimed that the widespread practice of squatting in Kingsey and Durham was the true cause "of the lawless spirit which gives rise to riots, personal attacks under disguises with threats of repetition if law is had recourse to."[74] This was an ironic statement given the role Vondenvelden had played in resisting Blanchard's attempt to evict a squatter in 1839, but it certainly helps to explain his unpopularity with one segment of the community.

As for the accusation concerning Vondenvelden's female servant, while sexual morality and the intimate life of the married couple were a dominant theme in charivaris everywhere, European historians have noted that there was seldom a single motive involved.[75] In this case, Vondenvelden's private transgression served as little more than a catalyst in an already volatile situation. An important part of that situation was clearly the political power struggle (in the sense of competition for local dominance) between Vondenvelden and Blanchard, though this could not have been deduced from the records that deal directly with the charivari.

Allan Greer has described how the charivari became a political weapon of intimidation during the Rebellion,[76] but in this case politics was not the whole story or Vondenvelden would surely have had some conservative allies. Perhaps the most important component was simply the desire of a significant part of the community to rid itself of an unpopular and disruptive force without transgressing certain culturally accepted norms. Thompson notes that "even when rough music was expressive of the most absolute community hostility, and its intention was to ostracize or drive out an offender, the ritual element may be seen as channeling and controlling this hostility."[77] Most charivaris may have initially been aimed at reintegrating their victims into the community by exacting public humiliation for their transgressions, but Vondenvelden was essentially an outsider who was not temperamentally inclined to accept such chastisement. Also, his legal training would enable him to continue to irritate the local petite bourgeoisie through the courts, and by opposing the implementation of institutional reforms which they supported.

It is somewhat ironic, then, that a reformer such as Blanchard, who would become the first mayor of the township, would resort to a rather violent ritual associated with traditional custom. Indeed, Carol Wilton has recently argued that Upper Canada's conservatives were more likely than the reformers to resort to collective violence for their own political purposes, an observation which E.P. Thompson has also made for early nineteenth-century England.[78] But the Kingsey situation does not entirely contradict this theory, for Vondenvelden was not above appealing to the masses himself, and he would encourage popular resistance to school taxes in the Nicolet area later in the decade. As a matter of fact, he also remained a thorn in Blanchard's side, for when the latter became a minor official he complained that the old "Etignoire" [sic] had interrupted him while he was reading a petition from the Archbishop of Quebec condemning the burning of the Montreal Parliament Buildings in 1849. According to Blanchard, Vondenvelden (who had become a municipal councillor) then began preaching annexation, thereby exciting the minds of the people so much that they were capable of being induced to follow the example of those who had rioted against school reform in St Grégoire and the neighbouring parishes.[79]

Blanchard and Vondenvelden depicted each other as manipulators of the guileless masses, but it is worth noting how each of these members of the local elite played their games according to the rules or rites of the common people. The various charivaris we have examined include references to blackened faces, tarring and feathering, river ducking, late night processions behind half-dressed victims, horse-shearing, and cattle dirking. These were forms of popular ritual, and Thompson claims that while though those who enacted them "may have long forgotten their mythic origins ... the rites themselves powerfully evoke mythic meanings, even if only fragmentarily and half-consciously understood."[80]

The Gaffney and Shurtliff cases remain frustratingly opaque because little is known about either of these families, but both charivaris reflected the limitations of the official legal system in the face of public apathy or hostility towards the victims of locally based intimidation. More significantly, the involvement of the respectable merchant Blanchard in this ritual, and the tacit approval of the legal authorities, suggest that in the Eastern Townships of the 1840s the dichotomy between "popular justice" and "state justice" was still not as sharp as historians have tended to assume. As we shall see in the following section, there was an even greater contradiction between what the state officially outlawed and the community condoned when it came to the movement of goods and chattels across the international border.

REGULATING CROSS-BORDER TRAFFIC

Smuggling may be a crime, but it demands a separate treatment from the court system simply because so many residents of the Eastern Townships, while they demanded tariff protection against American imports, nevertheless acted as if they had the right to make duty-free purchases in the United States. In other words, local residents made a distinction between the short-haul movement of goods intrinsic to a regional economy which straddled the international border, and the long-haul transportation of American products to Montreal where they might suppress the provincial market.[81] Furthermore, small-scale smuggling differed from "crime" as it is generally perceived insofar as those apprehended simply had their contraband goods seized by the customs officers rather than being jailed or tried in the courts. The inland customs ports were not an innovation of the 1840s, but it was not until that decade that even marginally effective efforts were made to curtail smuggling, at least as far as the border between the Eastern Townships and the United States was concerned.

The first customs port in the Eastern Townships was established in Stanstead in 1821. As noted earlier, Collector William Hamilton must have also established a presence in Sherbrooke, for his house there was burned down in 1822. Very little is known about Hamilton's tenure, but in 1826 a meeting of Stanstead Township residents, including magistrates and militia officers, strongly condemned his decision to charge a fee to all persons crossing the border on horseback or in carriages, even if they had no articles to market. American drovers, the meeting complained, were at the same time allowed to bring their cattle into Lower Canada at a much lower duty than required by law.[82]

Three years later, the touring Archdeacon George J. Mountain reported that at Stanstead forty Americans had rescued a herd of cattle from Hamilton even though the captain of militia had placed ten men at his disposal. Mountain added: "There appears to be a sort of border war here, and some of the residents upon the Marches have manifestly adopted the Rob Roy principle,

  – the simple plan
  That those may take who have the power
  And those may keep who can."[83]

Hamilton's problems did not only originate from the American side of the border, for in 1832 the perennially discontented Elmer Cushing and a number of Stanstead residents called for an investigation into the customs collector's office. Cushing later wrote: "I have been watching Mr Hamilton's doings under the strongest impressions that he was doing what would not stand the test of strict investigation."[84]

There are no more letters from Stanstead in the Customs and Excise collection at the National Archives prior to 1845, when a dozen Canadian ports were established from Hereford Township westward. Fortunately, we do have the personal letters of the man who succeeded Hamilton after his death in 1834.[85] Robert Hoyle's income originally consisted of a commission of 50 percent on all collections of up to £200 per year, but in 1836 the fees were eliminated by legislative enactment. Marcus Child informed Hoyle that his fellow Stanstead MLA, William Grannis, was to blame for the fact that the Stanstead collector's salary was lowered from £40, as originally projected, to £25. Later in the year, however, Hoyle mentioned to his wife Eliza that customs officials were also entitled to one-third the value of the goods they seized. Child had recommended that those assistant officers known as land waiters or landing waiters who were stationed at Hereford, Potton, and Stanstead receive £15 salary, but the assembly agreed to this provision only for Stanstead.[86]

From 1836 there is a four-year gap in Hoyle's correspondence to Eliza, who was apparently living with him in Stanstead during this period. For much of this time Hoyle was in command of two volunteer cavalry companies, suggesting that the chief role of the military units stationed at Stanstead during the Rebellion was to keep a close eye on the border.[87] However, the military presence appears not to have curtailed smuggling, for Hoyle reported in 1838 that a Derby innkeeper named Chase "notoriously keeps a regular depot of contraband articles of various kinds for the purpose of being smuggled into this province whenever safe opportunities offered."[88]

The correspondence between Hoyle and his wife resumes in 1841, when she went to visit her family in New York. He wrote to her in October of that year that he had collected $900 in duties during the third quarter alone.[89] A month later, however, he was complaining: "There is a deal of Smuggling going on I suspect, and I fear a growing contempt for the Revenue Laws." Hoyle reported that when a suspected informer named Caples had entered the Rock Island store of Holmes and Morrill, he had been warned that they "would give $100 to have any informer murdered or *lynched* if the information was against themselves, customers, or neighbors." A Derby Line merchant present in the store at the time had added that "he would turn out, and strip to his shirt to rescue any man that should be stopped or taken when smuggling." The sixty-year-old Hoyle reassured his wife that he himself was not about to take risks: "you will recall that my *bump* of *caution* is large."[90]

The local community also resorted to more sophisticated means of thwarting the customs' office, for Hoyle complained in November 1842 that the "whole nest of S — [smugglers] on Rock Island" were encouraging an individual caught with five dozen books to petition the government for the return of his horse, sleigh, and harness. In return Hoyle had "hinted they had better be still, or I will go for the fine of £100 cy."[91]

Commenting on his imminent retirement, the Stanstead collector observed: "On reflection cannot say that I have any misgivings, for I am not over and above, attached to either folks or place; they are a most selfish set of beings."[92] Hoyle's successor, British naval veteran James Thompson, did not find the community to be any more congenial. He complained in 1848, six years after his arrival, that Stanstead was "without society, a place of worship [he was obviously not a Methodist], or one peculiarity to make it a suitable or desirable place of residence." Six months later, Thompson referred to Stanstead as "a hornet's nest," and in 1851 he wrote that it was "a community where smuggling is popular and the population is shrewd and lawless and ever willing to aid smugglers."[93]

The close social and economic links between the communities on either side of the border posed a formidable challenge to customs officers. Thus, when individuals from the Stanstead area switched residences to Vermont and back again, they felt that they should not have to pay duties on the horses and cattle that had originated in Canada. Referring to one such request from an old man who had resided two years with a married daughter in Derby, across the line from Rock Island, Thompson wrote that "I fear should the petition be granted we shall have innumerable applications of a similar nature from the continued changing of residences from this Province to the neighboring State and back again, as well as the swapping of property."[94]

The collector for Sutton, Anson Kemp, was also vigilant when it came to cross-border migration, for in 1845 he seized the horse, sleigh, and buffalo robes of William Castle, who had arrived from Vermont with his wife and three children a month earlier. Castle protested that he and his family were simply visitors detained by illness, and he attracted the sympathy of the local MLA who reported that they had been left "in a destitute and distressed state." But Kemp replied that Castle had arrived planning to stay in Canada, and that he had refused the opportunity to pay the duty, choosing instead to have a friend bid his horse and sleigh in at the sheriff's auction for only £5 8s. 5d. A few days later Kemp reported that Castle had disposed of the horse and taken a farm, as predicted. The collector insisted that if this seizure were given up, "I shall be harassed in every future one."[95] Such tariffs were obviously very unpopular, however, and a new bill introduced in 1848 allowed immigrants from the United States to import livestock as settlers' goods. Thompson of Stanstead complained that "Many who come into the Province at this Port as Settlers return to the States again after a year or two and should such settlers be permitted to bring in an unlimited quantity of live stock free I consider it will be prejudicial to the Revenue."[96]

Whether or not he was exaggerating about the nomadic propensities of the border residents, Thompson did face a significant problem from farmers who owned land on both sides of the border. In 1845 William H. Holmes protested that four of his cows had been seized when he was returning them to Canada from his pasture in Derby. The cows were returned, but a couple of months later Andrew Patton, now elevated to the position of customs surveyor, reported his fourth seizure of the season from the farmer, though his 112 lambs were returned after John McConnell, Dr Colby, and several JPs supported his case.

Holmes continued his practice of herding livestock across the border without reporting to customs, and in the spring of 1846 the commissioner of customs finally decided to levy the punitive fine of £100 after the seizure of two pigs. But Holmes again had the last laugh, for Thompson himself intervened on his behalf this time by reporting that the smuggler's Stanstead property was mortgaged to its full value. As a result, the fine would simply lead him to transport all his moveables out of reach across the border.[97]

Holmes may have been particularly bold, but he was certainly not the only farmer engaged in livestock smuggling. In 1848 Thompson complained that "this system of sending Cattle in the Spring, or as soon as the feed is good into Canada, on uninhabited and back farms to pasture, in too many instances terminates in their being sold in the fall to the Canadian Drovers, who drive them off and the duties are evaded." The Stanstead collector claimed that from the Beebe Plain neighbourhood alone a herd of at least 150 cattle was collected in this fashion every fall.[98]

Millers, as well, had long tended to ignore the border, at least as far as the local economy was concerned. When Thompson attempted to collect duties on American grain brought to the Rock Island mill of Spalding and Foster, MLA John McConnell protested on their behalf that even during the War of 1812 inhabitants from the American side of the border had been allowed to grind their grain locally without interference. According to McConnell, when Spalding and Foster had erected their new flour mill at great expense a few years earlier, they had assumed that they would receive business from both sides of the border. In the face of such opposition, the Stanstead collector suggested that the millers proceed without interference on condition that they post a bond to ensure that none of the American flour remained in Canada without paying duty.[99]

This recommendation was accepted by the government, but a year later a similar problem emerged when John Gilman of Stanstead was charged duties for the first time on the Canadian lumber he brought back from his Derby sawmill. His protest was supported by two local notables, Dr Colby and Selah Pomroy, JP. Likewise, in 1847 Wright Chamberlin asked that Vermonters continue to be permitted to bring wool and cloth to be carded and dressed at his mills without paying duties.[100]

The government's response to these two petitions is not recorded, though in all likelihood it was favourable. A greater threat to the revenue was Horace Stewart's store which straddled the border in Beebe Plain for reasons that are not hard to imagine. In 1846 Thompson seized the horse and wagon driven by a farmer named Dudley Magoon on the grounds that he had purchased a jar of New England rum at Stewart's store. When Magoon's protest was supported by Marcus Child and two other JPs, Thompson replied that "the Magoon family which are numerous, and the Settlers in the Magoon settlement trade exclusively with Stewart and the Traders in the State of Vermont immediately on the province Line." Since "goods to a large amount are annually smuggled into this province in this small way," it was necessary to make the smugglers "suffer when detected."[101]

Like Hoyle ten years earlier, Thompson in 1848 described how local merchants stored their American wholesale purchases in a nearby Vermont depot from where they or their customers smuggled them into Canada in small quantities. He felt that the construction of a warehousing port at Rock Island would go a long way to reducing this practice, since the merchants would be able to pay duties on their goods only as they needed them. But Thompson's advice was not heeded, and, in the meantime, he complained that importers were contributing financially to the improvement of roads to rival ports where collectors charged lower duties than he did.[102]

Still more seriously, the local merchants were becoming increasingly adept at using the courts against him. Hoyle had admitted in 1842 that a seizure of tea was probably illegal because the magistrates had first placed the barn where it was stored under guard, "but a vast majority of the people think that the Custom House Officers are invulnerable." Only three years later, however, Thompson faced a legal challenge to his right to search premises for smuggled goods. When he attempted to seize forty chests of tea in Sherbrooke, the Queen's Bench refused to grant him or his men the writ of assistance required to enter the building where the goods were stored.[103] A year later the issue was still before the Queen's Bench where the merchants' counsel successfully argued that as the customs collectors generally did not make the actual seizures, the execution of a writ of assistance "would be placed in the hands of subordinate officers who might abuse its powers."[104]

The Stanstead collector still had not been issued a writ of assistance in February 1847, when Commissioner Dunscombe reported to the government that the ports in the District of St Francis were the only ones within the Province of Canada in this unfortunate position. By April the local magistrates were refusing to grant warrants for the searching of stores, making their own presence mandatory in any such operation.

Finally, almost a year later, in March 1848, the provincial judge of the district's Inferior Term of the Queen's Bench did grant Thompson the long-sought-after writ of assistance.[105]

Meanwhile, the Stanstead collector faced a different kind of legal threat in 1846 when the aggrieved parties in two cases threatened to sue in order to establish the right of the commissioners' courts to try cases involving property seized under the customs laws. Since these local courts were presided over by elevated JPs, some of whom themselves were involved in smuggling, Thompson had good reason to oppose their involvement in such cases. Furthermore, he and his men had failed to turn a blind eye to the activities of the local elite. In the fall of 1846, for example, an officer seized twenty-five windows in a Stanstead shop recently purchased by Wright Chamberlin, pioneer merchant, active tory supporter, and lieutenant-colonel in the militia. Not surprisingly, Thompson was quickly ordered by the commissioner to restore this property. Thompson also annoyed another influential pioneer in 1846 when he opposed Colonel Kilborn's request to bring back duty free the three tons of hops he had taken to be dried at a kiln in Derby.[106]

The Stanstead collector presumably won his point that smuggling cases should be kept out of the commissioners' courts, for neither he nor his fellow collectors ever referred to trials before the local tribunals in the Townships. This was just as well for them, since they were facing legal challenges in the neighbouring United States. In 1846, for example, Thompson was arrested by the Derby sheriff for destroying a pirated American edition ironically entitled *Moral Philosophy or the Duties of Man*. Thompson had apparently been unaware that he was standing on the American side of the line inside the local store when he made the seizure. He complained about "the mortifying and humiliating position of being obliged to defend his public conduct, in his official capacity, before the tribunal of a foreign nation," but at least the charge was eventually dropped.[107]

More serious was the situation faced soon afterward by the Barnston preventive officer, Aaron Workman, and his assistant. They were arrested in Canaan, Vermont, for having seized eight oxen and fifty sheep belonging to American residents. Released on bail, the two men were forced to return home without their sleighs and horses. In the case concerning the oxen, the Canaan court later found Workman liable for $28 in damages plus costs, bringing the total to nearly $100. Thompson felt that the grounds for appeal were weak, since no peace officer had been present at the time of the seizure, and Workman had not had a writ of assistance. The Canadian defendants nevertheless won an appeal in a Vermont court the following year. Officer Workman still had to face an action of trespass in the case concerning the sheep, but once again the judge dismissed the case against him.[108]

The customs officers of the Eastern Townships do not appear to have faced any other serious court challenges during the 1840s, but the local elites were still able to exert political pressure behind the scenes in a manner not easy to document. We have noted above how quickly the customs commissioner ordered Wright Chamberlin's windows restored, but there is nothing to suggest that the influential merchant did not have a legitimate grievance. More blatantly political was a case which took place at the smaller port of Sutton. Collector Benjamin Seaton decided in 1846 to make an example of a merchant named Nathaniel Pettis whom he suspected of being a frequent smuggler to his store in a remote part of Brome Township. Rather than following the usual practice of auctioning the seized tea, tobacco, and other articles, Seaton recommended the full penalty of £100. Soon afterward, the local MLA submitted a petition signed by two Episcopalian ministers, a JP, and the local establishment pillar, P.H. Knowlton, stating that the fine would "utterly ruin a loyal subject and otherwise a deserving young man and his family." Pettis was not only the local postmaster and school commissioner, he was the grandson of a United Empire Loyalist, in short, "a man of good character." All proceedings against him were subsequently suspended without protest on the local collector's part.[109]

Obviously not every member of the community enjoyed this degree of influence, and much more frequently documented than instances of political interference were the cases involving physical resistance to seizure of goods and chattels. In 1847, for example, a Stanstead preventive officer had his head split open with an iron bar, and the following year one of his co-workers, F.J. Parker, was knocked unconscious by an American who had been hiding five gallons of spirits as well as haying tools in his wagon. In 1851 Parker was again struck on the head and left semiconscious on the ice after seizing a young man's horse and sleigh on the grounds that he had not reported the three gallons of liquor and small piece of cloth he was carrying with him. But these were isolated instances. In the first Stanstead case, Thompson reported that the perpetrator was "one of those miserable wretches, not worth noticing," and in the last one he was the son of a prominent local doctor who was simply travelling from Vermont to visit his family.[110] More threatening to the authorities was the intimidation that took place on a broader, more organized scale.

The small port of Georgeville on Lake Memphremagog, which straddled the Canadian-American border, was a particularly troublesome spot for Thompson's men. In 1845, for example, preventive officer William McGowan discovered a party of ten to twelve men throwing stones at a fence in order to free the three steers he had seized across the lake. McGowan himself was then assaulted with stones, escaping only three hours later when two other men came to his rescue. When a second attempt was made to liberate the steers shortly afterward, Thompson quickly sold them even though he was supposed to wait thirty days before doing so.[111]

McGowan again met with local resistance in 1846 when Thompson supplied him with a boat at Georgeville to improve his effectiveness on the lake. Only four days after its purchase, the boat was taken from its landing place and, in McGowan's opinion, sunk in the lake "from a determination to frustrate any attempt to suppress the Smuggling carried on there." Thompson later reported that there was an organization of young men in Georgeville "to watch our motions and give information thereof." Certainly there was concerted resistance, for in 1850 a number of men blocked preventive officer Parker from inspecting some boxes carried from the lakeshore to the local store. Parker escaped without injuries, but soon afterwards McGowan was beaten while attempting to assist him in the same village. Their superior, Thompson, had obviously begun to take a certain amount of physical resistance for granted since he merely asked for permission to apprehend the parties involved if the violence were repeated.[112]

Another trouble spot was the village of Compton where members of the local community adopted the idiom of popular ritual in their campaign to intimidate the customs officers. In 1845 Thompson reported that Ford, the local preventive officer, had once been "tied to a tree, had his head shaved, ears cut, and was otherwise brutally treated." The offenders were never found despite the £25 reward offered by the government.[113] Perhaps not surprisingly, Ford's name does not appear again in the customs correspondence. However, preventive officer Workman would prove to be more resilient.

Most of Workman's activities were in the Hereford area, where he eventually moved, but in 1848 he was severely beaten by the Compton merchant, Charles E. Stimson. The prosecution's principal witness was the hostler of the tavern where Workman had taken refuge but, in Thompson's words, "he was bought off and sent to Boston." Thompson also claimed that some of the jury members were bribed, which presumably explained why Stimson was fined only £3. The following year Workman was once again attacked in Compton, this time while investigating whether four loads of goods had been declared at customs. He and his assistant were forced to flee for their lives after the latter was injured by a group of stone-throwing men. The two officers spent the night hiding in a ditch, and when they emerged the next morning they found Workman's hat atop an effigy erected in the centre of the village.[114]

These acts of violence, brutal as they were in some instances, never resulted in life-threatening injuries, nor did they serve to discourage such hardy preventive officers as Workman. In general, then, popular resistance to the customs officers conformed to a pattern of rough justice, with no resort to firearms and the local population careful to stay within the bounds of accepted violence. The aim was make the work of the customs officers as difficult as possible without challenging the authority of the state in too overt a fashion.

Indeed, the most serious challenge to that authority came not through resistance by means of the courts or physical violence, but through subversion by means of social pressure and corruption. The instances of political interference on behalf of the well-connected probably did little for the reputation of the customs office, and still more damaging were the suspicions that certain officers were in league with local smugglers. Such suspicions would turn officers in Stanstead and Hereford against each other, seriously impeding the effective operation of both inland ports.

To a certain extent, internal dissension was a structural feature of a system in which the preventive officers were more dependent than their superiors on the proceeds from the sale of seized goods. In one of his many petitions, Andrew Patton of Stanstead complained that even though he was the only land waiter overseeing "Sixty or Seventy miles of Frontier intersected by half as many roads," not to mention "an open water communication of three miles in width," he received only $60 in salary. Furthermore, he was obliged to employ an agent in Kingston to receive it for him, leaving a total of only $55 a year "which is barely enough to pay the Expenses of Keeping a horse which he must do or do nothing, for such is the simpathy [sic] of the people towards Smuglers [sic], that it is impossible to hire one [i.e. a horse] on Such bussiness [sic]."[115] Given their dependence on commission income, Patton and his fellow officers in the field objected when the collector relinquished goods which they had seized. In 1846, for example, Patton and James Young protested when Thompson returned the 14,000 shingles they claimed were manufactured from smuggled trees, and two months later another officer filed a formal objection when Thompson returned a horse he had seized.[116]

But the real trouble did not begin until 1848 when the Stanstead preventive officers came to suspect that Andrew Patton was sending them on wild goose chases in order to allow Knight, Kilborn and Company to smuggle goods from their Derby warehouse to their store in Rock Island. Acting on a tip, McGowan had set up a watch on the store one evening rather than following Patton's instructions to leave town on another mission. Late that night a number of men did unload a wagon and carry the goods into the back alley, but from his vantage point across the street McGowan was unable to observe which building they entered. Thompson went to Sherbrooke for a writ of assistance the following day, but the judge was absent and so he was forced to let the matter drop.

One evening the following year McGowan again suspected that Patton was sending him out of the way, and the following day he was taunted with the statement "that had he got the property that was smuggled that evening it would have kept him a year, but in all probability would have cost him his life." When an informant soon afterwards told McGowan that he had overheard someone say to Knight that "he had smuggled enough the other night for three months," the collector himself searched the store, stables and nearby tavern, as well as Patton's premises, but found nothing.[117]

Patton attracted this suspicion because his son was employed by Knight and Kilborn during this period. Indeed, he was elevated to partner in 1849, yet no one was willing to testify publicly against his aging father, and Thompson was concerned that the community would protest his search of Patton's premises. Under these circumstances, the collector reported, his hands were tied. The most that Thompson was ever able to do was to limit Patton's responsibilities. In May 1850, after forwarding one of the controversial customs surveyor's many requests for a raise in salary, Thompson added that "if his continued application for this increase could but be the cause of removing him, my comfort would be enlarged for I have lost all confidence in him, as have all the subordinates here, and the result is that I cannot with any degree of satisfaction absent myself even after the regular hours of business." Patton persisted for eleven more years, however, when he finally retired at the age of seventy-nine with his full salary of $375 a year.[118]

Meanwhile, McGowan and Dixon had uncovered evidence pointing to collusion between a wholesale merchant named Rowell from North Troy, Vermont, and customs collector McVey of Potton. In 1849 the two Stanstead preventive officers seized several chests of tea and tobacco in Frost Village and nearby Waterloo, after verifying that the Potton office only had records of a much smaller quantity being entered by Rowell, who had supposedly paid the duties in advance. Several days later, however, Rowell was able to produce returns from the Potton customs office recording imports to Canada exceeding the amount seized in the two stores. McGowan and Dixon then returned to Shefford Township where they were able to find still larger quantities of tea and tobacco that had been shipped to various merchants by Rowell. But this time collector McVey himself appeared in Stanstead with recent records of imports from Rowell's store which far outstripped all that the two officers had discovered on even their second tour. Thompson was clearly not anxious to inform on his Potton colleague, but McGowan and Dixon demanded a government inquiry.[119]

Marcus Child and the customs collector at neighbouring Sutton were appointed to investigate the charges against the Potton collector. They reported that his books were "regularly and neatly kept," and that "in every particular the Office work appeared to be well performed." While admitting that they were unable to determine from witnesses whether Rowell had shipped more goods across the line than he had paid duties on, the two investigators noted that 2,570 pounds of tobacco and 3,412 pounds of tea had been entered in his name at Potton, while McGowan and Dixon had seized only 342 pounds of the former and 950 pounds of the latter. The report therefore concluded that the allegations were unsubstantiated. However, it did criticize McVey for taking the customs stamp to Rowell's store in North Troy, and it noted that a case of dry goods supplied by Rowell to a Stukeley merchant had contained a type of shirting not mentioned in any of McVey's reports. The commissioners therefore concluded that if any entry had been made of this case of goods, it must have been a false one.[120]

A still more contentious internal dispute was about to erupt to the east, at the recently established port of Hereford. The conflict there was along structural lines, with a preventive officer who depended upon seizing goods for his bread and butter feeling thwarted by a customs collector who preferred not to make too many waves in the local community. But personality traits also played a role, and the dispute reveals how fine the line could be between zeal and intimidation on the one hand, and accommodation and corruption on the other.

We have already described how Workman was twice assaulted in Compton, but it was apparently the expenses entailed in the Vermont court cases which led him to sell his farm in Barnston and move to the backwoods of Hereford, where he was aware that smuggling went relatively unchecked. From Stanstead, Thompson had recommended him for a salaried position at that rather remote port, but he also warned that Workman would likely "not be equal to the opposition he would have to contend with, besides his not being esteemed by Mr Vincent [the local collector] with whom he would have to do business."[121]

Hereford's reputation to some extent reflected the fact that the local farmers were effectively cut off from the neighbouring townships for much of the year, forcing them to rely on the nearby Vermont and New Hampshire communities for their market. As a result, a tacit agreement existed with customs collectors on both sides of the border that the Hereford people would not have to pay duties on the goods they exported and imported. For obvious reasons, Hereford collector Robert Vincent never spelled this arrangement out to the commissioner, but he did make his priorities clear: "I have endeavored during my residence here to prevent disturbances – previously there were often Riots and bloodshed. I shall continue to exert myself to prevent these Border feuds."[122]

Workman later claimed that he too abided by these informal rules, and certainly there was no overt conflict between him and Vincent until late 1852, when construction of the St Lawrence and Atlantic Railway came close enough to affect the local cross-border traffic. The first clash of wills came when Workman seized ten trunks of ready-made clothes, ten bags of provender, and ten bags of oats, plus the horses and sleighs hauling the shipment. Vincent later reported that a railway contractor named Horner had made a previous arrangement with him to have these materials pass through Canada duty free. They were destined for his crew working just south of the border a few miles to the west of Hereford.

Workman was paid £10 to accompany the load to its destination, but he subsequently complained that the teamster would go no farther than a farm in Barford, about eight miles north of the border, using the condition of the roads as an excuse. He added that "a number of loades [sic] of Goods have passed and are still passing at this post without paying the duties or any Guarantee that the [sic] leave the province what ever."[123] To this Vincent replied that he had a witness to testify that the goods in question, which were obviously workers' clothing, were deposited at contractor Horner's storehouse in Norton, Vermont.

Concerning Workman, Vincent added in the same report that "no person thoroughly acquainted with him, would place any confidence in any statements he might make under any circumstances – and his dishonesty is proverbial – and in the discharge of his official duties his way and *manner* provokes hostility; and quarrels after ensue. I have had great difficulty in restraining those who have been ill treated by him, from their attempts at retaliation." The commissioner obviously accepted Vincent's explanation, for he ordered Workman to return half the money he had been paid to accompany the load of goods to Horner's depot.[124]

But Vincent was not satisfied with this small victory, and during the following months he began to collect affidavits testifying to his subordinate's abuse of authority. Two local justices of the peace swore that Workman even seized private letters as well as using "rough and improper language especially when in a state of intoxication (*as he frequently* is)." Furthermore, Workman was assisted by John O'Conner, "a man of notorious bad character and one who ever stands ready at the call of officer Workman to give or make any or all informations corresponding with the case then on hand." The point had been reached where "many people are afraid to travel across the line on the Road where said Workman resides."[125]

But the strongest language came from the collector on the American side of the border. While admitting that "it is delicate, and perhaps improper" for an officer in the u.s. customs to interfere in a Canadian matter, George Hartshore emphasized the privileges enjoyed by the Hereford residents in neighbouring Vermont and New Hampshire: "there is scarcely a day that the *strict letter* of our law would not require the seizure of some of their teams, or other property." But "they come to our stores and shops, mills, etc. etc. and return without molestation and without fear of molestation." Hartshore claimed that he was not asking for "reciprocal immunities," simply "a fair administration of your revenue laws." He concluded: "In a word, I complain that this officer Workman is so well understood to be *Capricious, Drunken, Extortionate,* and *Outrageously Abusive,* oftentimes that people fear to travel near him, and avoid him when they can, as they would avoid a *Robber.*"[126]

In addition to the affidavits, the customs commissioner received a petition signed by thirty-four magistrates, militia officers, and others in the St Francis District accusing Workman of extortion and drunkenness, and stating that "his general conduct and bearing would indicate that he takes more pleasure in annoying, oppressing and tyrannizing over the public than in preventing fraud to her Majesty's revenue in this Province."[127] Soon afterwards, the Sherbrooke and Stanstead MLAs, Sanborn and Terrill, added their support to the petition.

Rather than encouraging Workman to be more circumspect, the organization of this campaign caused him to become more defiant than ever of Vincent's authority. In late July 1853 he seized three barrels of gin and a keg of wine even though the wagon driven by Hiram Wright was accompanied by preventive officer Heath, who stated that it was destined for the railhead at Norton, Vermont. When Vincent tried to convince Workman to release the team and its cargo, the latter insisted on delivering them to the Stanstead collector.[128]

Workman finally came to his own defence in late September, claiming to be the victim of "a conspiracy headed by the said Robert Vincent Esq. and encouraged by the smuglers [*sic*] on the Frontier." He noted that the only evidence presented against him was a small number of affidavits, and he proceeded to tell his side of the story in detail. Workman denied ever having been drunk, or having extorted money from travellers, claiming that his compensation was always paid on Vincent's recommendation. As for the charge of seizing mail, he had merely offered to post two letters for a man was carrying them to Compton. Coming to the defence of his assistant, O'Connor, Workman described how the former had been persecuted as an informer by the burning of his barn with all his crops and farming equipment, the poisoning of his horse, the destruction of his sugar kettle and buckets, and the repeated breaching of his fences so that cattle would destroy his grain and hay. As for the recent incident concerning the liquor seized from Hiram Wright, Workman argued that preventive officer Heath was well aware that it was destined for Stanley's "groggery" on the Canadian side of the border. Since ordinary supplies were by this time being carried northward on the railway line from Portland to the construction crews, there was no reason for liquor traffickers to take the circuitous route through Hereford to Norton, Vermont. They must therefore be supplying a Canadian market.[129]

Workman was not being quite truthful, for he was doubtless aware that the liquor was destined for the railway crews then working south of the border because the state attorney had personally taken seventy militiamen and destroyed all the dram shops located near the railway construction crews on the American side of the border. This had not ended the drinking problem because the traffickers had responded by shifting their operations back across the border into Canada, one of them simply moving his tavern the required distance northward on rollers. According to High Constable Clark of Sherbrooke in July, the railway contractors were complaining that work was being brought to a standstill by "the constant drunkenness and Rioting of the men." Pointing specifically to Vincent, the constable added: "Our neighbours express great surprise and indignation the [sic] we should allow their grog sellers to cross the Line with their Liquors and openly sell it on this side to their annoyance and damage."[130]

Workman was also able to undermine the impact of the petition against him by pointing out that only thirty-four people had signed it even though six townships had been canvassed, and fifteen of the complainants were merchants or the sons of merchants, some of whose goods he had seized. As for Sanborn, Workman noted that he was the brother-in-law of one of the said merchants, that he had acted as Hiram Wright's attorney in the case of the seized liquor shipment (a presumably awkward position for a leading temperance advocate), and that he had vowed to have Workman dismissed after the latter publicly opposed him as an annexationist during the last election.[131] The other MLA, Terrill of Stanstead, subsequently withdrew his protest against the preventive officer, as did several of those who had signed the petition.

But Workman did not restrict his efforts to undermining the testimonials gathered against him. He also acquired signatures and letters of support from nearby American residents, as well as inhabitants of Hereford and Barnston and prominent members of the Eastern Townships elite. The Hereford petition was particularly damaging to the image that Workman's opponents had painted, for it pointed out that he served as the local postmaster, secretary-treasurer of the school commission, municipal roads surveyor, evaluator, and census enumerator. In addition,

Marcus Child wrote that "a more faithful and zealous preventive officer of the customs cannot be found on this frontier, although he may not on all occasions, & under all circumstances, have acted in the most prudent manner." W.L. Felton and High Constable Clark each wrote that Workman was the victim of a conspiracy, and James Thompson (who was now the Coaticook collector) noted that Workman had had to contend with "murderous attacks and waylayings, heavy law suits," and bribed juries before he moved to Hereford. Thompson added that he had never seen Workman "either drunk or unmanageable," and he concluded that the accusations were clearly designed to remove "out of the Smugglers way a determined opponent."[132]

Such testimony from a fellow customs collector was highly injurious to Vincent's reputation, and in early November the commissioner of customs, R.S.M. Bouchette, completely exonerated Workman. He wrote that "whatever may be Aaron Workman's faults he has in the present instance been the object of a conspiracy in which it is highly discreditable in Mr Vincent ... to have taken part." Bouchette added that Workman had refuted the vague charges against him "in a manner which I think it would have been impossible for him to do had he been the worthless character which he is represented to be in the Petition & some of the malevolent letters which accompany it." He had therefore "*proved* his innocence" and he should be promoted in rank and salary. As for Vincent, his "extreme weakness of character, seems to unfit him for his office on the Frontier." A couple of weeks later the Hereford collector was demoted to clerk and surveyor in the Stanstead office, though at the same salary of £100, and Workman was assigned as head of the Hereford post, though as sub-collector under the authority of Thompson in Coaticook. He would receive £75 per year plus a £15 expense allowance.[133]

Given the categorical terms of the commissioner's report, it may appear surprising that Vincent was simply demoted. The assertion that Workman had been the victim of a conspiracy implied that the Hereford collector, his American counterpart, and some of the local notables were acting in league with smugglers. But neither Workman nor his supporters ever stated outright that this was the case, and the commissioner declared that Vincent was weak rather than corrupt. While the Hereford collector's co-operation with the liquor traffickers in particular suggests that he may have been accepting bribes, his main concern appears to have been to maintain good relations with the neighbouring Americans. Not only were the respective roles of collector and preventive officer bound to engender a certain degree of conflict, but Vincent and Workman clearly had two very different personalities, the one rather accommodating (though obviously not towards his own subordinates) and the other fearless and uncompromising.

It is perhaps not surprising that the government would support the man who most clearly acted in the interests of the central state. However, it is somewhat ironic that the chief official of each inland customs port had more reason to be sensitive to local community pressures than did his subordinates, even though customs collectors were generally chosen from outside the districts they worked in. It would also be a mistake to assume that during the 1840s there was a deep sense of resentment in the region concerning the imposition of customs officers by the state. The St Francis District grand jury report of 1842 actually asked the legislature to adopt measures to suppress smuggling, which it claimed was "committed publicly and without any attempts at concealment." It argued that the revenue thus lost to the province "would amply repay an additional increase of officers along the line, and in the increase of the Public funds derived from imports, reduce the necessity of maintaining heavy taxation."[134]

Presumably the members of the local elites who sat on the grand jury were thinking less of their own activities than those of the American traders who crossed into the Eastern Townships en route to Montreal. There is certainly ample evidence to demonstrate that merchants as well as others in the border region actively avoided paying customs duties, as we have seen. Furthermore, the preventive officers were subjected to a considerable degree of public intimidation and violence. While the people of the border townships clearly tolerated the presence of the customs officers – indeed, they may even have welcomed their role in discouraging American competition in the local market – they also ensured that those officers interfered only minimally with their own cross-border transactions. In short, the daily operation of the inland customs ports was an informally negotiated process between the state's representatives and the communities in which they lived.

During the pre-industrial and early transition era of the Eastern Townships, alcohol abuse became a moral issue largely dealt with through moral suasion and public pressure rather than state prohibition or regulation. The destitute remained almost entirely at the mercy of their neighbours' generosity, and the great majority of those categorized as lunatics lived with their families or in other households. Only for those few individuals deemed so dangerous to themselves or others that they had to be incarcerated in the district jail was there a persistent demand that the state take a more active role by providing access to an asylum. In addition, there was clearly a high degree of tolerance for certain forms of smuggling, as well as "rough justice" and what might loosely be termed recreational violence. These activities aside, we saw in the preceding chapter that there was little serious crime in the Eastern Townships (at least as it was defined by the community at that time) until a rather dramatic change took place at mid-century. What the long-term impact of that change was is impossible to know without further study, but during the 1840s there obviously existed an effective equilibrium between traditional community-based sanctions and the state's laws, between the power of the crowd (if one can use this term in a largely rural setting) and that of the official authorities.

4 Origins of Local Government

Prior to their migration to the Eastern Townships, the early settlers had been accustomed to managing many of their own affairs in the New England town meetings. Surviving records reveal how this tradition was transferred to Newport Township, first settled in 1793. Newport's first public meeting, held in 1799, included "associates and other inhabitants," which suggests that the American "leader and associates" system of land grants had created a distinct and perhaps privileged group of settlers.[1] The meeting's first step was to form a committee to draft regulations "for keeping and maintaining good order etc. among the Inhabitants." The only other recommendation, aside from a provision for recording land grants, was that a public meeting should be held each September when a committee would be chosen "to manage the prudential affairs of the Association and to call any meeting upon any emergency."[2]

Future meetings dealt with the establishment of a cemetery (1801), the recording of births, deaths, and marriages (1802), and the building of a school house (1806), but the main focus was on establishing road links to the outside world. In 1802 the agents of a number of townships met at Ascot to draft a plan for constructing a public road from there "towards a market viz. to the river Nicolet." The subsequent Newport meeting resolved that four persons would be hired at a daily rate of one dollar, or one bushel of wheat, to complete that township's portion of the road. Reflecting the slow pace of development in the township, only eighteen settlers were listed as contributors. They were to pay the total sum of $50 by contributing 66 ½ cents per ratable poll, plus 55 cents on each ten acres of land.[3]

The following year the meeting arranged to build a road in the opposite direction to the Connecticut River "for the better conveyance of ye Produce of this Country and carrying on a more free and advantageous trade" with the United States. The same eighteen subscribers were to pay the labourers with 107 bushels of wheat, but they themselves constituted a high proportion of the fourteen-man work party. In subsequent years the annual meeting dealt mainly with local roads, but this system of local self-government was not to endure. The Newport minutes for 1810 note that the grand-voyer of Trois-Rivières had appointed a township surveyor and ordered the township's senior militia officer to have five individuals elected as overseers of highways and bridges, as had been provided for by the Constitutional Act of 1791.[4]

The law dictated that any new road had to be approved by the grand-voyer, whose fees and travelling expenses were to be paid by the petitioners for the road. The grand-voyer was also supposed to make a yearly tour of inspection, though this certainly did not include most of the Eastern Townships region. According to Ivanhoë Caron, the 1796 law making inhabitants legally responsible for all local roads was not recognized outside the seigneurial zone, and attempts to pass legislation to remove all doubts in the matter succeeded only in 1823.[5] Clearly, then, the settlers in the Eastern Townships were left largely to their own devices as far as road construction was concerned. A deputy grand-voyer was finally appointed for the St Francis District in 1829, but the inhabitants remained overwhelmingly hostile to the expensive and inefficient grand-voyer system. Meanwhile, with Newport's roads after 1810 under the control of a formal, state-sanctioned institution, subsequent township meetings were concerned largely with maintaining the cemetery and the school. The meetings appear to have ended in 1814, whether because of official hostility or local indifference is impossible to say.

Certainly, the extension of the grand-voyer system to the Eastern Townships reflected the administration's post-Revolutionary distaste for local democracy. The same applied to Upper Canada, but here the magistrates meeting in quarter sessions began to levy taxes for local public works as early as 1793.[6] In the Eastern Townships the inadequate transportation system would long remain dependent on sporadic grants from the provincial government. These grants were administered by appointed commissioners who were commonly accused of jobbing and directing road lines through their own properties.[7]

Unfortunately for the Eastern Townships, the municipal bill introduced by Ebenezer Peck of Sherbrooke in 1832 was rejected in the

Assembly by the spokesmen for absentee proprietors opposed to land taxes, as well as by the Patriotes who claimed that it was not compatible with the traditional grand-voyer system.[8] However, a greater degree of local control was permitted the same year when legislation enabled parishes, townships, or counties to elect road commissioners to take over the responsibilities of the grand-voyers within their boundaries. Even though the act was voluntary and due to expire three years later, the grand-voyer of Quebec later reported that the option "was adopted pretty generally in the townships."[9] But apparently because few parishes in the seigneurial districts took advantage of this bill, it was not renewed in 1835.

The formation of constitutional associations and corresponding committees during this immediate pre-Rebellion period was nevertheless leading to intensified political involvement at the local level. In 1838 a meeting of residents of the St Francis District, with Lieutenant-Colonel William Morris as chair and Samuel Brooks as secretary, demanded that internal communications "should be under the charge of local commissioners elected periodically by the proprietors, and that absentees as well as resident landholders should be compelled to contribute to the support of those roads."[10] That same year a petition from Kingsey Township presented the resolutions of a meeting which requested the power to elect persons every two years "to locate roads and bridges," pass bylaws for the good of the township, and fix rates for road work where required.

The recommendation of local taxes was clearly aimed at forcing absentee proprietors to contribute to road work, for the resolutions complained that the grand-voyer and his Eastern Townships deputy were a great expense to the settlers who remained "slaves to persons having great tracts of land granted to them, who never contribute any aid in Money, or Labour, etc." Resident farmers spent up to fourteen days a year working on roads fronting on the absentees' lots, in addition to building lengthy bridges carried away by the floods of the St Francis River during the spring when their time was most wanted on the land. Largely through the labour of others, the absentees' land had increased in value from three shillings an acre thirty years earlier to as much as twenty shillings an acre at the current time. The Kingsey petition claimed that these grievances had been ignored by both houses of the legislature because they represented the interests of the great landed proprietors, and warned that the situation "has often caused a great murmuring among us all."[11]

Likewise, the Melbourne notary, Daniel Thomas, recommended in 1840 that townships wishing to elect a road commissioner to perform the duties of the grand-voyer be allowed to do so. Thomas argued that "the actual Settler has by his labour upon such Roads greatly enhanced the value of certain wild lands without the *slightest* exertion or aid of the proprietors. The continuance of a burthen so unjust & oppressive would continue to drive intending settlers to other parts of America where persons are obliged to contribute to such improvements in proportion to the advantage which they derive from them." Finally, Thomas supported a system of local assessment over "the general one which now appears to be so much the rage" and he suggested that proprietors have only one year to redeem lots sold for non-payment of taxes on "leading *Market Roads* in the *Township Sections* of the province."[12]

These sentiments may have echoed the agrarian radicalism of the Rebellion era, but they also cut across class and political lines. As Carol Wilton has pointed out for Upper Canada, much of the pressure for administrative reform came from the local elites whose ties were with the Tory party.[13] W.B. Felton of Sherbrooke had himself supported the establishment of an escheats court, as well as local governing institutions, while Sherbrooke's constitutional association had subsequently elicited a promise from Lord Gosford that he would consider "any well digested plan for conferring on the chief Districts of the Province, Municipal Institutions for the management of internal affairs."[14] Under the ownership of a group of Sherbrooke entrepreneurs, the *Farmers' and Mechanics' Journal and St Francis Gazette* expressed hostility in 1839 to the proposal that the Special Council should have the power to levy taxes for "local improvements."[15] Even a large proprietor such as Shefford's Colonel Knowlton spoke out in favour of abolishing the grand-voyer system and giving each township the power "to alter and execute everything pertaining to highways." He added that the people of the Eastern Townships "are perfectly competent to manage their own affairs, and all road business might be left to them with great advantage."[16]

Knowlton's opinions appear in the appendix to the Durham *Report* concerning municipal institutions in Lower Canada. They are the only ones from an Eastern Townships resident to be recorded, simply because the two assistant commissioners in charge of the municipal inquiry had been unable to visit the rural areas of the colony.[17] Yet in their introductory remarks, William Kennedy and the francophobic editor of the *Montreal Herald*, Adam Thom, confidently claimed that all the "intelligent and experienced persons, both of British and Canadian blood," felt that comprehensive municipal reform was impracticable because of the ignorance prevailing among the habitants, "together with their deep-rooted dislike to every kind of tax and assessment." The two commissioners stated that the Eastern Townships offered better prospects for municipal institutions, "but, even in these localities, the state of education is very backward." To support this opinion, they quoted a gentleman from Frelighsburg in Missisquoi County who claimed: "The people are not anxious for municipal institutions, and if they receive them, they are prepared for a very limited power. I must warn you that the power of taxation, for any purpose whatever, would produce greatest dissatisfaction." He added that the one power that would be welcomed without reservation would be control of the roads, since the "expense, the trouble and vexation of procuring the establishment of a new road, are so great that individuals undergo them only when necessity absolutely compels them." These were clearly the self-interested views of a landed proprietor, for experience would prove that the general population was not opposed to taxation per se. Nevertheless, the unnamed "gentleman" did hit the mark when he claimed that roads would be by far the most important order of business.[18]

Kennedy and Thom were themselves not convinced by those of their witnesses who felt that "until education is generally diffused, a system of popular local government would do more harm than good." The two commissioners argued that it made no sense to allow the people to elect provincial representatives while being denied the right to choose municipal authorities, "and thereby gradually acquiring a disciplined knowledge of their social duties in the school of practical citizenship." Their report added that the rural population already elected overseers of highways for as many as nine sub-divisions within each parish or township, and these positions "require for their due performance as much education and intelligence as are required for the execution of most of the ordinary duties of a municipal character." Furthermore, because they held minor judicial powers, the popularly elected fence inspectors required a still higher degree of education. With the machinery for electing these local functionaries already in place, it would be a relatively short step to establish a municipal council composed of two elected officers from each parish or township sub-division.[19]

But Kennedy and Thom feared democracy almost as much as their conservative witnesses did, and the municipal system they envisioned was a highly centralized one. To begin with, they recommended two additional higher levels of local government, with county councillors being elected by those who possessed double the education and property qualifications required to elect the parish/township councillors, and the election of district councillors based on a still higher property qualification. There would be approximately eight municipal districts in Lower Canada under the supervision of a salaried executive head. And the duties of even these bodies would remain strictly circumscribed, with their operation defined by a municipal code and the district chief required to report to a provincial board of internal improvement as well as the government.[20]

Furthermore, while the two commissioners felt that the grand-voyers were not capable professionals, they were obviously convinced by arguments for the necessity of retaining a role for disinterested government officials. Kennedy and Thom suggested that in place of the grand-voyers, the crown should appoint an engineer to serve as each district's superintendent of roads and bridges. Appointed county superintendents would act as the engineer's assistants, holding the power (previously vested in the courts of quarter sessions) to draft procès verbaux at the monthly county council meetings.[21] The county superintendent would also appoint the parish or township surveyors, who would report directly to him. As for the thorny issue of local taxation, the commissioners' report stated only that absentee proprietors should be forced to contribute to public works, and "pecuniary payment" should completely replace joint labour.[22]

Like Kennedy and Thom, Lord Durham rejected the British government's long-standing fear of local government, and he complained that "The great business of the assemblies is, literally, parish business; the making [sic] parish roads and parish bridges." He added that "the utter want of municipal institutions giving the people any control over their local affairs, may indeed be considered as one of the main causes of the failure of representative government." If the British authorities had long blamed town governments in New England for fostering the American Revolution, Durham was suggesting that their absence from Lower Canada had contributed to the Rebellions of 1837–38: "The inhabitants of Lower Canada were unhappily initiated into self-government at exactly the wrong end, and those who were not trusted with the management of a parish, were enabled, by their votes, to influence the destinies of a State."[23]

As for the Eastern Townships, Lord Durham lamented the fact that the government had discouraged the American settlers from introducing their own municipal institutions, and claimed that the region presented "a lamentable contrast in the management of all local matters to the bordering state of Vermont, in which the municipal institutions are the most complete, it is said, of any part of New England."[24] Ironically, a similar view was expressed in 1848 by the former Patriote spokesman, E.B. O'Callaghan, who seems to have been unaware of the municipal reforms enacted since his departure for New York. O'Callaghan complained to Papineau that "Every thing almost must emanate from the seat of Government, there is scarcely any machinery in the Parishes, Towns or Counties for the political education of the People, who are ignorant (politically) because they have not those small municipal subdivisions wherein every one is called periodically to take a part in public matters, whether local or general."[25]

SYDENHAM'S DISTRICT COUNCILS ACT

As with most other matters, Charles Poulett Thomson (later Lord Sydenham) shared Durham's enthusiasm for municipal government, and he referred to the refusal of London to include local institutions in the Act of Union as "this almost destruction for all good purposes of the Bill."[26] But Thomson remained hesitant to trust the people with a substantial amount of local responsibility and power, and when his municipal bill did pass, it included only the more centralizing of Kennedy and Thom's recommendations. Several bills and a number of years would pass before the government finally devised a municipal system that was truly effective even in the Eastern Townships, where there was a strong desire to break out of the region's social and economic isolation.

Rather than the three-level system recommended by Kennedy and Thom, Sydenham's 1841 bill created only twenty-two district councils for all of Canada East. These district councils were rather unwieldy, particularly in the more thinly settled areas, though they functioned quite effectively in Canada West until they were replaced by a new system in 1849. They consisted of three government-appointed officials – the warden, clerk, and treasurer – as well as one or two representatives (depending on the size of the local population) elected at the annual meeting of ratepayers of each parish or township within the district. Elected at the same time would be the local assessors, collectors, surveyors, road overseers, fence viewers, drain inspectors, and pound keepers.

Despite the busy agenda, the public meetings were to be held only between 9:00 a.m. and 4:00 p.m., and they were not under any pretext to last longer than two days. Sydenham was presumably anxious to prevent the meetings from becoming forums of political dissent in this post-Rebellion era, but he appears to have been still more concerned to prevent election violence. The poll was to be open only the first day (which presumably meant that other matters could be dealt with the second day), and the returning officer had the authority to call upon militia officers and constables to assist in enforcing his orders. They could arrest "any person who is guilty of violence or engaged in an affray or riot, or any person armed with clubs, staves, or other offensive weapons, or carrying flags or wearing ribbons, cockades or badges, or preventing or endeavouring to prevent Electors from coming to the poll, or in any wise interrupting the Poll or the business of the Election."[27] We shall see that this stipulation would have limited effect in preventing violence in townships where deep-rooted political differences existed.

The district councils themselves were limited to four six-day meetings a year, except with the express permission of the governor, and no public works project could be started until it had been reported on by the district surveyor, who was appointed by the warden. If the cost of the project exceeded £300 it had to be approved by the provincial board of works. Most important, as far as central control was concerned, all district bylaws were to be reported to the governor, being subject to disallowance within thirty days, and any district council could be dissolved by the governor with the consent of the Executive Council. Severe as they were, none of these restrictions played a significant role in the failure of the district council system in the Eastern Townships, though the provincial government did intervene when district assessment bylaws contravened the law.

Sydenham's District Councils Act has been criticized for placing the essential powers in the hands of the government-appointed district officials. But the clerk was selected from a list of three names presented by the council, and both he and the treasurer were functionaries who took no direct part in council proceedings. The warden, on the other hand, was expected to exert a considerable degree of control over the quarterly meetings, but in each of the districts examined below he would prove relatively powerless against the defiant councils. Even his salary depended, in the governor-general's words, on securing "the respect and favourable consideration" of the councillors.[28]

Sydenham's bill had actually left the councils largely to their own devices as far as most matters were concerned. In September 1841 the perplexed warden from Portneuf wrote to his nephew, Edward Hale, who was the warden of the Sherbrooke District:

I thought we should have had some instructions from head quarters before this, but not a word; surely some calculation must be made & plan formed towards paying the District Officers, & the mode of assessment to which we must resort; the Executive must desire uniformity throughout the several Districts, as far as can be accomplished. I have little hopes that our french people will do anything, the new system is generally disliked & a great alarm is created at the apprehension of taxation so that if left to themselves & no requisition made by the Govern't no funds will be raised.[29]

As the elder Hale foresaw, in most of Canada East the new municipal councils were apparently rejected as "machines à taxer."[30] The reaction in the Eastern Townships was generally more positive, but here too the system accomplished little, in part because of the shortcomings outlined in Hale's letter. The English-speaking councillors of the Missisquoi and Sherbrooke districts did not hesitate to levy taxes, but their view of which sectors of the community should contribute to the local improvements, and how they should do so, conflicted with that of powerful local interests as well as with the law as interpreted by the provincial government.

The northern part of the region was incorporated into two other districts which overlapped the south shore seigneurial zone (see Map 4), and here the system was stymied by the resentment of the French Canadians at having the district seats placed in remote and thinly settled townships. Contrary to standard historical interpretations, in each of these four districts popular opposition was neither to the centralized structure of the district council system nor to the principle of taxation, but to the restrictions placed on the ways in which the councils wished to exercise their power.

THE MISSISQUOI DISTRICT AND THE GRAND LIST

The first meeting of the Missisquoi District Council was convened by Warden William Baker in the village of Nelsonville in Dunham Township on 7 September 1841. With fifteen councillors present, only St Armand West was not represented. Most of the townships had one member, but Dunham and Stanbridge each had two, while the more northerly Milton, Roxton, and Ely shared one. At the first meeting, separate committees of five drafted rules and regulations for council proceedings, then presented a road bill as well as reports on ways and means to raise money for the support of schools, the poor, and highways and bridges.[31] The Missisquoi councillors were clearly eager to bring the new system of district government into operation, and, with the success or failure of all their projects dependent upon the ability to raise funds, their most crucial committee was that on ways and means. Unfortunately for them, the strategy they proposed was rejected by the government as contrary to the law. And because the majority of the councillors refused to back down on this issue, very little of concrete value was accomplished during the four-year history of the council.

The major conflict involved the basis of the taxation system, with the councillors anxious not to have the burden fall entirely on the shoulders of the rural property holders. The committee of ways and means recommended, first, that all real estate be evaluated and taxed by township assessors, except wild lands, that would pay one penny per acre. The Sherbrooke District Council would come to grief essentially on this question of a wild land tax levy, but it was not the crucial issue in the more thickly settled Missisquoi district. Much more controversial was the council's declaration that all business assets, subsequently known as the Grand List, would be assessed at a recommended rate of 6 percent. The list would include bank and railway stocks, money on loan, money on hand over and above debts, all stock-in-trade, and all farming stock. The committee even presented a list of rates of taxation for each category of livestock. For example, a distinction was made between horses for work and horses for pleasure or profit by rating all those over two years of age at £5, unless they were worth £12 10s. or more, in which case the latter rate would apply. Subsequently defeated were amendments to value at £50 all stud horses kept for breeding purposes, and to exempt one pair of horses and one yoke of oxen for each farmer.[32]

On the third day of the council meeting it was declared that assessments would begin the following 1 June, with all residents to deliver to the assessors before 20 June, or the town clerk by 1 July, a schedule listing every animal and all other assets liable to be taxed. Otherwise, the local officers would assess them "as they may think to be right and just." Anyone submitting an incomplete list was to be rated twofold on *all* assessable property.[33] What socio-economic background most of the councillors came from is impossible to say, but their intention was clearly to collect funds from merchants as well as farmers and large landholders. Since household goods would not be taxed, only the artisans and liberal professionals would escape relatively lightly.

Subcommittees recommended that the 141 schools in the district be supported by an assessment based on the Grand List, and drafted procedures for initiating public works projects. Then the councillors declared by a vote of ten to four that they felt they had the power to authorize townships to raise money on the Grand List for keeping in repair roads and bridges, and so on, but they asked the warden to verify this. The committee on rates and fees also recommended a cautious approach for the time being. Its members declared that because the municipal ordinance is "a very great experiment involving an entire change in our local matters complicated in its provisions, and uncertain as to its advantages, or disadvantages to the country," it would have "far better prospects of a fair trial ... if the different parish and township officers were left to discharge their respective duties at present without imposing a tax upon the inhabitants for the purposes of remunerating them for their services."[34]

After the first four-day session had ended, Warden Baker could honestly report to the civil secretary that the councillors had "proceeded very orderly to business." In his opening remarks to the next meeting in December 1841, Baker congratulated the members on their accomplishments at the last session: "Your unanimity enabled you to effect more, I believe, than any other District."[35] He reported that their test bylaw on roads had not been disallowed, and that prompt action on their part was necessary since, in his opinion, the grand-voyer system had ceased to apply when the parish and township officers were elected.

Curiously enough, however, the solicitor-general later claimed that the grand-voyer system remained in force, except where it conflicted with the new ordinance. Furthermore, where Baker had suggested that each township might have the power to decide how to fund the construction of its roads and bridges, the solicitor-general stated that the municipal act "expressly excludes the exercise of any powers by the Parishes and Townships except those mentioned in it or to be specially conferred by the Legislature."[36] But the main point of conflict would concern the very basis of the taxing system.

Baker had defended the assessment bylaw in his report to the civil secretary, stating that because "some of the Council seem to be diffident of their abilities, I would wish that if it is not really inconsistent, it might be allowed." In addressing the second session, the warden went still further than the bylaw by arguing that "mechanical" and professional men should also be required to contribute towards schools and public improvements by introducing a tax on profits, rather than simply on assets. The Missisquoi Council proceeded to pass five bylaws based on the Grand List system, only to have the solicitor-general notify it four months later that "certain portions" were illegal since the courts could not recognize either monies in hand and on loan, or bank and railway stock, as personal property. Such a levy would be "of the nature of an income tax." Furthermore, the council had no authority to double the levy on those who failed to declare all their property, or to have those who refused to serve as assessors fined by a justice of the peace.[37]

In his opening comments to the third session of March 1842, Baker counselled restraint: "In your legislative capacity you will be called upon to exercise a degree of patience, and be willing to learn from your experience." He also admitted that because "the public seemed so clamorous," he had ignored the motion of the previous meeting to borrow money in order to pay the council's £68 14s. in expenses, including £28 2s. 6d. for the councillors themselves. Attendance nevertheless remained at eleven of sixteen, as in December, and three of the absentees were reported to be ill. Only one recently elected member had decided to flout the law by failing to take the oath. He eventually paid the legal penalty, and was replaced.[38]

The majority of the councillors remained unwilling to modify the tax proposals, and narrowly defeated a motion calling for a committee to draft a more restricted version of the Grand List in order to raise money for one year only. Their argument, as Baker later informed the civil secretary, was that "by leaving out what they called the shavers, men who kept money to let perhaps at 12 percent with a mortgage on the farm, the owners of Bank and Rail-Road Stock, the original Grantee of lands, who was exempt by the said Act and moreover as there seemed to be no way of collecting the tax on nonresident lands, the Farmers would be the principal contributors to the District expenses, which would bring a heavy burden upon that class."[39] The councillors were mistaken in assuming that the original grantees, like the seigneurs, were exempt from such taxes, but for all intents and purposes the absentee proprietors were immune because of restrictions on seizing land for back taxes.

After rejecting the conciliatory motion, the council petitioned the government to amend the municipal act "so as to make it lawful to impose a Tax on monies on hand, Bank and Rail Road Stock, debts due, and also to give power and authority to the District Councils to enforce their Bye Laws by imposing fines and penalties on persons for neglect of duty or non compliance with the requirements of such Bye Laws." Without such amendments, "the District Councils would be paralized [sic] and in many instances a dead letter." Additional resolutions criticized the regressive bill fixing school fees, demanded a protective tariff against American manufactures and produce, and requested that the council's expenses be defrayed. Finally, Baker was asked to raise the matter of district courts and jails, which were supposed to be financed by the province.[40]

The Missisquoi councillors continued to meet regularly until the district system was abolished three years later in 1845. They refused to alter their demand that the taxation system be expanded, with the result that road work proceeded on the traditional system of statute labour, with the council simply amending the surveyors' reports where necessary.

Somewhat surprisingly, there is no indication that the Missisquoi councillors resented the centralized structure of the municipal system, presumably because it allowed for more local initiative than has generally been assumed. It also enabled the agrarian interests to express themselves in a unified and forceful manner, which may help to explain why the new Municipal Act of 1845 introduced the radically localized parish and township councils. But the district-based system was also proving to be cumbersome elsewhere, and experience with the public school system was revealing a strong sense of localism, as we shall see. If the enthusiasm of the councillors contrasted sharply with the attitude of the school commissioners, it may have been because roads and bridges were of broader geographic concern than the one-room schools. Furthermore, the district council system could respond to local needs because it permitted councillors to levy special assessments on any township or locality, presumably upon the request of the ratepayers concerned.[41]

Upper Canadians were also obviously concerned about the narrow base of the taxation system, for in 1843 Hincks's assessment bill for Canada West adopted the New York practice of including income from any trade, profession, or employment. All the provisions in the Hincks bill were abandoned except for those dealing with real estate, but the taxes on personal property and income were reintroduced in 1850.[42] A year later LaFontaine's abortive municipal bill for Lower Canada took a similar step by introducing a tax on the businesses of merchants, professionals, and tradesmen, but this provision did not come into force until the passing of L.T. Drummond's bill of 1855. J.H. Aitchison claims that the people of Canada West objected to the inquisition that such tax assessments implied, but this clearly had not caused the Missisquoi District councillors undue concern. These delays were therefore probably due largely to opposition from the non-rural population, though the petite bourgeoisie in the towns and larger villages may have ultimately taken solace in the fact that they could establish their own municipalities whenever the rural majority threatened their interests.

THE SHERBROOKE DISTRICT AND THE LAND COMPANY

Lord Sydenham chose as warden for the Sherbrooke District the well-connected Edward Hale, a member of the Special Council who would soon be elected to the new province's first parliament. When first asked to serve, Hale urged the appointment of Colonel Morris in his place, as he felt the duties of warden and MLA would be incompatible. Besides, he informed his wife, the wardenship "would entail upon me much trouble and much abuse." Ultimately, Hale was convinced to accept the post, and he in turn recommended for treasurer Charles Towle of Lennoxville, "a man of very respectable character and connexions, long resident in that part of the country, and in independent circumstances."[43] For clerk, Hale submitted three names chosen by the council as required, but he later indicated his preference for the tory J.S. Walton of the *Sherbrooke Gazette.* Hale reported only that Walton had been a lieutenant on the frontier during the Rebellion, and that he had acquitted himself with satisfaction "upon occasions of a somewhat critical nature," but this was enough to secure the appointment. As district surveyor, Hale chose Joseph Pennoyer, son of the man who had run the initial survey lines for much of the region and been rewarded with a large share of Compton Township. In addition, Joseph's father, Jesse, had proven his British loyalty by serving as commanding officer of the Fifth Eastern Townships Militia Battalion during the War of 1812, but we can assume that Joseph was a competent surveyor in his own right because the British American Land Company had employed him to survey its main road line to Port St Francis.[44]

The elected councillors included influential conservatives such as Benjamin Pomroy of Compton, who had served as captain of the Queen's Mountain Rangers during the Rebellion; Samuel Brooks, who would be elected to the legislature for Sherbrooke in 1844; John McConnell, who would be returned for Stanstead in the same election; C.B. Cleveland of Shipton, who would oppose the liberal annexationist, John Sanborn, in the 1850 by-election; and Thomas Tait of Melbourne.[45] Most of these men were merchants, and therefore unlikely to follow the Missisquoi example of attempting to widen the tax base to include an assessment on profits. Instead, their main target would be the large landed proprietors, and especially the British American Land Company, even though it was intimately linked to the commercial and industrial development of Sherbrooke.

With the franchise restricted to those who owned property worth £2 a year or paid an annual rent of £5,[46] only thirty-three individuals voted at the Ascot meeting, and the returning officer from neighbouring Eaton informed Hale that it was "a matter of difficulty if not impossibility ... to discharge his duty consistently with the letter of the law, scarcely one in the settlement being qualified either to vote or hold office." But a councillor and township officers were elected in Eaton, after which the meeting "dispersed in a quiet orderly manner, the feeling being I should say among all the respectable part of the community decidedly in favor of the new system." Such was not the case in the perennially turbulent Barnston Township. After choosing their councillor in January 1842, the householders refused to elect any of their township officers.[47] In Bury, to the north, even the election of the councillor was controversial.

The first order of business of the Sherbrooke District Council was to consider a petition protesting the election of Bury's Thomas Bown on the grounds that he had acted as chairman and returning officer for his own election. After drafting elaborate regulations on contested elections, the council declared Bown's seat vacant.[48] But, with no other controversies or acts of defiance reported, it appeared that most of the townships in the Sherbrooke District had accepted the new municipal system quite readily.

Apart from establishing rules and regulations to govern its own meetings, and appointing a committee to recommend a system for constructing and repairing roads, no other business was transacted during the first session. Hale later informed the governor that he had not proceeded further because the municipal ordinances had not yet been distributed and "the public seemed somewhat nervous as to the extensive innovations at the outset." Also the number of councillors in attendance barely exceeded a quorum because some had been unaware that the day of meeting had been fixed by law. Despite these initial mix-ups, Hale was "enclined [sic] to think that no spirit inimical to the new system has so far attended its progress – on the contrary, I am decidedly of opinion that, accompanied by some degree of doubt natural with regard to what is not thoroughly understood, the feeling among the Inhabitants of this District and of the Eastern Townships is strongly in its favor."[49]

The minutes for the Sherbrooke District Council's second session have not survived, but Hale informed Daly that it had been "a most harmonious & industrious one – the members all punctual in attendance and working zealously & indefatigably." The council passed five broad-sweeping bylaws concerning the common school system, the assessment of real and personal property, the performance of statute road labour, and, most significantly, the taxation of wild land at a penny an acre. All assessments not paid by 1 May would result in sales by the district treasurer four months later. In addition, penalties would be imposed on assessors and road officers not performing their duties, and upon those resisting them, with magistrates having the summary authority to levy and collect the same. Like Baker in Missisquoi, Hale requested that if any of these enactments over-stepped the council's powers, legislative amendments be made to correct the situation.[50]

The Sherbrooke Council's bylaws brought a quick response from the British American Land Company's two Canadian commissioners. Peter McGill wrote in December that the uniform tax on wild lands "without reference to their locality or value is monstrous – and will be ruinous because land cannot be sold at present." His colleague, George Moffatt, added: "I was prepared for a tax on wild lands but not of the amount imposed and which will in my opinion defeat the object which the Council has in view. If the By-law is left in its operation it is clear that the Land Company cannot long continue theirs."[51]

The London-based company complained that it owned about 451,000 acres of wild land in the District of Sherbrooke, which would mean a yearly assessment of about £1,800. At the same rate, the 133,000 acres in Missisquoi and 112,000 acres in Nicolet would cost an additional £1,100 a year, yet only inhabitants could elect councillors. The company's officers were also well aware of the bylaw's dubious legality since the municipal act did not specify any summary or other particular mode for councillors to proceed against delinquent ratepayers as the Sherbrooke Council was attempting to do. Indeed, more than a hundred inhabitants of Shipton, Melbourne, Durham, Kingsey, and Ely had complained in a petition to the governor-general, when his municipal act was moving through the legislature, that there was no clause "to enable the Road Officers to sell in default of the performance of the accustomed Road duty a part of the Land to satisfy the same." On this basis, the land company informed the provincial secretary that the only recourse the district councils could have was the court system, and the Sherbrooke District bylaw should therefore be disallowed.[52]

A Quebec lawyer consulted by the council supported the land company's position insofar as the imposition of penalties and their summary recovery was concerned, declaring that the bylaw did not need to be disallowed by the provincial government for it to be rejected by the courts.[53] The Sherbrooke Council reacted in its next session by amending part of the offending bylaw in order to avoid invalidating the tax it had imposed. It nevertheless asked for authority to seize without the usual forms of legal process all lots on which taxes were more than six months in arrears, as well as to impose penalties on all transgressors against its bylaws. The councillors also wished to tax theatres, circuses, and public exhibitions (except for agricultural fairs), as well as billiard tables and auctioneers "in a similar manner as is now conferred upon the councils of the cities of Quebec and Montreal."[54]

In reaction to the Sherbrooke Council's determined position, the land company proposed that in lieu of taxes it would provide funds for the improvement of the Montreal Road in Orford Township. The precedent had recently been established when the government had allowed the company to direct half its land payments to officially sanctioned public improvements. The Sherbrooke District councillors agreed in June 1842 that the company could direct £100 towards the road in question as payment of the wild land tax in Orford Township,[55] but no further steps appear to have been taken in this direction.

The following September the company's Eastern Townships commissioner, John Fraser, wrote to Metcalfe that "our progress must be gradual owing to circumstances which are beyond our Control." He claimed that it was therefore impossible to collect enough money to pay for the company's share of the statute labour in the region. The Missisquoi Council had charged the company £145 for its share of a short road in Acton Township, the Nicolet Council had levied a still greater outlay for a range road in Wickham Township, and the company faced heavy expenses for its own road work in Bury, Roxton, Stukely, and elsewhere, besides its share of the general repairs of roads and bridges in the region. Fraser claimed that the land company was willing to conform to the current system of owners taking responsibility for roads passing through or near their land. But under the threatened imposition of a general wild land tax "in this depressed unfrequented region, the amount would be expended by the Majority of voices for improving the settled parts instead of developing the masses of back land paying most of the assessment. It would ensure our rapid ruin." In addition, the company land sold at peremptory auctions would fetch a small fraction of what the company had paid for it from "a new set of small Land Jobbers who would be far less indulgent and encouraging to emigrants and poor settlers than we have been." Though Fraser overstated his company's indulgence towards its settlers, there was no denying its poor financial condition, for it had surrendered over half a million acres to the government two years earlier. Experience in Upper Canada had also shown that land taxes could indeed produce a new generation of speculators in the more remote townships.[56]

But the Sherbrooke councillors remained unsympathetic to such pleas, and in June 1843 they appointed a committee of five "to enquire what measures are necessary to enforce the collection of the Wild Land tax" levied in 1841. In the meantime, the bridges over the Magog River in Sherbrooke, and the Massawippi River in Ascot Township, were repaired at the expense of the local ratepayers alone despite their importance to much of the outlying district.[57]

The request for extended powers to enforce wild land taxes was resubmitted by the Sherbrooke Council in September 1843, the last meeting for which minutes have survived. Even though the council remained without revenue for its officers, who frequently were given onerous responsibilities, fragmentary evidence suggests that the residents of the Sherbrooke District did generally conform to the municipal regulations, continuing to elect councillors and township officers.[58] For example, in January 1844 the clerk for Hatley Township reported that cold weather and poor roads had prevented several local districts from being represented at the annual meeting, thereby necessitating a special session in which the two local magistrates, with "such of the inhabitants as thought best to attend," appointed some of the township officers. But the residents of the relatively new British settlements in the union of Bury, Lingwick, and Westbury had been more conscientious, electing a clerk, two assessors, a collector, three road surveyors, twelve road overseers, three overseers of the poor, three fence viewers, three pound keepers, and five school commissioners, in addition to a councillor.[59]

The minutes of the annual meetings in Ascot Township from 1841 to 1845 indicate the degree to which these positions were rotated, ensuring that few farmers would escape the performance of their public duties. The clerk remained unchanged during the first four years, the same three assessors remained in office for the first three years, and one individual held the collector's position for two of the five years, while another was overseer of the poor for the first two years. But there was very little continuity with the two pound keeper and three road-surveyor positions, or the fourteen (twenty-four by 1845) annual overseers of highways, fence viewers, and drains inspectors. Between 1841 and 1845 seventy-seven different men filled the eighty-nine openings for the latter three roles, which were combined in one office.

In addition, despite the property restrictions, the position of councillor was sufficiently sought after in Ascot for three candidates to run for the single post in 1844. A protest was registered when Leonard C. Ball won by only four votes, another was registered in Bury the same year, and yet another in Eaton the following year. But only in Stanstead Township did partisan feeling cause serious conflict at the municipal level by 1845. That year P. Hubbard reported to Hale that no officers were elected by the annual town meeting because the time was taken up with "disputes between Mr Child on the one hand, and Messrs Gustin, Steele, myself, etc., on the other hand." Hubbard claimed that Child and his party had brought some fifty to sixty persons who were not eligible to vote and attempted to have them qualified "in the mass."[60]

The ongoing elections in the Sherbrooke District suggest that the local officers were fulfilling their functions to some extent, at least in certain townships, if only by assigning statute labour and enforcing local regulations. In one documented case, the system was effective enough to evoke an expression of outrage on the part of an English gentleman, James Laing, who had been ordered to clear a winter road by an overseer whom he claimed was a squatter. The Sherbrooke Council claimed that the law required no other qualification for local officers than residency, but Laing insisted that eligibility was legally restricted to those who held sufficient property to participate in the annual township meeting. He complained that respectable persons who wished to improve their lands could not find agricultural labourers because of the practice of squatting, and if such individuals were placed on the same level as bona fide purchasers of land, "then all end is put to the entry of *respectable* families and individuals to the country, and the Colonising of the Province very much retarded."[61]

Because most of the routine road work was organized by locally elected township officers, there was actually little for a council unable to raise any revenue to do except approve or reject such projects. The Sherbrooke Council's stubborn attempt to tax wild land continued to be stymied largely by the efforts of the British American Land Company's young Sherbrooke-based secretary, Alexander T. Galt. Galt wrote to Governor Metcalfe in November 1843 that, given its investments in the region, the company should not be subjected to the same penal taxes as the absentee proprietors who had neglected their duty. He also argued that because the Special Council had not had the authority to levy taxes itself, it could not confer this power on other bodies. The forthcoming repeal of the District Council Act should therefore be made retroactive to include all bylaws passed while it was in effect. Galt recommended that wild lands make a one-time only contribution based on their value, and that all other assessments be based on value as well.[62]

But Galt's plea had little chance of success at a time when Inspector-General Hincks was introducing a new municipal bill for Canada West which would be particularly hard on the absentee proprietors. It would allow the government to authorize advances from the Consolidated Revenue Fund to district treasurers of sums equivalent to the taxes in arrears on lands owned by non-residents. Provisions for collecting such arrears were necessarily made much more stringent than previously.[63] Galt wrote to his superiors in London that, in a conversation with him, Hincks had "immediately commenced a violent denunciation of all wild land owners," stating that "they had retarded the development of the province for years." Not only would they now have to contribute taxes "for schools and local purposes," but the government might soon find it necessary "to provide for the interest on the public debt by a direct tax on real property, wild and improved." Galt consoled himself that Hincks's "influence and measures are principally confined to Canada West, and from what I can learn the Ministry fear if the same steps were extended to Lower Canada the French-Canadians would speedily become dissatisfied with their administration." But he remained worried that "the feeling of hostility to the proprietors of wild lands has extended from the lower classes to the Executive."[64]

The Baldwin-LaFontaine resignations leading to the so-called Metcalfe crisis took place only four days later, thus ensuring that there would be no new municipal bill for Canada East before another election had taken place. As we saw in chapter one, Galt consequently decided to play his company's political card, and Metcalfe proved receptive to Galt's promise that the company would throw its full support behind his conservative ministry in the next election. The Sherbrooke Council's awareness of the new political development may explain why it refrained from attempting to collect the wild land tax. But the dynamic shifted somewhat again in 1844, when the energetic Galt became the land company's local commissioner. To end the region's economic isolation, he began to promote the construction of a railway from Montreal to the Atlantic seaboard.

Like Hincks in Canada West, Galt realized that the district council's taxing authority could be an important source of revenue for his pet project. At the end of the year the municipal secretary, J.S. Walton, informed Hale that the council had narrowly voted a £1,000 subsidy, "*supposing they had it,*" for the projected railway. In return, Galt had agreed to write to the principal land owners stating that "if *they will consent to pay the penny tax, he will do so!*"[65] But when the Sherbrooke Council expired with the new municipal legislation in 1845, it was nominally owed £8,531 in wild land tax and it in turn had incurred £455 in unpaid obligations, including £198 for Walton's salary, £75 for the construction of a bridge in the town of Sherbrooke, and £25 for the loss of a horse due to the alleged neglect of the road overseers.[66] As a pro-ministerial MLA,

Warden Hale had good political reason not to alienate Galt by encouraging the council to push for payment of the arrears. Furthermore, as Hale confided to his wife, his own large investments in Sherbrooke property and industries gave him every reason to hope that the company would "survive and prosper."[67] Whether the Sherbrooke District Council would have eventually come to life had a new radically decentralized municipal system not been introduced in 1845 is impossible to say, but it is likely that the need to finance railway construction would have led to some sort of compromise arrangement with the British American Land Company.

NICOLET AND THE DISTRICT SEAT QUESTION

Despite its name, much of the Nicolet District lay outside the south shore seigneurial zone, and inside the Eastern Townships. It extended up the St Francis River to Durham and Kingsey, as well as including much of the Bois-Francs area to the northeast. But the majority of the district's population did live in the seigneurial parishes, and the fact that each thinly settled township received the same representation as all but the most populous parishes therefore meant that the English Canadians were overrepresented in the council. Sydenham was clearly hoping that a major British influx would soon redress the ethno-cultural imbalance in the Nicolet Council and its neighbouring Chaudière counterpart.[68] But in 1841, Nicolet's councillors from the St Lawrence parishes still outnumbered those from the townships by approximately three to one, and they bitterly resented the choice of Drummondville in Grantham Township as the district seat. French Canadians had begun colonizing the northern townships, but Drummondville remained a struggling frontier village nearly three decades after it had been founded by Colonel Frederick George Heriot as a settlement for veterans of the 1812 War. While Heriot's influence may have helped to win the district seat, he would die in 1843 and Drummondville would fail to develop significantly until after Confederation.[69] Indeed, this stagnation reflected the failure of Sydenham's municipal act, for, as C.F.J. Whebell has pointed out, a local capital would normally become "a primary node in a communications network," with great efforts being applied "to consolidate all public institutions and offices, and many social institutions as well" in that location.[70]

With Colonel Heriot absent in England in 1841, his nephew R.N. Watts, who was the Drummond County MLA, recommended either Captain Cox or Major Menzies as warden. Watts gave three reasons for explicitly rejecting Captain James Brady, formerly of the Royal Scots Fusiliers and commander of the Durham Township volunteers during the Rebellion: Brady was not on good terms with Heriot, he had only lived in the province for three years, and he intended to leave once he could sell his farm. But Brady had acquired valuable experience as a staff member of the governor of Guiana, where he had become the colony's first stipendiary magistrate, and to Watts's considerable annoyance, he became Sydenham's choice for the district of Nicolet.[71] Brady's weaknesses would prove to be more serious than even Watts had suggested, though it is doubtful that anyone else could have made much progress either, given the circumstances.

Commenting on the council elections in late August 1841, the new warden informed the civil secretary that "the Electors throughout the District have conducted themselves at those meetings, with the greatest propriety and order, and it is gratifying to reflect, that notwithstanding the novelty of the Legislative measures introduced, the mass of the inhabitants have evinced everywhere a perfect acquiescence and readiness to meet the *intentions* of the Ordinances *as their own*."[72] Brady's optimism appeared to be well founded, for all but one of the twenty-three parishes and townships were represented at the first council meeting in early September. However, the first motion, presented by the representatives from St Pierre-les-Becquets and Nicolet, was to read a petition requesting removal of the district seat to the village of Nicolet. Brady intervened on the grounds that this question lay outside the jurisdiction of the council. In response, the members simply adjourned the meeting, declaring that there had not been sufficient time for "deliberations," and that they felt unprepared to draft legislation. Brady commented sardonically that he was not surprised "as two thirds of the Councillors are totally ignorant of the English language and generally speaking men of no Education, in fact some can neither read nor write." The result was that the representatives from Nicolet and St Pierre, who were both notaries, had "acquired a complete ascendancy over them and are their leaders."[73]

The movement to have the district seat changed only gained momentum after the council's adjournment, with a petition from ten parishes being presented on 17 September by K.C. Chandler, the seigneur of Nicolet. The petitioners pointed out that the 1831 census recorded these parishes with 21,873 people of a total of 24,405 in the district. Drummondville had only twenty-eight houses and 118 souls in 1831, and it had not grown since that time. The village also lay seventy miles distant from many of the petitioners, with only one road to the parishes and no direct road to ten of the fifteen townships. St Jean-de-Nicolet, on the other hand, had 104 houses, a college, and about seven hundred souls. It was the only port in the district, it lay at the mouth of two rivers, and it was a mere forty miles from the most distant townships and thirty-three miles from the furthest parish.[74]

In November the influential MLA for Nicolet, A.N. Morin, presented a statement to Governor Bagot in support of this petition. It claimed that the officer from the corps of Royal Engineers who had been instructed to trace the municipal boundaries and recommend council seats had chosen the village of Nicolet, which explained the district's name. Morin's petition was signed by a veritable who's who of influential Quebec merchants, politicians, and officials, all claiming to be proprietors within the Nicolet District. Certainly most if not all of them were land speculators in the Bois-Francs townships, which were closer to Nicolet than to Drummondville. A second petition from most of the same individuals claimed that for the two quarters ending 5 October 1841, the Drummondville postmaster had handled only 1,216 pieces of mail, while 3,095 letters and parcels had passed through the post office for Nicolet and neighbouring Port St Francis, information which one of the absentee proprietors, Deputy Postmaster-General Stayner, would have at his ready disposal.[75]

Despite the widespread opposition to Drummondville as the district seat, Brady remained confident that the council would do much to improve the transportation problem provided it "does its duty and imposes a tax on all wild lands."[76] At the second council meeting he stressed the need to make up for lost time by providing for district and parochial officers, the establishment and maintenance of common schools, and the raising of tax revenues. But Councillor Méthot of St Pierre-les-Becquets simply responded with a motion to vote on eight resolutions, the first of which voiced an objection to Drummondville as a convenient location for their meetings. On division, the motion passed by fifteen votes to six. Council then adjourned itself before action could be taken on the several roads petitions. Reporting the results to the provincial secretary, Brady rationalized that some confusion in the system was to be expected at the start, but he asked that the question of the district seat be settled once and for all.[77]

In self-defence, the pro-Drummondville forces noted that their town linked the French-speaking and English-speaking settlements and argued that the isolated town had been chosen as the district seat largely because the people of the area were characterized by "uniform loyalty and attachment to British rule and British connexion." The loyalty cry was a rather weak one at a time when Bagot was attempting to placate the French Canadians so that his government could operate more effectively, but redressing the grievances of one district would have created a precedent for all the others in which the municipal seat was an issue.[78] Representatives of the aggrieved majority nevertheless increased their efforts in the hope that Bagot would be more sympathetic than his predecessor had been. In January 1842 the governor received an anti-Drummondville petition from J.G. Barthe, MLA for Yamaska; D.B. Viger, MLA for Richelieu; C.S. Cherrier, a Montreal member of the Papineau clan who identified himself as a district proprietor; and several others. In February the seigneur Chandler, who was now identified as a lieutenant-colonel of the Nicolet militia, submitted another monster petition claiming that the choice of district seat represented "un grief sévère" for a large proportion of the population. A printed circular naming Chandler as committee president complained that the courts of justice would also be established in Drummondville because it was the district seat. It even claimed that the education of their children and the "bien-être de leur postérité" were at stake.[79]

Under these circumstances it is not surprising that the Nicolet District's municipal system began to break down even before the third meeting took place in the spring of 1842. Late the previous December, Brady had issued warrants to justices of the peace to have parish/township officials elected, but the officials in St Pierre and Gentilly, at the easternmost edge of the district, took advantage of a technicality to refuse the order. When the warden sent out corrected warrants, the chair of the meeting in St Pierre simply declared that he would not hold an election. When yet another warrant was sent to a new chair, he was told to discontinue the meeting because Brady did not have the power to authorize an election on any date other than the second Monday of January. The parish of Gentilly presented the same rationale for not electing parish officers, but its meeting did name five school commissioners so that it would be eligible for the government grant.[80]

Brady's opening address to the councillors who did appear nevertheless expressed the hope that their meeting would be "characterized by a spirit and temper more worthy a body on the wisdom of whose measures mainly depend the welfare and advancement of this fine District, than were displayed at our initiatory and last assemblies." Choosing an approach designed to appeal to the residents of the overcrowded parishes, he recommended the imposition of a uniform annual tax "on all lands whether wild or cultivated." The message was driven home with a quote from a despatch sent by Sydenham to Lord Russell: "On cultivated lands it would in fact be scarcely felt but it would operate as a penal tax on wild land and would compel the owners either to cultivate or dispose of it. If applied to local improvements such as the opening and maintenance of roads, the repairs of Bridges etc. it would be the greatest boon ever conferred on the Country."

Any persuasive effect Brady's remarks may have had was largely lost when he then retired from the meeting due to an undefined "indisposition." The councillors did proceed to pass resolutions and consider petitions concerning local roads, but they made no provision for taxation before the majority ended the proceedings with five resolutions concerning the location of the district seat. The acting chair, who was a French Canadian, reported to Bagot that the situation had become severely aggravated since the last session because of the movement of the district court and registry office to Drummondville. The council had decided to suspend discussion of all matters except roads until after the government had found a more convenient "chef-lieu."[81]

Brady could no longer express a sense of optimism in his missives to the provincial secretary, but he made his own bias on the district seat question perfectly clear by claiming that "This section of the District is nearly altogether peopled by hardy, loyal British Settlers, a very large body of whom volunteered for general service during the unfortunate rebellions of 37 & 38." A change from Drummondville would be considered "as a death blow to their interests." Brady had little cause to worry about this matter, since the governor-general declared in 1842, concerning the seat of Nicolet and several other districts in Canada East, that "such seeming inequalities ... will be in constant progress of correction from the increase of the population of the newer settlements." He would therefore "be reluctant, except for very strong evident reasons, to sacrifice the permanent interest of a whole Dt to the temporary advantage of any particular section of it." Furthermore, Bagot concluded, the law gave him no power to change the seats of the district courts, and there was therefore little point in moving the district council chambers.[82]

At the Nicolet Council's meeting in June, A.P. Méthot of St Pierre insisted on taking a seat even though he had been declared ineligible by the law officers of the crown. Brady replied that Méthot's presence made the council's proceedings illegal and he retired, leaving the councillors to pass yet another resolution condemning the choice of Drummondville as the district seat. Before adjourning, they also declared that under more favourable circumstances they would have petitioned the government for control of local revenues such as inn licences, river tolls, and fines, but they had no confidence in the three branches of the legislature as they currently existed.[83]

The September meeting, which had the surprisingly high number of twenty councillors present, appears to have avoided the topic of provincial politics while still refusing to set the machinery of local government in motion by passing an assessment bylaw. Brady reported that the councillors devoted all their time to reading petitions for the laying out of new roads, "all of which was fruitless, as none of the roads prayed for could be carried into execution without the aid of large pecuniary grants." At the December meeting, which Brady did not attend owing once again to "a severe indisposition," the councillors actually passed a certain number of bylaws, though to what effect is not clear.[84]

No more minutes from the Nicolet District meetings have survived, but Brady reported in January 1843 that the annual election of parish and township officers had taken place with "regularity and good order." The councillors met in June of the same year, but, with Brady again reportedly too ill to attend, the only new resolution was that the governor should appoint another warden. In response, Brady's wife reported to the civil secretary that she felt it her duty "to step out of my proper sphere" to report that most of the councillors were "narrow-minded, illiterate and ignorant." Not only had her husband faithfully discharged the arduous duties of warden for two years, but she could produce certificates from four physicians testifying that he suffered from a liver complaint and enlargement of the kidneys.[85]

By the following February James Brady was dead, and in September 1844 William Pitt of St François was finally chosen to take his place. The political tide had obviously turned against the Drummondville supporters, but the Executive Council decided that the forthcoming reform of the municipal system made it pointless to change the district seat at that time.[86] The district council system therefore ended with a considerable number of disappointed claimants from the Nicolet District, including the clerk who was owed £280 as four years' salary, the district surveyor who asked for £100 per year for three and half years, and Warden Pitt who claimed £50 for one year of his services.[87] Whether the Nicolet Council would have become an effective institution if the district seat issue had been solved is impossible to say. The fund-raising proposals of the June 1842 meeting suggest that a general assessment on land may have remained a contentious issue, though the stiff tax on undeveloped land would undoubtedly have proven popular to the French Canadians who were then colonizing the region's northern townships. Far from simply boycotting the district council as a "machine à taxer," the French-speaking members who constituted the majority clearly appreciated its potential value and attempted to reform it in such a way that it would best serve the interests of their communities.

RADICALISM AND FACTIONALISM IN THE CHAUDIÈRE DISTRICT

Taxation would be a more dominant issue in the poorer Chaudière District, even though the site of the council chambers was of crucial importance there as well. If the Nicolet District's municipal seat was merely inconvenient for the majority living in the south shore seigneuries, the village chosen for the Chaudière District's meetings was practically inaccessible at certain times of the year for the residents of the lower Chaudière and Etchemin valleys. Unlike Drummondville, the village of

Leeds was not on a major river artery, but on the poorly maintained Craig Road high in the hills of Megantic County.

The isolation of the largely British settlements in Leeds, and neighbouring Inverness, Ireland, and Halifax townships, was such that the French-Canadian councillors proposed dividing the district in two rather than moving the seat to their county. Furthermore, their protest movement was less focused on a single issue than was that of the Nicolet District, for they began to criticize the local judicial system, school taxes, and the centralized structure of the municipal system itself. Finally, unlike the Nicolet District, local resistance to the municipal legislation in the Chaudière District was not largely confined to the French Canadians.

In August 1841 a meeting in the predominantly Irish-settled parish of St Sylvestre in Lotbinière County declared that the District Councils Ordinance "may more correctly be intituled, An Ordinance to extend Government patronage, to enable the rich, who have already enough, to draw more out of the pockets of a poor peasantry, who can hardly procure for their own families a decent competency." The meeting attacked the property qualification for councillors, as well as their lack of power, and "Resolved unanimously, – That we will use all constitutional means within our reach to obtain the repeal of the said Ordinance, or, at least, to obtain such amendments as will render it worthy of the acceptance and thanks of a free, grateful and loyal people."[88] The following January a meeting of landholders in Frampton and Cranbourne, to the east of the Chaudière River, proclaimed that the area was settled by Irishmen "who have fled from their native land in consequence of the heavy burden of taxation," and they would not tolerate a similar oppression in the land of their adoption.[89] Finally, we shall see that the recently arrived Scots settlers in Inverness Township remained a thorn in the warden's side until the district council system expired with nothing of substance accomplished.

The French-Canadian protests also began in August 1841 when the inhabitants and proprietors of the Chaudière and Etchemin valleys presented a petition pointing out that they were seven-eighths of the district's population, and seven to thirteen leagues (approximately twenty to thirty-six miles) from the village of Leeds. During the spring and fall many of them could have no communication with the district seat because it was impossible to cross the Chaudière for two months of the year. The time and expense required to reach Leeds under the best of conditions would mean ruin "par les difficultés sans nombre qu'ils éprouveront à avoir une justice prompte & expéditive qui était le but de cette ordonnance."[90] As in Nicolet, then, opposition to the site of the district council was inextricably tied to the site of the district court. Soon after the protest petition was submitted, a select committee of the Legislative

Assembly recommended that the Chaudière district be divided in two, with Ste Marie as the district town for the eastern half, and Leeds confined to the western half.[91] Reasonable as the request may have been, Sydenham was clearly not willing to face the impact that compliance would have on the other districts of the province.

The Scots settlers of Inverness registered a protest of a different nature that same month. The problem originated with a perceived slight to Archibald McKillop, the man who acted as the spiritual and secular leader of these devout Congregationalist Highlanders from the Isle of Arran. It is doubtful that McKillop spoke for the Irish Protestant majority in the township, for he had been involved in a dispute with some of them over his attempt to control a local school in 1838.[92] He nevertheless informed Provincial Secretary Daly, who was the local MLA, that there was general indignation against the appointment of John Lambly of Halifax Township as district warden because of a statement he had made to the *Quebec Gazette* concerning a new road. McKillop claimed that he himself had originally defended the choice of Lambly, who was the son of the Quebec harbourmaster, because he could speak French.[93] Unfortunately for the new warden, however, he had made the faux pas of overlooking McKillop to chair the township's first annual meeting. The status-conscious Scot proclaimed that this slight to himself as the county's senior justice of the peace, as well as senior captain of militia, was "insulting to Governor, Council, Parliament, and myself."

Furthermore, McKillop claimed that one of the notices for the meeting was sent "under cloud of night past my house and chapel, which is the second place in the Township for publicity," to be posted near Somerset Township. He had attended the meeting only to declare that it was irregular, and to insist "that I would not be taxed by virtue of such meetings." While McKillop claimed that he regretted having to take this action, "as it had a tendency to raise people generally agt taxes," he made it clear that he would not tolerate state-sanctioned incursions on his local leadership role. If Lambly "chooses to consult me I shall freely help him by advice, etc., but if he follow out his own foolish way I shall not say a word more in his favour to the people – but shall call him our enemy, whatever effect it may have on the people."[94]

In his detailed report, the chairman of the meeting, Robert Cobban, revealed that McKillop had indeed stirred up local opposition to the tax assessment. Ignoring the admonition that the meeting should confine itself to electing the township officers, McKillop had made an entertaining and inflammatory speech in which he declared that "the tax could not be less than 6d per acre and leave anything to be laid out on the roads, after paying the salaries of officers who would be riding *in Painted Carrioles* [sic] *drawn by Arabian horses*!!!" At three or four shillings the tax would amount to £10 on his 600 acres, "a sum which he would never pay." McKillop then drove his point home by declaring that "he thought any of them would do very well if they could take down to Quebec in the fall, 3 or 4 fat sheep, and get as much for them as would pay their tax, – perhaps there would be 10/ or 12/6 over to buy pins which they would bring home to their wives to pin their rags together."

The loquacious McKillop then objected to the property qualification required for councillors, stating that "there were many poor men in the Township as clever as any one who was properly qualified and he did not see why there should be any distinction – for instance said he £300 worth of property would not make a man speak French, and as for himself, he said he would still be the same long-legged McKillop." Reflecting the mixed British composition of his township, McKillop declared that "he could get three old women, one Scotch, one English, and Irish woman, over a cup of Tea, to make better Laws than had been made by the Governor and Special Council." Finally, according to Cobban, McKillop pronounced "in an exalted tone of voice, I adjourn this meeting as it is illegal & you shall all go away home."

The chairman did manage to have a candidate for councillor nominated, but "after this all was tumult, riot & confusion." Cobban had attempted to restore order by arguing that the high property qualification was meant to spare those who would not have sufficient free time to hold public office, that the tax might be paid by working on the roads, that by assessing wild lands held by speculators, money would become plentiful in the county, that the councillors would not be paid for their services, and that they would have to pay the same taxes as other property holders – "all of which seemed to please them very well but at this moment a second rush from behind upset my table and crushed myself." Regaining his feet, Cobban declared John Campbell elected, "and if matters were ill before the people became savagely furious now." They demanded a poll on whether the majority favoured Campbell or not, which Cobban refused, but he could not convince them to elect township officers. Instead the chairman was seized by a man who called out "drag him away, haul him away," but he was then rescued by a militia officer. After demanding in vain that McKillop, as captain of militia, arrest the offending party, Cobban finally went home. His report added that "many of the people belonging to the Settl't brot sticks and cudgels with them, which was a thing quite unusual for them to do in attending meetings."[95]

Surmising that McKillop would submit his own version of the riotous events, Cobban asked for a government investigation. But, rather than attempt to play down his role in the violent affair, the defiant leader of the Arran settlers simply informed Daly once again that he would continue to oppose taxation until a notice was posted at his residence and another meeting held in the centre of the township. And Lambly should "take good care not to send among us another chareman and returning officer who poublicly insults the good people by comparing them with *hogs* and who tells severals to their faces that they should be declared *rebals* if they do not elect their officer in regard to taxing." McKillop then boasted that "my advice to the people would do more for the good of the county in facing rebals than both Lambly and Coban taken together, and I can do more at one meeting to make the good people of Inverness (particularly the Irish Orangemen) understand the real nature and the advantages of moderat assessment than they all can do."[96]

Under these circumstances John Campbell had decided that it would be prudent to decline sitting as the Inverness councillor. Referring to the "lawless mob" at the meeting, he asked "Sir when the [*sic*] do this in the bud what shall the do in the Green Tree."[97] But Lambly informed Campbell that he would be fined £10 if he resigned, and asked Cobban to convene a meeting of the justices of the peace to choose the township officers. He then decided to hold another public meeting instead, "so that the bad feeling which had been created might be destroyed." Lambly's change of mind appears to have followed his realization that Campbell was not qualified to be a councillor, since he was "only a Quit Renter without a freehold property."[98]

Not surprisingly, Cobban was passed over as chair this time, but he then decided to make some mischief of his own. He swore the formerly reluctant and ineligible Campbell in as councillor, and issued a summons for three JPs (none of whom had Highland names) to meet at his house. Here they declared the first meeting legal and proceeded to appoint the township officers, as originally planned. Meanwhile, the second public meeting elected McKillop to be councillor, and named its own list of officers.[99] At the root of the local conflict was clearly a power struggle between the Arran Scots and the other settlers in Inverness Township.

When Campbell and McKillop both appeared at the first district council meeting in September, Lambly gave McKillop the seat. However, Daly later informed him that Campbell was the legally elected candidate, after all, and that the second public meeting had overstepped its authority when it elected township officers.[100] But the warden faced a more serious problem than the factionalism within the British community of Inverness. The two councillors from Ste Marie presented the first motion of the meeting declaring that when institutions or "pretendus droits populaires" which were conferred for the sole benefit of the people proved to be subversive to those same ends, "il est du devoir de ceux pour qui de pareilles loix ont été passées de refuser leur coopération à l'exécution de ces loix par tous moyens légitimes." This was more radical language than had ever been resorted to by the Nicolet councillors.

Revealingly, all ten of the French Canadians voted for the resolution, while four of the anglophones opposed it. McKillop, however, and Matthew Donoghue of St Sylvestre, voted in the affirmative. They presumably wished to make a statement about their independence from the government, for they joined the English-speaking minority in voting against the next three motions. These resolutions protested against Leeds as a district seat, and against the appointment of township/parish officers by executive decree when local meetings failed to elect them. They also declared that no taxes should be paid until the district was divided or a more central location found for meetings. Most of the councillors then simply left the meeting, forcing an adjournment due to lack of a quorum. Lambly reported somewhat lamely that he had allowed the motions to be presented in order to reveal to the governor the grounds on which the majority refused to co-operate, and he declared that the system would never function until the district was divided.[101]

The warden nevertheless opened his report on the second council meeting on a positive note, stating that it had been "very favourable all things considered." After nominating three individuals from whom the governor was to choose a clerk, the council passed a resolution declaring that it would not proceed with taxation until the governor had acted on the resolutions adopted at the previous meeting. The division was nine to five, with Dr R.A. Fortier of Ste Marie the only French Canadian to vote with the minority.[102] The inhabitants of the seigneurial parishes remained defiant, and the district seat was not the only issue at stake. In St Sylvestre, which lay adjacent to Leeds Township, the annual meeting to elect a councillor and parish officers resulted in a near-riot because of deep-rooted ethnic, religious, and political divisions within the parish.[103] The local curé, J. Nelligan, led a procession of men armed with clubs to the meeting place, allowing only five individuals to cast votes during the first two hours. Edward Parker, a supporter of the municipal system, received three votes, while Ignace Gagnon, who opposed it, received two.[104]

In Ste Marie-de-Beauce the conflict centred on the two local councillors. P.E. Taschereau was the militia major and justice of the peace who had led the district council's opposition to the municipal ordinance, and R.A. Fortier was the recently appointed county registrar who had supported the warden at the previous council meeting. Taschereau was re-elected after speaking out strongly against taxation. He warned that it would soon be extended to finance the provincial government, and declared that the schools should be paid for by the government, as in the past.[105]

Meanwhile, the Chaudière District's local road maintenance system was breaking down. The township and parish road officers had no funds at their disposal, and they could not even procure the relevant official statutes, with the result that the inhabitants refused to keep the roads in repair. In March, Lambly was forced to admit that even in his own township the inhabitants had refused to elect a councillor or choose township officers. When the magistrates then took it upon themselves to name the local officers, those chosen to be assessors claimed exemption on the grounds that they were "but 'squatters' and consequently not voters."[106]

Under these circumstances, it is not surprising that the council attended to very little business in its March meeting.[107] The councillors nevertheless met again in June, passing the usual resolution to justify their refusal to put the local governing machinery into operation. The council also now advocated a strictly parish-based system of municipal government. Failing that, it insisted on appointing all the district municipal officers except the warden, on the right to assemble at the members' convenience, on the extension of the time period allowed for election of councilors, and on a considerable lowering of the property qualification. Nor were the councillors content with demands related directly to the municipal system, for they also protested against ordinances concerning registry offices and sleighs, and they claimed that the judicial system should be more expeditious and less costly. Finally, they declared that all schools supported by voluntary contributions rather than tax assessment should be eligible for a public allocation.[108] We shall see that this issue was a particularly contentious one throughout the Eastern Townships.

In forwarding the minutes for the June meeting, Lambly expressed his deep sense of discouragement. Having penetrated the forest,

and subdued a great portion of it, our hopes of something being done by the Government for the amelioration of our condition have ever supported us under all our privations. And now that we have placed in our hands the very Law that would fully accomplish all that the Country requires (with a trifling alteration), to have it now a nullity, by a set of men opposed to the Government, and in a great measure ignorant of its utility, knowing this and suffering as we do, we are I assure you sir almost ready to despond.[109]

If Sydenham's municipal ordinance could not be made to function in relatively homogenous American-settled districts such as Sherbrooke and Missisquoi, there is little wonder that it floundered in as artificial a district as Chaudière, with its old French-speaking seigneurial parishes in Beauce County and its struggling young British settlements in Megantic. As with Nicolet, the most fundamental issue appears to have been the location of the district seat. Despite their widely contrasting back-grounds, however, McKillop and Taschereau of the Chaudière Council both expressed a more radical critique of the district council system than did their counterparts in the more prosperous areas to the west and south. While the Missisquoi and Sherbrooke District councillors focused on widening the tax base beyond the agricultural population, the Chaudière councillors declared that the municipal system would have to be made more accessible and more locally accountable before they would consider supporting property assessments of any kind. This would be the aim of the new municipal act finally passed in 1845, long after the ineffectuality of Sydenham's district council system had become obvious.

5 Municipal Reform, 1845–51

The new municipal act, drafted by Denis-Benjamin Papineau, took the radical step of reducing the municipal corporation to the parish or township level. The Chaudière District Council had not been alone in making such a recommendation. In 1843 notary Daniel Thomas of Melbourne wrote to Edward Hale: "The necessity of some more stringent control over the Road officers & the absolute expediency of having an efficient authority at hand to regulate the internal improvements of the Township or Parish … seem to render it desirable that Township Councils should exist." But the opinion of the leading figures in the Eastern Townships was generally hostile to the idea of such a marked decentralization of authority. J.M. Taylor, also of Melbourne, wrote to Edward Hale in 1845 that "in our meagre population, it will be difficult to obtain a sufficient number of proper persons to fill the office of Township Councillors. According to my humble estimate of them, even our leading men are scarcely in the least cognizant that the *pro bono egomet* may be best served acting in the principle of the *pro bono publico*: hence I anticipate the narrow-mindedness of a partial, selfish, and even flagrantly unjust Township legislation." Taylor nevertheless advocated extending the franchise to all householders, including squatters, for he himself was a purchaser of improved but untitled land.[1]

According to Edward Hale, Alexander Galt of the British American Land Company was also concerned that township councils would be "less well disposed to the Company than even the District Council was."

But Galt had helped to ensure that the impact of the new municipal system on the large proprietors would be cushioned by lobbying successfully to have all land taxes based on value rather than superficial acreage. Furthermore, only residents could effectively be pursued for non-payment of taxes because personal property could be seized on short notice by judgment of the local circuit court, while five years' grace was permitted before landed property could be auctioned.[2]

The landed interests were not the only Eastern Townships spokesmen to be concerned about the decentralization of municipal authority. Reverend J. Anderson of Richmond declared that "few townships have the materials to compass it – there must be *education, knowledge,* and *a tact for business.*" Also, Sherbrooke's district councillors seem to have been generally opposed, and not simply because of their political ambitions. As leading entrepreneurs in the region, they clearly felt that their plans for economic improvement would be jeopardized. J.S. Walton reported to Hale that "all seemed to think it would be impracticable in many of our townships, & and that there would be such a want of co-operation between the different sections of the country that they would create great confusion!" Certainly, Thomas Tait of Melbourne and Benjamin Pomroy of Compton were of this mind, and Samuel Brooks of Sherbrooke wrote: "It is another [?] French abortion, and will never [?] do good here & I fear much evil."[3]

Because the municipal minutes and bylaws no longer had to be submitted to the provincial government for approval, any surviving records from this period remain in the local town halls or even in private homes. The only records I have discovered are the minutes and miscellaneous records of the Ascot Council, which appears to have included Orford Township and the town of Sherbrooke within its jurisdiction.[4] Fortunately, the *Stanstead Journal* began publication in 1845, and its columns cover the municipal meetings of Stanstead Township quite thoroughly. There are also petitions from various councils filed in the civil secretary's incoming correspondence.

The Ascot records reveal how the Sherbrooke notables quickly asserted their dominance over the local council, though this was obviously too narrow a field for their regional development ambitions. Without a secret ballot, each of the seven council positions technically had to be contested separately rather than declaring elected the seven men who received the most votes. In the first election, earlier negotiations resulted in six names being agreed upon unanimously "as a compromise by all parties." This left five candidates to present their names for the seventh position, and some of the losers were clearly unhappy with the pre-arranged proceedings, for they claimed that the election was illegal.[5] The council proceeded to meet in any case at a Lennoxville hotel.

Its first task was to select the mayor, with William Ritchie receiving six votes and L.C. Ball only one. Under the new regulations, the assessors, collectors, and other local officers were now named by council as well, rather than being elected at an annual public meeting. Once this task had been accomplished, the Ascot Council adjourned for three days so that committees could draft procedural regulations. These regulations proved to be surprisingly detailed and formal for a community that had never experienced local governing institutions. For example, a councillor who wished to speak was to rise and address the chair, every member present had to vote unless the council excused him, and no motion was to be entertained by council unless it was put in writing and seconded.[6]

During the following days the councillors passed a series of bylaws concerning roads and bridges, the taxation of traders and tavern keepers, the remuneration of township officers, the assessment of all immovable property within three months, and the internal regulation of the town of Sherbrooke. There was clearly some difficulty finding men to act as the local officers, for substitutions were noted for the positions of surveyor, overseer, and assessor. In September the council would rationalize this system, and conform to the deep sense of localism, by establishing five surveyors' districts and twenty-four overseers' districts within the single municipality. Meanwhile, the July session closed with the motion to place a notice on all bridges warning that a five shilling penalty would be imposed "for riding on the same faster than a walk."[7]

The local body was already making more progress than the district council had in its several years of existence. But a smaller theatre of operations certainly did not mean that controversy would be entirely eliminated, as the debate over the first major public works project was to demonstrate. The issue involved the building of a road and bridge laid out by the former district council. At least one member advocated an alternate route, but the council decided to make no change after receiving the report of three men chosen to investigate. At the following session, when the dissident councillor presented a petition complaining about this decision, it was rejected "on account of disrespectful language towards the council, & towards the Committee appointed by the Council."[8] This inaugural public works project also revealed the practical problems caused by the limited territory covered by each municipal council under the new system. The mayor of neighbouring Eaton informed Ascot that his council did not feel legally capable of contributing to any project not within its township boundaries, and the Compton Council rejected a motion to contribute one-third of the expenses for the same road and bridge. Finally, when several private individuals offered to pay one-third of the bridge construction costs themselves, the Ascot Council agreed to contribute £75 for the project on condition that those individuals also maintain the bridge for ten years.[9] It would appear, then, that the tradition of local voluntarism persisted despite the introduction of the municipal system in 1841.

Fortunately, other projects proved less controversial, and a considerable number of public works were set in motion despite the limitations of the municipal boundaries. For the pioneer industrial centre of Sherbrooke, however, the council's activities were somewhat surprisingly confined largely to fire prevention. Thus, in October 1845, it voted for the assessment of £25 within the town to purchase one hundred feet of water hose, twelve leather buckets, and four iron hooks and chains. It was not until December that Sherbrooke's limits were formally fixed for all bylaws and other regulations specifically relating to the town.[10]

As for the rural communities, during the September session Ascot Council had voted £258 for construction and repair of roads and bridges. The councillors' first bylaw had declared that all public work on roads and bridges would be borne by general assessment, but a local lawyer had advised that this was illegal.[11] The following year J.S. Walton suggested to Edward Hale, in his capacity as MLA, that if the councils had this authority, "it would remedy the worst feature – the unequal distribution of labor – & make municipal taxes less odious."[12] But the minutes of a June 1846 meeting of several Ascot overseers reveal that they were careful to distribute labour equally. Proprietors in each of their sub-divisions were assessed ten days' work on the local roads and bridges for every 200 acres, and two days' for every village lot they owned.[13] Given the flexibility of this system and the strong sense of localism that persisted in the rural communities, it is doubtful whether a general assessment would have been popular even though it would now operate at the township rather than the district level.

The limited municipal boundaries were of more immediate concern than the assessment system. Late in September the Ascot councillors met in special session to consider a petition from what had become a more co-operative Compton asking them to open those roads connecting the two townships which had been laid out by the late district council. The following December Ascot Council invited its counterparts in the District of St Francis to meet in convention in order to draft a petition for amending the municipal act. The Ascot councillors made their position clear prior to the meeting by proclaiming that they were "as a general principle in favour of large municipalities, reserving to each Township, or union, certain definite powers within their own limits."[14]

The outlying areas would prove to be less than enthusiastic about this threat to their autonomy, but representatives from eight townships did adopt two other Ascot resolutions at their joint meeting in January. These declared that municipal councils should have summary powers for the collection of taxes on wild lands, and the authority to have roads and bridges maintained by a general assessment on ratable property. A number of other resolutions were passed to similar effect, and each municipal council in the district was requested to pass them individually, thereby revealing how Sherbrooke's rising bourgeoisie was making its influence felt throughout the region.[15] Furthermore, MLAs Edward Hale and John McConnell were in attendance, and the two leading recommendations noted above were ultimately adopted in the 1855 municipal act. The long delay would prove frustrating to the pro-development forces in the Townships, but the provincial government would not be rushed by pressures from one region, and it certainly would not act on the municipal convention's resolution that "the Eastern Townships require a Municipal, School and Road Law, adopted to their peculiar wants and local situation, without reference to those parts of the Province where lands are held under Seigniorial or Feudal tenure."[16]

Meanwhile, the Ascot councillors had to attempt to work within the existing system as effectively as possible. Beginning in 1846, the leading role in this endeavour was taken by the newly elected William Locker Pickmore Felton, son of the late W.B. Felton and himself a local lawyer with political ambitions. While his father and uncles had benefited from government largesse as the most politically powerful family in the region during the pre-Rebellion era, the young Felton proposed that salaries and other allowances to municipal officers "be reduced to the lowest sum consistent with the public service." Then, the following year, he moved that a committee of three ascertain how statute labour could be more effectively assigned for the performance of road work.[17]

Ascot Council had certainly not been particularly successful in enforcing its regulations related to road work. As early as September 1845, it had proclaimed that each negligent surveyor and overseer of roads would be prosecuted, and the following January it declared that suits were to be launched against all delinquent rate payers. But overseers and surveyors continued to be dismissed and replaced without prosecution until May 1847. Then, when fines of 25 s. were imposed on two men, the council excused them from payment. Perhaps the reason was that the 1845 municipal act was about to expire, leaving Ascot with £39 in the treasury, nearly £65 owing in municipal taxes, and £12 13s. owing in town taxes, presumably for various licences.[18]

Whether there was concerted local opposition to municipal taxes in Ascot is impossible to say, given that most issues of the Sherbrooke newspaper have disappeared, but there is evidence of considerable resistance elsewhere in the region. For example, the *Stanstead Journal* records a public meeting in Hatley in November 1845 which censured the local council for not consulting the property holders on the taxation system.

Referring to the new schools act as well as the municipal act, those in attendance passed a resolution declaring "that the Inhabitants of this Township are opposed to taxation in every form whatever." The meeting had a semblance of local authority since it had been called to order by one militia captain and chaired by another, but letters printed in the ensuing issues of the newspaper indicate that not everyone in the township agreed with its participants.[19]

A similar public meeting held in Shefford Township elected a committee of five which in turn nominated nine men (including a gentleman, an esquire, and a militia captain) to draft the resolutions. Adopted unanimously, these resolutions criticized the local council for choosing assessors without consulting the wishes of the people, and "regardless of that opposition to an unequal direct taxation which exists in this Township."[20] Much of the hostility was clearly directed at school taxes, for we shall see that the people of the Eastern Townships clung to their tradition of voluntary support for local schools. Had the newly established school commissions been given separate taxing authority in 1845, it is quite likely that the municipal councils (though not the school commissioners) would have met with less opposition. Furthermore, the objection in Shefford, at least, was not to municipal taxation per se, but to the exclusive burden placed on landed property.

The pages of the *Stanstead Journal* reveal that, despite the popular desire to reform the municipal system, Stanstead's township council met regularly and passed a series of bylaws pertaining to roads and other local matters. In June 1846 it broadened its tax base by establishing licence fees for traders, shopkeepers, tavern keepers and temperance houses of entertainment, though these permits continued to be issued by provincial authorities. Those operating without a licence were to be fined £1 10s. In February 1847 the municipal secretary noted the bad state of the roads due to the inclemency of the weather, and asked that the road surveyors and overseers discharge their duties: "And it is hoped that this notice will be sufficient."[21] Judging from the number of warnings in the *Stanstead Journal* concerning stray horses, bulls, and other livestock, it would appear that any new sanctions introduced by the council failed to make much impression on the fence viewers, but correspondence to the civil secretary reveals that farmers did take road overseers to court for neglect of duty.[22]

The relatively prosperous townships of Ascot and Stanstead undoubtedly had two of the more dynamic municipal institutions in the region. Certainly, there were major shortcomings in the more recently settled townships to the north, especially because of the failure to lower the property qualification from £250 to a more reasonable level when the municipal bodies were reduced in size. Thus, in 1845 Daly was informed

that the Tingwick councillors, only some of whom met the property qualification themselves, had in turn been forced to appoint assessors with
the same deficiency. The result was that they had had "dooers [sic] shut
against them," and all operations were suspended until they could learn
whether or not they had the legal right to act.[23]

Likewise, the school commissioners of Bury, which had been settled
largely by immigrants from southern England during the 1830s, expressed concern that the municipal council would not be able to levy
the required school tax because not one of its members met the legal
qualifications. Two had been residents less than a year, one was an alien,
and none of the others held any real estate. The solution proposed by a
petition from members of the American-descended minority who had
drifted northward into the township was to annex part of long-settled
Eaton Township and call another election.[24] But Mayor McClintock
argued successfully that not only did Eaton lie sixteen to twenty-five
miles away from Bury's centre of population, but it was inhabited by
Anglo-Americans "whose opinions & feelings, respecting local government, are manifestly different from those entertained & felt by the
inhabitants of this Municipality."[25] McClintock himself did not speak for
the Highland settlers who lived further north in Lingwick, which was attached to Bury for municipal purposes. These Gaelic-speaking immigrants protested in turn that because they were unable to qualify as
councillors, they were not represented by the municipality.[26] Localized
as it was, then, the township council system clearly failed to satisfy all the
sectional interests in the younger colonization districts because of the
prohibitive property requirement.

Even from an older township such as Granby there came the
complaint that two "aliens," presumably Americans, had been elected,
thereby preventing British subjects from filling all the offices.[27] But the
issue of municipal representation was still more contentious where
French Canadians had taken up land in townships already partially settled by English-speaking families. There was no such controversy at first
in Milton Township, which was 79 percent French-speaking by 1844.
The local MLA simply reported after the first municipal election was delayed that "the Canadians [meaning French Canadians] should by honest right have the majority of the Councillors." Four of the seven names
submitted by Dr S.S. Foster were French, while fourteen freeholders
with English names recommended five of their French-Canadian co-
inhabitants to be appointed as councillors.[28]

But problems arose the following year, in 1846, when two election
meetings were held to replace two retiring councillors, one chaired by
the English-speaking senior councillor and the other by the French-
speaking mayor. The first meeting elected a French Canadian and an

anglophone, the second elected two French Canadians. A petition signed with thirty-seven English names and two French names claimed that only the first meeting had been advertised, and it alone had elected men who met the property qualification as well as being educated. It added that since people were refusing to perform the road labour assigned by the officers who had been appointed by Mayor Lacoste's two new councillors, the result was much litigation and confusion. Foster asked the provincial secretary "to put a stop this [sic] by some means at once," but the government's reply was that only the courts of law could decide.[29] In 1847 one of the original English-speaking councillors resigned on the grounds that three of his colleagues were incapable of signing their names, and the clerk could write only in French, "and that very incorrectly." The result, he claimed, was that a notary and a lawyer had declared all the bylaws "to be incorrect in spelling and diction and quite unintelligible."[30]

One step that could be taken when two groups of different national origin lived in different parts of the same township, and where numbers warranted, was to divide the township into two municipalities. This was the solution sought in Stukely, where the population of 1,151 was approximately half English-speaking and half French-speaking according to the 1844 census. A petition endorsed by the mayor and four councillors claimed that a broad belt of unsettled land divided the newer, mostly French-speaking settlers in the north from the longer-established English-speaking residents in the south. Because transportation was not good even on horseback, some school commissioners and councillors had walked a circuitous twenty-three-mile route through a neighbouring township in order to attend meetings in the north of Stukely in December 1846. In March, when the meetings were held in the south, no one from the north had been able to attend. Furthermore, the different languages made the transaction of business difficult, and assessors had to employ interpreters. However, a counter-petition claimed that the population was mixed throughout the township, and that the north and south were connected by several cross roads. The MLA, S.S. Foster, asked for time to "git [sic] the affair settled among the Inhabitants," but he later supported division of the township on the grounds that it would "prevent an Eternal Quarrel" between the two sections. The Executive Council accepted his recommendation a month later.[31]

The English-speaking residents in the townships of mixed national origin were not the only ones to complain of unqualified French-speaking councillors. In 1845 Louis Richard of Stanfold in the Bois-Francs reported that only two of his fellow councillors could read or write, and all but one were squatters. He complained that he did not wish to sit with them because they knew nothing about public affairs, and he would therefore have to shoulder all the responsibilities. He should therefore be allowed to resign without penalty, or have the other councillors replaced with those whose names he submitted to the government. They did not strictly meet the property qualification either, but at least they had land titles.[32]

Richard's complaint may have masked rivalry between local political factions, but a similar problem developed in the neighbouring township of Somerset. When the public meeting resulted in the election of councillors who were opposed to taxation, a rival group charged that the proceedings had been irregular because the chairman had failed to read the act due to illiteracy.[33] He had also accepted the votes of those who did not meet the property qualifications. The local curé, Charles Bélanger, was clearly behind the second group, and his letter to the civil secretary revealed that the problem was not that democracy had been thwarted, but that it had been served all too well:

Nos gens ne se sont assemblées aux jours marqués pour les élections que dans la voie de troubler le repos ou dénommer des personnes qui sont tout à fait opposés à l'exécution des lois, car presque tous ne voyent en celà que taile ou impôts. Que les chemins soient beaux, tant mieux, disent ils, mais nous ne voulons pas les faire ni les entretenir. Qu'il y ait des écoles, la chose peut être bonne, mais nous no voulons pas payer pour nos enfants; voilà le langage de la presque totalité.[34]

Bélanger submitted an alternate list of names and had his church-wardens and other allies draw up a petition supporting them, as requested by the civil secretary.[35]

Daly was clearly willing to make an exception to the provincial government's rule of non-interference when the functioning of the municipal and school systems was at stake, though the attorney-general prevented him from appointing the councillors recommended by the curé and the three justices of the peace of another Bois-Francs parish, St Norbert d'Arthabaska. The four notables had decided that a public meeting would upset the tranquillity that had recently been restored after the burning of a local school, but the attorney-general declared that councillors could be appointed by the province only when the local proprietors had refused to elect them.[36]

Opposition to the municipal system was not confined to the French-Canadian settlers in the northern townships. A similar attitude prevailed among the nearby British immigrants of Megantic County, whose resistance against the district council system we have already examined. In 1845, William Hall of Broughton Township complained that the local settlers had refused to elect councillors on the grounds that none met the property qualification, even though other places had elected less qualified men "than several that are here." Because Broughton's isolated location did not make union with another township feasible, a committee of the Executive Council simply declared that it could not "think of any method by which the difficulty can be removed."[37] Hall reported the following year that without any municipal structure of any sort, Broughton was in a "horrid state." Roads were impassable, "and the People say there is no Law to make them work, therefore they will not work." After yet another plea a month later, the government replied that the names Hall had submitted would be appointed councillors "with all practicable despatch."[38]

The settlers of Inverness Township did elect a council in 1845, but an informant complained to Daly that only one councillor "professes to think favourably of the Municipal Act."[39] In neighbouring Ireland Township Mayor Donald McLean complained that the settlers refused to vote to fill the council's vacancies in 1846, making it impossible to appoint township officers who could collect taxes. Even the justices of the peace "have availed themselves upon all occasions to embarrass and perplex your memorialist and Council serving vexatious protests upon their Acts, and rendering nugatory all legal proceedings that may have been deemed necessary for the enforcement of the assessment levied by the Council."[40] McLean's own irascible personality and accumulation of local offices were at least partly to blame for this situation, but it was clear to the government by 1847 that there were serious deficiencies in the municipal legislation that had been introduced two years earlier. A new act would address both the problems of property qualification and of inadequate co-ordination between townships. But the conundrum posed by the absentee proprietors would remain for future reform legislation.

THE 1847 MUNICIPAL ACT AND ITS AFTERMATH

Though many of the councillors must have been frustrated with the geographical limits to their authority, the convention of eight municipalities held in Sherbrooke in January 1846 was "decidedly opposed to" Edward Hale's recommendation that there should be bigger municipalities. The Sherbrooke entrepreneurs appear to have been essentially alone in their wishes for a more effective agency of regional development at a time when concerted attempts were being made to establish a railway link with Montreal. Eighteen months later, in June 1847, Hale, Samuel Brooks, J.S. Walton, J.G. Robertson, and G.D. Innes were among the town's notables who organized a public meeting which proposed a return to the district council system. To placate rural hostility to centralization, the

meeting (which was "very thinly attended," according to the unsympathetic *Stanstead Journal*), declared that such a council would be composed of representatives from township councils, though these local
bodies would act "in subserviency to, and in harmony with," the district
council.[41]

The Sherbrooke bourgeoisie was presumably pleased, then, when William Badgley's municipal act of 1847 eliminated the township/parish
councils completely, and declared that rural municipalities would
henceforth be organized at the county level. But the reaction from the
outlying townships was far from enthusiastic. Edward Tourneaux of Melbourne Township wrote to Hale that he would oppose Samuel Brooks in
the next provincial election in part because of the role he had played in
ending the township system before it had been given a fair trial: "Our
member did not consult, nor was time allowed to petition against it."
Likewise, a public meeting held in Eaton Township and chaired by the
former MLA, John Moore, declared that while it approved in principle
of the new municipal legislation, it regretted the abolition of township
councils. Those in attendance felt that small municipalities were better
adapted to the wants of the people in their section of the province, and
that they should have been given the same powers that were now vested
in the county councils. The editor of the *Stanstead Journal* wrote that
these resolutions probably expressed the sentiments of the majority in
the region.[42]

Aside from creating larger municipal entities, the only other significant changes introduced by Badgley's act were to reduce the property
qualification for councillors from £250 to £150 (which was still a prohibitive sum for many small proprietors), and to double the maximum
assessment allowed to six pence per pound of yearly property value.[43] In
lieu of municipal records for the 1847–55 era, the civil secretary's correspondence and the *Stanstead Journal* once again represent the main
sources of information concerning elections and meetings.

While the township councils had been abolished, councillors were still
elected on a township basis. The *Stanstead Journal* reported that at Stanstead Township's first public meeting under the new legislation the two
local councillors were elected by acclamation, and the civil secretary's
correspondence reveals the contests proceeded without major incident
in Ascot, Barnston, Melbourne, the village of Philipsburg, the union of
Wickham and Acton, and Bury. In the last township, however, Lemuel
Pope complained that his arch-rival, Hammond McClintock, was an
alien who had failed to pay his taxes. Likewise, a Sherbrooke correspondent blamed Orford's "dirty little clique" of Edward Hale,
H. Smith, W. Ritchie, and S. Brooks for irregularities in that township's
election of Smith and Griffith.[44] Finally, Durham Township's senior

justice of the peace complained that the secretary-treasurer had absented himself from the election, making it impossible for most of the inhabitants to pay the taxes imposed for a bridge, and thereby leaving them ineligible to vote. The reply from the civil secretary was simply that municipal councils now had the power to decide upon contested elections rather than having to rely upon the courts.[45]

These townships did at least elect councillors. No regular elections took place in the American-settled townships of Dudswell and Eaton, or in the union of Hereford, Clifton and Auckland, and in the French-speaking Bois-Francs no elections were held in Somerset, Arthabaska, or Chester, though this appears again to have been a decision taken by the local elite which simply submitted its choices to the civil secretary. In Megantic County the justice of the peace for Halifax reported that the population refused to elect councillors and, of the few inhabitants who assembled in Ireland, all but two or three were said to be determined to obstruct the election.[46]

With so many abortive and controversial elections even in Sherbrooke's long-established townships, it is perhaps not surprising that the county council made little progress at first. The *Stanstead Journal* reported in December 1847 that opposing elements within the Sherbrooke Council "bend their powers to obstruct and break down, rather than make the paths of legislation smooth and beneficial," and that "some lawyers have scared council from doing anything." A month later the grand jurors of the Queen's Bench, meeting in Sherbrooke, noted that many bridges in the district were "in a very dangerous condition," and regretted that "the majority of the Council of the County of Sherbrooke, refused to act." Once again, the following August they reported that "it was with some risk to life and limb that we made our way here to attend our duty." The Aylmer bridge in Sherbrooke was unsafe, the Lennoxville bridge was "entirely gone," the bridge over the Coaticook River near the Centre Village in Compton was "in a dangerous state," and the Lennoxville-Sherbrooke road "in a bad state of repair."[47]

The problem apparently stemmed from the fact that certain provincial statutes concerning roads and bridges were inconsistent with the municipal act. Considerable time was spent by the council in drafting proposals to present to the provincial government for a new road law specifically suited to the needs of the Eastern Townships, as well as debating whether or not to renew the old struggle with the British American Land Company.[48] The councillors eventually passed a resolution stating that even though the 1845 and 1847 municipal acts declared that any new bylaw could assess landed property on its value only, the Sherbrooke County Council was effectively a reincarnation of the Sherbrooke

District Council, therefore the original 1841 assessment of one penny per acre on wild land was again in force.

While Galt had little doubt that the Sherbrooke resolution was illegal, he complained that the courts which had the power to grant injunctions preventing sales of land for back taxes met in Sherbrooke only twice a year. The company would therefore have no other recourse but to take action against each purchaser at the sheriff's sales, a tedious procedure which would shake the confidence of settlers in all company titles. Galt asked the government to express the opinion that the course taken by the Sherbrooke Council exceeded its authority, but he was informed that "it forms no part of the duties of the law officers of the Crown to give opinions on matters such as this when the Crown is in no way interested." The outcome of this controversy is unclear, but Skelton claims that the British American Land Company henceforth assumed only "a moderate tax burden."[49]

The power to collect taxes in arrears proved necessary in the case of the Stanstead County Council. It was saddled by the courts with the £125 debt accrued by the former Hatley Township Council when it unsuccessfully sued sixteen individuals, presumably for non-payment of taxes or refusal to hold local offices.[50] Despite this setback, the Stanstead Council had a relatively productive history. The *Journal* claimed in December 1847 that the councillors transacted a great deal of business at their first meeting, the only unpleasant matter being the expulsion of a member for being illegally returned. Also, the location of a permanent place of meeting was a "delicate point," though most of the sessions would take place in Levi Bigelow's hotel in Georgeville or that of Dr Colby in Stanstead. Both men were councillors for much of this period.

The second meeting was reported to be routine except for the thorny question of collective responsibility for public works. The councillors prepared two draft bylaws concerning road taxes, one providing for taxation by the acre on land contiguous to the road in question, which was the traditional practice, and one levying a general assessment according to property value. Both would allow for payments in labour. A decision on which strategy to apply was held over for the next meeting, presumably to allow for consultation of the local residents as well as legal experts. But at the April meeting it was decided to obtain an opinion from the attorney-general. For the time being, the councillors simply decided that the county's deputy grand-voyer (the equivalent of the previous surveyor of roads and bridges), would rely on the good will of the roads petitioners for his remuneration.[51]

Both the 1845 and 1847 municipal bills clearly stated that assessments were to be according to value, rather than acreage, but in May the Stanstead Council decided to continue with the old system of taxation, imposing a limit of twelve days of statute labour for 200 acres lying alongside any laid-out road, and six days for each 200 acres lying "back from" such a road. Each village lot would be assessed at two days' labour on the local streets. Those who neglected their duty, or chose to pay cash instead, would be charged five shillings for each day's work they owed. The local surveyors, who were to visit the roads each May and September, could call for extra public labour if needed.[52]

This bylaw clearly reflected the entrenched sense of localism in the region, as well as an aversion to the assessment of property values even if the tax could be paid off by labour. Mayor Chauncey Bullock protested that the council had conformed to custom rather than law, and that the system it thereby perpetuated was "unequal, unjust, and insufficient," but he was the only member to oppose the bylaw. The following session Bullock introduced a bylaw for the Beebe Plain–Rock Island road which would provide for its construction not by statute labour but by assessment and rate on the whole township. Most of the councillors felt, however, that they had no authority to issue contracts for road work except by sanction of a public meeting. Bullock's parting shot in the September meeting was to move that the £115 owed to the municipality be levied by assessment and rate, but he was outvoted four to three.[53]

Councillor Levi Bigelow took up the cause a year and a half later at his township's annual public meeting. After listening to a number of speeches by the local notables on the question of whether building and maintenance of roads, "should be on the Valuation, or by days' work, as formerly," the meeting decided to adhere to the status quo. At the December 1850 council meeting, however, the motion to have road work estimated on the assessment role finally passed by a vote of six to four. A general bylaw to this effect was passed in March 1851, finally bringing Stanstead into conformity with the provincial regulation passed six years earlier. The editor of the *Stanstead Journal* approved, noting that the previous system had been "rather onerous upon the poorer class of householders."[54]

Another contentious issue concerned the local tavern licence funds which were collected by the receiver-general before being turned over to the county councils. In an attempt to prevent the passing of a motion in 1848 to have the money distributed among all the municipality's creditors, Bullock argued that Stanstead Township deserved a greater share than its counterparts because it contributed a greater proportion than the rest of the county. His motion was overwhelmingly defeated, however, when fellow councillor C.B. Cleveland objected: "The money received for show licenses was, it is true, paid in Stanstead; but look at the enormous amount the people paid the taverns in Stanstead, in consequence of attending those shows."[55]

The conflict between Bullock and Cleveland continued to mark the council meeting in March 1849, but both men had been replaced as members by June when the *Journal* reporter noted somewhat mischievously that the councillors had "listened patiently" and "argued soberly if not wisely." Council affairs became more routine from this time onward, but a discussion which revealed much about gender roles and attitudes took place in June 1850. The issue at hand was certainly trivial in the minds of most of the councillors, for it concerned complaints that Levi Bigelow's old shed was blocking the road to the new wharf then under construction in Georgeville. The problem emerged when council was informed that the complainants were women. The member who had seconded the motion to consider their petition immediately asked to have his name removed, and another left his seat until the debate was closed, stating that "he could not stand that." Bigelow himself proclaimed that women's petitions were inevitable, "but he begged of the Council to keep them back as long as they could, for they had to sit almost a week to receive and act on petitions from the men, and if they allowed petitions to be received from the ladies, they would have to sit from one quarterly meeting to the other; and that was not all; at the next election they must be represented by at least one Lady from each Township."

Neglecting to point out that there was no stipulation against women property owners voting at the municipal level of government, Bigelow noted to roars of laughter that the petitioners included "girls from 10 to 14 years of age, old maids and married women." The Georgeville innkeeper then "called upon the Lord to protect him and deliver him from this evil." When several councillors spoke in favour of receiving the petition in any case, Bigelow appealed to their sense of masculine pride by stating that "there must be something wrong with men, if they put their wives and daughters to ask for something they were ashamed to ask for themselves." Neither tactic worked, however, for the petition was received and a small blow thereby struck for women's rights during an era of significant reversals.[56]

We have seen in our discussion of the temperance issue that there was also some debate among the councillors concerning liquor licences, but, for the most part, Stanstead County's municipal government continued to operate smoothly. By 1851 lands in arrears for taxes had begun to be advertised in the local newspaper, and the annual budget had reached approximately £200.[57] Final decisions might be made at the county level, but the initiative for local improvements came from the sub-divisions within each township, and the mill rate varied accordingly.

As for the region as a whole, the municipal election returns for 1849–50 reveal that contests were held in all but two or three of the thirty-one townships listed, though that list included only one township from division number two of Drummond County.[58] Within that division it was reported that no elections had taken place in Tingwick or Wotton townships, reportedly due to apathy, or in Stanfold, Arthabaska, and the other Bois-Francs townships because of dissatisfaction that the county council meetings were to be held in Kingsey. The two Kingsey councillors were in an ironic position, given their township's opposition to Drummondville for the same reasons during the district council era, but they argued that the leading roads from Warwick and Wotton converged in Kingsey, even if it was at the edge of the municipality. Nevertheless, no public meeting was held to appoint local officers, and the road law became completely suspended.[59]

Drummond number two again failed to report a mayor or secretary-treasurer for 1851–52, and neighbouring Megantic County remained in essentially the same position. Councillors had evidently been elected in at least some of the Megantic townships, but a petition signed by residents from Halifax and four other townships in 1850 complained that there had still been no quorum for a council meeting. The petition blamed the bad state of the roads and requested that township councils be reinstated within a county-based system, with Megantic being divided in half like Drummond. Another petition from the opposite end of the sprawling county, near Lake St Francis, complained justifiably that the village of Leeds was too far away as the county seat and registry office, since it required fifty to ninety miles of travel through Dorchester and Lotbinière counties.[60]

The 1850 municipal reform act did address this problem by declaring that Megantic County would be divided in two once the boundary and two suitable municipal seats could be determined. As we noted in chapter one, however, this provision cost the county's MLA, Dunbar Ross, his seat even though he attempted to avoid alienating voters by leaving the choices to a local meeting with two delegates from each township. When a majority of two voted for the largely French-speaking township of Halifax as the seat for a northwestern division, the two delegates from Leeds reminded Ross that their township had strongly opposed the meeting as "an undue interference with the Government's prerogative as well as with the vested rights of this township" as the current municipal headquarters.[61] There were also protests from Tring, which lost the seat for the southeastern division to Forsyth, but the petitioners conceded that the most important matter was to have the division made without delay. The government did accept the will of the majority at the May meeting, but the arrangement was short-lived since new constituency boundaries were drawn for the Eastern Townships in 1853, when Leeds once again became the municipal seat for a much smaller Megantic County.[62]

The temporary division of Megantic into two municipalities in 1851 was not the only reform introduced between 1847 and the enactment of L.T. Drummond's sweeping Municipal and Road Bill in 1855. Much of the pressure came from the missionary priests of the Bois-Francs who demanded a system which would be more effective against the absentee proprietors who were said to be hindering French-Canadian colonization. But the reform ministry hesitated to extend the provisions of the Baldwin Municipal Act of 1849 to Canada East because of the hostile reception that compulsory school taxes were receiving. The government did, nevertheless, expand the taxing powers of Canada East's municipal authorities by legislation in 1850 by reducing from five years to six months the period allowed for payment of taxes before landed property would be seized. This bill also permitted any township with three hundred souls to declare itself a separate municipal body, as requested by a petition from Windsor, Brompton, Shipton, and Melbourne in 1849. Finally, it empowered councils to impose a small annual levy for unspecified general purposes.[63]

The following year, reflecting the degree of popular unrest in the province, councils were given the authority to repair or replace property or buildings damaged or destroyed "by any incendiary, mob, tumultuous assembly or riotous persons."[64] Further amendment of the act in 1851 took the important step of declaring that court judgments were no longer necessary before selling lands for taxes in arrears.[65] Significant as this reform was, LaFontaine had actually planned to introduce more wide-sweeping legislation in 1851. As with the 1855 act, his bill would have reinstated the township/parish level of government while maintaining the county councils as courts of appeal or revision as well as bodies to deal with larger projects. There was even a provision in the 1851 bill for five delegates from each county council to meet in order to discuss municipal works which involved the broader district.

These measures appear to have met with general approval in the Eastern Townships, though the Sherbrooke Council again opposed decentralization,[66] but the same cannot be said of the provision in the 1851 bill to introduce a government-appointed officer with the traditional title of grand-voyer to be given sweeping powers beyond the control of the municipalities. First proposed two years earlier by Dr Thomas Boutillier, who was the MLA for St Hyacinthe and a speculator in Eastern Townships wild land, the grand-voyer would appoint councillors in the event that the ratepayers refused to hold an election, and perform the councillors' duties if they refused to do so.[67] Even within the smoothest-functioning municipality, the grand-voyer would have powers that paralleled and surpassed those of the council, including the approval of any building to be constructed for municipal purposes.

This office was clearly designed primarily for the French-Canadian colonization zone, where the municipal system was failing to encourage development. The *Stanstead Journal* complained that such powers were "liable to be abused in the hands of incompetent or unprincipled persons." Likewise, a petition signed by 114 residents of Shipton, Melbourne, and vicinity protested that the bill "affects to give to the rate payers in the rural Districts of Lower Canada the control of their local improvements by means of a Council, but by reason of the extraordinary powers confided to a functionary called a Grand Voyer, the independence & consequently the usefulness of such Council, appears ... to be quite destroyed."[68] Finally, the Sherbrooke Council asked its MLA to prevent the bill from affecting the six Eastern Townships counties. Because the existing law was functioning in the region "without much difficulty," it would be unjust to tax its ratepayers to support a functionary "appointed by, and accountable to, the Executive alone."[69]

While wide-ranging reform was postponed in 1851, presumably because of opposition to the grand-voyers' powers, the government continued to feel pressured to make the settlement frontier more accessible to French-Canadian colonists. As a result, it introduced a provisional bill inspired by Thomas Fortier, MLA for Nicolet and chairman of the Special Committee, "to enquire into the causes which prevent or retard the settlement of the Eastern Townships." Known as "l'acte pour faciliter l'établissement des townships de l'Est dans le Bas-Canada," Fortier's amended bill would empower the province to collect land taxes in Nicolet, Megantic, Drummond, Sherbrooke, and Stanstead counties in order to apply the money to unfinished colonization roads leading into the region. Unoccupied or unimproved land would pay one and a half pennies per acre, while improved lots situated within a mile of these roads would pay one penny per acre, and other land a half-penny per acre.[70]

This bill reflected petitions from the Bois-Francs demanding taxes of tuppence per acre on all lots with less than five improved acres,[71] but it was no more popular in the southern townships than its predecessor had been. The grand jury for the District of St Francis declared that it had "heard with surprise and regret that it is the intention of Government to introduce a Bill into Parliament for the taxation of lands in the Townships for the purpose of making roads in other sections of the Province."[72] And the *Stanstead Journal* expressed uncharacteristic outrage:

A piece of gross tyranny and injustice! The tax proposed to be levied upon Shefford and Missisco Counties will amount to £1,000 annually, and what special advantage are they to receive from building roads not one of which enters their limits? Why should the improved farms in either of these counties, or Stanstead County be taxed to build a bridge over the St Francis between Wendover and

Grantham? or a road from Arthabaska through the Seigniories to the River St Lawrence? or the *Blandford Road*, leading through the *Fief Dufort*, to the St Lawrence? Is that road through the wild lands of the Townships? We should like to know upon what principle the Townships are to be taxed for these roads?[73]

With seigneuries paying no tax for the colonization roads passing through them, one correspondent stated bluntly that the bill was a plot "to settle certain wild lands in the Townships with French Canadians at the expense of the people who are already settled in the country." With the forthcoming election in mind, he concluded with the question, "Are the yeomanry of the Townships prepared to submit to such tyrannical interference with rights which have been granted them for the purpose of self-legislation upon their local affairs?"[74]

Fortier's bill did become an issue in the general election of December 1851, though we have seen that the deciding factor in Marcus Child's defeat as the government candidate in Stanstead was the route taken by the St Lawrence and Atlantic Railway. The protests were obviously effective in any case, for Fortier's bill never did pass. The *Stanstead Journal* was willing to concede in 1852 that where the influence of the large landed proprietors was too great, the government should pass a law taxing the wild lands of these younger counties "for the purpose of inducing the opening up of new Townships."[75] However, the key to collecting such taxes would be reform of the municipal system rather than its circumvention. The municipal councils had already gained the authority to auction lots for non-payment of taxes in 1851. To make even those in the colonization zone effective, Drummond's Municipal and Road Act of 1855 simply reinstituted the township/parish level of government in conjunction with the existing county municipalities (henceforth to consist of local mayors), and made each local council legally accountable for the maintenance of its roads and bridges.[76]

It took approximately fifteen years before a stable municipal system was established in Canada East, and there were many adjustments to make at the local level thereafter. From the start, however, residents in the longer-settled southern part of the Eastern Townships demonstrated a strong desire to bring such a system into effective operation so that they could break out of their social and economic isolation. In November 1848, for example, a correspondent to the *Stanstead Journal* wrote that taxes were "the price we pay for the security of life and property." He asked rhetorically, "Shall we deteriorate from our proud position and go back again to the scenes of the dark ages, through the fears of the no-tax men; or the narrow-minded selfishness of those who can see no merit or benefit in any measure that does not directly tend to increase the contents of their own purse?"[77] There was more hostility to municipal institutions in the northern British and French-Canadian colonization zones where property qualifications could only be met by a few individuals, broader community identities had not had time to develop, and impoverished settlers resented paying taxes while absentee proprietors escaped the same exactions.

Indeed, nowhere in the Eastern Townships were residents prepared to accept whatever municipal system the government decided to impose upon them. Finally, the ongoing attachment to road levies based on property location rather than assessed value may seem irrational, particularly given the enthusiasm with which district councils embraced the "grand list" during the early 1840s. It should be recalled, however, that the state authorities had insisted on limiting taxation to landed property. As a result, the general assessment system would impose an inequitable share of the burden for non-rural public works, including railway subsidies, on the farmers. On the other hand, it was to the farmers' advantage to have villagers contributing to the construction and maintenance of roads and bridges, and rural concerns were finally addressed when the 1855 reform act introduced a business tax and decentralized the municipal system once again. As we shall see in the following chapters, this was also the direction in which the people were pushing the public schools system during the 1840s.

6 The Demise of Voluntarism: School Reform to 1846

The government of Lower Canada first established an elementary school system for the population as a whole in 1801, with the founding of the Royal Institution for the Advancement of Learning. The governor-in-council appointed not only the central administrative body, but also the commissioners in any parish or township which wished to open a Royal Institution school. While the responsibility for hiring and paying for the teachers remained with the government, the commissioners oversaw the construction of school buildings, which were to be financed by the local population.

Any chance this highly centralized state initiative may have had for acceptance by the Roman Catholic hierarchy was nullified by the appointment of the colony's Anglican bishop as the Royal Institution's president. In addition, Protestant ministers were to act as school inspectors. No more than seventeen French-Canadian localities had established a Royal Institution school by 1824 when new legislation permitted the parish church councils (fabriques) to use one-quarter of their annual revenues to finance elementary schools.[1] This legislation obviously did not apply to the Protestant population, with its voluntarist system of church support, but there were forty-five Royal Institution schools operating within eighteen of the Eastern Townships during the 1820s.[2]

Significant as the Royal Institution's role may have been in the region, religious dissenters resented Anglican attempts to control education. The government's third initiative, the Assembly Schools Act of 1829, was therefore welcomed by the Eastern Townships, whose six newly established constituencies had increased the political pressure for school reform. The government would now provide school funds to five trustees (syndics) who had been elected by a public assembly of parish or township property owners. The legislation provided for a grant of one-half the cost of constructing each schoolhouse, to a maximum of £50, and towards each teacher's salary a subsidy of £20 a year plus 10s. for every student whose family could not afford to pay fees.[3]

The population was not required to contribute to the non-building expenses of the school system, but the government exerted a measure of control by insisting that the trustees submit an annual report to the Assembly before funds would be granted. It also created the position of school visitor in 1831 to ensure that the reports were accurate and the schools conducted in a satisfactory manner. This control was augmented considerably the following year when the teachers now needed a certificate of competence signed by a clergyman, a justice of the peace, and the senior militia officer, or at least two of the foregoing three. The new legislation also obliged teachers to keep a daily journal, and to draft yearly reports to be signed by the trustees as well as by their MLA. Finally, it specified the length of the school year, required students to be between the ages of five and fifteen if their parents were not to pay more than the 2s. fee (which had been reduced from 3s. 4d.), and limited the number who could receive free schooling to ten per school.[4]

With no established educational bureaucracy, the deputies enjoyed a good deal of influence within the new school system through their Permanent Committee on Education and Schools. Members of the Legislative Assembly now allocated the government grant to their respective constituencies, a source of patronage which Arthur Buller deplored in his report on education for the Durham commission. He claimed that the politicians exercised a power over the teachers, who depended upon them for their salaries, "which was too often propitiated by acts of political subserviency."[5] Furthermore, the deputies acted as school visitors, which allowed them to regulate local conflicts over the location of schoolhouses, mediate disputes between trustees and teachers, and make decisions about the boundaries of school districts. Although they shared the office of visitor with each county's legislative councillor, senior justice of the peace, highest ranking militia officer, and minister of the largest religious denomination, Buller claimed that the MLAs effectively controlled the whole power of visitation.[6]

Even if the Assembly schools system was susceptible to a degree of political abuse, it did allow for a substantial measure of local control through the elected trustees, and it did provide generous financial assistance in an era of increasing economic hardship. It would therefore become a popular option throughout the province, with nearly half the children aged six to thirteen enrolled in school in 1831 despite the Catholic clergy's resentment of its loss of influence.[7] According to the return of a school visitor in the county of Sherbrooke in 1831, there were fifty schools of various denominations for the 7,104 inhabitants.[8] During his visit of the previous summer, the archdeacon, George J. Mountain, commented:

It is gratifying to see the number of schools established throughout the townships, and increased by the late grants of the provincial parliament. Few or none of them, I believe, are inefficient. The teachers are generally Americans, and the books used are chiefly procured from the States. But no republican kind of objection to render obeisance seems to be inculcated among them, for the little barefooted boys and girls rarely fail to make their bow and curtsey to the traveler as he passes.[9]

A less flattering picture was painted by the Reverend J.L. Alexander of Leeds Township, who complained to the Assembly's Permanent Committee on Education in 1836 that grants were being distributed to districts with no school buildings; household heads were failing to supply firewood, thereby causing illness among the often malnourished and poorly dressed children; and poor salaries were confining teaching to the ignorant or the vicious and unprincipled who did more harm than good. Leeds may have been a particularly poor area of recent settlement, but similar observations were made in submissions to Buller from longer-established townships. John Grannis, who had sat as a reform MLA for Stanstead from 1834 until he resigned in 1837, claimed that in his township of Hatley several local teachers either had no certificates or were not qualified to teach, that the trustees were incompetent, and that the school visitors were shirking their duty.[10]

Grannis appears to have been largely concerned about the schools' effectiveness, and basically the same criticisms would be made about the school system in the 1840s and thereafter. A more fundamental critique was made by another reformer, Stephen Randall of Shefford Township. A former publisher of the *Hamilton Free Press*, Randall had been financially ruined by the Family Compact before retreating to his native Eastern Townships, where he became preceptor of the Frost Village Academy in the late 1830s. In his submission to the Buller commission the Anglican-educated Randall revealed himself to be an uncompromising critic of what he called the American schools system prevalent in the region. He began by stating that the defects could be summarized "in three words – bad schoolhouses – bad teachers – bad books." He then complained that the teachers were "generally American, hired by the month at wages less than those of a labouring man, boarded round as itinerants among the inhabitants who employ them, compelled to accommodate themselves to the prejudices and ignorance of the parents and to humour the indolent habits of the children, during their temporary engagement of three, or at most six months."

While Randall did not mention the political values imparted by the American teachers and their books, he considered that public grants without fundamental reform would be of no benefit. In a telling metaphor, he proclaimed: "As well might government attempt to convert the peasantry of the country into a well-disciplined army by giving them the pay of regular troops and leaving them to choose their own drill sergeants and field exercise." What was needed was "an active and efficient system of public instruction under the entire control and direction of the government ... The schoolhouses must be built, the books furnished, the teachers appointed and the rate of tuition fees and other emoluments established by the government." But Randall appears to have been less interested in social control of the masses than in establishing well-educated local elites. He stated that if there were insufficient funds to establish such a system for all, then the focus should be on the few: "In a certain sense of the word education may be said to be already general in the Eastern Townships as well as in the United States, since it is hardly possible to find a farmer or mechanic that has not been taught after a manner to read and write, yet of all the use the greater number make of these acquirements, they might as well have remained as ignorant as the French *habitans.*"[11]

Unfortunately Buller did not print the views of any of the people whom the schools actually served in the Eastern Townships. Certainly one cannot assume, as Serge Gagnon does, that the majority of the English-speaking people in Lower Canada were concerned about the liberal and democratic orientation of the education system.[12] Evidence suggests that schooling had made significant advances in the Eastern Townships during the 1830s, even if it was not of a nature to please educational reformers such as Randall. A report published by the Legislative Assembly in 1832 claimed that nearly all the school-age children in Sherbrooke and Stanstead counties were receiving an education that year, as compared with one in three for the province as a whole.[13] Less impressive is Allan Greer's estimate from the questionnaires submitted at Buller's request by fourteen English-speaking townships (mostly in the Eastern Townships region) that 55 percent of their school-age children were in school in 1836. But this was double the ratio reported for the French-speaking communities, and it does mean that virtually all the children in Sherbrooke and Stanstead could have been enrolled in school about four and half years – that is, half the time between the prescribed school ages of six and fifteen.[14] But whatever its successes or failures may have been, the publicly funded school system was moribund by 1836.

The Legislative Council had refused to pass an amended version of the school law which would have increased the allocation to schools and given the deputies even greater powers. As an alternative, the upper house's committee on schools advocated a central board to regulate educational affairs, an idea which clearly would not appeal to the Assembly. The result of the deadlock and the ensuing Rebellion was a steady diminution in government funding for the colony's schools from £25,612 in 1835 to only £3,390 in 1838. The impact was even more abrupt in the six Eastern Townships counties. Here funding declined from £4,801 (19 percent of the provincial total) in 1835 to £180 (5 percent of the total) in 1838.[15] The disruption caused by the Rebellion ensured that earlier levels of funding were not restored until 1843 (see Appendix, table A1, p. 243), though many schools had managed to remain open without government support. For example, all nine of Hatley Township's schools were operating in the fall of 1838, and in Sherbrooke County there were more schools than ever in 1840 due largely to local efforts.[16]

THE 1841 SCHOOL ACT

Buller's report to Lord Durham recommended sweeping changes to the education system, and in 1841 Lord Sydenham introduced a school act which would give ultimate responsibility for the schools to the Executive Council through the office of the superintendent of education.[17] Judging from the tenor of the Buller Report, the chief aim was to break the influence of the MLAs over the local schools, though not entirely for political reasons. The goal was also to implement a more efficient and effective educational system, but centralization would be hindered by the slow development of the state bureaucracy, and particularly by the fact that local ratepayers were not prepared to contribute towards schools without exercising some power of their own.

In order to avoid ethnic and religious tensions, the education office was soon divided in two, with effective control placed in the hands of an assistant superintendent for each section of the province. The choice for Canada East was Jean-Baptiste Meilleur, an American-trained medical doctor who had close links with the Catholic clergy despite being a former Patriote deputy.[18] Meilleur was responsible for apportioning monies from the public school fund to Sydenham's twenty-two district councils, each of which was to act as a board of education for its own territory. The district boards' duties were essentially of a financial nature: collecting taxes, which were to be levied for the first time; distributing the school fund; apportioning monies for school books; and reporting annually to the superintendent. The boards were also to establish their parishes and townships as school districts, which would each receive a share of the common school fund based on their numbers of school-age children. Each school district would have its own popularly elected commissioners, who would be responsible for overseeing construction of the schoolhouses, examining teachers whom they could also hire and fire, regulating the course of study, approving the textbooks, and visiting schools each month, as well as reporting to the district council.[19]

But, as the Sherbrooke District Council pointed out, this was an impossible work load for five unpaid officials (seven in those townships which had two municipal councillors), especially in townships with large numbers of schools.[20] From Barnston Township came the request that the number of visits required of the school commissioners be reduced. Likewise, J.S. Sabins, the recently retired principal of Sherbrooke Academy, argued that the number of commissioners was hardly adequate to visit all the schools in a thickly settled township such as Stanstead, especially since no remuneration was attached. He recommended that a commissioner be appointed to represent each local school.[21] The parish or township school districts of Canada East had since the early 1830s been sub-divided into units at the individual school level, confusingly called school districts as well. Thus, in the school district of Stanstead Township (which in turn lay within the municipal district of Sherbrooke), there were twenty-nine so-called school districts (known as school sections in Canada West), each with its own school. Sabin's recommendation for more localized representation would have resulted in unwieldy school commissions for such heavily populated townships as Stanstead, but it was later adopted in a modified form, as we shall see.

The aim of the local sub-divisions (which we will call sub-districts) was clearly to control the proliferation of schools by ensuring that their distribution conformed to a rational pattern within each township or parish, but they held a deeper significance to a population accustomed to seeing its contributions going strictly to the neighbourhood school. Sabins later made the interesting observation that "The people have generally resorted to the old method of management [by] local committees and the commissioners do but little else than sanction their proceedings. This seems the only method of successful operations here."[22]

Indeed, this was the system which had officially operated in Upper Canada prior to 1841, and it would be re-adopted there in 1843, yet it never appears to have been seriously considered by Meilleur. Perhaps one reason was that the parish, as an area designed to support a single church, was generally smaller than the rather arbitrarily defined township, which covered approximately one hundred square miles. Furthermore, the French Canadians had, since the French régime, been accustomed to electing church councils and paying assessments at the parish level, while the township had little political significance prior to the 1840s in Canada East. In any case, it was the threat that reform legislation posed to the strong sense of localism in the Eastern Townships that fuelled the opposition movement there.

And if the township school commission was considered too far removed from the local level, still further was the district council, which held exclusive taxing powers as of 1841. As Buller pointed out, by the eve of the Rebellion even the Assembly had become concerned about the level of dependency on the annual government grant. While Serge Gagnon claims that Lower Canada's English-speaking minority imposed the school tax in order to avoid subsidizing the schools of the less affluent French Canadians from the general revenue, the fact was that local school assessments had been considered by the Legislative Assembly's education committee as early as 1831. Its abortive bill of 1834 would have empowered the majority of inhabitants in a parish or township school district to impose a local school tax.[23] But the distinction between empowerment and compulsion was a crucial one, and Buller reasoned that the only way to ensure that French Canadians would send their children to schools designed to eradicate their cultural identity would be to force them to pay school taxes. The initiative would still have to come from the local level, however, since Buller favoured the American system of requiring each school district to raise by assessment on all its property holders a sum at least equivalent to the grant it was entitled to from the public treasury.[24] Presumably a district could choose not to pay such taxes, but only at the cost of sacrificing the government grant.

While Buller's proposal was adopted by the 1841 school act, any chance it had of succeeding was negated by the structural weaknesses of the district municipal system which undermined the sense of local control that existed in the American system. The most common cry from the Eastern Townships was that the schools should be entirely separated from municipal control. The general population feared that local monies, once sent to the district treasurer, would be directed to other than local purposes. Although Superintendent Meilleur supported compulsory education, he had written letters to the press in 1838 opposing school taxes, and he reported in 1843: "I know the invincible repugnance of the people to having the power of taxing them confided to persons who might make use of it for other purposes than those of education without their consent, also their strong objections to have their money carried out of their usual place of residence."[25]

Meilleur was pragmatic enough not to insist on the letter of a law whose basic flaw was so readily apparent. With most of the district councils inoperative, he appointed special commissioners in each district to distribute school subsidies according to the matching-grants system, and he instructed that the local funds need not be raised by tax assessment. Conforming schools were to have operated nine months during the year with an attendance of at least fifteen students per day, and to have submitted regular reports, but Meilleur stated that he would be willing to accept "good and sufficient" excuses for non-compliance. While conforming schools would be entitled to the traditional maximum of £20 each, assuming that this did not exceed the district's total allowable grant based on school-age population, independent schools were also allotted funds based on the local contributions they had received. Because the officers appointed by the district wardens to report the number of children aged five to sixteen were "tardy and often incapable persons," the maximum entitlement for each district was fixed according to its total population in the long-outdated 1831 census.[26]

This maximum was essentially meaningless for most districts in 1842 since local school contributions in Canada East amounted to only £9,024, while £30,000 had been set aside for school purposes. But the situation was quite different for the two municipal districts which fell almost exclusively within the Eastern Townships – Missisquoi and Sherbrooke. The former received £700 15s. of a £942 allowable maximum, and the latter its full £905 entitlement. The only other district aside from Sherbrooke to receive its maximum allowable grant was Sydenham, while the cities of Montreal and Quebec, with their greater sources of private wealth, were the only two districts to receive nothing in 1842.

A closer look at these two Eastern Townships districts reveals that in Missisquoi twenty schools operated under the schools act and twenty-two were considered to be independent (see Appendix Table A2, p. 244). Meilleur later wrote that their teachers "had refused to submit to the control of the School Commissioners."[27] They apparently paid no penalty for doing so, since each of the fourteen non-conforming schools in Dunham Township received the full £20 grant to which conforming schools were entitled. The eight independent schools in Potton received a total of only £20 15s., but this was all that their supporters had contributed. Presumably, the conforming schools each raised at least £20 to match the government grant; certainly, in Granby Township the local contributions were close to £28 per school. In addition, there were forty-one schools in Missisquoi for which no contributions were reported or credited, which must have meant that they were not in operation.

In the neighbouring municipal district of Sherbrooke, 4,472 students were taught in 146 schools scattered among thirteen township districts. Without the census-based ceiling of £905, these schools would have been entitled to £2,198, since this was the amount of money they raised locally, and all had conforming status. Meilleur's reliance on an out-dated enumeration exacted a heavy penalty on this growing frontier district with its keen interest in education.[28] While all the Sherbrooke municipal district's schools which received grants were listed as conforming, however, this term was interpreted rather loosely. The warden and MLA, Edward Hale, wrote that "the provisions of the law have been more or less fulfilled, perhaps in none has it been found practicable to fulfil [sic] all."[29]

Characteristically, Hale took a rather conservative approach towards the education system, claiming that the local inhabitants would always maintain schools, with or without government aid. Thus, in his home township of Orford, there had been no urgent need for a school to operate under the authority of elected commissioners because there was already an academy and a small independent school, presumably the one operated by the Church of England's Society for the Propagation of Christian Knowledge. Hale simply ignored the fact that Orford and Ascot townships were the site of the burgeoning industrial centre of Sherbrooke whose labouring newcomers, mostly French Canadians, were in no position to support schools without government assistance. In 1844 a French-speaking commissioner reported that there was still only one school to serve the growing population in Orford due to the poverty of the inhabitants and the lack of capable teachers.[30]

As for neighbouring Ascot, five local notables complained that the district council should have allocated their township a grant for 1842 despite the fact that no schools had been reported in operation. The statute simply stated that funds would be distributed according to the number of children resident between the ages of five and sixteen, information which they had reported. The complainants argued that the purpose of the Common Schools Act was not to maintain schools but to establish them. In Sherbrooke and other parts of Ascot three to four hundred children "either have no schools to attend, or are unable from poverty to attend the schools within their districts." Parents were willing to erect schools if they could receive help, but the result of Meilleur's policy was that "competence will be helped, and poverty left destitute."[31] It nevertheless appears that some schools were operating in Ascot in 1842, for a Sherbrooke resident wrote to Meilleur that the problem lay with the district council's decision to distribute the fund based on the length of time the schools were in operation, with no reference to the number of children in the schools. The Ascot commissioners had apparently failed to report the enrolment, and editor J.S. Walton of the *Sherbrooke Gazette* reassured Meilleur that it was through their "neglect or *obstinacy* that the Reports were not made out."[32]

A more justifiable complaint came from the local school district of Clifton, Hereford and Auckland, which was deprived of a subsidy for sending a letter to the education office rather than filing a report with the district council.³³ But, while neither the Clifton or Ascot school districts were funded for any of the schools they had in operation in 1842, in at least one case the authorities erred on the side of generosity. The combined district of Bury, Lingwick, and Westbury received full compensation in 1843 for two schools which were taught by the same teacher for three days each per week. Rather than paying this individual a double salary, the school commission in 1844 sought permission from Meilleur to devote half its grant to deficiencies in pay for other teachers, or to the purchase of books.³⁴

Many such irregularities may have slipped through the cracks in 1842, but Meilleur was already engaged in a campaign to have the school commissioners conform to the school act as closely as practicable. Thus, Compton Township was eventually recognized as having sixteen conforming schools in 1842, but the superintendent had threatened to withhold the grant on the grounds that the school returns were not properly filled out. In return the chairman, the Reverend C.P. Reid, complained that they had not received the required forms until the last quarter of the year. He also publicly accused Meilleur of counseling him to break the law by suggesting that school commissions should assume the duties of municipal councils when the latter refused to provide property assessments. However, J.S. Sabins of Sherbrooke reassured Meilleur that the Compton commissioners had become generally well disposed towards him since his tour of the Townships the previous fall. It had left an impression "which will not be easily effaced *even by the influence of a clergyman of the established church.*" The ever-scrupulous Meilleur nevertheless asked Sabins to write a letter to the local press in his support. He confided bitterly that the school commissioners of Compton "can boast of being the only ones, *in the whole Province!* whose conduct has been to me a subject of persecution and grief."³⁵

Another of the Reverend Reid's objections to the school regulations was that they required a minimum attendance of fifteen students per day despite "the fearful sickness" that was then raging. Provision would be made in 1846 for "periods of epidemic or contagious diseases,"³⁶ but in 1844 the chairman of the Brome Township school commission pointed out that attendance levels varied from season to season, as they reflected the labour needs of parents, weather conditions, and the state of the roads. Rather than requiring a daily attendance of fifteen students, the education office should take the yearly average into account. But the same policy appears to have remained in effect until 1849, when a local school district was only required to have fifteen school-age children within its boundaries, even if fewer attended during the year.[37]

Local residents also complained about the length of the school year, for much the same reasons. From Stukely, for example, a number of leading citizens protested that it was impossible to have children attend a school for nine months of the year. Six months would be more reasonable. Likewise, the district council of Sherbrooke declared formally that the prescribed school year was impracticable "in the Country sections of this District, where from the limited circumstances of the people they are called upon to avail themselves of the labour of their children for their agricultural pursuits."[38] Meilleur was convinced by these arguments, and in his report of December 1842 he recommended that the school year be reduced to six months. After the 1843 school bill failed to pass, Meilleur informed a school commissioner that he would recommend that schools open for less than nine months should receive a grant. The 1845 school act did officially reduce the school year, though only by one month to eight months.[39]

Meanwhile, the district councils of Sherbrooke and Missisquoi also protested in 1842 about the fees of 1s. 3d. per month levied for each student, and a petition from Compton Township complained of "the hardly to be understood complexity and complication of the requirements" as well as "the burdensome drudgery" imposed on the school commissioners. Reverend Fleming and others from Melbourne stated simply that the act was not suitable to the Eastern Townships, "where the settlements are in most cases new, and the settlers for the most part poor."[40]

Despite the outpouring of criticism, and not only from the Eastern Townships, Meilleur took comfort in the degree to which the people of Canada East had been brought into conformity within a year of the school act's implementation. He claimed in his report for 1842 that parish and township school districts had been established with or without the sanction of the district councils, school commissioners had been almost universally elected for 1842 and 1843, sums had been raised – voluntarily or otherwise – for the common schools, and reports had been submitted either to the district warden or directly to the superintendent of education. The main obstacle to the fulfilment of the letter of the law was the lack of co-operation on the part of the municipal councils for reasons not connected with the education system. Without waiting for authorization from the government, Meilleur recommended to the school commissions that they take over the municipal councils' task of drawing up tax assessments.[41]

Meilleur's compromises with the schools act helped to ensure that only twenty-three of more than 1,300 schools in Canada East were reported to be independent in 1843, as compared with nearly half in 1842. An additional thirteen claimed dissentient status. In the Missisquoi municipal district, the number of schools increased from forty-two in 1842 to ninety-nine in 1843, with all but ten categorized as conforming schools in the latter year. Local contributions in Missisquoi multiplied at a still higher rate, from £700 15s. to £2,240 14s. 3d. but the government grant increased by only £241 because the £942 ceiling remained despite Meilleur's recommendation to use the recent census as a basis for allocation of the schools grant (see appendix, Tables A2 and A3).[42] The 2,522 students who were enrolled in Missiquoi represented 41 percent of that district's children between the ages of five and sixteen as enumerated in 1842,[43] a ratio which would increase substantially by the end of the decade.

Once again there were no independent schools in the Sherbrooke District in 1843, but curiously enough the number of public schools in operation there declined from 146 to 121. Ascot Township actually reported five schools for the first time, but elsewhere the decrease was greatest among the longest-settled townships.[44] It is not that there were fewer schools open in 1843 but rather that their reports were submitted too late, for Meilleur was now enforcing a 29 July deadline. Despite the drop in its number of schools reported, the Sherbrooke District still more than qualified for its severely limited grant of £905. In sharp contrast, the region's northern townships, within the Chaudière and Nicolet municipal districts, reported only twenty-two schools with 533 students. For the first time, however, a number of these schools were located in the Bois-Francs area, then being colonized by French Canadians.

A more detailed picture of how the schools system actually operated is provided by the report submitted in 1842 by the Sherbrooke District Council.[45] All but twelve of the 152 teachers were listed as British subjects by birth, a surprisingly high ratio given the complaints about American teachers during the pre-Rebellion period. Some of the schools, and not necessarily the largest, were taught by more than one person, suggesting that they were employed consecutively rather than at the same time. The common practice had been that men taught the older children during the winter term, and women the younger ones during the summer. Archdeacon Mountain reported in 1830, for example, that in Melbourne Township the master of the Royal Institution school

teaches himself only in the Winter, some Winters in one part, others in another part of the Township, and during the Summer provides four women, paid out of his own salary, all teaching at once in difference places. This is the kind of system universally preferred & very generally adopted in the Townships where the stouter boys cannot be spared for School during the labours of the Summer, and the girls and lesser boys can of course be taught equally well by women – the former thus learning also the use of the needle.[46]

It appears that by the 1840s teaching was no longer subcontracted in the public schools system, with the result that school commissions complained that they were forced to pay the male teachers at the end of the winter term, long before receiving the school grant, yet they were not allowed to borrow money to do so.[47] It may follow that one reason why teaching in the Province of Canada was becoming feminized was that the subsidy system made it much easier to pay a single teacher at the end of the school year, and it was more affordable for women to teach the older winter classes than for men to take over the younger summer ones.[48] Already, according to the Sherbrooke District's report for 1842, most schools were taught by single individuals who were responsible for students of all ages, and female teachers outnumbered males by eighty-four to sixty-eight, even if one assumes that all those identified by initials in place of Christian names were men.

The Sherbrooke report also indicates that men were not paid more than women based on gender. Comparing the first two teachers listed for Barnston and Barford, for example, Amanda Lock of school district number one received £12 18s. 6d for teaching twenty-two children for four months, while Pierce Wheeler of district number four received £15 15s. for teaching twenty-nine students for five months.

One would expect another criterion for differential salaries to be education and experience, though nearly all the teachers simply reported "one" as their number of qualifications, whatever that may have meant. Only in Stanstead Township was there a significant number listed as having two or three, but this does not appear to have made much impact on salaries. For example, John P. Lee, listed as a three, received £33 15s. for teaching thirty-six and a half students (eight of them older than sixteen), during a nine-month period, while Mary Batchelor, who was only qualified as a one, received almost as much as Lee (£31 15s.) for teaching half as many students, all under the age of sixteen, and for a shorter period of time (eight months). Such individual discrepancies should not be too surprising given that teachers were hired at the local level, their salaries constituted most of the school costs, and voluntary contributions (as well as assessments) would vary from place to place and from one year to the next.

Table 6.1 suggests, however, that in comparing one school district to another, the variation in the average teacher's salary largely reflected the number of students and the length of time they were taught. Thus, the two teachers in Barford Township received the same average salary as the fifteen in the Eaton school district where the average number of

Table 6.1
Selected Date (expressed in means) for the School Districts in the Sherbrooke Municipal District, 1842

School District	Schools	Students	Months taught	Salaries (£)
Barnston	23	30.7	4.3	12.7
Barford	2	26.0	3.7	10.0
Compton	16	29.7	5.2	13.4
Eaton, Newport, Ditton, & Clinton	15	26.5	3.7	10.0
Dudswell	4	19.8	9.0	23.9
Hatley	12	45.6	8.3	27.0
Shipton	10	38.5	6.2	19.5
Windsor	2	23.0	2.5	6.8
Bury, Lingwick, & Westbury	6	41.7	7.0	15.8
Brompton	3	31.3	5.0	13.5
Melbourne	8	32.0	5.9	17.1
Stanstead	29	22.4	7.0	22.7
Totals*	130	30.3	5.8	17.2

* The averages for the municipal district as a whole were calculated from each individual entry rather than from the above school district averages, which accounts for the slight discrepancies in results.
Source: Annual Report to the Superintendent of Education by the Municipal Council of the Sherbrooke District, for the year ending 31st December 1842, no. 141, LR, E13, ANQQ.

students and months taught was almost the same. The teachers of relatively prosperous Stanstead Township were somewhat more favoured, with their relatively high salaries and light teaching loads, but differences in wealth from one township to another were generally reflected in the number of months the schools remained open rather than in teachers' salaries. Finally, Table 6.1 reveals that with an average salary of £17 for an average work period of less than half a year, teachers' monthly remuneration in the Sherbrooke District in 1842 was not far below the reported average of £36 per year for Canada East in 1846–47.[49]

There were also columns in the district council's report concerning the general progress and proficiency of the students, as well as the conduct of the teachers. For most of the Sherbrooke District these were simply listed as "good," though Richard Smith of Dudswell was said to be "indifferent" while the other teacher in the same school, Amanda

Smith, was rated as "quite good." Meilleur's expectations were clearly unrealistic if he thought that more detailed information on teachers would be provided by single unpaid commissioners who were obliged to visit all the schools in their respective townships. It certainly appears, however, that in the Townships of the early 1840s female teachers were beginning to be considered no less competent than their male counterparts, though it is also likely that parsimonious commissioners simply refused to pay men a higher salary than women.[50] Both explanations are reflected in the decision of the East Farnham school commissioners to defeat a motion in 1845 stating that "a man teacher should receive more wages than a woman teacher, as he considers a man teacher more competent at all seasons of the year." Not surprisingly, the township's annual report for the year ending 1 July 1846 records that only four of the twelve teachers were men.[51]

We have seen that Meilleur resorted to the 1831 census because the district councils failed to enumerate the number of school-age children in 1842, but the commissioners for several townships did so, making it possible to calculate their enrolment rates in 1843. In Stanstead Township there were 1,271 children of school age, with an enrolment of 642 within this age range. (Meilleur's statistical report claimed a total of 733, with no age specified – see appendix, Table A3.) In neighbouring Barnston and Barford, the ratio was similar, for the census submitted by this school district's commissioners recorded 860 children aged five to sixteen, while Meilleur's statistical report claims that there were 418 students enrolled during the year. Much the same picture emerges from a report for Dunham Township in the Nicolet municipal district for the school quarter ending 30 September 1842. It lists 140 students aged five to sixteen attending seven schools, or slightly more than half the 258 children of that age range in the township.[52]

These ratios, likely as high as any in the region at that time, are similar to those noted above for a number of townships in 1836. More meaningful would have been data on enrolment between the ages of five or six and eleven or twelve. But given that 103 students within the Sherbrooke municipal district (3 percent) were older than sixteen in 1842, it is clear that not everyone viewed formal education as something to be acquired in a regimented fashion. Stanstead deputy Ebenezer Peck informed the Assembly's Committee on Education in 1832 that most children began to work the land at the age of eight or nine, and could thereafter only attend classes during the winter. As a result, many were not ready to pursue superior studies at the age of fifteen. To take one example, when the sixteen-year-old John McGregor was apprenticed to a Shipton tanner in 1835, his contract stipulated that he would be provided with suitable school books and "with the privilege and tuition of the District School for eight weeks of each of the *four* following winter seasons."[53]

Furthermore, the meaning of the enrolment statistics is somewhat ambiguous. Meilleur insisted that they be based on the daily attendance rather than the number actually enrolled in each school. It is unlikely that many commissioners adhered to this regulation in 1842, nevertheless the enrolment ratios in the townships examined above do not mean that half the school-age population attended classes for the full school year. Theoretically, nearly all school-age children could have attended classes for one session or the other of the school year when government statistics suggest that only half were enrolled.

No detailed school reports were published for 1844 and 1845, but the table providing data for each municipal district (see appendix, Table A4) reveals that in Sherbrooke and Missisquoi there was a steady growth in the number of schools and of students. Popular enthusiasm for public schooling appeared to be increasing. In April 1844, for example, the chairman for Eaton Township wrote to Meilleur that only a year earlier he had "found great appathy [*sic*] and negligence on the part of the parents all they seemed to care was to do just enough to get the Government Allowance as it would help them to pay their teacher at the next meeting of the Commissioners." But each commissioner called the parents together on his next visit and delivered "a short lecture on the importance of education." As a result, "we found on our last visit at the close of the winter term that the scholars had made considerable progress in their studies and that the teachers had been faithful in the discharge of their respective duties and the parents seemed to take more of an interest in the right education of their children."[54]

THE 1845 SCHOOL ACT

The Metcalfe constitutional crisis of 1843 had disrupted the government's plan to reform the school act that year, but all educational matters were finally removed from the hands of the municipal authorities by the school act of 1845. Furthermore, in recognition of the persistent strength of localism, the number of representatives in each township or parish school commission was to reflect the number of school subdistricts, with a minimum of five and a maximum of nine members.[55] The intention was clearly to permit most schools to have their own commissioner, or to share one with a neighbouring sub-district.

Much to Meilleur's displeasure, Denis-Benjamin Papineau had also bowed to the popular will by adding the voluntary option to the school bill at the last minute, though such contributions were supposed to be collected by 1 August, which was before the fall harvest when farmers were likely to have surplus funds. Interestingly enough, compulsory assessments were no longer a contentious issue in Canada West where the public had long been subjected to taxes by the road laws. There, the alternative to property assessment was considered to be the rate bill, known simply as student fees in Canada East where they remained compulsory but fixed at a relatively low level. Indeed, these fees went directly to the teacher, and could not be counted towards the sum raised to match the government grant.[56]

Meilleur was also upset by what he called a clerical error. It apparently left municipal councils (now operating at the parish/township level) with the responsibility of authorizing a property assessment list if one had not been previously ordered. In Meilleur's opinion, this limited school commissioners to the power of assessing for the construction of schoolhouses. Even within this restricted domain his advice was that they avoid litigation by resorting to voluntary contributions or, what he termed in one instance, "zealous voluntary sacrifice" of the local inhabitants.[57]

The taxation authority for schools in Canada West remained in the hands of municipal councils rather than school commissions without any apparent problem. But the municipal system seems to have continued to be rather ineffective throughout much of Canada East prior to the passing of Drummond's reform bill in 1855. While this was not true of much of the Eastern Townships (as we have seen), the official restoration of the voluntarist option – circumscribed though it may have been – appears to have ensured that the assessment function of municipal councils would remain irrelevant as far as school funding in many areas was concerned.

The school commissioners for Ascot did request that the municipal council levy a school assessment in 1845,[58] but many spokesmen from the Eastern Townships clearly felt that the well-entrenched voluntarist system had operated effectively enough for local educational needs. Referring to the abortive school bill of 1843, Stanstead's MLA, Marcus Child, wrote to his wife:

Mr Neilson & Black of Quebec, Jones of Missisquoi and myself, spoke against one part of the bill – that was, give us power to raise one half & we will do it – "*but dont compel us to do so – by the force of executive power against the will of the people*" – Compulsion is not agreeable in any thing – not even in a good one, and therefore – I defended the District of Sherbrooke from the imputation that such a provision in the law would cast upon us – We did not deserve it – we supported our schools from the settlement of the county in 1795 to the year 1829 – without any aid from Gov.t and from 1829 to 1836 we felt very grateful for public aid, which we received from the Prov.l Legislature. and our habits of attention to schools, that we brot with us to the country, – had found us in a situation to receive the greatest benefit from that aid – our schools were established – and hence the money granted could be at once, and well expended.[59]

James Reid, the Anglican minister for St Armand East, expressed the same sentiment in 1845: "I have known the Townships for 33 years, and during the whole of that long period ... I have had something to do with the superintendence of common schools, and therefore can testify from my own personal knowledge that coercive taxation for the maintenance of schools is both uncalled for and deplorably injurious. The people can, and are willing to, support their schools in the usual way. If our fellow subjects of french extraction require that method, let them have it, without putting us under the same yoke."[60]

That Child and Reid were articulating popular opinion was demonstrated by several disputes which arose as a result of the ambiguity of the 1845 schools act. In one case, the Shefford school commissioners quickly seized upon their newly established authority to have a tax levied by the municipality. In response, a public meeting chaired by militia captain D. Wood pointed out that the legislation also provided for the option of a voluntary subscription equal to the eligible government grant: "It is the opinion of this meeting that this clause expresses the desire of an indulgent Government to meet the wishes and provide for the wants and exigencies of the people according to their feelings and circumstances, a point which has been overlooked in this township by the board of School Commissioners and by the Municipal Council." The meeting protested further that assessors had been appointed and penalties imposed without steps being taken to determine the amount of money required for municipal and school purposes, "without consulting the wishes of the people, and regardless of the well known opposition to an unequal direct taxation which exists in this township." The final resolution stated that the inhabitants should proceed immediately to raise by voluntary subscription an amount equal to the government school grant.[61]

Opposition to taxation was expressed still more forcefully in Melbourne Township when an election was called for school commissioners as well as municipal councillors. According to the chairman, "the fear of taxation operated so thoroughly upon the more ignorant portion of the meeting that there was an organized opposition to the election of any officers either municipal or educational." Municipal officials were eventually elected after "some manifestations of riotous conducts," but the justice of the peace decided to dissolve the meeting at this point "rather than endanger the peace of the community."[62]

It is difficult to judge exactly where the roots of the local hostility to taxation lay, for no reasons were recorded in the petitions and correspondence. Speaking of his jurisdiction as a whole in 1846, Meilleur wrote darkly that systematic opposition to the school law came from "certain persons whose previous conduct in affairs of a public and common interest, as well as their social position, afforded grounds for expecting from them an altogether different conduct, in respect to a measure of vital necessity for the country." The tax assessment system would presumably spread the burden more widely, yet Marcus Child noted in 1843 that the school contributions had come from the wealthier farmers, and the commissioners for Barnston and Barford reported that "the monies that have been paid in many instances have been paid from a few individuals a great number not being able to pay."[63] By spreading the burden more widely, the tax assessment should have lightened the burden on the local elites. Perhaps they feared that the decline of voluntarism would undermine their community prestige, including their moral right to control the school commission. It may be significant, for example, that the names of the school sub-districts and the schools themselves had been personalized. Thus, Archdeacon Mountain noted while on his official tour of the region in 1829: "I preached ... in a back part of Melbourne, called according to the fashion of the country, the *Gallup District,* after a family who are the principal settlers, – (the *District* being the space within which the families reside whose children attend the School within those limits.)" Likewise, in 1844 a Methodist New Connexion missionary reported that he was to preach in Sergeant's schoolhouse in Stukely on 9 February, Scott's schoolhouse in Dunham on 14 February, and so on.[64]

As for the region's northern frontier, to be examined in detail in the following chapter, there was little reason for the settlers to embrace compulsory assessments as long as municipal and school authorities remained legally incapable of enforcing payment on the absentee proprietors who owned most of the land. In short, while some of the local notables clearly played a leading role in organizing the opposition to taxation, it appears unlikely that a small minority could have manipulated the movement against a system which had little to offer the general population. Rather, the main problem faced by Meilleur was more probably that the local elites initially refused to co-operate with the state in overcoming the deeply imbedded popular distaste for taxation.

Nor was this distaste simply based on material considerations, for the element of compulsion would naturally be unpopular in any community which had long operated on the voluntary principle. In Canada West opponents to free schools even charged that the idea of taxing people with no children was tyrannical and socialistic, since it took away from the working man the dignity of educating his own children, and it impinged on the right of local property holders to self government.[65]

However, localism was the most pervasive and persistent factor in the reaction of the Eastern Townships to the introduction of taxation. The families of each local community were simply concerned lest the revenue they contributed should be spent elsewhere. The superintendent himself recognized this when he criticized the unwieldy district council system in 1843: "The inhabitants of a Parish or Township will always be reluctant in carrying the amount of their taxes, sometimes a considerable distance, in order there to deposit it in the hands of a man they hardly know, and over whom they have no control ... . The people there are accustomed to transact their business 'en famille,' and an order of things so natural ought not to be done away with."[66]

Meilleur was also aware that the voluntarist system operated at a strictly local level, with the money any family contributed being directed towards its neighbourhood school rather than to a common educational fund for the township. Thus, in 1844, he recommended to the Shefford school commission that its more affluent local school districts might contribute "on behalf of the teachers of poor school districts, to ... make up a sum so as to equalize the government allocation." Another example of how school funding operated at the local level is provided by a letter from the Reverend C.P. Reid of Compton in 1846 asking: "Is it possible to lay a rate for building a school house on the particular district for which it is designed or must such rate in all cases be levied on the whole municipality?" His fellow commissioners "would not believe it possible but that each individual school District was obliged to build and keep in repair its own school house." Also, no one would pay taxes for the benefit of a school in another district even though it lay within the same township. Reid obviously did not approve of this entrenched localism, but he concluded that, as far as the Eastern Townships was concerned, the school act "in a great degree needs to be remodeled. It is not at all suited to the peculiar habits of thought that prevail among the American part of the population."[67]

The commissioners of Brome Township clearly agreed, and they were more sympathetic than Reid to the principle of local responsibility for school construction. Their spokesman remarked that work on several schools then under construction would come to a standstill if the whole municipality had to be assessed for them:

I greatly fear that what has heretofore been cheerfully done, will hereafter be accomplished step by step, at the end of legal proceedings. Several Districts in this township have, at their own expense, by the aid of what they have received from the Government, provided themselves with good and expensive houses; if these are now obliged to aid in building school houses for others who are much more able than themselves, and from whom they received no assistance, we think that the injustice will be palpable and it cannot fail to beget an immense amount of popular disgust, resistance and ill-will.[68]

Rather surprisingly, Meilleur ceded to the localist impulse insofar as the construction and repair of schools was concerned. He admitted that it would be unjust to oblige those who had built schoolhouses at their own expense to contribute to other districts from which they had received no assistance.[69] This principle would be formally adopted in the 1849 school bill.

Localism was carried even further in Shefford Township where, in 1844, school sub-districts sent their petitions for grants to build new schools directly to the education office. The school commission chairman, H. Robinson, complained to Meilleur in a rather pompous manner:

We by no means desire to be officious, nor would we knowingly obtrude our interference where it might not be profitable or acceptable, but, we cannot bear the responsible office to which we have voluntarily and legally pledged ourselves, and stand indifferent to proceedings connected therewith which cannot fail, in the issue, to produce dissatisfaction, and of consequence disorder among the people, retard the progress of education, and abuse the confidence by disparaging the responsible office of the school commissioners.[70]

The situation deteriorated when one of the township's school sub-districts, despite having no legal status as a corporation, hired a teacher whose qualifications the school commission had rejected. Meilleur himself was caught out when he sent money directly to the sub-district in question where, according to Robinson, the teacher's father was encouraging the inhabitants to rebel against the commission. That body's decision not to hire the teacher had clearly been motivated by political infighting, for his father was none other than the MLA, Dr S.S. Foster, who, was challenging the commissioners' decision to levy a tax assessment. Meilleur attempted to justify his own action by writing that it was "time for the exercise of an indulgence which cannot be continued in future to the same extent, all parties concerned being now apprised of their powers and duties respectively." A furious Robinson replied that the authority of the school commissioners had the same legal basis as did Meilleur's own as assistant superintendent. He also questioned Meilleur's motives: "Shall it be said that the Head of the Department is venal – is open to corruption from interested motives – makes use of or rather abuse of authority to maintain office? or shall we ascribe it to imposition which is but another name for incapacity?"[71]

Meilleur appears to have acted in good faith, for in his own defence he pointed out that he had received a statement from two preceptors of academies as well as a clergyman to the effect that the young Foster held a certificate of qualification. Furthermore, the school in question had been presented as having independent status, under the control of three respectable men. The government had continued to subsidize such schools to a limited extent in 1843. Meilleur insisted that "all this was done with legal and Governmental authority, in good faith, and without the least suspicion of giving thereby the slightest offense to the local School Commissioners." He concluded by stating that "The general tone of your letter is quite derogatory, and in future, I will feel it my duty not to correspond with you, unless you are pleased to do it according at least to the common rules of politeness."[72] Imbroglios such as this one undoubtedly encouraged Meilleur to adhere to the strict letter of the regulations as closely as possible, and legislation soon ended any ambiguity about how local monies were to be raised.

THE 1846 SCHOOL ACT

The inadequacy of the voluntary contributions in much of the province, coupled with the confusion over assessment responsibilities and resistance to taxation, resulted in a rapid repeal of the 1845 law and the promulgation of the first permanent act in 1846. This law would form the basis of Quebec's school system for more than a century. Meilleur had not been able to persuade the government to enact compulsory education, but the act did provide a strong inducement for parents to send their children to school by making monthly fees apply to all parents of school-age children, whether or not their children attended classes. However, there appears to have been no practicable way to enforce this much-resented policy against those whose children stayed home, so the fees effectively acted as a disincentive for poor families with large numbers of children.[73]

More enforceable was the new regulation specifying that school commissioners, now elected for a period of three years, must order a property assessment, and that they were liable to a fine of up to £5 if they failed to do so. They were also required by law to initiate prosecution against any proprietor who refused to pay school taxes. Reflecting custom and the lack of cash in the rural areas, both the annual assessments and the monthly fees could be paid in produce at prices fixed by the school commission.[74] The 1846 school law also centralized state control by providing for appointed boards of examiners in Quebec and Montreal to determine, among other things, which textbooks could be used in schools, and to examine teachers applying for certificates of qualification.[75] Most significantly, however, the new legislation effectively completed the move begun in 1845 towards locally levied school taxes. The rumblings noted above for that earlier year were an indication that the policy would not be welcomed in the Eastern Townships. And, elsewhere in the province, schools became subject to arson and vandalism, though the Guerre des Éteignoirs (Candle-Snuffers' War) would not break out in earnest until 1850. Comparatively peaceful as the resistance was in the English-speaking communities of the Eastern Townships, the situation nevertheless called for all the skills of diplomacy that Meilleur could muster.

The outline of the story appears in the statistics compiled by the education office. Despite the problems associated with the 1845 schools act, the number of schools in the territory covered by the former municipal districts of Sherbrooke and Missisquoi had increased slightly, from 255 during the first term in 1845 to 275 a year later. Enrolment had stabilized at 7,980. In Canada East as a whole, the number of students had actually increased substantially during this period, from 59,389 to 69,887 (see appendix, Table A5). But the legislation of June 1846 brought a dramatic reversal. Enrolment in the government-supported schools of the six Eastern Townships counties dropped from 9,017 for the scholastic year ending in July 1846 to 6,964 during the following term. The number of schools funded declined from 316 to 234 (26 percent), which was a more marked movement than in Canada East as a whole where schools receiving grants declined from 1830 to 1632 (21 percent) (see appendix, Table A6). There is no way of knowing how many schools continued to operate without the government grant, but correspondence from commissioners in the Eastern Townships suggests that few closed their doors in that region.

Official enrolment dropped or remained stable in every Eastern Townships county except Shefford, where it grew from 1,593 to 1,785, though the number of conforming schools there decreased from forty-eight to forty. A closer examination reveals that official enrolment in several of Shefford's townships actually declined slightly, but the number of students in Shefford Township grew dramatically from 253 in six schools to 587 in eleven schools. The Shefford Township anomaly can clearly be explained by the conflict over schools which had taken place within that township in 1845, as we saw above. Chairman Robinson's early attempt to introduce tax assessments had apparently cleared the way for a general compliance a year later.

Elsewhere, the number of Drummond County's subsidized schools declined from twenty-six to twelve, Megantic's from sixteen to three, Missisquoi's from sixty-one to fifty-eight, and Stanstead's from eighty-two to twenty-seven. Clearly then, some of the most prosperous communities with the longest-established schools were the most adamantly opposed to the new schools legislation. But in Sherbrooke County the

number of schools remained the same, at eighty-three. The support
of the town of Sherbrooke's rising bourgeoisie can be detected in the
Ascot Township figures, where the number of schools actually increased
from eleven to fifteen. In nearby Brompton, Melbourne, Compton,
Bury, and Hereford the number of schools also increased very slightly,
from thirty-seven to thirty-eight, though all these townships were initially
recorded in Meilleur's official report as having no conforming schools
in the fall of 1846.[76] Obviously, then, they had submitted reports which
were even later than usual, which would suggest some degree of opposition to the new legislation.

The Melbourne correspondence reveals how deep-seated the popular
opposition to the school bill was even in a township which the statistical
tables recorded as conforming. We have seen that an attempt to elect
school commissioners in Melbourne was aborted as early as 1845. Those
subsequently appointed by Meilleur later pleaded that there had not
been time to make up the required eight months of schooling during
the 1845–47 school year, and that attendance fell below fifteen in some
schools because of the dispersed settlement pattern and the necessity
felt by older students to work during the harvest. The sum of £110 had
nevertheless been raised through taxation, a claim which obviously convinced Meilleur to reverse his rejection of the commission's return for
1845–46, since Melbourne received the full £70 grant for which it was
eligible.[77]

But the taxation principle was yet to be accepted permanently in Melbourne, for the local school commission admitted that a public meeting
in December 1846 had voted "not to pay any rates of any description."
The commissioners' court subsequently rejected attempts to enforce
payment on the grounds that not all the wild lands had been assessed, as
required by law. The school commission compensated for the taxation
shortfall by allowing "each district to make up in wood for the fire, and
board for their teacher the amount required by law." Meilleur was initially unsympathetic to this breach of the regulations, but he eventually
agreed to submit the case to the government, "with little or no hope of
success." Once again, though, the commissioners' persistence resulted
in a grant. In 1848 they were able to write that there had been "on the
whole less opposition to the law this year than formerly."[78] As we shall
see, however, trouble would erupt in Melbourne once again in 1851.

The only township in Sherbrooke County not to receive a grant during the 1846–47 school year was sparsely settled Windsor, where the
school commission reported that "the general feeling of the population
is, they would rather give by voluntary subscription than by a compulsory tax." In the spring of 1847 Meilleur took a hard line, encouraging
the secretary-treasurer to find some inhabitants who would sue the

school commission for breach of duty. If this failed to succeed, he should send the education office the names of five local persons "of energy and influence" within the municipality who were well disposed towards the schools act, as well as the names of three others qualified to be assessors.[79] The property qualification of £250, which the Legislative Assembly had inserted into the 1846 act against Meilleur's wishes, was an obvious stumbling block in such a poor township. Meilleur therefore effectively negated it by writing to Windsor that this provision was merely meant to protect the inhabitants "against those who might be put in office without any interest in the locality." Therefore anyone elected as a school commissioner or assessor who was "as well qualified in point of properties as the other inhabitants of the township generally are" could be considered acceptable "according to the true interest and purpose of ... the present school act." As of the fall of 1848, however, neither Windsor's municipal council or the school commission had ordered the drafting of a valuation role. Only in the spring of 1850 would the township finally receive a grant for three schools serving fifty-five students.[80]

In Stanstead County resistance to the 1846 school act was more widespread than in Sherbrooke, and not because of settler poverty. In Bolton and Hatley townships the number of schools remained stable, but in the long-settled border townships of Barnston, Stanstead, and Potton they dropped from fifty-four to zero. The chairman of the Stanstead Township school commission was Marcus Child, who had defended the voluntarist principle as the county's MLA in 1843. Child informed Meilleur in August 1846 that the people opposed assessments: "And in accordance to their feelings & habits (which do them honor) I wish to propose one simple question for your early consideration & answer – that is – *If the Township of Stanstead raises by voluntary means – a sum equal to the portion of the School Fund to which they would be entitled – in lieu of doing so by compulsory assessment, could they be entitled to receive that portion of the public funds?*" Meilleur insisted in his reply that "a regular assessment for educational purposes is the most easy, the most just, the most certain and the most satisfactory means to be resorted to" in raising funds for schools.[81]

This response did not satisfy Child, who insisted that the people would prefer to forego the grant rather than accept being assessed. Meilleur did not express much sympathy, stating simply that since the legislation applied to the entire province, "those of a particular locality have no just reason to consider themselves insulted by the said law, because they might have been more zealous than those of other localities to find some of the necessary means wherewith to procure, to our interesting youth, the benefit of an education."[82]

Child may have disagreed with this logic, but Meilleur was well aware that he would never advocate resistance to constituted authority.

Indeed, the aging political veteran would become the district's first schools inspector in 1852, and the evidence suggests that the ongoing resistance in Stanstead Township did not emanate from the school commissioners. They called a public meeting in October 1846 "for the purpose of taking the opinion and advice of the people in respect to assessments upon their real property under the present school law," but then refused the *Stanstead Journal*'s request that the results of the meeting be published. Instead, they appointed a school manager for each sub-district and imposed a tax of 11/100 of 1 percent on real estate as well as a school fee. The following month, the secretary-treasurer, D. Mack, reported to Meilleur that after frequent meetings he and his colleagues had also allotted to each member of the board a share of the schools for his particular "care, management and inspection," drafted and circulated rules and regulations for the schools, held public examinations for teachers, and appointed three evaluators who were ordered to draw up assessments.[83]

The ongoing problem, as far as the schools act was concerned, lay with the assessors, and the public's attitude towards compulsory taxes. Child reported to Meilleur in January 1847 that the board of commissioners was working "in good faith," but making "poor progress." There was still no evaluation of rateable property in Stanstead as late as June. One assessor had simply refused to act when informed that the school commission was not authorized to pay for his services, stating that he would prefer to pay the penalty. Stanstead Township's schools had nevertheless remained open, as before, with £644 spent for their operation during the scholastic year. Of this amount, £494 had already been raised by voluntary subscription, the remainder being equivalent to the last government grant and presumably representing a debt to the teachers. Mack expressed the hope that Meilleur would once again consider the township to be entitled to this grant, and the school commission petitioned the governor-general to the same effect. Meilleur stood firm, however, arguing that "the School act is so explicit on the subject, and the inducement to deviate from it so great, that it would be dangerous for the Gov.'t to depart from it *entirely* as the case would be, in behalf of Stanstead."[84] In 1847 Stanstead Township once again received no assistance for its schools (see appendix, Table A7).

The superintendent probably realized that compliance was inevitable since the conflict itself had ensured that the voluntarist principle could no longer function effectively. According to the Stanstead municipal councillor, Chauncey Bullock of Georgeville, the dilemma faced by the school commissioners was that "Some will have nothing to do with the law, others will do nothing without it, and between the two contending parties our schools and school houses are going to ruin." Part of the problem, in Bullock's opinion, stemmed from confusion about the regulations. He felt "confident that all further opposition to the law will cease with the People" if only Meilleur would settle the questions about whether or not the school commission was obliged to provide a school in each sub-district, whether or not the whole township had to contribute to the building of a school in a particular sub-district, and so on. Once again, the strong sense of localism reflected in these concerns appears to have been at least as important a force as hostility to the principle of compulsion itself. Meilleur informed Bullock that any school commission which refused to provide a sub-district with a school room immediately, or a schoolhouse within four years, was subject to a fine. And schoolhouses were supposed to be built by a tax levied on the whole municipality. But he reluctantly conceded, as he had to the Reverend Reid of Compton two years earlier, that the tax might be levied only on the sub-district in question in cases where the other districts in the municipality had constructed their schools by voluntary contribution.[85]

Meilleur may have had to cede to local pressures as far as school construction was concerned, but in his campaign to enforce compliance with the 1846 school bill he was also able to use the expense of constructing suitable schools to the state's advantage. Each school district was entitled to a building subsidy equivalent to the share of the annual grant it had failed to collect, for whatever reason, since 1842.[86] Because the school districts which resisted the enforcement of the compulsory assessment regulation after 1846 were thereby effectively accumulating a school building fund, the pressure to conform ultimately was much greater than if this money had simply been sacrificed. Stanstead Township provides a good example. When the commissioners requested funds for school construction in 1847, Meilleur replied that they had collected the full grant between 1842 and 1845. But he was obviously aware that the township had received nothing for the 1846–47 school year, and he was therefore able to use the accumulated fund to break down resistance to the 1846 school bill. He stated somewhat coyly that if the commissioners would soon comply with the regulations, "I might be able to ask His Excellency's warrant for a certain sum in their favor."[87]

The municipal authorities had, in fact, finally completed a property assessment in December 1847, though the school commissioners hesitated to levy a tax right away because the regulations stated that this could only be done each May. In June 1848 the township's school commission was finally able to submit its report for the last six months of 1847. Emphasizing the pressing need of the commission for funds, D.W. Mack expressed the hope that Meilleur would "take into consideration the difficult task of the Commission acting in opposition to the wishes of the people, ... or of convincing them of the necessity of giving up their former habits and usages and adopting new ones." Meilleur could afford to be conciliatory, and in September he sent Mack a draft for £85 17s. 7d. for the last six months of 1847 and the first six months of 1848. A year later Mack was able to report an improvement in attendance and the length of time that the schools were kept open, many of them "from one to two months more than the law requires." As late as 1853, however, the commissioners were still facing an uphill battle in the local courts against recalcitrant rate payers.[88]

Another of the more persistent centres of opposition to the 1846 school law was Stanstead's rather turbulent neighbouring township of Barnston. Here the school commissioners had appointed three evaluators as early as July 1846, but as of November they still had not drawn up any assessments. The community's chief spokesman was the colourfully loquacious Baptist minister, James Green. As secretary-treasurer of the school commission, he reported that the assessors had "refused to face the rage of that political storm" which had earlier "devastated the town." The commissioners in turn had feared that if they should attempt to force the assessors to do their duty, "they would subject themselves to the contempt and ill will of the people generally and thus render themselves useless in office or that which is worse, subject the system of Education to odium and contempt." Meilleur's instructions in 1846 that these men should be fined had obviously been ignored.[89]

Green, who would play a prominent local role in the British American League in 1849,[90] laid the blame for the spirit of resistance at the door of the municipal election of December 1846, when "political party spirit so far predominated in the annual meeting of the inhabitants of the municipality that all the work was done illegally and the election of councillors was a complete failure."[91] However, the *Stanstead Journal* reveals that the Baptist minister himself had played a dominant role in Barnston's school protest. His committee presented resolutions, unanimously approved by a town meeting held on 21 December, declaring that the school act was not suited to the needs of the Eastern Townships. They demanded a much more decentralized system, with a superintendent of common schools for each township municipality elected at the annual general meeting. This official would take charge of school property, examine teachers and issue certificates of qualification, visit all schools at least once a term, decide on the boundaries of school districts, establish model or girls' schools if necessary, distribute the government grant, decide all disputes between the people and the commissioners, and meet other superintendents in the same county once a year. As a board of education, the superintendents of each county would allot the government grant, devise means to promote a uniform course of instruction, approve books to be used in the schools, and judge all disputes between commissioners and individual superintendents. Finally, the chairman of this board would report annually the state of education to the legislature.

Clearly, there would be no role for a provincial superintendent in such a decentralized system, though Canada West had had less powerful government-appointed district superintendents since 1843. Surprisingly enough, taxes were not even mentioned in the Barnston resolutions, though they did declare that the two school commissioners in each township would prosecute those refusing to comply with the vote of the district meeting for fuel, board, money or produce, or in any way contravening the intention of any vote of a majority of the voters.[92] Presumably, then, the matter of how local funds were to be raised would be left entirely to the people.

Green may have been envisioning himself as the obvious candidate for the locally powerful role of superintendent, but his ideas did attract support elsewhere. Although he was a government supporter, the provincial MLA, John McConnell, chaired a town meeting in Hatley in January which adopted the Barnston resolutions. The following March, the *Stanstead Journal* printed "An Address to the People of the Eastern Townships" which declared that the school bills had all been worthless except for one or two clauses, and that the people of the Townships had been "borne down by a multitude ignorant of our situation and wants." Signed by Green, McConnell, and a number of notables from Compton and Stanstead, as well as Barnston, the address asked that the Barnston and Hatley resolutions be taken up by other townships.[93]

Nothing more would be heard of the Barnston resolutions until nearly two years later, in January 1849, when a county meeting held at Langmayd's Flat in Hatley Township included education as one of the themes it wished to address. John McConnell and James Green addressed the meeting on the school law, and Green chaired the committee on the school act, which presented resolutions declaring that no school law should deprive the local districts of any part of the management of their schools, and that the only officer superior to sub-district managers that could possibly be of use would be a county superintendent. An entirely new demand was that the Eastern Townships should have a normal school for the training of its teachers: "The immense sums which are now lavished upon the useless office of General Superintendent, should be immediately appropriated to the support of those schools," which should be made the nucleus of the whole educational system.[94]

Meanwhile, no school commissioners were nominated in Barnston until January 1848, though this had not prevented Green from petitioning for school funds six months earlier.[95] He later reported that students had been constrained to pay fees throughout this period, which suggests that Barnston's schools, like those of Stanstead, did remain open without government assistance. By April 1848 the community's landholders had been assessed and were awaiting their share of the school grant. Meilleur agreed to bend the regulations by providing the grant for as early as the first six months of 1847 provided the matching sums required were raised in the prescribed manner.[96]

The story did not quite end here, however. After a year of peaceful compliance, Green reported in September 1849 that "on account of some dissatisfaction in the people things of late have not been pleasant and many schools have [been] kept which have not reported to the commissioners." The commissioners had to borrow part of the sum re-quired to operate their schools during the fall of 1849, a step which Meilleur condemned as irregular, though he agreed to accept the re-turn on the understanding "that I will not do the same in future." In June 1850 the now compliant Green issued an official notice that taxes back to the 1848–49 school year were due by 1 July; thereafter, "pay-ment in every instance will be constrained."[97]

While local custom ensured that the tax assessment system would be unpopular in the well-established townships, it was basically unfeasible in those areas with large quantities of wild land. Edward Hale explained the problem as follows to Meilleur in 1846. Apparently in order to com-pensate for the land owned by absentee proprietors, the legislation allowed school commissions to assess taxes 15 percent higher than the sum needed to equal the school grant they were eligible for. But Hale pointed out that in Sherbrooke, as in many other municipalities, "15 percent will by no means cover the deficiency and as we can only as-sess equally all Property to the exact amount, it is also certain that we shall not collect it." In other words, the delinquent resident proprietors would more than cancel out the 15 percent margin allowed because of absentees. Hale therefore wished to know if the difference could be made up by school fees or voluntary contributions.[98] Meilleur replied that school fees (whose ceiling was fixed at two shillings per month) were distinct from the amount required to obtain the grant, and that the quantity of wild land in a school municipality was irrelevant since the grant was based on the number of school-age residents.

The superintendent was probably correct in assuming that the more unimproved land there was in a municipality, the smaller its school-age population would be, but this did not solve the problem for townships with large numbers of renters or squatters. Meilleur declared that occu-piers of land owned by absentees should not be exempt from taxes, but it would be difficult to enforce such assessments given that the delin-quents could not be punished by the sale of land which they did not own. This problem appears to have occurred to Meilleur a few days later, for he attempted to offer Hale a loophole when he suggested that those inhabitants "immediately interested in the effectual operation of the schools" might raise the required sum, "exclusively of others." Presumably he was referring to voluntary contributions, but while the "others" clearly included the absentee proprietors, Meilleur did not mean that the commissioners need not assess their property. He added that wild lands should be charged with a special mortgage to be paid sooner or later for educational purposes.[99] The Ascot school commission did collect the required sum, though by including school fees, which ran counter to the regulations – a fact which Meilleur apparently chose to ignore since the school district received its grant and the commissioners continued to follow the same practice in 1848.[100] A similar complaint about the difficulty of taxing absentees was made by Hatley Township, among others in the area,[101] but the absentee proprietor problem was most intractable in the townships to the north, as we shall see in chapter seven.

One of the few townships not to object to some aspect of the 1846 school bill was thickly settled Eaton. In 1847 the Eaton commissioners remarked:

While many townships express great dissatisfaction with the present school act, we have found no difficulty in working it and keeping up our schools. In some points we think it might be amended for the better, but we should be unwilling to have it repealed altogether and we are confident that if those townships or parishes who are now loud in condemning the act would turn to and make the most of it, they would have much less cause to complain.[102]

As late as January 1848, however, the grand jurors for the criminal term of the Queen's Bench for the St Francis District declared that the 1832–33 schools act had been "much better adapted to the wants and wishes of the people." They objected in particular to the £1,200 yearly salary for Meilleur, a sum they stated to be sufficient to sustain sixty schools under the current act.[103] As in the pre-Rebellion era, the majority of the American-descended residents in the heart of the Eastern Townships was clearly antagonistic to the imposition of highly paid government officials, particularly when the policies they implemented were unpopular. But we shall see that the people in these long-settled townships would gradually accommodate themselves to compulsory taxes, even if it was on their own terms. The more recently arrived British and French-Canadian settlers in the peripheral townships proved to be less compliant.

7 Peripheral Settlements and Later Developments

THE BRITISH-SETTLED PERIPHERY

Just as not all American-settled townships resisted the schools legislation, likewise not all the English-speaking townships that did so were of American origin. A complicating factor in the British-settled northeastern area was the role played by the Church of England's Newfoundland and British North America School Society, which opened parochial schools after the publicly funded system was disrupted by the Rebellion.[1] In 1843 this British-based society, which had begun to receive provincial government grants in 1840–41, reported two schools with 30 students each in Ireland Township, two with 156 students in Leeds, and one with 35 students in Inverness. Outside Megantic County it also claimed 385 students in the St Francis Tract of the British American Land Company, 368 in the town of Sherbrooke, and 237 in various other localities within the proximate area.[2] This activity would do little to enhance popular incentive to support public schools, at least on the part of the Anglican settlers.

It was no accident, for example, that the only township in the Chaudière Municipal District not to elect school commissioners by 1843 was Halifax, where the Newfoundland Society supported three or four independent schools. Indeed, no conforming public schools are recorded for Halifax until six appear in the education office's list for the second term of 1849, and some of these were operated by the French Canadians in the township.[3] British settlers in the other Megantic County townships would prove still more recalcitrant than those of Halifax, but Superintendent

Meilleur was largely content to leave these isolated settlers to their own devices.

In May 1846 the school commissioners of Inverness Township reported to the education office that because their municipal council was not in effective operation their school had been supported by "liberal" contributions from the people. They added that they were satisfied with the schoolmaster, the regularity of his daily journal, and the improvement of the scholars. With the local settlers being generally satisfied as well, the commissioners believed that the teacher was entitled to the full government allotment, but Meilleur evidently rejected their report. When the 1846 bill requiring tax assessments, rather than allowing voluntary contributions, came into effect, the Inverness commissioners made it clear that they were not enthusiastic about its provisions. They informed Meilleur in the fall of 1846 that they would "attempt to work the law, notwithstanding the many obstacles that will have to be overcome, owing to the great opposition of the people, as they think the law very unjust and oppressive to the poorer classes of the inhabitants, while the land speculators which are very numerous here, pay comparatively nothing." The people also objected to the compulsory fees for young children many of whom could not attend school, "it being impossible for them to walk two and three miles through a bush road, as well also we have a very large river without bridges, running through this municipality."[4]

While the law provided for fines against commissioners who refused to enforce the regulations, there was little the state could do when the people of any district refused to elect a school commission except to impose such a body on them. This Meilleur avoided in the English-speaking townships, though we shall see that school commissions, like municipal councils, were commonly appointed in the Bois-Francs. The one return entered for Inverness prior to the end of our study period was for a single dissentient school in the spring term of 1850. On his first visit in 1852 Inspector J.S. Clarke reported that he was "pained to learn" that there was only one school open within the township, and its supporters had not received any government assistance.[5]

Much the same response came from neighbouring Ireland Township, though here four public schools had operated during the first term of 1846 (see appendix, Table A5), and the commissioners appear to have exerted greater efforts to implement the new legislation. In January 1847 they informed Meillleur that "certain persons" had alarmed the inhabitants at a public meeting by stating falsely that the commissioners "were intending to compel the payment of 1s. 3d. per head for each resident child within the limited ages prescribed by law and that without exception – stated also that if the people refused to pay a school tax, the commissioners could not collect it – but that if they paid a fraction of tax or assessment in any shape, he would afterwards be liable to unrestricted taxation." This meeting had been called just before the appointed time for the public examination of the schools so that the people could be advised to keep their children at home.

The commissioners had argued in vain that the amount contributed by "those accustomed to support the schools" would be halved by tax assessments. Some of the less well-to-do would clearly now be required to share the burden, but once again, according to the commissioners certain members of the local elite were to be found at the head of the protest: "It is to be regretted that some persons have been found countenancing these dangerous misrepresentations who from their rank and official standing, better things were expected of them."[6] Ireland Township had been settled in part by retired military men, and it is possible that the notables referred to were former officers who owned large land holdings on which they would have to pay substantial tax bills.

The Ireland commissioners expected that the situation would soon be resolved since "the more sensible people now see their error and are coming to a better mind," but they were being much too optimistic. The school commission subsequently resorted to legal proceedings against several proprietors, a majority having refused to pay the tax assessment. As a result, some of these individuals sabotaged a meeting called in July 1847 to elect two new commissioners. They blocked the steps to the school where the meeting was to be held, "threatening violence to the persons and property of those commissioners who attempted to carry the law into effect." Reporting on these events the following January, the secretary-treasurer added that two of the commissioners had "countenanced the opposition on the part of the people."[7]

There matters rested until three years later, when a Protestant clergyman from Upper Ireland finally asked permission to establish a dissentient school. Meilleur replied that such a step would be very irregular in a district where the majority, being opposed to the school law, were without school commissioners or any school in operation. He remarked bitterly that the legislature, "by giving them a school law as liberal and benevolent as that which is now in force, could not foresee such blindness or indifference to their most lively interest." Nevertheless, the superintendent agreed to the proposal provided that the trustees submit their names, the date of their election, the names of the dissentients, and the number of their children. After the school had been taught for four months, the trustees were to submit a return declaring that the inhabitants had contributed a sum (no mention was made of tax assessment) equal to the legislative grant they were eligible for. As late as 1852 there was only one school open in Ireland Township, and it was operated independently of the school law.[8]

Like Ireland Township, neighbouring Leeds received a school grant for several schools which were open during the first term of 1846; indeed, the Buller report had mentioned an operating schools network during the 1830s.[9] But here again the British settlers obviously rejected compulsory taxation, though no correspondence to or from the township has been preserved for the period between July 1846 and April 1850. On the latter date, trustees elected by thirteen Irish Catholics and a French Canadian asked that their school be given dissentient status. They noted that they had not been able to notify the chairman of the school commission, as normally required, because "there is no such personage – no election for school commissioners having taken place in this municipality for some years past." Finally, in January 1851, Meilleur was informed that an election of school commissioners had taken place in Leeds, and that three public schools supported by £47 in voluntary contributions had been in operation throughout the previous year.[10] Meilleur provided assistance for only the Catholic dissentient school in 1850, but the government did subsidize four public schools in Leeds for the first term of 1851. These schools were obviously popular, since they reported an average attendance of thirty-five students each. Unfortunately, delays in the delivery of the subsidy meant that the commissioners were unable to pay the teachers, and all the schools but one had to close their doors during the second term of 1851.[11]

It is impossible to say exactly why the settlers of Megantic, who were mostly of British birth, opposed taxation even more ardently than those of American descent in the townships to the south. The two most important factors were probably poverty and the scourge of absentee proprietorship. Most of the large proprietors were probably residents of Quebec City who could resist the increased pressure to pay taxes through the same political machinery that won votes for the Quebec politicians who ran for office in this county. More research is needed to gain a clearer understanding of the social dynamics on this heterogeneous frontier, but it is clear that the local elites were themselves rather divided and restricted in influence, and that the settlers needed little prompting to resist compulsory taxation when government regulations effectively allowed large-scale speculators to pay nothing.

Furthermore, the Newfoundland Society probably continued to operate a number of schools in the area, since its decline in Canada East did not begin until the 1860s. This society certainly created a nuisance for Meilleur in the St Francis Tract, where the population included not only the original Anglican settlers from southern England, but a small number of American-descended families and a rapidly growing group of Scots Presbyterians from the Isle of Lewis. At the centre of the controversy was William King, superintendent for the Newfoundland and

British North American Society in the Eastern Townships, and school-master in the building erected by the British American Land Company in the village of Robinson. Claiming in 1841 that the settlers were too poor to clothe their children, much less pay for their education, King asked for and apparently received a government grant. But the days of special status for the Church of England had passed, and King's ordination the following year would jeopardize his control over the local school.

When the Anglican bishop requested the title to the "public and common School-house at Robinson Village," Meilleur protested that it was "a large and handsome framed building, with a spacious school room, and a dwelling house for the teacher" erected by the company at public expense out of its improvement fund. The superintendent had no objection to the Anglicans continuing to use the building on Sundays, but he supported the elected school commissioners' request for a teacher "not submitted to any particular clerical jurisdiction." He insisted to the governor-general that "in a fine Township like Bury, capable of maintaining in comfort more than ten times its present number of inhabitants, it is impossible to say what future disadvantage and discontentment might arise from permanently relinquishing a Public Institution, intended and granted for the equal good of all, to the exclusive Control of any one Church denomination."[12]

But King would not give up so easily. Two years later, in March 1844, several commissioners representing the school district of Bury, West-bury, and Lingwick complained to the Sherbrooke District Council that King was withholding the building from public use even though he was their chairman. The warden, Edward Hale, drafted an agreement whereby King would retain possession of the dwelling part of the building, and use the school portion for Sunday services, in return for $20 per year from the Newfoundland School Society fund. This sum would go towards the operation of the school under the control of the commissioners, though King would decide who would be the teacher.[13] Meilleur concurred, but King rejected Hale's generous compromise, and no progress was made during the following two months.[14]

Indeed, King's resolve had been strengthened by his failure to be re-elected to the school commission. In April the commissioners complained to Meilleur that thirty-six children were forced to attend classes in the front room of a shoemaker's shop while the village schoolhouse was intermittently serving only six or seven students, including King's own offspring. The matter was finally referred to the governor-in-council in May, but King was still in possession of the school in November of 1845. The commissioner complained that about fifty children were thereby deprived of an education, while only three were attending King's classes.[15]

King was not without his supporters, for he and his slate were re-elected to the school commission in 1845. However, his opponents refused to recognize this result, and they elected their own council two months later.[16] The persistent clergyman then had himself elected to the newly established township council, and his last recorded intervention in school affairs was to persuade one of the assessors appointed by the school commission to ignore his instructions. The commissioners sought Meilleur's permission to prosecute, but we have seen that the 1845 school bill left exclusive taxing powers in the hands of the municipal councils. The commissioners also suggested that the Scots of Lingwick, who were seeking independent status for their township, be urged to establish a dissentient school instead. They were all Presbyterians, and "having once had this power in their own hands they feel jealous of loosing [*sic*] it, and thus give a great deal of trouble."[17] But the government had assumed that dissentient status would be given only to a Protestant minority within a Catholic school district, or vice versa, and the commissioners elected in Lingwick ultimately accepted the status quo in return for an equal share of the school grant.

There remained the problem of collecting the taxes that would make the Bury-Lingwick school district eligible for such a grant.[18] In the spring of 1847 the school commission informed Meilleur that it had sued twenty individuals in the Bury commissioners' court for non-payment of their assessments. A judgment had been obtained against ten of those charged, but the others had hired an eminent attorney from Sherbrooke. The lawyer argued that the assessment of wild land taxes was invalid because the commissioners had reached a compromise with the British American Land Company whereby it would pay a much smaller amount than if each of its lots had been assessed at its full value. In response, the commissioners claimed that otherwise the company would have refused to pay anything, necessitating a long and expensive law suit. They added that even if they could have won such a case, they would not be allowed to sell company land equivalent in value to the assessment for an additional five years, "thus entirely defeating the main intention of the Act, viz. to have schools in active & successful operation."[19] Meilleur felt that the commissioners had a good case, but the lawyer's argument was evidently successful, since the chairman noted in 1850 that his board had only ever succeeded on one occasion before the commissioners' court. Consequently, "as some of the leading men advise the rest not to pay their taxes," the school commission had fallen into debt, presumably by borrowing money to pay the teachers' salaries.[20]

Incurring this debt, which Meilleur ordered the school commissioners to reimburse at once,[21] would explain why Bury and Lingwick were able to continue operating most of their schools and to claim the government grant despite the recalcitrant taxpayers. As we shall see, the 1849 school bill gave the school commissioners more direct authority to enforce assessments, but the school returns from two years later show that there were still only five schools operating in the Bury-Lingwick school district, with 132 students. The result was ongoing protest from inhabitants who were required to pay taxes although they lived in sub-districts which had no schools.[22] As late as 1853 there were only six schools open in the nine sub-districts within Bury, Lingwick, and Westbury owing to the defalcation of the former secretary-treasurer and the ongoing refusal of absentee proprietors to pay school taxes.[23] While the progress of public schooling in the St Francis Tract was therefore more advanced than in the British settlements of Megantic County, the land company's very presence represented an obstacle to further development. Indeed, many inhabitants of both districts were apparently quite willing to use the existence of large tracts of privately held land as both an excuse and a legal crutch for resisting payment of school taxes.

DISSENTIENT SCHOOLS

While the question of sectarian schools caused some controversy among the mixed Protestant settlers of Bury and Lingwick, it was a potentially more contentious issue in those townships inhabited by Catholics as well as Protestants, especially since language difference was generally also a factor. With French Canadians from the seigneuries south of the St Lawrence beginning to expand more rapidly into the region in the 1840s, there were a number of mixed-population townships on the frontier of English-speaking settlement. To accommodate such municipalities in an era when the Protestant and Catholic sectors were not yet separated, the schools legislation in 1841 allowed religious minorities to establish dissentient schools. These would be operated by their own trustees and receive a proportional share of the school grant.

The 1846 school act added that the entire amount of monies raised by assessment on the dissentients, together with a due proportion of the building fund, should be paid to their school trustees.[24] Finally, the 1849 school bill added that if the dissentients were dissatisfied with the share of the local taxes given them by the school commission, they could collect their own assessments, receive school fees, and enjoy the principal privileges of a corporation.[25] Often caught in the middle were the Irish Catholics. They had to pay school taxes and fees to the Catholic system in those townships or parishes where the French Canadians formed the majority, even though they generally wished to send their children to the English-language dissentient schools which also required fee payments.

Meilleur clearly preferred that all children attend the public schools, particularly where the population was too small and poor to support two school systems conforming to the regulations.[26] The mixed settlements on the Eastern Townships frontier were far from affluent, but linguistic differences presented a formidable barrier to common schools. The Catholic priests would also play a role in discouraging such institutions, not only on principle but because they were acutely aware that the French-Canadian newcomers were in a minority within the Eastern Townships, and therefore presumably susceptible to assimilation and apostasy. Finally, the establishment of a dual system locally was generally not impractical since most of the French-speaking and English-speaking settlers lived in different corners of the mixed-population townships.

Such was the case in Megantic's Ireland Township, which had 559 English-speaking inhabitants and 132 French Canadians in 1844. A year later, Meilleur recommended to Ireland's school commissioners that they provide for Catholic representation in the next election, since the means of support would be too limited if the schools were divided according to religious faith.[27] In the meantime, however, the French Canadians had established their own school of twenty-five students without informing the clerk of the municipality, as required for dissentient status. The school commissioners nevertheless informed Meilleur that they had no objection to such a school, and that they were quite willing to compensate the teacher. Meilleur gratefully concurred, stating that the above-mentioned regulation was not generally enforced, and that the indulgence practised had resulted in "a great sum of good."[28] The benefits of such good will were short-lived, however, for we have already seen that the 1846 school bill resulted in all the public schools in Ireland being closed until at least 1853.

Relations between the French and English Canadians proved to be less harmonious in Kingsey Township, on the lower St Francis River. In 1843 the school commission consisted of a Protestant minister, a Catholic priest, and two laymen, one of whom was English-speaking and the other French.[29] There were evidently distinct schools for the two groups, but Hubert Robson, the missionary priest for the area, was clearly uncomfortable with such an arrangement. In May 1844 Meilleur advised the Reverend John Butler that if Robson, in his capacity as a school commissioner, rejected the grant issued for "the schools of his persuasion," then the other commissioners should distribute it themselves according to the table he had enclosed.[30] Meilleur later learned that a meeting of the Kingsey Catholics held in Robson's house had already elected him and three others as dissentient trustees of the township's Catholic schools. The superintendent informed Robson that he regretted the difficulties which had led to the division of the schools, but he realized that it was sometimes necessary for one group to protect itself "contre l'intolérance ou l'égoisme des autres sectes." It would appear that the Catholics felt that they were not receiving their fair share of the grant, for Meilleur promised that there should be no such difficulty in the future.[31] But the school commissioners continued to interfere, reporting in 1845 that they had withheld the grant from the two Catholic schools because they had not remained open the required nine months, and one of their teachers could not even write his own name legibly.[32]

The whole situation became further complicated by the revelation in the 1844 census that the French Canadians were actually the majority in Kingsey Township, outnumbering the English Canadians by 1,036 to 832. The Catholics therefore technically had no right to establish dissentient schools since these were intended to protect religious minorities against the proselytism of the majority. Meilleur could only ask the commissioners to share the 1844 grant with the Catholic schools and attempt to reach an agreement that would make dissentient schools unnecessary. He also assured Robson's successor, the Reverend Charles Tardif, that during the next election of the school commissioners the French-Canadian majority would be able to exercise its full influence. An added incentive to rejoin the school commission was the fact that as long as the Catholic schools remained dissentient they would not be entitled to government grants for school construction.[33]

When the election held several months later was declared illegal because of minor irregularities, the two returning officers acted upon Meilleur's advice by submitting a common list of names to be appointed to the school commission. It consisted of only three French Canadians, including the new curé, and six of British origin, including two clerics. Presumably not all the Protestants were meant to be appointed, and the ratio was not a crucial matter in any case, since Meilleur recommended that the two groups manage their schools separately. Kingsey would therefore have a dual system in all but name, with the groups submitting their reports to each other to be jointly signed at the end of each school year.[34] However, this sensible arrangement failed to appease the English-speaking commissioners, who complained that their Catholic counterparts were not qualified, and Meilleur was forced to inform them in October 1845 that they could not legally resign their posts. By the spring of 1846 the Protestants of one of the school sub-districts had acquired dissentient status (see appendix, Table A5),[35] but the two populations seem to have managed thereafter to settle their differences within a single school commission as no dissentient schools are recorded throughout the later 1840s.

Harmful as the ethno-religious rivalry may have been to the development of public schools in Kingsey, it appears that later in the decade a greater problem was the resistance to taxation by such landed propri-etors as William Vondenvelden. Certainly, the disputatious lawyer played an important behind-the-scenes role in the Guerre des Éteignoirs of the Berthier area, which was his second home.[36] While he was far from uni-versally accepted as a community leader in Kingsey, as we have seen, Vondenvelden was still capable of stirring up mischief among the poor settlers already resentful of taxes. When the school inspector reported in 1853 that there were only eight public schools open in Kingsey's four-teen districts, he blamed "the opposition of a few leading persons, who object to the payment of School-rates." In addition, the curé of the turbu-lent township criticized both the district inspector and Superintendent Meilleur for failing to overcome "the obstacles and the slight opposi-tions shewn by the people, who have become arrogant through the con-tempt they have been permitted to evince towards the law."[37]

To the immediate south, Reverend Trahan was still less satisfied than his Kingsey counterpart because the 1,500 French Canadians within his jurisdiction of Ely, Melbourne, Shipton, Windsor, and Tingwick still did not have a single Catholic school in 1853.[38] But the French Canadians could at least look forward to increased numbers and population den-sity. Foreshadowing developments elsewhere in the region, the Protes-tants of Milton Township (adjacent to the seigneury of St Hyacinthe), were already on the decline during the 1840s. Unlike their counterparts in Kingsey, Milton's English Canadians were too small a minority (197 of a population of 937 in 1844) to exercise much influence on the school commission. When the commissioners took possession of a Prot-estant school for the Catholic population in 1845, Meilleur made his displeasure quite clear: "Je regrette infiniment que des catholiques don-nent ainsi prise contre eux à ces gens qu'il est de l'intérêt de la charité, de la paix, et de l'éducation même de ne jamais heurter parce que, tôt ou tard, il en résulte du mal pour les uns comme pour les autres."[39]

One of Milton's four schools was listed as dissentient for the 1845–46 school year, but there was still one small group of Protestants who com-plained that their children were being deprived of an education. As a re-sult, Meilleur wrote to the Milton school commission: "I think it to be duty [sic] to represent to you that, as public men and christians, you are held to endeavor to offer, under the operation of the said law, an equal facility of instruction to resident children of every origin or creed." He recommended that the commissioners appoint a bilingual teacher for the school district in question. Milton's steadily diminishing Protestant population would find itself increasingly at the mercy of such good-will gestures, for with a drop from 106 students in 1850 to only 44 a year later, their government grant was becoming too small to operate the three dissentient schools.[40]

Assuming that the language issue could have been solved with exclusively French or English schools in homogenous sub-districts, and bilingual teachers in the others, dissentient schools should not have been necessary if the government had followed Buller's strong recommendation that a curriculum be designed to accommodate Catholics as well as Protestants. But the prospect of minimizing the role of religion in the schools was vehemently opposed not only by the province's Catholic Church but by many Protestants as well. Buller pointed out that the Irish National System had adopted a text of biblical extracts "acceptable alike to Catholics and Protestants," but he admitted that his suggestions had met with implacable opposition from the Anglican clergy in particular.[41] Three years later, in 1841, members of various Protestant denominations submitted petitions insisting on the use of the full text of the Bible (obviously the King James version) in the classroom.[42] Under these circumstances, the provision for dissentient status represented a reasonable compromise solution, particularly as it avoided the issue of equitable representation on the school councils, and the cases examined above suggest that it did serve to ease tensions within ethnically and religiously mixed townships. Given the population transition that was already beginning to take place in certain parts of the region, as well as the religious-based violence in other parts of British North America, relations between French-speaking Catholics and English-speaking Protestants in the Eastern Townships were remarkably peaceable.

FRENCH-CANADIAN SETTLEMENTS

Under pressure from the Catholic hierarchy, but also reflecting the prominent role played by the Protestant clergy, the schools legislation of 1845 declared that the curé or resident minister of the most numerous religious denomination would automatically be a school commissioner. This provision was dropped in 1846, but clerics now became school visitors, charged with arbitrating disputes between teachers and commissioners. They also gained the right to choose books dealing with religious or moral issues, and each teacher was required to obtain a certificate of morality from the local curé or minister before being tested by the board of examiners, established in 1846. Finally, the £250 property qualification instituted for all school commissioners in 1846 was dropped in 1849 for clerics who wished to stand for this office.[43]

These alterations won the Catholic Church's strong support for the school reforms, but the local priests were not able to prevent militant opposition to school taxes from erupting in Nicolet and Yamaska counties. Though there was less violence in the neighbouring Bois-Francs townships, the Guerre des Éteignoirs also made an impact there. This frontier zone had been slow to respond to the 1841 school act, for a resident of Somerset reported to the government in 1843 that his school district had not yet been divided into sub-districts. The result was that "nous ne pouvons faire régler aucune affaire ce qui nous met dans la plus grande gène." However, the Somerset colonists had contributed £2 10s. per month to maintain one school since 1842. From that year there had also been a school with twenty-five to thirty students in nearby Blandford and Maddington.[44] The only other two schools reported for the Bois-Francs in 1843 were in Stanfold and Arthabaska (see appendix, Table A3). Considering the poverty of these recent settlers, the merchant James Goodhue of Bulstrode was being overly harsh when he complained in 1843 that "the people have no Enterprise or Public Spirit." Goodhue claimed that he himself supported compulsory taxation, but in 1846 the curé of St Norbert d'Arthabaska complained that the chief obstacles to its implementation were the "Bourgeois."[45]

During the tumultuous fall of 1846 the number of schools in Stanfold actually increased from two to four, and in Somerset from two to three. Only in Arthabaska was there a decline, from two to one. It is unlikely that any taxes had been paid in this township, for the secretary-treasurer, P.N. Pacaud, informed Meilleur in March 1847 that his predecessor appeared not to have kept any records of local contributions.[46] In his capacity as a justice of the peace, this former commissary-general of the Patriote army[47] reported that the 1846 school bill had caused "Beaucoup d'effervescence chez un grand nombre d'hommes mal avisés." The school in sub-district number two had been razed in January 1847, after law officers had several times been prevented by threats of force from executing judgments against individuals who had refused to pay their assessments. Rumours suggested that there were also plans to destroy the other three schools and the chapel.[48]

The chief magistrate for Trois-Rivières, who was Pacaud's brother and himself a large proprietor of Bois-Francs land, wrote to the attorney-general that he could not interfere because his jurisdiction did not extend to the district in question. He then contradicted himself by stating that the Arthabaska fugitives could easily slip into either the District of Quebec or the District of St Francis since their borders lay nearby.[49] The government responded with the offer of a £50 reward for apprehension of the instigators, but instead it received a rather defiant petition with 160 names attached demanding the dissolution of the legislature:

Un peuple jadis heureux se trouve accablé par l'infortune. Il est trahi par ses propres Représentants, le sol est soumis à une taxe dont la collection va être cause d'un pillage universel en faux frais de toute espèce, et cette taxe a été imposée sans l'aveu et à l'insue du peuple. Dans notre douleur, nous n'avons qu'un espoirs [*sic*], c'est la bienveillance de notre Reine au nom de laquelle nous implorons le souvenir de sa parole royale donné au Canada par sa promesse faite en 1841, que le voeu de la majorité serait le guide et l'inspiration de son gouvernement en cette Province ... Nous voulons bien l'éducation, mais nous ne pouvons consentir qu'elle soit accompagné de la privation de la liberté Constitutionelle.[50]

A subsequent petition with 123 names charged that the 1846 school bill penalized those who preferred to send their children to seminaries or convents, sapped the industry and voluntary zeal of the inhabitants, and created a group of officials who cost more than they were worth.[51]

In June, Secretary-Treasurer Pacaud was able to report that "les enne-mis du Bill des Ecoles ... sont en pleine déroute,"[52] but he still did not feel confident enough to call the election necessitated by the division of the small township into two municipalities (presumably following parish boundaries) the previous year. Instead, he provided Meilleur with the names of those who should be appointed to the school commission, adding that under the circumstances the curé preferred not to be in-cluded.[53] Meilleur finally appointed the new commissioners in August, thereby making it possible to use the courts to enforce tax assessments. The parish of St Norbert d'Arthabaska was credited with three schools for the fall term of that year, and in 1849 the secretary-treasurer reported that they were "recommandables sur tous les rapports." Furthermore, the contributors who were formerly so opposed to the schools bill were now "les premiers à le soutenir." There were, however, still no schools re-ported for the offshoot parish of St Christophe, even though its curé had submitted a list of names to be appointed commissioners in 1848.[54]

To the northeast, the Reverend Charles E. Bélanger of Somerset also played a leading role (at least at the outset), acting as secretary-treasurer and submitting a list of names to be appointed school commissioners in 1845.[55] He claimed that the vast majority opposed taxes for any pur-pose, but the three local schools were the only ones within Megantic County to be reported as conforming to the new schools act in the fall of 1846. The chief obstacle to the expansion of public schooling in Somerset, as elsewhere in the Bois-Francs, was poverty, exacerbated by absentee proprietorship. In March 1847 Charles Prince, who was Som-erset's justice of the peace and captain of militia, wrote to the civil secre-tary that the local settlers could not afford to pay the taxes now required by law: "J'ai eue aujourd'hui la douleur de condamner douze personnes de payer leur cotisation, ainsi que la taxe mensuelle de leurs enfants, ces personnes n'ont rien, du tous, il faut donc faire saisir le peut qu'ils pos-sède pour le soutien de leurs enfants et le vendre." Prince added that most families in the Bois-Francs could not clothe their children well enough to send them to school: "Je suis et je serai toujours le premier à encourager l'éducation dans notre pays, mais là où il n'y a rien on ne peut rien."[56] Prince was obviously influenced in his official capacity by community opinion, but not sufficiently to overlook official regulations. Legal coercion clearly continued to be applied, for in 1851 a JP for Stanfold Township claimed that during the previous six months he and his counterpart had signed sixty-four "actions" launched by the school commissioners, for which forty-six judgments (presumably favourable to the school commission) had been rendered.[57]

Under these conditions it is not surprising that in 1845 the teachers in Somerset's two schools were paid only £8 and £10 6s. for five and six months of work, respectively. These salaries were about half those in Stanstead County, even though class sizes were comparable.[58] In a pioneer township such as Somerset, the chief priority was inevitably the construction of adequate school buildings. In 1846 the commissioners submitted a request for £40 to expand and repair five existing schools and £60 to erect a sixth. They noted that "grande misère malgré la bonne volonté" was preventing the settlers from assuming the costs themselves.[59] Government funds were available for this purpose, but the commissioners found it difficult to provide proper documentation for the land transfers. A year earlier, Meilleur had replied to an angry Reverend Bélanger that he would not adopt "le même ton sur lequel il vous a plu de m'adresser, d'abord, parce qu'il n'est pas dans mes habitudes de le faire pour personne, et ensuite parce que j'ai trop de respect pour vous de le faire." The problem, Meilleur claimed, was that his office had not been sent a registered deed transferring land to the schoolhouses, and he was in no position to break the rules.[60] Unfortunately, absentee proprietorship and isolation from the nearest registry office presented formidable obstacles to the Bois-Francs commissioners.

In 1847 the Somerset commissioners were still facing the same problem concerning the land deed, though they desperately needed the £60 subsidy they had been counting on because they had invested £130 in their school buildings. They had been forced to suspend work on a sixth school, "vue l'indigence où sont exposés les chefs de famille de cette arrondissement," but an increasingly impatient Meilleur refused to bend the regulations.[61] He replied that he could not grant aid to the school buildings due to irregularities in procedure, and he complained to Somerset's secretary-treasurer that failure to conform to all the "réquisitions et formules" was adding to postage costs and increasing the work in his office. In September the Somerset chairman, a local surveyor named F.L. Poudrier, finally travelled to Montreal armed not only with affidavits from people stating that the superintendent had promised the money in May, but also with legal judgments against the commission on behalf of those who had done the work. He warned Meilleur that if the money was not forthcoming the following afternoon, he would submit his complaint to the governor-general accompanied by those of other school commissions: "Je suis bien mortifier d'avoir agir de cette sorte, mais je suis un pauvre homme je ne puis payer de ma propre argent cette somme."[62]

But Meilleur was unbending and Poudrier informed him in November that, after their unsatisfactory interview, the civil secretary had promised the money once the governor returned. Meanwhile, two of the commissioners were threatened with losing the little they had "par la mauvaise foi des personnes qui ont faits ces travaux." The matter was evidently settled to the Somerset commission's satisfaction, however, for two years later its chairman reported that one of the buildings had been expanded for use as a model school.[63] Poudrier had obviously gained the respect of the local population, for he won a large majority of Somerset's vote in the 1851 provincial election.

Aside from poverty, absentee proprietorship was the main obstacle to raising school taxes in the northern townships, and in 1851 the curé of Drummondville articulated the same complaints made by Hale for Sherbrooke County. Largely because non-resident landowners paid no taxes, the commissioners in Drummondville and area were left with a budget of less than £80 to cover the expenses of six to seven schools, making it necessary to charge higher monthly fees. Nor could they exempt those families who lived too far away from schools for their children to attend them. As a result, according to the Reverend Dorion, the very small number of wealthy proprietors (presumably residents) were able to rely in their anti-tax campaign "upon the poor class and some discontents of the middle classes." He feared that the opposition, which was "extremely active at the last election," would be able to elect a majority "unfavorable to the cause of education."[64]

Absentee proprietorship was also a major problem in the townships farther east, bordering on the Beauce region, where the compulsory assessment introduced in 1846 made a still greater negative impact than in the Bois-Francs. The mixed-language township of Broughton had supported one school until the 1846 school bill was passed, but none thereafter until the autum of 1849. The single school (whether Catholic or Protestant is not clear) still had only forty students in 1851, though the population had reached approximately six hundred by that time. In 1852 the inspector was informed that the school had been discontinued "owing to the small compensation allowed by the Government to the Teacher."[65]

As a French-language school municipality, neighbouring Tring included the townships of Lambton and Forsyth, both lying on the newly built Lambton colonization road. Here the number of schools listed in Meilleur's report dropped from four to zero in 1846. But the chairman did report in December of that year that two schools were open in the township, and that "malgré le mauvais exemple des paroise voisine tout le monde ysi parais ases satisfait de la cotisation." The problem was that the assessment was supposed to include wild lands, and two-thirds of Tring was wooded militia grants owned by absentees whose identities were unknown. There would be no new assessment until October 1847, but Tring was credited with two schools for the first term of that year. Two years later the chairman reported that yet another assessment was about to be made, and asked whether "les Grands Propriétaires de terres (bourgeois) résidant v.g. à Québec ou à Montréal" could be forced to pay their taxes in Tring. The commissioners had apparently done some research in the registry office in order to identify the speculators, for the chairman reported in November that he was submitting his returns late because "je n'ai pas pue retirer avant ces jour ci le montant de se cotisation des Bourgeois résidant à Québec et ailleur."[66]

There was initially sufficient harmony in Tring for its commissioners to be elected by the settlers rather than appointed by Meilleur, as in the Bois-Francs. But by 1849 internal conflict had developed over the location of schools, with the former commissioners accusing their successors of conflict of interest, and vice versa. The main problem appeared to be that the previous chairman had built a school on his own land in anticipation that he would be reimbursed by the government, and the new commission wished to change the site. Perhaps it was for this reason that the curé decided to become directly involved in the local administration of the schools. He appears to have exerted a calming influence, since the chairman was able to report in July that the 1849 election had been very quiet, contrary to expectations, with the two candidates being elected unanimously.[67] In 1852 the school inspector reported visiting two well-built schools in Tring, one managed by a woman with "good order and discipline" despite its nearly sixty students, and the other recently opened with her sister as teacher.[68]

One can only speculate as to why the French-Canadian colonists in the Eastern Townships generally conformed to the school reforms more readily than the British immigrants in the neighbouring northern townships. Their material conditions were no better, and the absentee proprietors presented a similar problem in all the peripheral townships in terms of tax collection. Also, speculators were accused with stirring up opposition in the Bois-Francs as well as Megantic County. The crucial difference may have been the greater cultural cohesiveness of the French Canadians and the concomitant stronger position of their local elites. Whereas Megantic's Protestant population consisted of Scots

Congregationalists and Covenanters, as well as Irish Anglicans and Methodists, the Catholic priests of the Bois-Francs had no religious rivals to challenge their authority. In contrast to the British settlements, the priests and local liberal professionals therefore tended to speak with one voice, and they all appear to have agreed that the government should impose school commissions on the colonists. Of course, it was because of popular opposition to the school reforms that such a step was deemed necessary in the first place. But if the Bois-Francs colonists did not mount as effective a resistance campaign as the habitants of St Grégoire and its neighbouring communities, it was doubtless because of their greater poverty and the fact that the farmers in the seigneurial parishes were able to make common cause with the seigneurs and their agents against land taxes and the increasing dominance of the village notables, including the curés.[69] In sharp contrast, there was no long-standing landed elite in the nearby frontier townships, and the missionary priests were able to pose as champions of the settlers against the oppression of the absentee proprietors.

THE 1849 SCHOOL BILL

Despite the quick rebound in school enrolment after resistance to the 1846 schools act had died down in the spring of 1847, Canada East was slow to surpass the level it had attained prior to the passage of that legislation. There were nearly 70,000 students reported for the scholastic year ending in July 1846, but the figure remained stalled at around 67,000 during the next three years (see appendix, tables A5–A9). This no doubt explains why in 1849 the government passed yet another school bill, one which represented a curious combination of increased coercion and conciliation. On the one hand, it increased sanctions against those who resisted school taxes. Thus, only those who had paid the tax would be legally entitled to vote for school commissioners; the steps school commissioners should take to prosecute those owing taxes or monthly fees were spelled out more clearly; fines were increased to £2 10s. for school commissioners who neglected to order a property assessment; and penalties were instituted against anyone who prevented the taking of an assessment, which included the right "to enter in and upon any property."[70] Clearly, the state had moved well beyond merely withholding the school grant as a means of forcing compliance with its regulations, though the Megantic example reveals that it could do little else where the inhabitants refused to elect a school commission and it dared not attempt to impose one.

On the other hand, in conformance with Meilleur's desire to make the new harsher regulations more palatable, the 1849 bill declared that commissioners could once again receive voluntary contributions to match the government grant. Only if they had not done so by 10 September of each year were they required to levy taxes in the usual manner, and with the increased sanctions listed above. While this provision might appear to represent a major concession to the voluntarist principle which Meilleur and the government had worked so hard to undermine, it still required the commissioners to assess property values, and they were to receive the voluntary contribution as one payment only, rather than in instalments.[71] The government no doubt realized that few school municipalities would return to voluntarism under these conditions. Certainly, the editor of the *Stanstead Journal* was not impressed with the concession. He wrote that "what has constituted the most objectionable feature of the School Law in this part of the Province, viz. the principle of taxation, remains still in force." The amendment did not alter the fact that "taxation is to be the basis of the School Law." Robinson concluded with the hope that "those who have hitherto opposed its working, will see the necessity of making the best they can of it, trusting to the future to obtain measures more suited to their views, and not interpose obstacles which will only retard the cause of education."[72]

One major advantage of the new regulations, at least according to Meilleur's interpretation, was that school commissioners could now collect voluntary contributions to compensate for the taxes not paid on wild lands.[73] The 1849 bill also yielded to the strong sense of localism with which Meilleur had been forced to comply unofficially as far as the building of new schools was concerned. It declared that school commissioners could raise contributions for the erection of schoolhouses by local districts rather than by municipalities as a whole, "according to the necessity and circumstances." Families could therefore continue to exert pressure on their school commission to have their tax dollars for building purposes remain within the immediate neighbourhood. Furthermore, decisions of school commissions relating to the limits of school districts and the site of a schoolhouse could now be appealed to Meilleur. With the colonization parishes obviously in mind, the new schools act also exempted municipalities which found themselves unable to pay sufficient taxes due to indigence. More minor revisions included the section which stated that monthly fees were compulsory in future only for children aged seven to fourteen years, though children as young as five and as old as sixteen could still attend school provided they paid the fees. Indeed, Meilleur suggested to the Eaton school commissioners in 1851 that they should allow those older than sixteen to attend, especially when the school was not crowded: "The friends of education ought to facilitate to our youth every means of instruction."[74]

But these concessions did not negate the impact of the increased sanctions in the minds of many inhabitants throughout Canada East. In 1850 the Guerre des Éteignoirs became marked by riots and other forms of popular resistance in Nicolet and Yamaska counties, as well as Île Bizard, west of Montreal. While much of the violence took place in the Nicolet parish of St Grégoire, one informant told LaFontaine in November that Drummondville was the only place in the general area that had not had a disturbance.[75] To prevent the popular resistance from spreading, LaFontaine presented a bill to the legislature in July which would have represented a complete concession to voluntarism.[76] However, much to Meilleur's relief, the government bill was withdrawn before second reading, presumably because the repressive military action and court proceedings had begun to make their impact on the disaffected parishes.

Canada East was therefore left with a more coercive system than Canada West, at least after 1850 when Ryerson's school bill left to the annual meeting of local householders and landowners the decision as to whether they would match the government school grant by a property assessment or by a rate bill (fees), or a combination of the two.[77] Ryerson wrote to his assistant in 1851: "I am satisfied I have adopted the best course in having the battle of free Schools fought in each city, town, & school section rather than in attempting to fight it in the Legislature." Instead of resorting to compulsion, he would use persuasion through his *Journal of Education* and the school superintendents. The result was that by 1871, when compulsory property assessment was finally introduced in Ontario, 4,244 of 4,400 school sections had already adopted it voluntarily.[78] Of course, the rate bill was a form of taxation as well, and Ryerson had not given the residents of Canada West the option of resorting to the system of voluntary contributions defended so strongly in Canada East. He was clearly confident that a population which had become accustomed to paying municipal taxes would not object for long to adding schools to the list. Meilleur, on the other hand, presumably feared that an open-ended rate-bill system would represent too great a barrier to school enrolment, particularly in the troubled economic context of the 1840s. Nor does it appear that anyone in the Eastern Townships defended this rather inequitable system, and during the 1850s there would develop widespread hostility throughout Canada East to fees of any kind.[79]

More surprisingly, there was no apparent support in the region for LaFontaine's concessionary bill of 1850. An official in the education office forwarded a letter to LaFontaine from the school commissioners of Dunham presumably opposing the 1850 bill, since he added, "on a paru croire que c'était dans cette partie du Pays qu'on désirait d'avantage les changements projetés, et que là ils pourraient y travailler avantageusement." Also, a Hatley correspondent later wrote that "The school bill presented in the last session by Mr Lafontaine could not have been brought into operation in any manner or shape whatever in this quarter of the province, chiefly owing to the absurd principle of voluntary contributions and much satisfaction was felt when it was withdrawn." And from the Reverend Green of Barnston (whose chief complaint had never been the tax system per se), came the statement that the feeling was universal that if "LaFontaine's bill presented at the last session had become law, it would have put a stop to the schools at once."[80] Finally, the *Stanstead Journal* labelled the new school bill a retrograde movement, and claimed that the people of the Townships wanted alterations to the current law, not its repeal. Not surprisingly, the newspaper resented the stipulations in LaFontaine's abortive bill that the government through the superintendent would appoint school commissioners, determine the number of schools in each municipality, and fix teachers' salaries when expedient. But its main objection represented a complete reversal of the position taken throughout the Eastern Townships since 1841:

The manner of raising the School Money, viz., by voluntary contributions, is not only absurd, but unjust. There are those in every community who are sufficiently benevolent to give freely for any object in aid of education, but unfortunately they are not usually those who have the most of this world's goods. The selfish, the grasping, the penurious, never will voluntarily contribute if they can avail themselves of the charity of their more benevolent neighbours.[81]

Part of the reason for this surprising turn-about was doubtless a sense of resentment that, after ignoring the peaceful objections from the Townships for years, the government appeared quick to respond to the violent protests in the French-Canadian parishes. Furthermore, LaFontaine's bill did not even allow school municipalities to retain the assessment option if they chose to do so. Most important, however, must have been the sense of frustration at the government's apparent readiness to change the rules once again, just when most of the region had adapted to the previous ones. A year later, when the editor of the *Stanstead Journal* heard that the school laws were once more about to be overhauled, he wrote that this was

a hobby quite apt to be ridden by our legislative doctors too much. What we want is a sound, practical common school system, simple enough at least to be interpreted by a well read lawyer, and with not more provisions than can be comfortably contained in a moderate sized quarto of fifty pages; then, whether exactly in accordance with the views of A B and C or not, give it a fair trial. We want stability.[82]

Nor was there any groundswell of support in the region for John McConnell's school bill, introduced in July 1851, even though it would have made assessment optional.[83] Throughout the province the principle of voluntarism was evidently being surrendered, for 90 percent of Canada East's school municipalities reported property assessments in 1855. And when permitted the following year to assess higher than the annual government grant, the majority of the school commissions soon did so in order to lower or eliminate the school fees.[84]

Despite the Guerre des Éteignoirs, then, the 1849 bill clearly had the desired effect as far as local school support and student enrolment was concerned. After having declined from the peak of 69,887 in 1845–46, the number of students in Canada East increased steadily each term from the fall of 1849 to the spring of 1851, when it reached 79,284 (see appendix, tables A5–A11). However, there had been much less movement in the Eastern Townships. Here, the enrolment peak of 9,017 achieved just prior to the 1846 legislation was restored quite quickly, but not much additional progress was made during the next several years, largely because near-maximum ratios had already been achieved in the more populous counties. Student numbers in the Townships remained steady at about 10,000 until the spring of 1850, then increased somewhat to 11,446 a year later. By 1851 the equivalent of 100 percent of the school-age children (five to fifteen years) were enrolled in Stanstead County, 91 percent in Missisquoi, 65 percent in Sherbrooke, and 62 percent in Shefford. Only in Drummond (29 percent) and Megantic (23 percent) were the ratios below the provincial average of 45 percent, but the enrolment in both these counties had increased substantially by 1861.[85] Evidently, then, the schools act of 1849 had made a limited though positive impact on the region as far as participation in public schooling was concerned.

The state had won a signal victory in imposing the school tax system on a rather reluctant population, but the generally more willing acceptance of municipal assessments (though only on a project-by-project basis) suggests that there was not a deep-seated opposition to taxation in principle. Since schools were a more localized concern than roads and bridges, however, it is not surprising that ratepayers in one sub-district would resist a system in which they might have to subsidize the schools elsewhere in the township. As for the residents of poorer sub-districts, they had reason to fear that their schools might be closed under a more centralized system, and their children forced to travel long distances in the name of educational improvement. The result, as the school inspectors discovered, was that school commissions tended to allow taxation and other school matters to be managed at the individual school level. In this sense, Meilleur's victory was only partial, for the localized version of the tax system would certainly perpetuate the local sense of independence from outside authority as well as make it difficult to improve education standards in poorer communities. But most school districts did accept taxation, and it appears that they did so not only because of their desire to gain the government subsidy, but because they were ultimately convinced that it was a more equitable and efficient system than the old voluntary one.

MODEL SCHOOLS

The type of instruction Meilleur wished is reflected in his suggestion that commissioners choose teachers who could teach reading, writing, arithmetic to the rule of three, the elements of grammar and geography, and the first general notions of science. In 1852 he strongly recommended the recently printed "Teacher's Guide" as a means of saving money on school books and efficiently imparting "both theory and practice" to students. Observing that the liberal professions had become overcrowded with the idle, while "some of the honest branches of industry are almost abandoned," Meilleur stressed that instruction should be geared towards producing well-educated mechanics, manufacturers, and farmers. Rather than receiving highly scientific training which would only render them vain and contemptuous of authority, children should be taught to respect "the humble but honourable and lucrative" calling of their parents.[86]

One method Meilleur favoured to such an end was to instill the habit and taste for manual labour, though it is clear that he had independent producers rather than an industrial proletariat in mind. His chief instrument in preparing boys for the labour market was to be a model school for each township and parish, and the 1849 school act dictated that the school commissioners should set aside £20 of the annual grant for this institution. Meilleur had written three years earlier that such a school would "offer to children [meaning boys] already advanced in their education, the means of terminating a course of studies adapted to the ordinary wants of society." The students would study Latin and history, but they should also learn the art of design and how to trace on maps the quickest and most secure routes "to those countries the natural and artificial productions of which serve to sustain commerce," how to compose letters on practical subjects, how to make out receipts and draw up promissory notes, and how to keep accounts by single and double entry. Last but not least, the model schools should inculcate "a knowledge of the principles of agriculture."[87] As for the girls, the local commissioners could establish for them a school "upon a superior footing" which would be eligible for the same share of the school subsidy as the other schools in the parish or township.[88]

Model schools would obviously hold more attractions than girls' schools for local taxpayers, especially in rural areas, but Meilleur had no power to enforce their establishment and few of either type were opened during our study period. The chief problem was money combined with localism, since townships wishing to open a model school were informed that there were no special funds for that purpose, and that it would require £150 in local support.[89] The residents of Compton raised £300 for a model school in 1849, but they also asked the government for a special grant to help pay the expenses.[90] In 1852 the inspector for Shefford and Missisquoi counties observed that the school commissioners in each township generally "consider it an injustice to appropriate as large a share of funds for the benefit of one District." In any case, many of the elementary schools already taught the same subjects that would be offered in the model schools.[91] Not surprisingly, the few attempts to open such institutions aroused considerable local opposition.

When Melbourne Township's school commissioners decided to build a model school in 1851, a local meeting convened by a JP demanded that they resign and that auditors be appointed to examine their books. Meilleur was informed that "A feeling of great excitement had been got up by the crying and misrepresentations of a few individuals who have set themselves in opposition to the commissioners, several threats and manoeuvres were used to intimidate the latter from pursuance of their duty and it has been said by some that if the tax is enforced the house would be burned." To make matters worse, there were only two magistrates, one of whom opposed the school act and refused to hear any case in which the commissioners were concerned. Nearly every ratepayer had refused to contribute unless compelled to do so by law, but the circuit court would not sit until the following September.[92]

Meilleur replied that the commissioners should suspend construction of the model school as well as the special assessment, at least until the excitement had died down. If it persisted, the project should be abandoned and the government grant of £122 10s. returned. Meanwhile, everything possible should be done to keep the elementary schools open, including a call to Major John to bring his police force.[93] The stand-off continued into the following month, however, when Meilleur received a protest petition with sixty-nine signatures, said to be the majority of the freeholders in Melbourne. They accused the commissioners of withholding funds from the teachers for months and even years while money was given to private individuals, avowedly on loan, but with no account given to the committee of inspection. Because the secretary-treasurer, Udolphus Aylmer, had refused to co-operate by opening all the books, the petitioners were able to charge further that he had failed to keep any vouchers, receipts, or accounts for each separate district as required by statute. There wasn't even any means to determine the cost of building the model school, which had been the main impetus for the protest. The petitioners further complained that this project should not have been a priority when there were sub-districts still without schools.[94]

In response, the commissioners denied all the charges and stated that the memorialists were only a small minority of the population. They asked Meilleur to send someone to inspect their accounts and investigate the charges "reflecting upon their individual characters." Otherwise, they would "feel bound to petition the Governor General to relieve them from their arduous, thankless, and unpleasant duties."[95]

The results of this altercation are not known, but the situation became tense when the leader of the Melbourne protesters, James Reddie Laing, attempted to flout the law by having an entire new slate of commissioners elected at the annual public meeting. When Laing refused to leave the room, the chairman had a justice of the peace swear in some special constables in order to carry the troublesome English gentleman to the Sherbrooke jail for eight days. The order was not carried out, but Laing nevertheless demanded satisfaction for the fact that the "miserable and contemptible" school commission chairman had ordered a British subject to be incarcerated while exercising his rights. Meilleur's unsympathetic answer was that Laing would have to resort to the courts because school commissioners in the execution of their duties were beyond the control of the provincial government.[96] Under these circumstances, it is not surprising that in November 1851 Meilleur regretfully approved the sale of the model school building. But the school commissioners appear to have won the struggle in the end, for the following July Inspector Child reported that twenty boys were attending classes in an unfinished building for which a substantial debt was still owed to the contractor.[97]

Local support for model schools was stronger in Barnston Township in 1850 than it was in Melbourne, but there too the expenses involved represented a major hurdle. Because the school commissioners had missed the 31 July deadline for levying the required £150 tax, Meilleur suggested that they resort to voluntary contributions. In a rather stunning reversal from a few short years earlier, the school commissioners rejected the voluntarist option as being inequitable. They argued that because the enemies of education and the wealthy opposed construction of a model school, even though they would undoubtedly send their children to it if one were built, all ratepayers should be forced to contribute their share. Secretary-Treasurer Green added that local support would be stronger if girls were allowed to attend.[98]

A month later, the Reverend Green submitted an ambitious plan, with ten rooms and an apartment for the teacher on the first floor, six rooms on the second floor, and thirteen smaller rooms in the attic for student boarders. The assumed cost was £400 to £500, with half that amount expected from the government. But Meilleur had consented to only a £150 grant, leading Green to complain that if the commissioners were prevented from fulfilling their contractual obligations they would become "a public laughing stock." Construction did come to a halt in March 1851, but the school appears to have been completed because a year later the rather desperate commissioners requested additional funds to enable them to pay off their £75 debt for the building. Inspector Child reported in July that Barnston was "sufficiently populous and wealthy to sustain the School, and I trust that when the feeling becomes more harmonious among the people, it will prosper."[99]

Despite their difficulties with financing the construction and repairs of elementary schools, the school commissioners of French-speaking Somerset Township took steps in 1849 to expand one of their buildings for use as a model school, and to accommodate girls in a separate room. The lot had been free, but they had invested £54 in the building and they wished to hire a qualified second teacher at £35 per year. They had also spent £13 for books and school supplies and planned to lay out another £10 3s. for maps, etc. Otherwise, the commissioners claimed, the students would be in the same situation as those in the neighbouring parishes, with nine or ten sharing each book. Once again, however, they failed to provide the education office with a deed, and it would appear that no extra grant was forthcoming as Somerset received only £23 17s. 10d. for its five schools for the first six months of 1850. In July the commissioners informed Meilleur that without his assistance the model school would be suspended despite the good will of the population.[100] What happened thereafter is not known, but the ambition shown by Somerset is quite remarkable in view of the few attempts made to open model schools in the American-settled area to the south. Clearly, the strong sense of localism was as strong an impediment in these older townships as was the lack of resources.

ACADEMIES

Another reason that greater attempts were not made to open model schools in the southern townships was presumably that the local elites were already served by a number of academies, both in the Eastern Townships and in Vermont, where many of them sent their children. While privately operated, those in the Eastern Townships had depended upon the government for assistance ever since the first ones had opened their doors in the late 1820s. In 1838, for example, the Special Council had provided £100 grants to each of twenty-one of these institutions throughout Lower Canada, including Stanstead Seminary, even though it was then serving as a winter barracks for the frontier troops.[101] In the spring of 1839 inhabitants of Stanstead also opened a "superior English School" taught by a graduate from the University of Edinburgh. While it claimed to be operated "on terms accessible not to the rich alone, but likewise to the worthy poor," the twelve proprietors probably failed to receive the £100 grant they applied for, since their school is not heard of again.[102]

Also in 1839, Sherbrooke Academy received £200, half of which was to liquidate debts, and the Anglican minister of Lennoxville and Sherbrooke was granted a one-time allocation for his seminary. In addition, Shefford and Waterloo academies were added to the list of subsidized academies, partly in order to train elementary school teachers because there were no normal schools in the province.[103] The Anglican minister of Waterloo, Andrew Balfour, had recently opened his academy with this purpose largely in mind, and in 1841 he claimed that about half the twenty-four students thus prepared to become teachers had been engaged as such. Three years later Balfour reported that his institution had an advanced class of eight training as teachers, five of whom would be ready to take winter schools when they opened.[104] No formal arrangements for training teachers in Canada East would be made until the next decade, and the role of the academy would remain rather ambiguous. While it was more than an elementary school and less than a college, the academy (whose Upper Canadian equivalent was the grammar school) was not intended to be an institutional link between these two institutions. Its curriculum was both classical and practical, and it served students from the ages of six to twenty-three.[105]

The return submitted by the Reverend Joseph Anderson for Richmond Academy in 1841 gives a good indication of how one such institution operated in the Eastern Townships. Anderson reported that he was the only teacher, and that the very full curriculum consisted of writing, arithmetic, English grammar, geography, book-keeping, "meseration," gauging, the elements of land surveying, geometry, trigonometry, algebra, and so on, plus Latin and Greek. The previous October the average number of students in daily attendance had been ten boys and two girls, four of whom were under the age of ten. Some of the boys boarded in the village. The yearly charge for "a merely English and Mercantile education" was £4, and double that amount for a mathematical and classical education. This fee structure should have produced £40 from his twelve students, but two were "free scholars," and "owing to causes over which I have but little control I scarcely receive the half of this sum." Anderson also claimed to have spent £5 fitting up a schoolroom, yet he had received no government grant.[106]

In 1844, however, Meilleur informed a Sherbrooke resident that £100 had been voted during the previous session for each existing academy. It was his private opinion that £50 per year would continue to be available for an academy in each county, provided it was placed under the control of the school commissioners.[107] Three years later the *Stanstead Journal* noted that for some years past Charleston Academy had been in a very low state, despite a liberal allowance from the government, but it was now well established, with 113 students. The newspaper added: "It is gratifying to note that there is one Academy in the Eastern Townships, that is doing well," since too many families sent their children to their Vermont competitors. It suggested that more efficient teachers should be employed, and that the fees be kept within the range of all who desired an education.[108]

Such an aim became more feasible in 1847, when the government appears to have finally established a policy of regular grants to the academies from the Jesuit Estates' Fund, which was now subsidizing Protestant as well as Catholic education in Canada East.[109] Thus, Charleston and Shefford academies, the non-denominational "seminary" at Stanstead, and the high school in Dunham each received £100, while the Sherbrooke Academy received slightly more, and £50 went to the British North American School Society of Sherbrooke. In addition, £100 was granted jointly to Andrew Balfour's school in Waterloo and the Bedford Academy. Finally, in the words of the *Stanstead Journal*, that "exclusive establishment at Lennoxville," Bishop's College, received its first subsidy of £250.[110]

Despite the expansion of the academy system in the Eastern Townships, New England institutions continued to advertise in the region's press. Three examples are the Derby Academy, which proclaimed that it offered anatomy and physiology illustrated by a mannikin (at an extra charge of 50 cents); the Lamoille County Grammar School of Johnson, Vermont; and the Orleans County Grammar School, also in Vermont. Indeed, in 1848 the *Stanstead Journal* rather self-servingly attributed the formerly "dormant and lifeless" state of the Stanstead Seminary largely to the fact that it had not followed the American example of soliciting students in the press: "In this day of Railroads and Magnetic Telegraph, it has become a 'fixed fact' that no institution, enterprise, or individual, can 'go ahead,' to use a Yankee phrase, without keeping their claims before the public." But the local school had reportedly learned the error of its ways and its enrolment had increased significantly to 117 students during the academic year. By 1849 that number had reached 143. Two years later the principal identified enrolment by gender: seventy-four males and sixty-nine females. It is not clear if they tended to be in different programs, but the academies were evidently providing an education for girls that Meilleur's blueprint for model schools would have largely precluded.[111]

The range of programs in the Stanstead Seminary might have been narrower than in the American institutions, but at least the fees were slightly lower – $2.00 for "English Branches," and $2.50 for languages during the eleven-week winter term, plus $1.25 per week for board in "good families." The Reverend Twilight of Richmond Academy, which had a similar fee schedule, advertised the total annual costs as £20 5s. ($81) per student, including board and lodging. Such a sum was clearly beyond the reach of most families of the time. In 1849 the Stanstead Seminary attempted to increase its appeal to the elite by hiring a French teacher as well as an instructor in instrumental music, charging $1.00 for a single course of twenty lessons of the former, and $8.00 for the latter, with use of an instrument. The following term it acquired a "new and elegant Philosophical and Chemical Apparatus," and claimed that it would be organizing a teachers' institute for a week.[112]

Beginning in 1851, Meilleur attempted to define a precise role for the academies as schools for students on their way to college, and to bring them under greater government control. He was removed from office before his suggestions could be fully implemented, but the academies were nevertheless subjected to the scrutiny of the school inspectors. Thus, in 1852 Marcus Child reported that Richmond and Compton academies were vacant, not having received any government aid, but the reason was presumably their failure to conform to required standards. A founder of the Stanstead Seminary, Child nevertheless had sent his daughter to a New England college and his son to Montreal High School, and he was quite critical of the region's privately operated institutions.[113] In 1853 Child reported that the three academies in the St Francis District (Stanstead, Hatley, and Sherbrooke), were taught by young students from the New England colleges "who come to this country, not to make teaching a business, but to raise funds, which will enable them to complete some professional study." The inspector contradicted the Stanstead Seminary's claim that its curriculum was "designed to be sufficient to qualify Students to enter any of the American Colleges." According to him, the instruction given in these institutions was "not in conformity to the law, neither is it such as to prepare students for College, for teaching, nor for any of the ordinary pursuits of business." Child, who had quite recently converted from Methodism to Anglicanism, recommended cutting off the academies' grants if the situation were not amended, perhaps by uniting them as collegiate schools with the Church of England's Bishop's College.[114]

Child's counterpart in Shefford and Missisquoi counties, Rotus Parmelee, was of essentially the same mind. In 1853 Parmelee reported that the five academies in his territory were all taught by competent and qualified teachers, but they were not well attended. Except for the few studying the classics, they offered the same subjects as many of the elementary schools. For higher education, most youths from the Eastern Townships still attended colleges in the United States. Consequently, the money contributed by the government to the academies, if directed to the elementary schools instead, "would subserve the Educational interests of the public much more effectually, and give more general satisfaction." Parmelee nevertheless felt that a smaller number of academies, "better endowed, better supplied with fitting apparatus, and Teachers, in the different departments of Academical Education, and thus made attractive and popular, would be a great public benefit."[115]

Clearly, then, the Eastern Townships academies were somewhat anachronistic, but by 1855 there were thirteen such Protestant institutions in the region, as well as a Catholic college in Sherbrooke. While most of them served students of both genders, two were exclusively for girls and several others held separate classes for females, as funds permitted. In 1855 they employed forty-three teachers (an average of three per school) and served 942 students (an average of sixty-seven per school).[116] Their most useful function may have been to produce teachers for the local public schools, though they were obviously also designed to provide the rudiments of a commercial training as well as a classical education for the children of the local elites. Several of them would perform the latter function as privately endowed institutions well into the next century.

INSPECTORS

The position taken by Child and Parmelee concerning the academies is a good example of how the school inspectors could serve to augment state control over the education system. The provision for inspectors in Canada East was not made until 1851, even though Arthur Buller had supported the idea in 1838, and district supervisors had been crucial to the success of the school reforms in Canada West since 1843. Bruce Curtis has argued that the knowledge collected by inspectors "was an inevitable precondition to state educational administration, for no state agency could govern schools about which it knew nothing."[117]

It is difficult to understand, then, why Meilleur and the legislators of Canada East waited so long to introduce inspectors into their school system. There was certainly support for the idea in the Eastern Townships. As early as 1838 Archibald McKillop of Inverness Township had recommended that rather than have elected trustees, the government should appoint a manager for each township whose role would be to determine whether the schools, which would be organized entirely by local initiative, deserved a government grant.[118] Five years later J.S. Sabins of Sherbrooke suggested the appointment of district directors, while the Reverend Alexander of Clifton recommended district inspectors or supervisors, and another Reverend Alexander, this one from Leeds, suggested a board of examiners for each county to examine the teachers and the schools, the elected school commissioners "being generally incompetent to the task." Perhaps Meilleur simply had too much faith in his own powers of persuasion and coercion to feel the need for such intermediaries. Certainly, he must not have taken kindly to the demand by a Barnston town meeting in 1847 that elected township superintendents essentially assume his duties, or the recommendation by the Honourable P.H. Moore of St Armand West that a resident English-speaking supervisor be appointed for the entire region.[119]

Provision for county superintendents in Canada East does appear to have been included in an abortive school bill for 1847,[120] but in his annual report for 1849 Meilleur mentioned the possibility only in a negative way. He emphasized how important it was for "all friends of the cause, above all of the Clergy, the Visitors, and School Commissioners," to keep a watchful eye on the local schools, thereby avoiding the costs involved in appointing "stipendiaries."[121] But the official visitors, whose mandate was not clearly defined by law, had little incentive to become embroiled in local controversies of this nature, and the school commissioners were often too poorly educated to interfere in the classroom. The outbreak of violence soon afterwars spurred critics to charge that the chief superintendent "n'est autre chose qu'une machine à payer et à enregistrer des rapports et des reçus. Quant à son autorité, à son droit de surveillance, ils sont *nuls*, ou plutôt il n'en possède réellement pas."[122] In 1850 Meilleur himself recommended the appointment of a deputy superintendent as a kind of itinerant assistant who would gather statistics, examine accounts, and investigate complaints. But the only practicable course would be to establish a corps of school inspectors, and Meilleur finally suggested this the following year.[123]

John McConnell's bill, introduced in June 1851, would have adopted Canada West's system of municipally appointed county superintendents, but the government opted for a much more centralized system of state-appointed officials. Meilleur's initial instructions required that they visit all the schools under their jurisdiction every three months. They were to report the number and type of schools in operation, their enrolment, the number of children of school age in each local school district, and the manner in which school monies had been divided by the commissioners. This task involved examining the assessment roles and account books, as well as taking note of debts and credits, "and of the means they have at their disposal to acquit the one and call in the other." The inspectors were also to determine whether the school grounds were cultivable and recommend the planting of fruit and forest trees, as well as the maintenance of "order and cleanliness throughout."

But Meilleur's prime concern was clearly the teachers, whose "morality and literary qualifications" were to be noted by the inspectors. The inspectors' reports were also to specify the teachers' gender, marital status, age, degree of instruction, and "the kind of School which they keep," as well as whether or not they had passed an examination before one of the boards of examiners. Those who could not produce documented proof of qualification and morality were to be tested by the inspector, who could issue a temporary certificate. Female teachers were not to be exempt from this examination even though the 1846 school bill did not require them to appear before a board of examiners. The inspectors were also to report on the subjects taught in each school, the books used, and the method of instruction.

Finally, it was the duty of the inspectors to investigate local opposition to the school law and attempt to resolve all such "difficulties," using "the greatest circumspection" in doing so. Wherever possible in such matters they were to "consult the wishes of the majority," and to join with the local school visitors as "a species of tribunal of arbitration." They were also to encourage the closing of inferior schools in poor or remote areas, informing the families that their children would benefit more from attending good schools even if it were less frequently and for shorter periods of time. Such tasks required diplomacy, for the inspectors were not simply to be gatherers of statistical data; they were expected to "do their utmost to render the Law popular, in endeavouring to show the people the great advantages they cannot fail to derive from it."[124]

The inspectors of Canada East, who held all the powers and authority of the chief superintendent within their sphere, acted much more directly as state agents than had the district superintendents of Canada West. And the contrast was even more marked after 1850 when the district superintendents were replaced by less socially influential school inspectors at the individual township level. According to Gidney and Lawr, these men, who were appointed by county councils, often had "strong local loyalties which would qualify their effectiveness as agents of the central government."[125] As full-time state-appointed officials responsible for large territories, Canada East's inspectors may have felt fewer divided loyalties, but their effectiveness was inevitably compromised by the large number of widely scattered schools for which they were responsible.

The aging Marcus Child, for example, was assigned nineteen townships with 207 elementary schools, two model schools, six independent schools, and seven academies and colleges. The Reverend J.S. Clarke had to inspect the Protestant schools in Quebec City and southward to Megantic County, a territory including approximately five hundred miles of mostly very poor roads which passed through large stretches of unsettled wilderness. Finally, the forty-nine-year-old Vermont native, Dr Rotus Parmelee, reported in 1853 that his jurisdiction covered 220 schools with 7,595 students within Missisquoi and Shefford counties, that part of Stanstead County lying west of Lake Memphremagog, and the Protestant communities of the upper Richelieu valley.[126] The task of compiling regular and accurate reports under such conditions was a daunting one, to say the least.

Analysis of the impact made by the inspectors lies beyond the time frame of this study, although Dufour reports that they were generally well received, and that they helped to convince the general population to accept the property-tax system.[127] For our purposes, however, the first reports of the Eastern Townships inspectors provide a useful impressionistic survey of the public schools system in the region at mid-century. Child admitted in his first quarterly report, dated 31 July 1852, that he had not yet visited most of the schools, but he had inspected the registers and accounts of each municipality. It had been impossible to fill all the blanks in the tables he had been provided, "owing to the imperfect manner in which the School-law has been carried into effect in this District," but he could attest that the treasurers' accounts were generally well kept. The registers were also legible for the most part, but "in other respects quite imperfect, and to explain what was necessary to make them conformable to the Law, engaged a good deal of my time and attention." Failure to conform to such legal requirements had caused the loss of a number of the commissioners' law suits, though most of the assessments had been collected without costs. The main exception remained the absentee proprietors.

Child had also found that the school fees were not generally fixed according to law, with the inhabitants simply making up the balance for that part of the teacher's salary not covered by assessments and the government grant. The teacher's boarding expenses were generally apportioned among the more affluent families in each district. Child encouraged the school commissions to vary school fees according to the means of the parents, the ages of their children, and the course of instruction, rather than levying the uniform rate of two shillings per month. The following year, in June 1853, the somewhat discouraged inspector reported that there was "no part of the school commission's duty well and correctly performed in this District (St Francis)." This former champion of voluntarism now advised withholding the grant from every municipality "which did not comply with the law as you have instructed them to do."[128] As for the teachers, Child found in 1852 that those employed during the summer months were generally well-qualified females "of unblemished moral character." They kept daily journals according to the forms provided, though not in duplicate as required. Since many of those who taught during the winter were men, it was necessary, according to the 1849 school bill, that they appear before a board of examiners before 1 July 1852. Most could ill afford the expense of a journey to Quebec or Montreal. There was a general wish, therefore, that such a board be established in the Eastern Townships.[129]

Rotus Parmelee, the inspector for the area to the west of the St Francis District, was still more forceful on this point. He claimed that the requirement for male teachers to travel outside the region for qualification "is part of a system of centralization that has long, too long, prevailed in Canada, but, alas, it is friendless in this locality. And were I to use, in reference to it, every adjective in Webster's Dictionary, expressive of dislike, contempt, or even abhorrence, I should not be amenable to the charge of using hyperbole or even exaggeration." While males were not eligible for employment unless they held a diploma, "no Law can compel young men to teach." There was therefore little choice but to employ females or forego the government grant. Parmelee did not even support a local examining board, such as existed in Canada West, because he felt that such institutions were superfluous: "A teacher who knew only the rudiments of grammar and arithmetic to the rule of three "would command little respect as a professional man" in a community "where old and young are educated, and where in almost every School there are more or less scholars with a thorough knowledge of Grammar and Arithmetic in all its parts."[130]

Indeed, Parmelee was generally sanguine about the state of education in his territory of nineteen municipalities. On his first tour he found that most of the school buildings were "of a superior kind, both as to construction and arrangement," and many of the teachers taught "thoroughly and efficiently" much of the curriculum for a model school. Parmelee also found that the secretary-treasurers kept correct accounts, but, aside from the clergy, "the appointment by Law of School Visitors is a mere dead letter." Nor did most of the school commissions examine the classes or their teachers. Like Child, Parmelee felt that the chief weakness in the system lay with the members of these school commissions. He stated that he was reluctant to criticize, since the faithful discharge of their unpaid duties "necessarily subjects them to censure." However, he had found that in many of the municipalities the school commissions had transferred to the local school manager, or individual commissioner living closest to each local district, the task of hiring of teachers and the collection of a sum from those attending school sufficient to make up the deficiency in the grant.[131] Even where the tax was

levied, the collection and disbursement were carried out at the local district level rather than passing through the hands of the secretary-treasurer: "Thus, the Commissioners, in their corporate capacity, throw the
responsibility upon the Commissioners, in their individual capacity, or
upon the local Managers, as the case may be; they, in turn, perhaps, call
for the scholar-tax unsuccessfully, are annoyed by duns from the Teachers, and resolve to give themselves no further trouble in a matter for
which they are not paid." Consequently, arrears of up to a year were not
uncommon.[132]

Parmelee's reports must have confirmed the education office's worst
fears, for localism and even voluntarism were clearly too deeply rooted in
many communities to succumb to government regulation in a few short
years. However, he claimed in his second and third reports that his visits
had resulted in progress being made in many municipalities. Parmelee
wrote in 1853: "I would here bear testimony to the urbanity with which I
have invariably been treated by the Commissioners and Secretary-Treasurer. They have received the suggestions my duty prompted me to make
to them, respectively, in a good spirit, solacing themselves, I presume,
with the reflection, that though their works are not perfect, they are, at
least, quite as good as the pay." Parmelee clearly considered himself to be
not only a state agent but also a spokesman for the people of his district.
He concluded his report of March 1853 by stating that "in acts there has
been no opposition to the Laws in my Circuit, but in opinion there has,
and the inhabitants are waiting in confident expectation that the Parliament will so far modify them, as to remove what is objectionable, supply
what is lacking, and adapt them to the wants and interests of every portion of Eastern Canada."[133]

J.S. Clarke of Quebec City submitted much less optimistic reports
for the remote townships in Megantic County, as did Inspector Bourgeois for Drummond County. In 1853 Bourgeois reported that the
teachers in Drummond taught only reading and writing, never having
studied grammar, arithmetic, or geography themselves. Here, as the
curé of Drummondville had also reported, the "éteignoirs" persisted
in their opposition to taxes, no matter what the system of education.[133] As for Megantic, Clarke wrote in the spring of 1852 that "I
cannot forbear expressing my profound grief, not only at the lamentable *want* of Education in the Townships through which I have passed,
but, what is still worse, at the mournful *willingness* to want it, which
almost invariably prevails." The only hope was that the more enlightened would "submit to self-denial, and self-sacrifice, for the sake of
these less favored of their fellow-creatures, who, sunk low in ignorance,
know not, alas! how much they lose while the treasures of knowledge
are unlocked."[134]

Clarke's bleak description was supported by a local minister named Henry Roe who wrote in 1852: "Most of the masters are not competent to teach the elements of reading and writing. I am persuaded that there is not a single municipality in Megantic, ... in which the provisions of the act are carried out in good faith."[135] The post-Rebellion school reforms may have furthered the cause of education in the more prosperous townships, but in Megantic they had simply closed the doors to what once had been a considerable number of institutions. Clarke to the contrary, the local settlers were not indifferent to education, and his successor reported in 1853 that if the taxation system was reformed so that it was not based on the superficial extent of land, "almost every municipality in the county of Megantic would immediately put the law into operation."[136] Certainly, until the commissioners gained the authority to collect taxes owing on the large tracts of unoccupied lands through sheriff's sale, there would be little hope of progress.[137]

Nor, it appears, had major advances been made in schooling within the longer-established communities, since there was still little more than the basic education which had already been available to most children prior to the Rebellion. The state had made greater inroads in the area of financial support. Voluntarism had been sacrificed on the altar of equity and uniformity, much as it had been without even a struggle in Canada West, though in that section of the province there remained a somewhat limited local choice between taxes for all householders on the one hand, or only the parents of school-age children on the other. The result of the state-sanctioned taxation would inevitably be a weakening of that sense of mutual obligation, as well as patronage by local elites, which had characterized pioneer communities.

But community pressures had ensured that individual schools in the Eastern Townships, and perhaps elsewhere in Canada East, were not only managed but financed at the local level by individual commissioners or appointed managers rather than by the school commission as a whole, despite the law's stipulations to the contrary. In other words, the schools system operated in a manner closer to that of Canada West than the regulations of the two sections would have led one to believe. Even the curriculum remained largely a matter of local discretion. In 1843, for example, Meilleur simply gave the Compton school commissioners the unnecessary advice to avoid school books objected to by any religious denomination when there were children "of mixed persuasions." More pointedly, he added that American books should be rejected for the same reasons that American teachers were disqualified by law.[138] The 1846 school bill did state that all books must be approved and recommended by the boards of examiners, but there was no such body in the Eastern Townships during our study period. Marcus Child reported in 1852 that because the people of the St Francis District had "imperceptibly acquired the control of the Schools in all their departments," it was difficult to bring them "under any system or uniformity in books." Those used were chiefly American, even though he did not fail to urge the use of the Irish National series.[139] In short, at mid-century the families concerned were still essentially in control of who would teach their children, how much they would be paid, what subjects would be taught, what books used, and whether to raise additional funds to improve their school. Indeed, the local school would remain a vital social institution in the rural communities of the Eastern Townships until the era of consolidation began after the turn of the century.[140]

Conclusion

Accompanying and underlying the major economic and constitutional changes of the 1840s in the Province of Canada was the establishment of locally based systems of government for municipal and school purposes. Lords Durham and Sydenham felt that municipal councils were an essential training ground for the exercise of responsible government at the provincial level, but more importantly, they were crucial to the expansion of the transportation network. Likewise, a more literate, better-trained population was seen by the governing elite as necessary for the effective operation of responsible government as well as the newly industrializing economy.[1]

As a rule, historians no longer blindly equate the march of industrial capitalism and the development of the modern state with human progress, but rather tend to emphasize the coercion of the dominant class. Necessary as this correction to the old liberal historiography is, the "new" social history has, in the words of Greg Marquis, "ignored or neglected the question of the popular legitimacy of state institutions." Marquis calls for "a more sophisticated approach sensitive to the complexities and ambiguities of popular attitudes towards the law."[2] Thus, while the expansion of the civil court system may have weakened the bonds of community by appropriating and formalizing arbitration, the widespread demand for commissioners courts to facilitate small debt collection also reflected the ongoing importance of mutual credit networks in the Eastern Townships.

As for criminal law, its addition to the responsibility of the St Francis District Queen's Bench in 1843 was more a matter of convenience for local jurors than the result of any outcry about increasing crime, even though Sherbrooke was beginning to industrialize at this time. The town's elite did actively promote temperance in the early 1840s, but this movement was more long-lived in the rural communities where community mores continued to be enforced largely through social pressure, including the charivari in extreme cases. This may have been a violent era, but at least until 1850 physical altercations were probably no more common or serious than they had ever been. Certainly, the use of guns and knives was virtually unknown. Where the interventionist steps taken by the state were deemed to be of low priority, or even obtrusive, as in the attempts to suppress counterfeiting and smuggling by the border population, little progress was made.

Only in the case of compulsory taxation for schools did the state win a clear-cut victory over the wishes of the local majorities. The outspoken defence of voluntarism after it was effectively ended by the 1846 school bill reveals the degree to which schooling had been associated with religion and public morality by the largely Puritan-descended population. Yet school assessments were generally accepted before legislation stiffened sanctions in 1849, and only the northern French-speaking townships were touched by the violent resistance movement known as the Guerre des Eteignoirs. The rather abrupt shift in popular attitude suggests that most people came to accept property assessment as a more equitable and dependable method by which to fund schools, just as it had proven to be for local roads and bridges.

But the state's role remained limited in scope, and the notion of equity stopped at the boundaries of the local sub-district as far as education was concerned. Contrary to the official regulations, each family's taxes generally went exclusively to support its neighbourhood school, and each school was supervised on a largely independent basis by the nearest school commissioner and one or more local managers. This profound sense of localism was not only a product of several generations of settlement and intermarriage in the older communities, but of isolation, ethnic clustering, and poverty in the peripheral colonization zone. The missionary priests and local liberal professionals were eventually able to persuade the French-Canadian settlers to conform to the school and municipal regulations. But social fragmentation continued to be so marked in the Irish and Scots settlements of Megantic County that they remained largely outside the operation of the public school system by the end of our study period.

Cultural values combined with economic circumstances therefore played a more important role than ethnicity in determining group responses to state formation in the Eastern Townships. And even though there was inevitably political conflict at the local level between English-speaking Protestants and French-speaking Catholics, there appear to have been few if any armed clashes such as took place between the Scots and Irish Protestants in Inverness Township. The two main linguistic groups appear to have generally maintained a wary distance from each other, with French Canadians willing to wait until they had established a clear majority before demanding a controlling voice in municipal councils and Protestants anxious to migrate elsewhere once this process had taken place. The situation was potentially more explosive in the culturally critical area of schooling, but the provision for dissentient status for religious minorities largely resolved the problem of mixed schools districts. Differences were eventually settled even in volatile Kingsey Township, where a longstanding politically motivated charivari failed to ignite an ethnic conflict.

It should be noted that this study is not suggesting that the Eastern Townships was somehow representative of the province as a whole, or that the government was particularly responsive to demands from this region. In both cases nothing could be further from the truth, which suggests that other parts of Canada East must have been making similar demands as far as municipal, school, and judicial reforms were concerned. But, because of their long struggle against economic, social, and political isolation, the people of the Eastern Townships were quite likely more receptive to the general thrust of institutional reform than was the majority elsewhere in the province.

Finally, while the basic tenets of the liberal creed of progress were widely accepted in the Eastern Townships, and presumably elsewhere in the province, it does not follow that farmers and villagers were willing to surrender all their political power to the urban bourgeoisie. They would accept taxation only if they felt it would serve their purposes and if they had direct input into the expenditure of the funds collected. Nor does it follow that individualist and materialist values overshadowed moral community-based ones. The people of that era could hardly be expected to foresee the slippery slope that increased integration into the market economy would eventually lead to. We should therefore heed Rusty Bitterman's advice against adopting a Durkheimian analysis in which "the forces of 'modernization' induce 'anomie and alienation' and common folk respond defensively at best they can."[3] In the final analysis, no matter what their motivations were, the people at the local level clearly exerted an important influence on the evolution of the educational, legal, social welfare, and public works systems. To examine state formation only from the perspective of the government and its legislation is therefore to leave oneself open to a fundamental misunderstanding not only of the dynamics involved but of the impact institutional reform made on social and economic development in general.

Data on Government-Funded Schools in the Eastern Townships, 1831–51

Table A1
Government Monies Expended (£.s.d.) for Education in the Eastern Townships Counties, 1831–43

	Drummond	Megantic	Missisquoi	Shefford	Sherbrooke	Stanstead	Total	Lower Canada
1831	220/12/0	91/13/6	664/11/0	251/12/10	788/14/2	2,298/8/8	4,315/11/4	25,242/10/3
1832	178/10/2	219/5/3	707/3/9	422/0/8	604/14/6	1,146/18/1	3,278/12/5	29,461/8/9
1833	210/18/0	266/10/7	502/16/0	268/19/0	778/6/6	1,277/10/0	3,305/0/1	19,833/0/11
1834	211/10/0	336/17/3	620/11/0	380/8/7	974/15/0	1,296/16/0	3,820/17/10	22,233/0/2
1835	188/20/0	324/1/0	790/13/0	452/4/0	1,690/18/5	1,354/12/3	4,800/12/8	25,611/13/3
1836	250/14/0	196/4/0	393/6/0	302/3/6	649/16/0	693/17/0	2,486/0/6	22,431/16/4
1837	175/14/6	158/0/6	351/3/6	222/17/6	414/3/0	751/1/6	2,073/0/6	12,648/1/1
1838	–	–	–	–	–	180/0/0	180/0/0	3,389/18/9
1839	–	–	–	270/0/0	270/0/0	90/0/0	630/0/0	3,753/6/6
1840	–	–	–	180/0/0	135/0/0	90/0/0	405/0/0	4,529/3/11
1841	–	–	–	180/0/0	145/0/0	180/0/0	505/0/0	3,066/10/0
1842	160/0/0	–	700/15/0	180/0/0	45/0/0	905/0/0	1,990/15/0	11,152/19/9
1843	199/8/6	590/4/4	942/0/0	180/0/0	[a]	905/0/0	2,816/12/10	20,288/18/6

[a] Sherbrooke total included with Stanstead.
Source: JLAC, vol. 4 (1844–5), Appendix PP, no. 4.

Table A2
Elementary Schools of the Eastern Townships Receiving a Government Grant (£.s.d.) in 1842

Municipal District	Conforming Schools		Independent Schools		
	No.	Grant	No.	Grant	Total Grant
MISSISQUOI					
Bay Missisquoi W.	10	200/0/0	–	–	200/0/0
Brome	4	80/0/0	–	–	80/0/0
Dunham	–	–	14	280/0/0	280/0/0
Granby	5	100/0/0	–	–	100/0/0
Potton	1	20/0/0	8	20/15/0	40/15/0
Total	20	400/0/0	22	300/15/0	700/15/0
SHERBROOKE					
Barnston/Barford	18	[not recorded]	–		
Barford	2		–		
Compton	16		–		
Eaton/Newport					
/Clinton	15		–		
Dudswell	5		–		
Hatley	14		–		
Shipton	18		–		
Westbury/Lingwik	6		–		
Windsor	2		–		
Melbourne	12		–		
Stanstead	29		–		
Brompton	3		–		
Clifton	6		–		
Total	146	905/0/0	–		905/0/0
NICOLET					
Durham	7	140/0/0	1	20/0/0	160/0/0

Source: JLAC, vol. 3 (1843), Appendix z.

Table A3
Elementary Schools of the Eastern Townships Receiving a Government Grant (£/s/d) in 1843

Municipal District	Conforming schools	Independent schools	No. of students	Paid to teachers by inhab.	Paid for support of schools	Allowed from public fund
CHAUDIÈRE						
Leeds	2	–	44	62/0/0	67/0/0	35/11/2
Jersey	1	–	20	15/0/0	20/0/0	15/0/0
Somerset	2	–	65	23/4/7	48/10/10	21/5/8
Broughton	1	–	25	2/10/0	3/5/0	2/10/0
Ireland	2	–	40	52/15/0	52/15/0	35/11/2
Total	8	–	194	155/9/7	191/10/10	110/0/0
MISSISQUOI						
Dunham	13	–	250	168/16/9	338/2/6	Total
St Armand E	8	–	165	180/10/10	203/15/10	amount
St Armand W	10	–	219	266/4/0	266/4/0	apportioned
Stanbridge	2	9	280	196/10/0	228/10/0	to the
Stukely	4	–	73	56/11/1	56/11/1	municipal
Brome	9	–	163	122/13/3	169/7/3	district
Farnham	4	–	83	30/7/6	61/13/6	allowed
Milton	2	–	68	30/16/3	67/12/3	
Bolton	7	–	238	83/13/0	155/14/3	
Potton	6	–	488	164/18/4	204/6/3	
Granby	9	–	174	163/13/5	186/8/4	
Sutton	8	–	135	106/8/0	106/8/0	
Shefford	7	1	186	169/18/0	196/1/0	
	87	10	2,522	1,740/0/4	2,240/14/3	942/0/0

Table A3   (Cont'd)
Elementary Schools of the Eastern Townships Receiving a Government Grant (£/s/d)
in 1843

Municipal District	Conforming schools	Indepen-dent schools	No. of students	Paid to teachers by inhab.	Paid for support of schools	Allowed from public fund
NICOLET						
Acton	–	1	22	2/17/6	2/17/6	2/17/6
Arthabaska	1	–	26	3/2/6	3/10/8	3/2/6
Blandford	1	–	20	12/0/0	22/0/0	12/0/0
Grantham	1	–	16	19/0/0	19/0/0	19/0/0
Kingsey	4	–	81	69/3/6	77/16/0	53/16/4
Stanfold	1	–	26	1/12/6	3/0/0	1/12/6
Durham	6	–	148	138/10/0	174/6/9	119/9/0
Total	14	1	339	246/5/10	302/10/11	211/17/10
SHERBROOKE						
Stanstead	29	–	733	822/1/7	936/14/7	
Dudswell /Windsor	4	–	58	34/4/10	35/12/2	The total
Brompton	2	–	50	45/0/0	49/0/0	amount
Tingwick	1	–	21	6/10/0	16/5/0	apportioned
Hereford	2	–	46	19/5/0	22/0/0	to the
Clifton	3	–	50	19/0/0	21/12/6	municipal
Compton	12	–	285	267/2/6	289/7/6	district
Hatley	14	–	331	294/7/1	343/12/1	is
Ascot	5	–	128	120/10/6	152/9/3	allowed
Bury/ Westbury/ Lingwick	2	–	33	5/5/0	6/7/6	
Shipton	11	–	220	248/5/10	344/18/1	
Eaton/ Newport	11	–	253	166/10/0	186/10/0	
Barnston/ Barford	16	–	418	284/0/0	345/19/0	
Melbourne	9	–	377	126/8/4	157/2/2	
Total	121	–	3,003	2,457/10/8	2,907/9/10	905/0/0

Source: JLAC, vol. 4 (1844–5), Appendix z. There is a column for dissentient schools in this table, but none were recorded for the Eastern Townships.

Table A4
School Returns for 1844 and First Part of 1845

	Municipal district	Children in School	Schools controlled by commissioners	Dissentient schools	Paid to teachers by inhab.'s	Government grant
1844	Missisquoi	3,621	110	2	2,286/1/10	972/4/8
	Sherbrooke	3,594	139	–	2,351/1/1	954/17/7
	Total	7,215	249	2	4,637/2/11	1,927/2/3
	Canada East	61,030	1,811	21	37,278/4/9	25,409/9/9
1845	Missisquoi	4,011	119	–	977/18/7	484/11/1
	Sherbrooke	3,967	136	–	985/11/9	474/13/5
	Total	7,978	255	–	1,963/10/4	959/3/6
	Canada East	59,389	1,722	15	18,151/12/1	12,713/16/6

Source: *JLAC*, vol. 5 (1846), Appendix P

Table A5
Eastern Townships School Returns for the Scholastic Year Ending 1 July 1846

Counties	Students	Under commissioners	Dissentient	Grant (£.s.d.)
DRUMMOND				
Aston	20	1	–	11/14/0
Arthabaska	37	2	–	51/11/6
Durham	197	7	–	84/0/8
Grantham	48	3	–	46/19/2
Kingsey	171	6	1	95/1/6
Stanfold	58	2	–	47/19/0
Tingwick	89	3	–	33/9/0
Wickham	25	1	–	15/9/9
Total	645	25	1	386/4/3
MEGANTIC				
Broughton	39	1	–	17/2/9
Ireland	91	4	–	39/4/4
Leeds	183	5	–	69/7/5
Somerset	48	2	–	47/15/8
Tring	120	4	–	23/17/10
Total	481	16	–	197/8/0
MISSISQUOI				
Dunham	339	17	–	127/0/9
Frelighsburgh	359	7	–	63/2/2
Philipsburgh	250	10	–	69/14/0
Stanbridge	542	18	–	132/16/2
Sutton	368	9	–	74/12/10
Total	1,858	61	–	467/5/11
SHEFFORD				
Brome	324	10	–	79/15/0
Ely	32	1	–	19/12/2
Farnham	458	12	–	93/1/11
Granby	301	11	–	69/14/0
Milton	155	3	1	46/2/9
Shefford	253	6	–	88/6/4
Stukely	70	4	–	44/6/6
Total	1,593	47	1	440/18/8

Table A5   (Cont'd)
Eastern Townships School Returns for the Scholastic Year Ending 1 July 1846

Counties	Students	Under commissioners	Dissentient	Grant (£.s.d.)
SHERBROOKE				
Ascot	265	11	–	108/18/3
Brompton	66	3	–	16/19/5
Bury	102	5	–	56/7/1
Compton	522	15	–	105/5/9
Dudswell	126	5	–	21/8/5
Eaton	475	13	–	90/19/1
Hereford	32	2	–	33/2/4
Melbourne	246	10	–	70/0/7
Shipton	297	17	–	103/6/3
Windsor	50	2	–	11/17/3
Total	2,181	83	–	618/4/5
STANSTEAD				
Barnston	331	17	–	125/4/6
Bolton	343	14	–	68/4/4
Hatley	400	14	–	83/10/9
Potton	301	8	–	59/9/8
Stanstead	884	29	–	171/17/2
Total	2,259	82	–	508/6/5
Eastern Townships	9,017	314	2	£2,618/8/0
Canada East	69,887	1,817	13	£26,097/12/2

Source: JLAC, vol. 6 (1847), Appendix FF

Table A6
Eastern Townships School Returns for the Last Six Months of 1846

Counties	Students	Under commissioners	Dissentient	Grant (£.s.d.)
DRUMMOND				
Arthabaska	41	1	–	25/15/9
Aston	–	–	–	–
Durham	192	7	–	42/0/4
Grantham	–	–	–	–
Kingsey	–	–	–	–
Stanfold	129	4	–	23/19/6
Tingwick	–	–	–	–
Upton	–	–	–	–
Wickam	–	–	–	–
Total	362	12	–	91/15/7
MEGANTIC				
Broughton	–	–	–	–
Halifax	–	–	–	–
Inverness	–	–	–	–
Ireland	–	–	–	–
Leeds	–	–	–	–
Somerset	82	3	–	23/17/10
Tring	–	–	–	–
Total	82	3	–	23/17/10
MISSISQUOI				
Dunham	310	16	–	63/10/5
Frelighsburg	373	7	–	31/11/1
Philipsburg	218	10	–	34/17/0
Stanbridge	482	16	–	66/8/1
Sutton	447	9	–	37/6/5
Total	1,830	58	–	233/13/0

Table A6   (Cont'd)
Eastern Townships School Returns for the Last Six Months of 1846

Counties	Students	Under commissioners	Dissentient	Grant (£.s.d.)
SHEFFORD				
Brome	422	11	–	39/17/6
Ely	–	–	–	–
Farnham	315	10	–	46/11/0
Granby	292	11	–	34/17/0
Milton	96	4	–	23/1/4
Shefford	587	11	–	44/3/2
Stukely	73	4	–	23/3/3
Total	1,785	51	–	211/13/3
SHERBROOKE				
Ascot	399	15	–	54/9/1
Brompton	69	3	–	8/9/9
Bury	171	7	–	28/3/6
Compton	473	16	–	52/12/10
Dudswell	116	5	–	10/14/2
Eaton	456	13	–	45/9/6
Hereford	64	3	–	16/11/12
Melbourne	200	9	–	35/0/4
Shipton	223	12	–	51/13/2
Windsor	–	–	–	–
Total	2,173	83	–	305/11/0
STANSTEAD				
Barnston	–	–	–	–
Bolton	302	12	–	34/2/2
Hatley	430	15	–	41/15/4
Potton	–	–	–	–
Stanstead	–	–	–	–
Total	732	27	–	75/17/6
Eastern Townships	6,964	234	–	£942/8/2
Canada East	60,685	1,611	21	£11,859/13/9

Source: JLAC, vol. 7(1848), Appendix P

Table A7
Eastern Townships School Returns for the First Six Months of 1847

Counties	Students	Under commissioners	Dissentient	Grant (£.s.d.)
DRUMMOND				
Arthabaska	38	1	–	25/15/9
Aston	–	–	–	–
Durham	201	9	–	42/0/4
Grantham	–	–	–	–
Kingsey	131	5	–	47/10/9
Stanfold	162	4	–	23/19/6
Tingwick	–	–	–	–
Upton	–	–	–	–
Wickam	–	–	–	–
Total	532	19	–	139/6/4
MEGANTIC				
Broughton	–	–	–	–
Halifax	–	–	–	–
Inverness	–	–	–	–
Ireland	–	–	–	–
Leeds	–	–	–	–
Somerset	149	3	–	23/17/10
Tring	94	2	–	11/18/11
Total	243	5	–	35/16/9
MISSISQUOI				
Dunham	355	17	–	63/10/5
Frelighsburg	382	8	–	31/11/1
Philipsburg	264	10	–	34/17/0
Stanbridge	491	16	–	66/8/1
Sutton	447	9	–	37/6/5
Total	1,939	60	–	233/13/0

Table A7 (Cont'd)
Eastern Townships School Returns for the First Six Months of 1847

Counties	Students	Under commissioners	Dissentient	Grant (£.s.d.)
SHEFFORD				
Brome	449	11	–	39/17/6
Ely	–	–	–	–
Farnham	433	12	–	46/11/0
Granby	285	10	–	34/17/0
Milton	218	4	2	23/1/4
Shefford	574	11	–	44/3/2
Stukely	85	5	–	22/3/3
Total	2,044	53	2	210/13/3
SHERBROOKE				
Ascot	341	13	–	54/9/1
Brompton	53	4	–	8/9/9
Bury	171	7	–	28/3/6
Compton	473	16	–	52/12/10
Dudswell	121	5	–	10/14/2
Eaton	505	15	–	45/9/6
Hereford	57	3	–	16/11/2
Melbourne	200	9	–	35/0/4
Shipton	288	19	–	51/13/2
Windsor	–	–	–	–
Total	2,209	91	–	303/3/6
STANSTEAD				
Barnston	350	18	–	62/12/13
Bolton	349	15	–	34/2/2
Hatley	319	16	–	41/15/4
Potton	–	–	–	–
Stanstead	–	–	–	–
Total	1,018	49	–	138/9/9
Eastern Townships	7,985	277	2	£1,061/2/7
Canada East	68,133	1,708	19	£12,510/2/1

Source: JLAC, vol. 8 (1849), Appendix OO

Table A8
Eastern Townships School Returns for the Last Six Months of 1847 and
First Six Months of 1848

County	1847			1848		
	Schools	Students	Grant	Schools	Students	Grant
Drummond	23	649	139/6/4	24	671	139/6/4
Megantic	6	268	35/16/9	6	263	35/16/9
Missisquoi	62	2,126	233/13/0	60	1,924	233/13/0
Shefford	55	1,844	188/10/0	28	897	102/1/6
Sherbrooke	82	2,356	294/13/9	84	2,467	294/13/9
Stanstead	88	2,284	254/3/3	89	2,350	254/3/3
E.T.	316	9,527	1,146/3/1	291	8,572	1,059/12/7
Canada East	1,741	67,257	12,283/12/10	1,653	66,579	11,637/2/4

Source: JLAC, vol. 8 (1849), Appendix OO

Table A9
Eastern Townships School Returns for the Last Six Months of 1848 and
the First Six Months of 1849

County	1848			1849		
	Schools	Students	Grant	Schools	Students	Grant
Drummond	26	688	139/6/4	25	739	139/6/4
Megantic	5	196	35/16/9	5	218	35/16/9
Missisquoi	59	1,830	233/13/0	74	2,244	233/13/0
Shefford	62	1,948	188/10/0	58	2,062	188/10/0
Sherbrooke	80	2,316	278/3/7	75	2,330	278/2/7
Stanstead	94	2,599	254/3/3	90	2,626	254/3/3
E.T.	326	9,577	1,129/12/11	327	10,219	1,129/11/11
Canada East	1,750	67,152	12,030/19/3	1,713	68,422	11,605/17/3

Source: JLAC, vol. 9 (1850), Appendix U

Table A10
Eastern Townships School Returns for the Last Six Months of 1849 and
the First Six Months of 1850

| | 1849 | | | 1850 | | |
County	Schools	Students	Grant	Schools	Students	Grant
Drummond	27	685	139/6/4	23	627	113/10/7
Megantic	19	719	96/16/8	15	486	71/19/5
Missisquoi	71	2,146	233/13/0	72	2,308	233/13/0
Shefford	68	1,898	188/10/0	67	2,065	188/10/0
Sherbrooke	75	2,118	294/13/9	81	2,270	284/1/3
Stanstead	91	2,258	254/3/3	89	2,620	254/3/3
E.T.	351	9,824	1,207/3/0	347	10,376	1,145/17/6
Canada East	1,817	68,994	12,645/8/0	1,879	73,551	12,693/1/5

Source: JLAC, vol. 10 (1851), Appendix KK

Table A11
Eastern Townships School Returns for the Last Six Months of 1850 and
First Six Months of 1851

| | 1850 | | | 1851 | | |
County	Schools	Students	Grant	Schools	Students	Grant
Drummond	27	928	162/0/3	30	1,124	162/0/3
Megantic	15	597	92/14/4	21	838	123/1/4
Missisquoi	71	1,930	233/13/0	68	1,991	233/13/0
Shefford	65	1,849	188/10/10	59	1,966	188/10/0
Sherbrooke	89	2,772	300/12/5	91	2,792	294/13/9
Stanstead	100	2,700	254/3/3	96	2,735	254/3/3
E.T.	367	10,776	1,231/12/1	365	11,446	1,256/1/7
Canada East	2,005	74,857	13,064/9/7	1,991	79,284	12,926/14/7

Source: JLAC, vol. 11 (1852–53), Appendix JJ

Abbreviations

ANQM   Archives nationales du Québec à Montréal
ANQQ   Archives nationales du Québec à Québec
ANQS   Archives nationales du Québec à Sherbrooke
CEHMS   Canada Education and Home Missionary Society
CHR   *Canadian Historical Review*
DCB   *Dictionary of Canadian Biography*
ETRC   Eastern Townships Research Centre, Bishop's University
HP   Hale Papers, McCord Museum, Montreal
JLAC   *Journals of the Legislative Assembly of the Province of Canada*
LE   Lettres expédiées
LR   Lettres reçues
NA   National Archives of Canada
QDA   Quebec Diocesan Archives
RHAF   *Revue d'histoire de l'Amérique française*
SHS   Société d'histoire de Sherbrooke
SPC   *Statutes of the Province of Canada*
STAS   Sherbrooke Total Abstinence Society
UCA   United Church Archives

NATIONAL ARCHIVES OF CANADA

MG24 A27   Lord Durham Papers
MG24 B14   Papiers LaFontaine
MG24 B141   Robert Hoyle Papers
RG1 E1   State Books, Province of Canada

RG1 E5   Records Put By, 1839–67
RG1 A1   Civil Secretary's Correspondence, Lower Canada, 1838
RG4 B24   Stipendiary Magistrates
RG4 B26   List of Magistrates in Commission, Lower Canada, 1845–
RG4 B30   Education Records, 1767–1856
RG4 B36   Municipal Records, 1694–1867
RG4 B37   Annexation Addresses, 1849–50
RG4 B72   Election Records, 1792–1866
RG4 C1   Provincial Secretary's Correspondence, Canada East, 1839–
RG4 C4   Provincial Secretary's Correspondence, Miscellaneous
Correspondence
RG7 G14   Governor General's Correspondence
RG16 A1   National Revenue – Customs, Excise, Correspondence and Returns

ARCHIVES NATIONALES DU QUÉBEC À QUÉBEC

E13   Fonds Éducation

Notes

INTRODUCTION

1 Jacques LeGoff, "Is Politics Still the Backbone of History?" *Daedalus* (Winter 1971): 5.

2 See Jean-Marie Fecteau, *Un nouvel ordre des choses: La pauvreté, le crime, l'État au Québec, de la fin du XVIIIe siècle à 1840* (Outremont, Qué.: vlb éditeur, 1989).

3 *Statutes of Lower Canada*, 36 Geo. III, cap. 9, ss. 25 and 26.

4 Bernier and Salée argue that the Legislative Council impeded the Patriotes' attempts at decentralization, but they fail to mention that a 1832 bill allowing parishes and townships to elect road commissioners to take over the responsibilities of the grand voyers was permitted to expire three years later because few parishes had taken advantage of its provisions. Furthermore, Papineau and the Rouges remained unenthusiastic about municipal reform in the later 1840s. See Gérald Bernier and Daniel Salée, "Social Relations and Exercise of State Power in Lower Canada (1791–1840): Elements of an Analysis," *Studies in Political Economy* 22 (Spring 1987): 120; and J.I. Little, "Colonization and Municipal Reform in Canada East," *Histoire sociale / Social History* 14, no. 27 (1981): 95, 118.

5 For a similar perspective, see Chad Gaffield, "Children, Schooling, and Family Reproduction in Nineteenth-Century Ontario," *CHR* 72 (1991): 162–8.

6 Michael B. Katz, "Origins of the Institutional State," *Marxist Perspectives* 1, no. 4 (Winter 1978): 6, 15.

7 Ian Radforth, "Sydenham and Utilitarian Reform," in *Colonial Leviathan: State Formation in Mid-Nineteenth-Century Canada*, edited by Allan Greer and Ian Radforth (Toronto: University of Toronto Press, 1992), 66, 70.

8 Bruce Curtis, "Representation and State Formation in the Canadas, 1790–1850," *Studies in Political Economy* 28 (Spring 1989): 63.

9 Ibid., 62, 72–3.

10 Colin Gordon, ed., *Power/Knowledge: Selected Interviews & Other Writings, 1972–1977* (New York: Pantheon Books, 1981), 98, 142, 168.

11 Curtis, "Representation," 74.

12 On the concept of the Eastern Townships as a region and the role of the Sherbrooke bourgeoisie, see Jean-Pierre Kesteman, "Une bourgeoisie et son espace: Industrialisation et développement du capitalisme dans le district de Saint-François (Québec), 1823–1879" (PhD dissertation, Université du Québec à Montréal, 1985), 66–88, 92–3.

13 See G.F. McGuigan, "Administration of Land Policy and the Growth of Corporate Economic Organization in Lower Canada, 1791–1809," CHA *Report* (1963), 65–73.

14 On the concept of neighbourliness, see Keith Wrightson, *English Society 1580–1680* (London: Hutchinson, 1982), 51.

15 In his recent study of local settlement patterns in Quebec, geographer Louis-Edmond Hamelin fails to appreciate the sharpness of this contrast between the seigneurial zone and the southern townships. See *Le rang d'habitant: Le réel et l'imaginaire* (Ville LaSalle: Hurtubise, 1993), 105, 108.

16 *Lord Durham's Report*, edited by Gerald M. Craig (Toronto: McClelland and Stewart, 1963), 78.

17 Elwood H. Jones, "Localism and Federalism in Upper Canada to 1865," in *Federalism in Canada and Australia: The Early Years*, edited by Bruce W. Hodgins, Don Wright, and W.H. Heick (Waterloo, Ont.: Wilfrid Laurier University Press, 1978), 22–26.

18 Bruce W. Hodgins, "Disagreement at the Commencement: Divergent Ontarian Views of Federalism, 1867–1871," in *Oliver Mowat's Ontario*, edited by Donald Swainson (Toronto: Macmillan, 1972), 57. See also Paul Romney, "From the Rule of Law to Responsible Government: Ontario Political Culture and the Origins of Canadian Statism," Canadian Historical Association, *Historical Papers* (1988), 95–6.

19 See Gérard Bouchard, "La dynamique communautaire et l'évolution des sociétés rurales québécoises aux 19ᵉ et 20ᵉ siècles: Construction d'un modèle," *RHAF* 40 (1986): 53, 57.

20 According to the 1851–52 *Census Reports*, the Anglicans in the Eastern Townships numbered 15,109 and the Methodists 13,545. Françoise Noël, *Competing for Souls: Missionary Activity and Settlement in the Eastern Townships, 1784–1851* (Département d'Histoire, Université de Sherbrooke, 1988), 87, 128.

21 Kesteman, "Une bourgeoisie," see especially 92, 316, 352–8, 687–703.

22 Marcus Child's testimony of 1834, cited in Matthew Farfan, *The Stanstead Region 1792–1844: Isolation, Reform, and Class on the Eastern Townships Frontier* (Ottawa: Townships Publications, 1992), 47–8.

23 Farfan, *Stanstead Region*, 48–51; J.I. Little, ed., *The Child Letters: Public and Private Life in a Canadian Merchant-Politician's Family, 1841–1845* (Montreal and Kingston: McGill-Queen's University Press, 1995), 12–15.

24 Since Stanstead was a two-member constituency prior to 1837, the number of votes cast are divided in half for that period. The data are from the introduction to Little, ed., *Child Letters*.

25 Ibid., 12; Farfan, *Stanstead Region*, 50.

26 *Farmers' & Mechanics' Journal and St Francis Gazette*, 22 Apr. 1841, quoted in Farfan, *Stanstead Region*, 52.

27 The voting qualifications were first mentioned in the 1845 bill (8 Vict., cap. 40, s. 9), and they remained unchanged as of the 1855 bill (18 Vict., cap. 100, s. 26).

28 Michael Braddick, "State Formation and Social Change in Early Modern England: A Problem Stated and Approaches Suggested," *Social History* 16, no. 1 (1991): 4–5.

29 Allan Greer, referring to Gramsci, makes this argument for the developments leading up to the Lower Canadian Rebellion. Allan Greer, *The Patriots and the People: The Rebellion of 1837 in Rural Lower Canada* (Toronto: University of Toronto Press, 1993), 9.

30 Keith Wrightson, "Two Concepts of Order: Justices, Constables and Jurymen in Seventeenth-Century England," in *An Ungovernable People: The English and Their Law in the Seventeenth and Eighteenth Centuries* (London: Hutchinson, 1980).

31 On the role of social pressure in the French-Canadian parishes, see Greer, *The Patriots and the People*, 98–100. For a useful discussion on the toleration of circumscribed violence in pre-industrial communities, see Benoît Garnot, "La violence au village dans la France du XVIIIe siècle," in *De France en Nouvelle-France: Société Fondatrice et Société Nouvelle*, edited by Hubert Watelet and Cornelius Jaenan (Ottawa: Les Presses de l'Université d'Ottawa, 1994).

32 Marcus Child to My Dear Wife, Legislative Assembly, 3 Oct. 1843, in Little, ed., *Child Letters*, 59.

33 Jeffrey L. McNairn, "'A united public opinion that must be obeyed': The Creation of Public Opinion in Upper Canada, 1836–1844" (paper presented to the annual meeting of the Canadian Historical Association, 1995).

34 See Andrée Dufour, "La scolarisation au Bas-Canada, 1826–1859: Une interaction état-communautés locales" (Ph D thesis, Université du Québec à Montréal, 1992); Allan Greer, "The Birth of the Police in Lower Canada," in *Colonial Leviathan*, 17–49; and Wendie Nelson, "The 'Guerre des

262   Notes to pages 17–19

Éteignoirs': School Reform and Popular Resistance in Lower Canada, 1841–
1850" (MA thesis, Simon Fraser University, 1989).

CHAPTER ONE

1 See Maurice O'Bready, *De Ktiné à Sherbrooke. Esquisse historique de Sherbrooke des
   origines à 1954* (Sherbrooke: Université de Sherbrooke, 1973), 7; Wilbur H.
   Siebert, "The American Loyalists in the Eastern Townships of the Province of
   Quebec," Royal Society of Canada, *Proceedings and Transactions*, 3rd series, 7
   (1913), section 2, 3–41; and Thomas C. Lampee,"The Missisquoi Loyalists,"
   Vermont Historical Society, *Proceedings* 6, no. 2 (1938): 81–135.

2 See Gerald F. McGuigan, "La concession des terres dans les cantons de l'est
   du Bas Canada (1763–1809)," *Recherches Sociographiques* 4 (1963): 71–89.

3 O'Bready, *De Ktiné*, 22; Joseph Bouchette, *A Topographical Description of the
   Province of Lower Canada* (London: W. Fadon, 1815). Another unofficial survey suggests that there were 26,916 inhabitants in the region in 1819. Ivanhoë Caron, "Colonization of Canada under the British Domination (from
   1815 to 1822)," in Province of Quebec, *Statistical Year Book* (Quebec: King's
   Printer, 1921), 537.

4 Bouchette, *A Topographical Description*, 356–7.

5 Louise Dechêne, "Observations sur l'agriculture du Bas-Canada au début du
   XIXe siècle," in *Évolution et éclatement du monde rurale: France-Québec xviie–
   xxe siècles*, edited by Jean-Pierre Wallot and Joseph Goy (Montréal: Presses de
   l'Université de Montréal, 1986); Cyrus Lebourveau, *A History of Eaton* (n.p.,
   1894; reprint, Sherbrooke: Page-Sangster, 1965), 14.

6 Quoted in Helen Taft Manning, *The Revolt of French Canada, 1800–1835. A
   Chapter in the History of the British Commonwealth* (Toronto: Macmillan, 1962),
   192–3.

7 Fernand Ouellet, *Histoire économique et sociale du Québec, 1760–1850* (Ottawa:
   Fides, 1966), 287. See also Marie-Paule Rajotte LaBrèque, "Les Canadiens
   et les Cantons de l'Est, 1820–30," *Journal of Eastern Townships Studies* 2
   (1992): 3–14.

8 In 1831 £14,625 in public improvement grants (20 percent of the provincial
   total) was spent in five of the six Eastern Townships counties, but the amount
   dropped to £90 in 1832 and £934 in 1833, becoming insignificant thereafter. *JLAC*, vol. 4 (1844–45), appendix PP, no. 3. See also J.I. Little, "Imperial-
   ism and Colonization in Lower Canada: The Role of William Bowman
   Felton," *CHR* 46 (1985): 519–20; Fernand Ouellet, *Lower Canada 1791–
   1840: Social Change and Nationalism* (Toronto: McClelland and Stewart,
   1980), 154.

9 J.I. Little, *Nationalism, Capitalism, and Colonization in Nineteenth-Century Quebec: The Upper St Francis District* (Kingston and Montreal: McGill-Queen's University Press, 1989), 36–47.

10 Ibid., 47–63; Jean-Pierre Kesteman, "Une bourgeoisie et son espace: industrialisation et développement du capitalisme dans le district de Saint-François (Québec), 1823–1879" (PH.D. thesis, Université du Québec à Montréal, 1985), 437–56.

11 Jean-Pierre Kesteman, "Les travailleurs à la construction du chemin de fer dans la région de Sherbrooke (1851–1853)," *RHAF* 31 (1978): 525–46.

12 Kesteman, "Une bourgeoisie," 563–5.

13 Ibid., 566.

14 Ouellet, *Histoire économique*, 359–68; R.L. Jones, "French-Canadian Agriculture in the St Lawrence Valley, 1815–50," in *Approaches to Canadian Economic History*, edited by W.T. Easterbrook and M.H. Watkins (Toronto: McClelland and Stewart, 1967), 121–3, 126.

15 Kesteman, "Une bourgeoisie," 297.

16 Sawmills were much the dominant industry, numbering 213 in 1844 and 327 in 1852. L. Chevalier, "L'industrie manufacturière de l'Estrie"(MA thesis, Université de Montréal, 1962), 77.

17 Kesteman, "Une bourgeoisie," 176.

18 Ibid., 282, 284.

19 Ibid., 136.

20 For details, see J.I. Little, "British Toryism amidst 'a horde of disaffected and disloyal squatters': The Rise and Fall of William Bowman Felton and Family in the Eastern Townships," *Journal of Eastern Townships Studies* 1 (Fall 1992): 13–42.

21 *British Colonist*, 26 Jan. 1826.

22 See S.J.R. Noel, *Patrons, Clients, Brokers: Ontario Society and Politics, 1791–1896* (Toronto: University of Toronto Press, 1990). More analogous to the Eastern Townships is the image of Upper Canadian politics depicted in Robert Fraser, "'All the privileges which Englishmen possess': Order, Rights, and Constitutionalism in Upper Canada," in *Provincial Justice: Upper Canadian Legal Portraits*, edited by Robert L. Fraser (Toronto: University of Toronto Press, 1992).

23 J.I. Little, *The Child Letters: Public and Private Life in a Canadian Merchant-Politician's Family, 1841–1845* (Kingston and Montreal: McGill-Queen's University Press, 1995), 12–13. Matthew F. Farfan, *The Stanstead Region 1792–1844: Isolation, Reform, and Class on the Eastern Townships Frontier* (Hull: Townships Publications, 1992), 29–30.

24 The contents of this pamphlet are reprinted as "An Address by Marcus Child," Stanstead Historical Society, *Journal* 6 (1975): 16–24.

25 Denyse Beaugrand-Champagne, "Les mouvements patriote et loyal dans les comtés de Missisquoi, Shefford, et Stanstead, 1834–37" (MA thesis, Université du Québec à Montréal, 1990), 46.

26 *Vindicator and Canadian Advertiser* (Montreal), 20 May 1834. Quoted in ibid., 49.

27 Little, *Child Letters*, 15; Kesteman, "Une bourgeoisie," 510, 535.

28 *Missisquoi Standard*, 9 May 1836.

29 Edward Hale to Peter McGill (copy), Sherbrooke, 22 Feb. 1836. The Bank of Montreal would finally express an interest in opening a Sherbrooke branch in 1840, when it asked Hale to be the manager. A. Simpson to E. Hale, Quebec, 8 Jan. 1840, HP, McCord Museum.

30 M.F. Colby, "Electors of Stanstead," 26 Dec. 1836, Political Tracts, 1836–51, Colby Papers, Stanstead Historical Society.

31 William Ritchie to W.P. Christie, Stanstead, 8 Mar. 1838, vol. 532, 1838, p. 30, RG4 A1, NA.

32 For further details, see Little, *Child Letters*, 17–18; and B.F. Hubbard, *Forests and Clearings: The History of Stanstead County* (Montreal: Lovell, 1874; reprinted Bowie, Maryland: Heritage Books, 1988), 12–16.

33 See Louis-Philippe Audet, "Edward Hale," *DCB*, vol. 10; and Monique Choquette-Habel, "Edward Hale, un des fondateurs de la première société organisée de Sherbrooke, 1801–1875" (MA thesis, Université de Sherbrooke, 1985).

34 E. Hale to F.G. Heriot (copy), Jan. 1838; F.G. Heriot to E. Hale, Melbourne, 29 Jan. 1838; Lt Col. John Eden to E. Hale, Montreal, 5 Feb. 1838, HP. Gosford had ignored the request for arms made by the Hon. Robert Jones as colonel of the Missisquoi battalion (*Missisquoi Standard*, 10 Apr. 1838), and a "loyal meeting" held in Compton in January 1837 had complained that "we alone of the inhabitants of the Townships are unprovided with efficient military authority to take such steps as many be deemed necessary for the welfare and prosperity of the Township." *Sherbrooke Gazette*, 28 Dec. 1837.

35 E. Hale to Eliza, Stanstead, Sat. morning; E. Hale to Col. A. Gugy (draft), [30 June 1845], HP.

36 J.G. Robertson to E. Hale, Sherbrooke, 13 Apr. 1846, HP.

37 E. Hale to Attorney-General (copy), 2 Aug. 1839; E. Hale to Civil Secretary (copy), Sherbrooke, 30 Aug. 1839; C.M. Montizambert to E. Hale, Montreal, 2 Sept. 1839, HP.

38 Draft reply to R.N.Watts to E. Hale, Montreal, 27 Nov. 1839, HP.

39 See, for example, E. Hale to William Ritchie (draft), [Apr. 1840], HP. In this letter, Hale refers specifically to "my friends Peasely, Pierce, Pomroy, Smith, Kilborn, etc."

40 E. Hale to C. Murdoch (draft), Sherbrooke, 20 May 1840, HP.

41 Draft reply to C.D. Day, 24 Aug. 1840, HP; Jacques Monet, "Bartholemew Conrad Augustus Gugy," *DCB*, vol. 10.

42 Public Good, "The Modern 'Pious Aneas' and His Trojans, or Lieutenant Colonel Gugy and The Demonstrations of the Unemployed," Fonds Bartholomew Conrad Augustus Gugy, P075/000/000/003, ETRC.

43 E. Hale to Eliza, Montreal, 7 Jan, 1840, HP.

265 Notes to pages 29–33

44 E. Hale to Eliza, Sherbrooke, 24 Aug. 1840; E. Hale to C.D. Day (draft),
5 Oct. 1840, HP; Charlotte Thibault, *Samuel Brooks, entrepreneur et homme politique de Sherbrooke, 1793–1849* (Département d'histoire, Université de Sherbrooke, 1985), 58, 63.

45 J.S. Walton to E. Hale, Sherbrooke, 22 December 1840; E. Hale to Eliza,
Montreal, 27 Dec. 1840, HP.

46 E. Hale to Eliza, Montreal, 19 Jan. 1841; J.S. Walton to E. Hale, 25 Jan. 1841,
HP. The proposed railway was to run from Sherbrooke west to the Richelieu,
where it would connect with the Champlain and St Lawrence Railway at
St John's. Gerald J.J. Tulchinsky, *The River Barons: Montreal Businessmen and
the Growth of Industry and Transportation, 1837–53* (Toronto: University of Toronto Press, 1977), 130.

47 Hollis Smith to E. Hale, Lennoxville, 20 Feb. 1841; E. Hale to John Davidson (draft), 27 Feb. 1841; John Davidson to E. Hale (private), Montreal,
23 Feb. 1841; 3 and 5 Mar. 1841, HP. For further details on the Sherbrooke
contest, see Thibault, *Samuel Brooks*, 86–91.

48 Michael E. McCulloch, "English-Speaking Liberals in Canada East, 1840–
1854" (PH.D. thesis, University of Ottawa, 1986), 126.

49 On the crucial role played by Sydenham throughout most of Lower and Upper Canada during the 1841 election, see Irving Abella, "The 'Sydenham'
Election of 1841," *CHR* 47 (1966): 326–43.

50 S. Sewell Foster vs Alphonso Wells, Shefford County Poll Book, 1841, 103 –
11/01–04, ANQM.

51 Andrew Robinson to E. Hale, Montreal, 5 Apr. 1841, HP.

52 Quoted in Farfan, *The Stanstead Region*, 52.

53 McCulloch, "English-Speaking Liberals," 127–8.

54 Ibid., 127, 129; J.G. Clapham to Lord Sydenham, Quebec, 27 Feb. 1841,
3361– 4, vol. 23, RG4 B72, NA.

55 E. Hale to Eliza, Kingston, 12 July 1841, HP.

56 E. Hale to Eliza, Kingston, 2 and 14 Aug. 1841, HP.

57 Draft letter, Sherbrooke, 21 Dec. 1841; E. Hale to J.B. Forsyth (draft),
Sherbrooke, 4 Jan. 1842; E. Hale to D. Daly (copy, private), Sherbrooke,
22 Feb. 1844, HP.

58 Memo of Agreement between the British American Land Company and
G.F. Bowen and Edward Hale, 19 Mar. 1846; E. Hale to Eliza, Montreal, 26
and 29 Mar. 1846; G.F. Bowen to E. Hale, Sherbrooke, 8 May 1846, HP.

59 W. Morris to Livingston Morris, 5 Apr. 1845, Morris Papers, McCord Museum.

60 M. Child to D. Daly, Kingston, 24 July 1841, no. 1321 1/2, 1841, RG4 C1.

61 M. Child to D. Daly, Kingston, 22 July 1841, no. 329 3/4, p. 5161, 1840–41,
RG4 C1; Little, *Child Letters*, 21.

62 See Noel, *Patrons, Clients, Brokers*, 15–16, and chapter 5. Child may well have
learned the rules of the game prior to the Rebellion, for his first running

mate, Ebenezer Peck, was by the 1840s said to be teaching the "Canadian" theory and practice of party organization to the Illinois Democrats. Peck later became a friend of Abraham Lincoln and a founder of the Illinois Republican Party. Senator N.P. Lambert, "Ebenezer Peck, Stanstead's Parliamentary Representative for Lower Canada," SHS *Journal* 13 (1989): 51–3.

63 P. Hubbard to E. Hale (confidential), Sherbrooke, 8 July 1841, HP.

64 See, for example, Robert Hoyle to Eliza, Stanstead, 10 Apr. 1842, MG 24, B141, NA.

65 Wright Chamberlin et al. to E. Hale, Stanstead, 22 Dec. 1843, HP.

66 E. Hale to D. Daly (draft), Kingston, 26 Oct. 1843; E. Hale to Capt. Higginson (draft), Sherbrooke, 13 Sept. 1844, HP.

67 M. Child to D. Daly, Stanstead, 10 Mar. 1844, no. 1050, 1844, pp. 3518–19. T.A. Stayner to D. Daly, Montreal, 10 July 1844, no. 2434, 1844, p. 8880; M. Child to C. Dunkin, Stanstead, 8 Aug. 1844, p. 8882; M. Child to D. Daly, Stanstead, 27 Aug. 1844, no. 2514, p. 9196, RG4 C1.

68 M. Child to Provincial Secretary, Stanstead, 19 Mar. 1849, no. 708, 1849, RG4 C1. Sanborn of Sherbrooke and McConnell of Stanstead both complained that the former practice of consulting the MLAs concerning appointments was no longer followed. *Stanstead Journal*, 6 June 1850.

69 M. Child to A.N. Morin, Stanstead Plain, 3 Dec. 1851; draft reply, Quebec, 8 Jan. 1852, no. 2274, 1851, RG4 C1; *Stanstead Journal*, 10 Jan. 1850.

70 M. Child to F. Hincks, Stanstead, 22 Apr. 1850, vol. 339, RG16 A1, NA.

71 W.F. Parker to Sir (copy), Lennoxville, 22 July 1852, vol. 341, RG16 A1. The younger Parker had indeed caught Tuck smuggling some cloth in 1850, and in 1856 he was replaced after the captain of the *Mountain Maid* complained that he was "impiously profane and abusive in language, filthy, intemperate, ungentlemanly and a disgrace of the public service." Quoted in D.N. McIntosh, "Customs in Stanstead County," SHS *Journal* 11 (1985): 66.

72 E. Hale to Eliza, Kingston, 14 June 1841, HP.

73 Quoted in McCulloch, "English-Speaking Liberals," 125.

74 E. Hale to Eliza (copy), Kingston, 15 July and 27 Aug. 1841, HP.

75 Ibid., 21 Sept. 1842.

76 *Missisquoi Standard*, 18 May , 30 June, 24 Nov. 1835.

77 Petition of merchants, mechanics, and other inhabitants of Village of Philipsburgh and vicinity [1838], 83, vol. 542, RG4 A1.

78 E. Hale to Eliza (copy), Kingston, 3 Oct. 1842, HP.

79 Ibid., 8 Oct. 1843.

80 Marcus Child to Lydia, Leg. Ass., 9 Oct. 1843; 20 and 24 Oct. 1843, in Little, *Child Letters*, 66, 72, 77; Jones, *History of Agriculture*, 132.

81 See Little, *Child Letters*, 68–9, 79, 82–3, 96, 106, 113.

82 E. Hale to Eliza, Kingston, 18 Nov. 1843, HP.

83 Quoted in K.D. Hunte, "The Development of the System of Education in Canada East, 1841–1867, an Historical Survey" (MA thesis, McGill University, 1962), 95.

84 Watts was either absent or he abstained from voting. McCulloch, "English-Speaking Liberals," 210–11.

85 A.T. Galt to Metcalfe, Kingston, 1 Dec. 1843, 6183–9, vol. 12, RG7 G14, NA; Oscar Douglas Skelton, *Life and Times of Sir Alexander Tilloch Galt* (1920; reprint ed. Toronto: McClelland and Stewart, 1966), 57–9.

86 P. Hubbard to E. Hale, Stanstead, 30 Sept. 1843.

87 E. Hale to A.T. Galt (draft), 1844, HP.

88 E. Hale, to Capt. Higginson (draft), Sherbrooke, 27 Feb. 1844, HP; Thibault, *Samuel Brooks*, 68–71, 107–9.

89 E. Hale to Capt. Higginson (draft), Sherbrooke, 13 Sept. 1844, HP.

90 McCulloch, "English-Speaking Liberals," 263–5, 240–3, 330–1.

91 E. Hale to Edward Hale [uncle], Sherbrooke, 25 Oct. 1844, HP.

92 A.T. Galt to E. Hale, Sherbrooke, 9 Dec. 1844; B. Pomroy to E. Hale, Compton, 23 Dec. 1844, HP.

93 Tulchinsky, *River Barons*, 128–33, 138–44.

94 A.T. Galt to E. Hale, Sherbrooke, 14 June 1847, HP.

95 McCulloch, "English-Speaking Liberals," 324–7, 333–6; E. Hale to Eliza, Montreal, 5 June 1847, HP.

96 E. Hale to Eliza, Montreal, 15 Apr. 1846, HP. Hale was devastated by the death of his young daughter of erysipelas in 1842.

97 Thibault, *Samuel Brooks*, 121–2; *Stanstead Journal*, 6 Jan. 1848.

98 McCulloch,"English-Speaking Liberals," 352– 3, 361, 377– 8; Jacques Monet, *The Last Cannon Shot: A Study of French-Canadian Nationalism, 1837–1850* (Toronto: University of Toronto Press, 1969), 264.

99 P.H. Knowlton to E. Hale, Brome, 10 May 1848, HP; McCulloch, "English-Speaking Liberals," 346, 353–4.

100 A.T. Galt to E. Hale, Sherbrooke, 11 Nov. 1848, HP. On the completion of the St Lawrence and Atlantic Railway, see Tulchinsky, *River Barons*, 158–65.

101 *Stanstead Journal*, 12 Apr. 1849. The tariff was on cattle and agricultural products (with the exception of wheat and Indian corn).

102 *JLAC*, vol. 8 (1849), 113. For details, see Skelton, *Life and Times*, 24– 6.

103 *Stanstead Journal*, 29 Mar. 1849.

104 Ibid, 15 Nov. 1849.

105 Ibid., 22 Nov. 1849.

106 Ibid., 7 and 14 Mar. 1850.

107 Ibid., 10 Jan. 1850.

108 Ibid., 4 Apr. 1850.

109 *JLAC*, vol. 10 (1851), appendix A.

110 *Stanstead Journal*, 30 Jan., 6 Mar. 1851.

111 Ibid., 3 Jan. 1850.

112 The main reason for the decision to avoid the village of Stanstead was the concern that it was too close to rail communications with Boston, which might siphon off the Montreal-Portland trade. *Stanstead Journal*, 26 Dec. 1850; Tulchinsky, *River Barons*, 164–5.

113 *Stanstead Journal*, 4 and 18 Dec. 1851.

114 On the construction of this railway, see J. Derek Booth, *Railways of Southern Quebec*, Vol. 1 (Toronto: Railfare, 1982), chapter 1.

115 McCulloch, "English-Speaking Liberals," 544–5, 548; *Stanstead Journal*, 7 Mar. 1850.

116 *Stanstead Journal*, 20 Oct. 1851.

117 McCulloch, "English-Speaking Liberals," 518; *Stanstead Journal*, 20 Nov. 1851.

118 McCulloch, "English-Speaking Liberals," 514–15; *Stanstead Journal*, 31 July, 2 and 16 Oct. 1851.

119 McCulloch, "English-Speaking Liberals," 518–19.

120 Ibid., 520; *Stanstead Journal*, 31 July 1851; Writ and Return, Drummond County, 4107–14, RG4 B72.

121 *Stanstead Journal*, 18 Dec. 1851.

CHAPTER TWO

1 Sir C.P. Lucas, ed., *Lord Durham's Report on the Affairs of British North America*, 3 vols (Oxford: Clarendon Press, 1912), vol. 2, 125–6. During the early 1830s provision was made for county courts wherever courthouses and jails were erected, but because half the expense had to be met by local rate-payers, this had been done in only two counties, l'Acadie and St Hyacinthe. Lucas, *Lord Durham's Report*, vol. 3, 160–2.

2 Donald Fyson with the assistance of Evelyn Kolish and Virginia Schweitzer, *The Court Structure of Quebec and Lower Canada, 1760 to 1860* (Montreal: Montreal History Group, 1994), 65.

3 J.H. Terrill to E. Hale, Sherbrooke, 11 Mar. 1840, HP, McCord Museum.

4 Petition of J.H. Terrill to Metcalfe, Sherbrooke, 15 Jan. 1844, no. 2973, 1844, RG4 C1, NA. In 1844 the new high constable was granted a salary of £30 per year. State Book C, 548, 20 Sept. 1844, RG1 E1, NA.

5 Lucas, ed., *Lord Durham's Report*, vol. 2, 126–9, 130–1.

6 Despite its name, the quarter sessions of the St Francis District was held only twice a year prior to 1853. For details, see Fyson, *The Court Structure*, 44, 59–62; and Frederick H. Armstrong, "The Oligarchy of the Western District of Upper Canada 1788–1841," Canadian Historical Association, *Historical Papers* (1977), 91–3.

7 Fyson, "Criminal Justice," 32, 355. A similar argument for Upper Canada is made in Susan Lewthwaite, "Violence, Law and Community in Rural Upper Canada," in *Essays in the History of Canadian Law, vol. 5, Crime and*

Criminal Justice, edited by Jim Philipps, Tina Loo, and Susan Lewthwaite (Toronto: The Osgoode Society, 1994), 326–6.

8 Lucas, *Lord Durham's Report*, vol. 2, 131; vol. 3, 160.

9 Ibid., vol. 3, 235; vol. 2, 133. On the role of the militia in pre-Rebellion Lower Canada, see Allan Greer, *The Patriots and the People: The Rebellion of 1837 in Rural Lower Canada* (Toronto: University of Toronto Press, 1993), 100–7.

10 Brian Young, "'The Business of Law' in Missisquoi and the District of Bedford before 1861," *Proceedings of Missisquoi Historical Society* 20 (1990): 12–15. On this question, see Evelyn Kolish, "The Impact of the Change in Legal Metropolis on the Development of Lower Canada's Legal System: Judicial Chaos and Legislative Paralysis in the Civil Law, 1791–1838," in *Papers Presented at the 1987 Canadian Law in History Conference*, Carleton University, 8–10 June 1987, 319–58; and John E.C. Brierly, "The Co-Existence of Legal Systems in Quebec: 'Free and Common Socage' in Canada's 'pays de droit civil,'" *Cahiers de droit* 20 (1979): 277–87.

11 Young, "The Business of Law," 15; Petition of the inhabitants of Shefford, Granby, Farnham, Brome, Dunham, St Armand East and West, 10 Apr. 1846, no. 1422, 1846, RG4 C1.

12 Petition of inhabitants of County of Shefford, no. 551, 1848; Petition of inhabitants of counties of Missisquoi, etc., Shefford County, May 1851, no. 1255, 1851, RG4 C1.

13 Quoted in Matthew F. Farfan, "Court Reform in Early Nineteenth Century Stanstead," *Stanstead Historical Society Journal* 14 (1991): 64.

14 Petition of W.B. Felton et al. to Andrew Cochrane, 18 Sept. 1822, RG4 A1, NA.

15 Farfan, "Court Reform," 65.

16 *British Colonist* (Stanstead), 16 Mar. 1826.

17 The Society's rules and regulations are printed in *Stanstead Journal*, 6 Sept. 1845.

18 Little, "British Toryism," 26–7; *Montreal Gazette*, 22 Feb., 4 Mar. 1830.

19 Fyson, *The Court Structure*, 85–6.

20 Farfan, "Court Reform," 64; *British Colonist*, 25 Nov., 16 and 30 Dec. 1824, 27 Jan. 1825. The Provincial Court of the St Francis District held five terms per year at Sherbrooke, as compared with only two for the district Court of King's Bench.

21 Jean-Pierre Kesteman, "Silas Horton Dickerson," *DCB*, vol. 8.

22 J. Chamberlain to S. Walcott, Frelighsburg, 5 Jan. 1838, 68, vol. 529; William Ritchie to S. Walcott, Stanstead, 10 Jan. 1838, 119, vol. 529; Ed Cox to Stephen Walcott, Kingsey, 15 Jan. 1838, 153, vol. 530, RG4 A1.

23 J.S. Jones to Col. Rowen, Compton, 5 Apr. 1838, 56, vol. 533, RG4 A1.

24 Wm Ritchie to S. Walcott, Stanstead, 27 Jan. 1838, 251, vol. 530, RG4 A1.

25 J.S. Jones to Earl of Gosford, Compton, 28 Oct. 1837, 146, vol. 552, RG4 A1.

26 List of magistrates in the District of Montreal, 1 Dec. 1837, 117a, vol. 532, RG4 A1. A year later, the number of magistrates increased slightly to thirty-four in twelve townships. Office of the Secretary of the Province, Que., 20 Dec. 1838, 287, vol. 556, RG4 A1; *Missisquoi Standard*, 13 Sept. 1836.

27 According to the *Quebec Gazette* of 2 Jan. 1839, sixteen men from Ascot, Stanstead, Durham, and Barnston townships were in the Sherbrooke jail because of their suspected rebel sympathies.

28 Morris had entered the army in 1793, at the age of thirteen, serving in India, Newfoundland (where he married the chief justice's daughter), Canada, and Ceylon, before settling in Lennoxville. He died in 1851. A Copy of William Morris's Statement, 1906, Morris Family Papers, McCord Museum; *Stanstead Journal*, 5 June 1851.

29 Fyson, *The Court Structure*, 12, 14.

30 Petition of inhabitants of District of St Francis, Sherbrooke, 21 Aug. 1838, 53ff, vol. 549, RG4 A1.

31 The individuals named were Edward Hale for Orford, Morris himself for Ascot, Selah Pomroy for Stanstead, Daniel Thomas for Melbourne, and the district customs officer, Robert Hoyle, for Stanstead. Public meeting of District of St Francis held at Paige's Hotel in Sherbrooke, 29 Jan. 1839, 309, vol. 567, RG4 A1.

32 Petition of C.P. Elkins [n.d.], 136, vol. 558, RG4 A1.

33 P.H. Moore to Civil Secretary, St Armand [no no.]; Alex. Kilborn to Capt. Goldie, Stanstead, 5 Feb. 1839, 7 May 1839, vol. 4, RG4 B24, NA.

34 Allan Greer, "The Birth of the Police in Canada," in *Colonial Leviathan: State Formation in Mid-Nineteenth-Century Canada*, edited by Allan Greer and Ian Radforth (Toronto: University of Toronto Press, 1992), 21.

35 Affidavit of Edward Thomas, Montreal, 22 Oct. 1839, vol. 3, RG4 B24.

36 Draft reply, 16 Oct. 1839, to letter sent by A. Gugy to Major Goldie, Montreal, 15 Oct. 1839, vol. 3, RG4 B24.

37 A. Gugy to Major Goldie, Montreal, 15 Oct. 1839; A. Gugy to Chief Secretary, Montreal, 30 Oct. 1839, vol. 3, RG4 B24; W. Baker to T.W.C. Murdoch, Esq., Montreal, 8 Nov. 1839, no. 42, 1839–40, RG4 C1; draft letter to Lt Col Gugy, 19 Nov. 1839, vol. 3, RG4 B24.

38 A. Gugy to civil secretary, Montreal, 15 Nov. 1839, no. 162, 1839–40, RG4 C1.

39 A. Gugy to Capt. Pringle [n.d.], rec'd 19 Nov. 1839, no. 340, 1839–40, RG4 C1.

40 Petition of John Lord et al., Sherbrooke, 28 Jan. 1840, no. 649, 1839–40, RG4 C1.

41 Attorney-General Ogden to C. Montizambert, Montreal, 5 Dec. 1839, no. 341, 1839–40, RG4 C1.

42 Ibid.

43 Draft reply to letter of 7 Dec. 1839, no. 340, 1839–40, RG4 C1.

44 Fred'k Weiss to civil secretary, Sherbrooke, 28 Jan. 1840, no. 650, 1839–40, RG4 C1. In 1838 Sheriff Whitcher noted that the grand jury had recommended lathing and plastering the jail ceilings in order to make the cells warmer and to prevent the prisoners from communicating with each other through the open spaces in the floors. In addition, a 66-foot section of the brick wall surrounding the jail had fallen due to frost action, necessitating an estimated cost of £95 5s. for all repairs. C. Whitcher to C. Buller, Sherbrooke, 14 June 1838, 213, vol. 538, RG4 A1.

45 Petition of John Lord et al., Sherbrooke, 28 Jan. 1840, no. 649, 1839–40, RG4 C1.

46 Draft memo to J.C. Spencer, Esq., 30 Apr. 1840, no. 1794, 1839–40, RG4 C1.

47 Col. Nickle to civil secretary, Charleston, 3 Dec. 1839, no. 334, 1839–40, RG4 C1.

48 Draft letter to W. Coffin, 12 Dec. 1839, vol. 6; draft letter to Lt. Col. Gugy, 23 Dec. 1839, vol. 3, RG4 B24; E. Hale to Eliza, Montreal, 27 Apr., 3 May, 7 June 1840, HP.

49 Michael E. McCulloch, "English-Speaking Liberals in Canada East, 1840–1854" (PH.D. thesis, University of Ottawa, 1986), 74.

50 See, for example, P.E. Leclerc and A.M. Delisle to Charles Ogden, Clarenceville, 3 Jan. 1839; Capt. Gratton to Lt Griffin, Clarenceville, 3 Feb. 1839; C. Goodsil to W.F. Coffin, Clarenceville, 13 June 1839, vol. 6, RG4 B24.

51 N.R. Woods to Dear Friend, Potton, 1 Mar. 1838, cited in H.N. Muller III, "Trouble on the Border, 1838: A Neglected Incident from Vermont's Neglected History," *Vermont History* 44 (1976): 101; memorial of Harvey F. Elkins, Montreal, 20 Mar. 1838, 104, vol. 532, RG4 A1.

52 Quoted in *Quebec Gazette*, 24 Dec. 1838.

53 Petition of Susan Elkins to Governor-General Elgin, Potton, 22 Dec. 1846; memo of committee of Executive Council [n.d.], no. 2433, 1847, RG4 C1. Moses Elkins was the brother of Salmon Elkins who was in turn the father of Harvey and Ralph, and grandfather of Hector, the three men involved in the February shooting. Muller, "Trouble," 101. For a detailed account of this incident, see Rev. Ernest M. Taylor, *History of Brome County, Quebec*, 2 vols. (Montreal: John Lovell, 1937), vol. 2: 6–11.

54 *Missiskoui Standard*, 2 Apr. 1839. Greer (*The Patriots*, 253) claims that arson was not used as a weapon of popular pressure in the immediate pre-Rebellion period, which raises the possibility that Colborne's scorched-earth policy set the example for such reprisals.

55 Affidavit of William Burroughs, 26 June 1839, vol. 4, RG4 A1.

56 See Lewthwaite, "Violence, Law, and Community," 366; Fyson, "Criminal Justice," 113, 348.

57 J. Brady to D. Daly, Drummondville, 25 Jan. 1842, 2174, Nicolet District, RG4 B36, NA.

58 Memorial of Alexander Mackenzie, Danville, 2 Dec. 1842, no. 3052, 1842, RG4 C1.
59 R.N. Watts to Sir, Drummondville, 20 Sept. 1843, no. 1833, 1843, RG4 C1.
60 List of magistrates in commission, District of St Francis, 6 Oct. 1845, vol. 1, RG4 B26; List of magistrates whose qualifications have been filed, Sherbrooke, 2 Mar. 1846, no. 611, 1846, RG4 C1. Two other magistrates on the latter list resided outside the St Francis District. Fyson estimates that in the District of Montreal "the proportion of inactive, unqualified justices stayed steady at slightly under a third ("Criminal Justice," 113)."
61 Greer, "The Birth of the Police," 18; Greg Marquis, "Doing Justice to 'British Justice': Law, Ideology and Canadian Historiography," in *Canadian Perspectives on Law and Society: Issues in Legal History*, edited by Wesley Pue and Barry Wright (Ottawa: Carleton University Press, 1988), 50.
62 Paul Romney, "From the Rule of Law to Responsible Government: Ontario Political Culture and the Origins of Canadian Statism," Canadian Historical Association, *Historical Papers* (1988), 97, 118.
63 See J.M. Beattie, *Crime and the Courts in England, 1660–1800* (Princeton, N.J.: Princeton University Press, 1986), 318–31. Beattie writes that in eighteenth-century England grand jurors "were the authentic voice of the country, the spokesmen of that broad political nation that the parties fought to influence and that all governments had to appease and appeal to" (ibid., 322).
64 Presentment of Grand Jury, St Francis District, 4 Feb. 1842, no. 455, 1842, RG4 C1. While the court is not identified, these reports must have been for the General Sessions of the Peace (also known as the Court of Quarter Sessions) until the end of 1843 when the district Queen's Bench was given authority over criminal cases.
65 Presentment of Grand Jury, District of St Francis, 5 Oct. 1843, no. 2191, 1843, RG4 C1.
66 Jurors for Court of Queen's Bench, St Francis, no. 2884, 1844; no. 2605, 1848; no. 2884, 1844; Report of James B. Johnston, Physician of Gaol [n.d.]; Report of G.F. Bowen [n.d.], no. 354, 1850, RG4 C1.
67 Dr Wolfred Nelson Commission, *JLAC*, vol. 11 (1852–53) appendix HH.
68 Presentment of Grand Jury, St Francis District, 4 Feb. 1842, no. 455; Calendar of Prisoners in Sherbrooke Gaol, 31 Dec. 1842, no. 167, 1843, RG4 C1; *JLAC*, vol. 8 (1849), appendix J.
69 Presentment of Grand Jury, District of St Francis, 5 Oct. 1843, no. 2191, 1843, RG4 C1.
70 W.F. Coffin to E. Hale, Ste Marie de Monnoir, 21 Feb. 1840, HP.
71 Except where noted, the following account is based on the documents in no. 2950, 1848, RG4 C1.
72 Affidavit of Daniel Delaven, Troy, NY, 26 Nov. 1844, HP.
73 E. Hale to P.A. Barker (draft), Montreal, 26 April 1845, HP.

74 Beattie claims that "the character of the prisoner (in the sense of both his dispostion and his reputation) was especially important and was often crucial to the outcome of the trial" (*Crime and the Courts*, 440).

75 Fyson, The Court Structure, 32. See, for example, the petition signed by A.T. Galt, B. Pomroy, J. Pennoyer, and 144 others. Memorial of inhabitants of Compton Township, Compton, 7 Oct. 1843, no. 2288, 1843, RG4 C1.

76 Calendar of Criminal Proceedings and Report of Jurors, Court of Queen's Bench, St Francis, August session, 1844, no. 2884, 1844, RG4 C1. The documents for the Blanchard case are in no. 2066, 1849. On local response to the trial, see Little, *The Child Letters*, 56.

77 *Stanstead Journal*, 7 and 21 Mar. 1850; documents in no. 353, 1850, RG4 C1.

78 John Weaver, "Crime, Public Order, and Repression: The Gore District in Upheaval, 1832–1851," *Ontario History* 8, no. 3 (1986): 202–4. This argument echoes that in Douglas Hay, "Property, Authority and the Criminal Law", in *Albion's Fatal Tree: Crime and Society in Eighteenth-Century England* (London: Allen Lane, 1975).

79 *Stansdead Journal*, 12 Sept., 10 Oct. 1850.

80 The documents in these cases are in no. 3178, 1845; no. 1779, 1850; and no. 206, 1851, RG4 C1 respectively.

81 See Beattie, *Crime and the Courts*, 445–6.

82 R.N. Watts to Sir, Montreal, 10 Oct. 1845; Petition by magistrates, etc., Melbourne, 29 Sept. 1845; Petition to governor-general, Kingsey, 3 Oct. 1845, no. 2797, 1845, RG4 C1.

83 Attorney-General Smith to D. Daly, Montreal, 13 Oct. 1845, no. 2797, 1845; report of G.F. Bowen et al., 24 Oct. 1845, RG4 C1.

84 See Jean-Marie Fecteau, *Un nouvel ordre des choses: la pauvreté, le crime, l'État au Québec, de la fin du XVIIIe siècle à 1840* (Outremont, Qué.: VLB éditeur, 1989), 249–52; Weaver, "Crime."

85 F.C. Gilmour to D. Daly, Granby, 25 Apr. 18, no. 1309, 1845; E. Clark to R.B. Sullivan, Montreal, 28 June 1848, no. 2029, 1848, RG4 C1; *Stanstead Journal*, 20 Apr., 13 and 20 July 1848. In May a Rock Island resident was also arrested with counterfeit bills and two sets of dies for "hard money." *Stanstead Journal*, 18 May 1848.

86 Presentment of Grand Jury, Aug. 1848, no. 2605, 1848, RG4 C1; *Stanstead Journal*, 31 Aug. 1848.

87 *Stanstead Journal*, 25 Jan. 1849; Gaol calendar, St Francis District, Oct. and Nov. 1849, no. 3052, 1849; Dec. 1849, no. 54, 1850, RG4 C1.

88 *Stanstead Journal*, 27 Sept. 1849.

89 Quoted in ibid., 5 Apr. 1850. The context suggests that the passage is from the Montreal, not the Sherbrooke, *Gazette*. Ingram's sentence is not known, but, as in the Toussaint case, the *Stanstead Journal* (4 Apr. 1850) supported executive clemency. The following month the sentence was reduced to two years in the Montreal jail. Ibid., 2 May 1850.

90 Affidavit of E Clark, 4 Jan. 1850, no. 116, 1850, RG4 C1.
91 Documents in no. 370, 1850, RG4 C1.
92 Much of the following account is from affidavits and *Sherbrooke Gazette* clippings filed with no. 2328, 1850, RG4 C1.
93 *Stanstead Journal,* 5 Sept. 1850.
94 E. Clark to James Leslie, Sherbrooke, 25 Oct. 1850, no. 2328, 1850, RG4 C1; *Stanstead Journal,* 3 Oct. 1850.
95 Several were also dismissed in Missisquoi County. *Stanstead Journal,* 14 and 28 Feb. 1850; 1276–7, vol. 4, RG4 B37, NA.
96 *Stanstead Journal,* 6 June 1850.
97 Petition of Clergymen, etc. [n.d.], no. 1436, 1850; E. Clark to J. Leslie, Sherbrooke, 5 May 1850; Memo to McClintock, May 1850, no. 931, 1850, RG4 C1.
98 J.S. Sanborn to J. Leslie, House of Assembly, 28 July 1851, no. 1597, 1851; M. Child to A.N. Morin, Stanstead Plain, 3 Dec. 1851, no. 2274, 1851, RG4 C1.
99 Gaol calendar, Sherbrooke, December 1850, no. 31, 1851, RG4 C1.
100 Thomas Christie to Sir, Melbourne, 24 June 1851, no. 1376, 1851, RG4 C1.
101 Jean-Pierre Kesteman, "Les travailleurs à la construction du chemin de fer dans la région de Sherbrooke (1851–1853)," *RHAF* 31 (1978): 527; Presentment of Grand Jury, St Francis District, 6 Oct. 1851, no. 1968, 1851, RG4 C1.
102 George N. Ridgway to J. Leslie, Dudswell, 19 Sept. 1851, no. 1907, 1851; J.S. Sanborn to A.N. Morin, Sherbrooke, 29 Nov. 1851; Petition of residents of Dudswell Township, 26 Nov. 1851, no. 2261, 1851, RG4 C1.
103 For details, see *Stanstead Journal,* 7 Aug, 11 Sept. 1851.
104 Cited in ibid., 7 Aug. 1851.
105 Presentment of Grand Jury, St Francis, 16 Dec. 1851, no. 2333, 1851, RG4 C1. In March the solicitor-general offered a £100 reward for information leading to the arrest of Sprague's murderer(s). Solicitor-general's draft, 22 Mar. 1852, filed with no. 562, 1852, RG4 C1.
106 Kesteman, "Les travailleurs," 527, 530–1, 535, 543.
107 Cited in *Stanstead Journal,* 1 Jan. 1852.
108 T. McGovern to A.N. Schweizer, Sherbrooke, 23 Dec. 1851; A.T. Galt to A.N. Morin, Sherbrooke, 24 Dec. 1851; A.T. Galt to A.N. Morin, Sherbrooke, 25 Dec. 1851; draft reply, Que., 19 Jan. 1852, no. 2410, 1851, RG4 C1.
109 Nelson Report, *JLAC,* vol. 11 (1852–53) appendix HH.
110 Presentment of Grand Jury, St Francis District, 14 Feb. 1852, no. 381, 1852, RG4 C1.
111 This charge was laid in May 1851, but Thompson had also been convicted of selling liquor without a licence in 1845. He died before his commission could be revoked in 1852. Draft letter to Thompson, Toronto, 20 May

1851; E. Clark to J. Leslie, Toronto, 8 July 1851; [cover note], 29 Aug. 1852, no. 381, 1852, RG4 C1.

112 Presentment of Grand Jury, St Francis District, 14 Feb. 1852, no. 381, 1852, RG4 C1; Kesteman, "Les travailleurs," 543.

113 The *Sherbrooke Gazette* had recommended in December that a police force be stationed along the railway construction line. *Stanstead Journal*, 1 Jan. 1852.

114 It is not clear when coroners were appointed for the St Francis District, but in 1842 the warden of the Nicolet District complained that no provision had been made for such officers, with the result that their duties were assumed by the captains of militia. These officers seldom deemed it necessary to hold inquests, and when they did so there was generally either no investigation or one "so imperfectly conducted as to pervert the intentions of the criminal law into a mere mockery." James Bready to civil secretary, Drummondville, 31 Aug. 1841, 2029, Nicolet District, RG4 B36.

115 Report of R.B. Johnson, Special Magistrate, Sherbrooke, 5 Apr. 1852, filed with no. 562, 1852, RG4 C1.

116 Kesteman, "Les travailleurs," 543–4.

117 Weaver, "Crime, 177–83.

118 Greg Marquis, "The Contours of Urban Justice, 1830–1870," *Urban History Review* 15, no. 3 (1987): 270.

119 Bruce Mann, *Neighbours and Strangers: Law and Community in Early Connecticut* (Chapel Hill: University of North Carolina Press, 1987), 9.

120 Fyson, *The Court Structure*, 85–6, 91.

121 Presentment of Grand Jury, St Francis District, 5 Feb. 1842, no. 455, 1842, RG4 C1; 9 Sept. 1842, Missisquoi District, vol. 6, Municipal Records, RG4 B36.

122 Petition of inhabitants of Barnston and Barford, Barnston, Sept. 1842; M. Child to D. Daly [n.d.], no. 2500, 1842, RG4 C1.

123 Petition of inhabitants of Stanstead County, Stanstead, 15 Sept. 1843, no. 1945; Petition of inhabitants of Stanstead, no. 2055, 1843; Petition of inhabitants of Granby to Legislative Council, Granby, 15 Sept. 1842, no. 2535, 1842; Memorial of inhabitants of Compton Township, Compton, 7 Oct. 1843, no. 2288, 1843, RG4 C1.

124 A similar point is made in Douglas McCalla, "Rural Credit and Rural Development in Upper Canada, 1790–1850," in *Patterns of the Past: Interpreting Ontario's History*, edited by Roger Hall, William Westfall, and Laurel Sefton MacDowell (Toronto and Oxford: Dundurn Press, 1988), 43.

125 Issue Book, Division Court no. 3, Stanstead (1842–44), ANQ à Sherbrooke.

126 Fyson, *The Court Structure*, 88.

127 Marcus to Lydia, Legislative Assembly, 5 Dec. 1843, in Little, *The Child Letters*, 134.

128 The petitions listed in the index to RG4 C1, 1848, are from Kingsey
     (nos 2011 and 2744), Stanstead (no. 821), Barnston (no. 883), Shefford
     (no. 2444), Dunham (no. 2445), Arthabaska (no. 2204), Halifax (nos
     2346 and 3265), and Melbourne (no. 1830). For 1849 they are Bury
     (no. 1012), Ireland (no. 404), Somerset (no. 836), Sutton (no. 867), and
     Farnham (2795). These petitions are listed as having been filed with the
     Commissioners of Small Causes papers, which were not found.

129 *JLAC*, vol. 11 (1852–53), appendix YY.

130 Fyson, *The Court Structure*, 79.

131 J.W. Hallowell to E. Hale, Sherbrooke, 14 Oct. 1843, HP.

132 The bill presented by the clerk for the Stanstead circuit court in May 1844
     was £19 10s., though not all the claims were accepted by the administra-
     tion. Expenses … no. 3545; Petition of C.P. Elkins, Nov. 1844, no. 3546,
     1844, RG4 C1.

133 Petitions of C.P. Elkins, Stanstead, 20 June 1844, no. 2086; and Nov. 1844,
     no. 3546, 1844, RG4 C1.

134 Judge Fletcher to D. Daly, Sherbrooke, 20 Feb. 1844, no. 778, filed with
     no. 1110, 1844, RG4 C1.

135 Fyson neglects to mention the number of circuits in the St Francis District
     prior to 1855, when there were five, with three to six circuits annually in
     each of them. Each county became a circuit in 1857 (*The Court Structure*,
     80–1).

136 No. 2252, 1848, RG4 C1.

137 Petition of inhabitants of Shipton, Melbourne, and vicinity [received 9 July
     1851], no. 1455; F.C. Cleave to J. Leslie, Richmond, 21 July 1851,
     no. 1560, 1851, RG4 C1.

138 Thomas Tait to E. Hale, Melbourne, 1 Nov. 1843, HP

139 Though the plumitif for the non-appealable or summary cases (which gen-
     erally involved sums under £10) does not record the professions of the par-
     ties involved, it is likely that farmers were more heavily represented at this
     level. There were 322 appealable cases by 19 Dec. 1849. Plumitifs, Stan-
     stead Circuit Court, 1844–55, 1844–65, ANQS.

140 Statement requested by the Honourable Legislative Council, Sherbrooke,
     9 Sept. 1847, no. 2169, 1846, RG4 C1.

141 Petition of Andrew Muir, Jr, et al., Montreal, 18 May 1846, no. 2836, 1846;
     Petition of merchants and traders of Montreal, 23 Sept. 1846, no. 2834,
     1846, RG4 C1.

142 Petitions of C.P. Elkins [n.d.]; and Sherbrooke, 28 Apr. 1847; S. Brooks to
     D. Daly, Sherbrooke, 2 Oct. 1846; Memo by C. Dunkin, 10 Nov. 1846,
     no. 2834, 1846, RG4 C1.

143 See the correspondence in no. 2834, 1846, RG4 C1.

144 Tina Loo, *Making Law: Order and Authority in British Columbia, 1821–1871*
     (Toronto: University of Toronto Press, 1994), 3–4.

145 On the pre-Rebellion era, see Brian Young, *The Politics of Codification: The Lower Canadian Civil Code of 1866* (Montreal and Kingston: McGill-Queen's University Press, 1994), 21–30.

CHAPTER THREE

1 For a useful overview, see Reginald G. Smart and Alan G. Ogburne, *Northern Spirits: Drinking in Canada Then and Now* (Toronto: Addiction Research Foundation, 1986), chapter 1.

2 Rev. Edward Cleveland, *A Sketch of the Early Settlement and History of Shipton, Canada East* ([Richmond]: S.C. Smith, 1858), 35–6.

3 Ian R. Tyrrell, *Sobering Up: From Temperance to Prohibition in Antebellum America, 1800–60* (Westport, Conn.: Greenwood Press, 1979), 209. The Rechabites were introduced to the United States from Great Britain in 1842, and from there spread to Canada in 1846. F.L. Barron, "American Origins of Ontario Temperance, 1828–1850," *Canadian Review of American Studies* 11, no. 2 (1980): 140–1.

4 *Stanstead Journal*, 4 July 1850.

5 Memorial of Sherbrooke Temperance Society [n.d.], no. 1037, 1842, RG4 C1, NA.

6 Samuel Brooks to E. Hale, Sherbrooke, 25 Apr. 1845, HP, McCord Museum.

7 E. Clark to D. Daly, Stanstead, 17 June 1845; memo by Attorney-General Smith to D. Daly, Montreal, 19 July 1845, no. 1834, 1845, RG4 C1.

8 Presentment of Grand Jury, District of St Francis, no. 563, 1845; tavern licences issued, District of St Francis, 5 Apr. 1845 – 5 Apr. 1846, 5 Apr. 1846 – 5 Jan. 1847, no. 117, 1847, RG4 C1.

9 C. Bullock to D. Daly, Georgeville, 3 June 1845, RG16 A1, NA.

10 Presentment of Grand Jury, Sherbrooke, 20 Aug. 1847, no. 2956, 1847; E. Clark to J. Leslie, Sherbrooke, 5 Oct. 1848, no. 2917, 1848, RG4 C1.

11 *Stanstead Journal*, 31 July 1851.

12 Ibid., 19 Sept. 1850; Jan Noel, "Temperance Campaigning and Alcohol Consumption: A Case Study from Pre-Confederation Canada," *Contemporary Drug Problems* (Fall 1994): 416.

13 Colby had purchased thirty-nine barrels of whiskey from J.W. Molson in November 1848. Family correspondence file, Colby Papers, SHS.

14 *Stanstead Journal*, 10 Apr. 1851.

15 A.J. Wright to Bro. Colby, Boston, 27 Nov. 1850, Miscellaneous letters file, Colby Papers.

16 *Stanstead Journal*, 17 Apr. 1851.

17 Ibid., 18 Sept. 1851. The *Journal* declared itself in opposition to the Maine law on 27 May 1852.

278 Notes to pages 87–9

18 Ibid., 20 Mar. 1851; Petition of Stanstead Municipal Council, 1 June 1851, no. 1113, 1851, RG4 C1.

19 The applicant would also have to prove that he held property valued at at least £100, and provide a security of £100 plus two sureties of £50 each for his good behaviour. *Stanstead Journal*, 3 Apr. 1851. Petition of Municipality of County of Shefford, 9 June 1851, no. 1113, 1851, RG4 C1.

20 Barron, "American Origins," 143– 5. See also T.W. Acheson, *Saint John: The Making of a Colonial Urban Community* (Toronto: University of Toronto Press, 1985), 152. Under the township council system of 1845–47 only Shipton appears to have petitioned for the right to grant liquor licences. Petition of municipal council of Shipton, 6 Apr. 1846, 6670–3, no. 1233, 1846, RG4 C1.

21 *Stanstead Journal*, 15 Jan. 1852, 18 Mar. 1852.

22 Jean-Marie Fecteau, *Un nouvel ordre des choses: La pauvreté, le crime, l'État au Québec, de la fin du XVIIIᵉ siècle à 1840* (Outremont: VLB éditeur, 1989), 39.

23 One exception is the Dorcas Society to which Lydia Child belonged in Stanstead during the 1840s. See J.I. Little, ed., *The Child Letters: Public and Private Life in a Canadian Merchant-Politician's Family, 1841–45* (Montreal and Kingston: McGill-Queen's University Press, 1995), 33, 113, 117. For a description of this society, see Kate Douglas Wiggin, *My Garden of Memory: An Autobiography* (Boston and New York: Houghton Mifflin Company, 1929), chapter 37. I am indebted to Virginia Careless for this reference.

24 David R. Murray, "The Cold Hand of Charity: The Court of Quarter Session and Poor Relief in the Niagara District, 1828–41," in *Canadian Perspectives on Law & Society*, edited by Wesley Pue and Barry Wright (Ottawa: Carleton University Press, 1988), 184.

25 The chair of the public meeting for this purpose in Stanstead was the mayor, Elisha Gustin. *Stanstead Journal*, 4 Mar., 22 Apr. 1847.

26 Lydia to Marcus, Stanstead, 8 Oct., 7 Nov. 1843, in Little, *The Child Letters*, 64, 96.

27 Fecteau, *Un nouvel ordre*, 42–4.

28 W. Monsell to Sir, Beebe Plain, 29 Aug., 23 Sept. 1847; W. Monsell to D. Daly, Beebe Plain, 12 Nov. 1847, no. 2938, 1847; A.T. Galt to D. Daly, Sherbrooke, 22 Dec. 1847, no. 4283, 1847; W.H. Fowler, m.d., to Prov. Sec., Montreal, 13 Mar. 1848; Report of A.C. Buchanan, 20 Mar. 1848, no. 791, 1848, RG4 C1.

29 Presentment of Grand Jury, Sherbrooke, Aug. 1848, no. 2605, 1848, RG4 C1. *Stanstead Journal*, 30 Aug., 6 Sept. 1849. The Aylwins lived in Quebec prior to the judicial appointment. Mrs Aylwin, the daughter of W.B. Felton, clearly did not have a strong constitution, for Marcus Child wrote in 1843 that "she is but the shadow of herself – and I think not long for this world." Marcus to Elizabeth, Legislative Assembly, 21 Nov. 1843, in Little, *The Child Letters*, 115.

30 Petition of the Roman Catholic Clergymen of Megantic County, 25 Feb. 1848, no. 848; Petition of inhabitants of Halifax Township, 29 Feb. 1848, no. 717, 1848, RG4 C1.

31 J.I. Little, *Crofters and Habitants: Settler Society, Economy, and Culture in a Quebec Township* (Montreal and Kingston, McGill-Queen's University Press, 1991), 52–4. On public subscriptions in Lower Canada, see Fecteau, *Un nouvel ordre*, 48–51.

32 Petition of Ebenezer Kilborn and Henry Hollister, Barnston, 25 Aug. 1845; Petition in support of foregoing, 30 Aug. 185; writ against Hollister, 29 Mar. 1845; James Smith to D. Daly, Montreal, 19 Sept. 1845, no. 2513, 1845, RG4 C1.

33 Silas Perkins to Governor Cathcart, Hatley, 7 Apr. 1846; reply, 28 May 1846, no. 1917, 1846; Robert Slatter to Governor-General, Inverness, 8 Jan. 1847, no. 163, 1847, RG4 C1.

34 Memorial of Members of Eaton Council and others of Eaton Municipality [n.d.], 5077–8, no. 921, 1846, RG4 C1. Of 6,825 personal petitions submitted to the governor of Upper Canada between 1815 and 1840, only 266 were for poor relief. J.K. Johnson, "Claims of Equity and Justice: Petitions and Petitioners in Upper Canada, 1815–1840" (paper presented to the annual meeting of the Canadian Historical Association, 1990), 26.

35 Marcus to Lydia, Legislative Assembly, 6 Nov. 1843, in Little, *The Child Letters*, 95.

36 C.M. Montizambert to E. Hale, Montreal, 21 Sept. 1839; James Cary to E. Hale, Montreal, 13 Nov. 1844, HP.

37 State Book D, 92 [1844], RG1 E1, NA.

38 Presentment of Grand Jury, St Francis District, 11 Jan. 1845, no. 563, 1845; 21 Aug. 1845, no. 2513; 24–30 Sept. 1845, no. 2816, 1845, RG4 C1.

39 Sheriff's requisition, no. 3384, 1846, index to RG4 C1; Petition of inhabitants of St Francis District, 31 Mar. 1846, no. 1221, 1846; Presentment of Grand Jury, Sherbrooke, Aug. 1848, no. 2605, 1848, RG4 C1.

40 C.A. Richardson to J. Leslie, Stanstead, 17 Jan. 1850, no. 145, 1850, RG4 C1.

41 Elizabeth L. Beach to J. Leslie, Dunham, 16 July 1851; draft reply, Toronto, 4 Aug. 1851; Dr H.S. Brown to J. Leslie, Dunham Flats, 5 Aug. 1851; draft reply, Que., 10 Feb. 1852, no. 1596, 1851, RG4 C1.

42 Report of Jas. B. Johnson, Physician to the Gaol, Dr Wolfred Nelson's Commission, *JLAC*, vol. 11 (1852–), appendix HH.

43 Presentment of Grand Jury, District of St Francis, 14 Feb. 1852, no. 381, 1852, RG4 C1; Canada, *Census Reports*, 1851–52, vol. 1. Rainer Baehre argues that the plight of the insane in Upper Canadian jails was the main force behind the move to establish mental asylums in that province. "Imperial Authority, and Colonial Officialdom of Upper Canada in the 1830s: The State, Crime Lunacy, and Everyday Social Order," in *Law, Society, and the State:*

Essays in Modern Legal History, edited by Louis A. Knafla and Susan W. Binnie (Toronto: University of Toronto Press, 1995), 197–205.

44 Petition of inhabitants of Stanstead County [n.d.], no. 808, 1848, RG4 C1.

45 For a useful survey of the various perspectives on the rise of the asylum, see André Cellard, *Histoire de la folie au Québec de 1600 à 1850* ([Montréal]: Boréal, 1991), 133–41.

46 Wrightson notes that these two concepts "had their origin in a shared concern with the maintenance of social harmony," but that they also had "markedly different implications in different situations." "Two Concepts of Order: Justices, Constables and Jurymen in Seventeenth-Century England," in *An Ungovernable People: The English and their Law in the Seventeenth and Eighteenth Centuries*, edited by John Brewer and John Styles (London: Hutchinson, 1980), 22.

47 In an exhaustive search of judicial records and newspapers, René Hardy found fewer than seventy cases throughout the province prior to 1850. René Hardy, "Le charivari: Divulguer et sanctionner la vie privée?" in *Discours et pratiques de l'intime*, edited by Manon Brunet and Serge Gagnon (Québec: Institut Québécois de Recherche sur la Culture, 1993), 50–1. See also his "Le charivari dans la sociabilité rurale québécoise au XIXe siècle," in *De la sociabilité. Spécificité et mutations*, edited by R. Levasseur (Montréal: Boréal, 1989).

48 For a useful description of the various forms of "rough music," see E.P. Thompson, *Customs in Common: Studies in Traditional Popular Culture* (New York: The New Press, 1993), 478–88.

49 Petition of C.P. Elkins and T. Turton, Sherbrooke, 15 Aug. 1838, 269, vol. 545, RG4 A1, NA.

50 E. Hale to Eliza, Kingston, 15 Aug. 1841, HP.

51 Memorial of Thomas Gaffney, Shipton settler, and son James [n.d.]; Solicitor-General to D. Daly, Montreal, 15 May 1846, no. 735, 1846, RG4 C1.

52 See the maps showing spatial distribution in René Hardy, "Le charivari dans l'espace québécois" in *Espace et culture / Space and Culture* (Sainte-Foy: Les Presses de l'Université Laval, 1995).

53 *Stanstead Journal*, 28 Feb., 16 May 1850.

54 Ibid., 3 and 10 July 1851.

55 Ibid., 24 July, 14 Aug. 1851, State Book M, 36, 12 Apr. 1852, RG1 E1. The depositions are referred to in a letter by C. Bullock dated 9 Sept. 1851.

56 See Hardy, "Le charivari: Divulguer," 49; Hardy, "Le charivari dans la sociabilité," 64–5; and Thompson, *Customs in Common*, 485.

57 John E. Hare, "William Vondenvelden," *DCB*, vol. 5.

58 Wendie Nelson, "The 'Guerre des Éteignoirs': School Reform and Popular Resistance in Lower Canada, 1841–1850" (MA thesis, Simon Fraser University, 1989), 73–8, 95, 104.

59 Phillip Hewett, *Unitarians in Canada* (Toronto: Fitzhenry and Whiteside, 1978), 26; Aegidius Fauteux, *Patriotes de 1837–1838* (Montréal: Les Éditions des Dix, 1950), 115–16.

60 F.B. Blanchard to Civil Secretary, Kingsey, 3 Jan. 1839, 59, vol. 566, RG4 A1.

61 Petitions of Alexis Noël and J.B. Cormier to Governor Colborne, Kingsey, 9 Sept. 1839, vol. 5, RG4 B24, NA.

62 W.C. Hanson to Major Goldie, Nicolet, 15 Oct. 1839, vol. 5, RG4 B24.

63 William Vondenvelden to D. Daly, Berthier, 24 Jan. 1841, no. 2142, 1842, RG4 C1.

64 Affidavit of William Vondenvelden of Kingsey, 13 Sept. 1841, no. 2142, 1842, RG4 C1.

65 Memo by E. Hale, Sherbrooke, 13 Sept 1841, no. 2142, 1842; Memorial of William Vondenvelden of Kingsey to Lord Sydenham, Sherbrooke, 14 Sept. 1841, no. 2142, 1842, RG4 C1.

66 W. Vondenvelden to D. Daly, Kingsey, 27 Sept. 1841, no. 2142, 1842, RG4 C1.

67 Memo to Commissioner of Police, Montreal, 6 Oct. 1841, no. 2142, 1842, RG4 C1.

68 William Vondenvelden to D. Daly, Three Rivers, 24 Oct. 1841, no. 2142, 1842, RG4 C1.

69 William Vondenvelden to D. Daly, Berthier, 6 Dec. 1841, no. 2142, 1842, RG4 C1.

70 Memo to Edmund Cox, Esq., 10 June 1842; memo to Mr Ermatinger, 10 June 1842, no. 2142, 1842; memorial of W. Vondenvelden to Bagot [n.d], no. 2142, 1842; W. Vondenvelden to Bagot, Berthier, 16 July 1842, no. 2142, 1842, RG4 C1.

71 W. Vondendvelden to Col. Hanson, Berthier, 6 Aug. 1842; Hanson to C. Dunkin, Nicolet, 14 Aug. 1842, no. 2142, 1842, RG4 C1.

72 Memo to Lt Col Hanson, Police Magistrate, 22 Aug. 1842; W. Vondenvelden to C. Dunkin, Sherbrooke, 25 Aug. 1842, no. 2142, 1842; W. Vondenvelden to D. Daly, Berthier, 20 Sept. 1843, no. 2142, 1842, RG4 C1. The index to RG4 C1 lists a letter (not found in the file) written by Evans and Vondenvelden on 16 Jan. 1844 informing the government that Blanchard should not be appointed to this position because he had been indicted before the Court of Queen's Bench at Trois-Rivières.

73 Petition of Wm Vondenvelden to Colborne, Kingsey, 12 Mar. 1838, 9, vol. 532, RG4 A1.

74 W. Vondenvelden to D. Daly, Berthier, 24 Apr. 1843, no. 2142, 1842, RG4 C1.

75 See Hardy, "Le charivari: Divulguer," 52. The complex nature of the charivari makes Hardy's division between those relating to private life and those having a political origin somewhat problematic, as he himself demonstrates on pp. 56–7.

76 Allan Greer, *The Patriots and the People: The Rebellion of 1837 in Rural Lower Canada* (Toronto: University of Toronto Press, 1993), 242–57.

77 Thompson, *Customs in Common*, 485.

78 Carol Wilton, "'Lawless Law': Conservative Political Violence in Upper Canada, 1818–41," (paper presented to the annual meeting of the Canadian Historical Association, 1994); Thompson, *Customs in Common*, 526.

79 F. Blanchard to J. Leslie, Kingsey, 21 Jan. 1851, no. 1773, 1850, RG4 C1.

80 Thompson, *Customs in Common*, 509.

81 On the latter traffic, see Reginald C. Stuart, *United States Expansion and British North America, 1775–71* (Chapel Hill: University of North Carolina Press, 1988), 106– 7,114–16.

82 D.N. McIntosh, "Customs in Stanstead County," *Stanstead Historical Society Journal*, 11 (1985): 52; *British Colonist*, 18 May 1826.

83 G.J. Mountain to Mary Mountain, Yamaska Mountain, 13 Feb. 1829, Eastern Townships Visitation, G.J. Mountain, case 2, folder 13, QDA, ETRC.

84 E. Cushing, Stanstead, 28 Nov. 1832, vol. 339, RG16 A1, NA.

85 See Françoise Noël, "'My Dear Eliza': The Letters of Robert Hoyle (1831–1844)," *Histoire sociale/Social History* 26, no. 51 (1993): 115–30.

86 R. Hoyle to Sir Charles Bagot, Lacolle, 25 Jan. 1842, Militia Documents 1837–40; Child to R. Hoyle, House of Assembly, 23 Feb. 1836; R. Hoyle to Eliza, Stanstead, 17 Apr. 1836, M. Child to R. Hoyle, House of Assembly, 23 Feb. 1836, Correspondence, MG24 B141, NA.

87 Noël, "My Dear Eliza," 118; R. Hoyle to Bagot, Lacolle, 25 Jan. 1842, MG24 B141.

88 Quoted in H.N. Muller III, "Trouble on the Border, 1838: A Neglected Incident from Vermont's Neglected History," *Vermont History* 44 (1976): 100.

89 R. Hoyle to Eliza, Stanstead, 10 Oct. 1841, MG24 B141. The duties for the first quarter of 1842 dropped to $788. Ibid., 10 Apr. 1842.

90 Ibid., 7 Nov. 1841.

91 Ibid., 21 Nov. 1841.

92 Ibid., 27 Mar. 1842.

93 J. Thompson to J.W. Dunscombe, Stanstead, 6 June 1849, vol. 340, RG16 A1.

94 Ibid., 24 Apr. 1847, vol. 339, RG16 A1.

95 Jacob DeWitt to Provincial Secretary, 20 Feb. 1845; Petition of William Castle, Sutton, 17 Feb. 1845; affidavit by Castle, Windsor, Vt.; A. Kemp to Commissioner of Customs, Sutton, 3 and 10 Mar. 1845, vol. 346, RG16 A1.

96 J. Thompson to J.W. Dunscombe, Stanstead, 18 Mar. 1848, vol. 340, RG16 A1.

97 Petition of William Henry Holmes to Governor-General, [n.d.]; J. Thompson to J.W. Dunscombe, Stanstead, 9 Sept. 1845; Petition by Holmes, Stanstead, 1 Dec. 1845; Dunscomb's report, Montreal, 13 Feb. 1846; A. Patton to J.W. Dunscomb, Stanstead, 23 Feb. 1846; J. Thompson to J.W. Dunscomb, Stanstead, 8 June 1846, vol. 339, RG16 A1.

98 J. Thompson to J.W. Dunscomb, Stanstead, 15 Aug. 1848, vol. 340, RG16
   A1.

99 J. McConnell to Provincial Secretary, Montreal, 26 Mar. 1845; Dunscomb's
   Report, 14 May 1845; Attorney-General's Report, 17 May 1845; Governor-
   General in Council, 8 June 1845, vol. 339, RG16 A1; State Book D, 377,
   9 June 1845, RG1 E1.

100 Petition of John Gilman, Esq., of Stanstead Township, 19 Mar. 1846; Petition of Wright Chamberlin, Stanstead, 28 May 1847, vol. 339, RG16 A1.

101 J. Thompson to J.W. Dunscombe, Stanstead, 12 Sept. 1846, vol. 339, RG16
   A1.

102 J. Thompson to J.W. Dunscombe, Stanstead, 24 Jan. 1848, vol. 340, RG16,
   A1; McIntosh, *The Collectors*, 65.

103 R. Hoyle to Eliza, Stanstead, 4 Apr. 1842, vol. 339, MG24 B141; J. Thompson to J.W. Dunscombe, Stanstead, 1 and 8 Sept. 1845, vol. 339, RG16 A1.

104 J. Thompson to J.W. Dunscombe, Stanstead, 3 Sept. 1846, vol. 339,
   RG16 A1.

105 Report by J.W. Dunscombe, 13 Feb. 1847; J. Thompson to J.W. Dunscombe, Stanstead, 13 Apr. 1847, vol. 339; J. Thompson to J.W.
   Dunscombe, Stanstead, 27 Mar. 1848, vol 340, RG16 A1.

106 J. Thompson to J.W. Dunscombe, Stanstead, 22 Sept. 1846; Petition of
   Wright Chamberlin, Stanstead, 24 Sept. 1846; J. Thompson to J.W.
   Dunscombe, Stanstead, 5 and 15 Oct. 1846, vol. 339, RG16 A1.

107 J. Thompson to J.W. Dunscombe, Stanstead, 21 Nov. 1846, vol. 339, RG16
   A1; McIntosh, "Customs," 57.

108 J. Thompson to J.W. Dunscombe, Stanstead, 26 Dec. 1846, vol. 339, 5 Mar.
   1847, 5 Jan. 1848; J. Thompson to J.W. Dunscombe, Stanstead, 4 Nov.
   1848, 15 Nov. 1848, 11 May 1849, vol. 340, RG16 A1.

109 Benjamin Seaton to Commissioner of Customs, Sutton, 4 Nov. 1846; Petition submitted by S.S. Foster, 8 Dec. 1846; draft memo to Dr Foster, MPP,
   vol. 346, RG16 A1.

110 J. Thompson to J.W. Dunscombe, Stanstead, 10 Nov. 1847, vol. 339;
   J. Thompson to J.W. Dunscombe, Stanstead, 16 July 1848, vol. 340;
   J. Thompson to R.S.M. Bouchette, Stanstead, 2 July 1851, vol. 341,
   J. Thompson to J.W. Dunscombe, Stanstead, 17 Nov. 1847, vol. 339; Peti-
   tion of Joseph Foord, 12 June 1851, vol. 341, RG16 A1.

111 J. Thompson to J.W. Dunscombe, Stanstead, 8 Oct., 5 Nov. 1845, vol. 339,
   RG16 A1.

112 J. Thompson to J.W. Dunscombe, Stanstead, 15 July, 3 Sept. 1846, vol. 339;
   F.J. Parker to J. Thompson, Georgeville, 17 Nov. 1850; J. Thompson to
   J.W Dunscombe, Stanstead, 19 Nov., 23 Dec. 1850, vol. 341, RG16 A1.

113 J. Thompson to J.W. Dunscombe, Stanstead, 28 Oct. 1845, vol. 339, RG16
   A1; State Book D, 115, 20 Jan. 1845, RG1 E1. For a description of the incident, see McIntosh, "Customs," 53–4.

114 J. Thompson to J.W. Dunscombe, Stanstead, 2 Apr. 1848; Aaron Workman
to J. Thompson, Hereford, 14 Nov. 1849, vol. 340, RG16 A1.

115 Andrew Patton to E. Hale, Stanstead, 19 Oct. 1843, HP. A year later, the
newly appointed customs collectors for Compton and Eaton would each be
paid $300 a year, though this sum was to cover the cost of office rent,
books, and blank forms. Unattached officers received no salary. State
Book C, 410, 5 June 1844, RG1 E1.

116 A. Patton and J. Young to J.W. Dunscombe, Stanstead, 19 Aug. 1846;
J. Thompson to J.W. Dunscombe, Stanstead, 17 Oct. 1846, vol. 339, RG16
A1, NA.

117 J. Thompson to J.W. Dunscombe, Stanstead, 31 July 1849, vol. 340,
RG16 A1.

118 J. Thompson to J.W. Dunscombe, Stanstead, 6 Aug. 1849, vol. 340;
J. Thompson to J.W. Dunscombe, Stanstead, 10 May 1850, vol. 341, RG16
A1; McIntosh, "Customs," 58.

119 Matthew Dixon to J.W. Dunscombe, Georgeville, 13 Dec. 1849;
W. McGowan to J.W. Dunscombe, Stanstead, 17 Dec. 1849; J. Thompson to
J.W. Dunscombe, Stanstead, 17 Dec. 1849, vol. 340, RG16 A1.

120 Report to Gov.-Gen. Elgin enclosed in Marcus Child and Benjamin
Seaton to J.W. Dunscombe, Stanstead Plain, 16 Mar. 1850, vol. 341,
RG16 A1.

121 J. Thompson to J.W. Dunscombe, Stanstead, 17 Feb. 1849, vol. 340, RG16
A1.

122 R. Vincent to Commissioner of Customs, Hereford, 10 Jan. 1853, vol. 122,
RG16 A1.

123 A. Workman to Commissioner of Customs, Hereford, 22 Dec. 1852,
vol. 122, RG16 A1.

124 R. Vincent to Commissioner of Customs, Hereford, 10 Jan. 1853; draft
memo to A. Workman, [n.d.], vol. 122, RG16 A1.

125 Affidavit of James Munn, JP, Hereford, 6 July 1853; affidavit of William
Rich, JP [n.d.], vol. 122, RG16 A1.

126 Affidavit of Geo. W. Hartshore, Port of Canaan, 6 July 1853, vol. 122, RG16
A1.

127 Petition … , 9 July 1853, vol. 122, RG16 A1.

128 R. Vincent to Commissioner of Customs, Hereford, 24 July 1853, vol. 122,
RG16 A1.

129 A. Workman to R.S.M. Bouchette, Hereford, 25 and 26 Sept. 1853,
vol. 122, RG16 A1.

130 E. Clark to R.S.M. Bouchette, Sherbrooke, 9 July 1853, vol. 122, RG16 A1.

131 A. Workman to R.S.M. Bouchette, Hereford, 25 and 26 Sept. 1853,
vol. 122, RG16 A1.

132 M. Child to R.S.M. Bouchette, Stanstead, 10 Sept. 1853; W.L. Felton to
A. Workman, Sherbrooke, 12 Sept. 1853; E. Clark to A. Workman,

Sherbrooke, 4 Oct. 1853; J. Thompson to R.S.M. Bouchette, Coaticook, 30 Sept. 1853, vol. 122, RG16 A1.

133 Draft memo, 9 Nov. 1853; draft memo, 27 Nov. 1853, vol. 122, RG16 A1.

134 No. 455, 1842, RG4 C1.

CHAPTER FOUR

1 See Gerald F. McGuigan, "La concession des terres dans les cantons de l'Est du Bas-Canada," *Recherches Sociographiques*, 4, no. 1 (1963): 71–89.

2 28 Sept., 3 Oct. 1799, 18–23, Newport, First Records, Province of Lower Canada, 1800, in possession of Lionel Hurd, Eaton Corner.

3 Ibid., 2 Sept. 1802, 43, 22 Nov. 1802, 45.

4 Ibid., 12 Sept. 1803, 46–50; 1 and 10 Aug. 1810, 81–4; Alain Baccigalupo, *Les administrations municipales québécoises des origines à nos jours: Anthologie administrative*, tome 1, *Les municipalités* (Montréal: Les Éditions Agence d'Arc, 1984), 53.

5 C.P. Lucas, ed., *Lord Durham's Report on the Affairs of British North America*, 3 vols. (Oxford at the Clarendon Press, 1912), vol. 3, 175, 191; Ivanhoë Caron, "Colonization of Canada under the British Dominion (from 1815 to 1822)," *Statistical Year Book* (Quebec: King's Printer, 1921), 538, 541.

6 J.H. Aitchison, "The Development of Local Government in Upper Canada, 1783–1850" (PhD thesis, University of Toronto, 1953), 230–1; George M. Betts, "Municipal Government and Politics, 1800–1850," in *To Preserve and Defend: Essays on Kingston in the Nineteenth Century*, edited by Gerald Tulchinsky (Montreal: McGill-Queen's University Press, 1976), 225–7.

7 See Lucas, ed., *Lord Durham's Report*, vol. 3, 177–8.

8 *Montreal Gazette*, 2 Feb. 1832.

9 Lucas, ed., *Lord Durham's Report*, vol. 3, 182.

10 Petition of inhabitants of District of St Francis, 53ff, vol. 549, RG4 A1, NA.

11 Kingsey Committee to Charles Buller, Esq., 30 May 1838, 184, vol. 543, RG4 A1.

12 D. Thomas to E. Hale, Melbourne, 2 Apr. 1840, HP, McCord Museum.

13 Carol Wilton-Siegel, "Administrative Reform: A Conservative Alternative to Responsible Government," *Ontario History* 78 (June 1986): 105–25.

14 *Missiskoui Standard*, 31 May 1836.

15 *Farmers' and Mechanics' Journal and St Francis Gazette*, 31 Aug. 1839; Charlotte Thibault, *Samuel Brooks, Entrepreneur et Homme Politique de Sherbrooke, 1793–1849* (Département d'Histoire, Université de Sherbrooke, 1985), 84–5.

16 Lucas, ed., *Lord Durham's Report*, vol. 3, 191.

17 Jacques Monet, *The Last Cannon Shot: A Study of French-Canadian Nationalism, 1837–1850* (Toronto: University of Toronto Press, 1969), 19.

18 Lucas, ed., *Lord Durham's Report*, vol. 3, 138, 144.

19 Ibid., 139, 227–8.

20 Ibid., 234–5.

21 The procès verbal described the road and named the persons appointed to make it and keep it in repair.

22 Lucas, ed., *Lord Durham's Report*, vol. 3, 231–3, 235–6.

23 Ibid., vol. 2, 92, 113.

24 Ibid., 114–15.

25 E.B. O'Callaghan to L.J. Papineau, Brooklyn, 10 Mar. 1848, vol. 3, p. 4344, Papineau Papers, MG24 B2, NA.

26 Quoted in Michael Ernest McCulloch, "The Defeat of Imperial Urbanism in Québec City, 1840–1855," *Urban History Review* 22, no. 1 (1993): 17.

27 Instructions for the use of Chairmen at Parish of Township Meetings, 1841, HP.

28 D. Daly quoting Sydenham in his letter to J.A. Lambly, 6 Sept. 1841, vol. 11, 17, Municipal Letter Book, Municipal Records 1694–1867, RG4 B36. RG4 B36, NA.

29 Edward Hale to E. Hale, Portneuf, 2 Sept. 1841, HP. See also the letter of 1 Oct. 1841.

30 A.D. DeCelles, "The Municipal System of Quebec," in *Canada and its Provinces*, vol. 15 (Toronto, 1914), 293; Baccigalupo, *Les administrations*, 66–7.

31 Minutes of the Proceedings of the Council for the Municipal District of Missisquoi [hereafter Missisquoi District Minutes], 7 Sept. 1841, vol. 6, 2314–25, RG4 B36.

32 Ibid., 2326–8, 2334.

33 Ibid., 2349–52.

34 Ibid., 2338–43, 2346, 2352.

35 William Baker to Civil Secretary, Dunham, 14 Sept. 1841, 2363–4; Missisquoi District Minutes, vol. 6, 2382, RG4 B36.

36 Missisquoi District Minutes, vol. 6, 2398; solicitor general's report, vol. 12, 23, Municipal Letter Books, RG4 B36.

37 Missisquoi District Minutes, vol. 6, 2387–8; note on solicitor general's report, 29 Jan. 1842, vol. 6, 2405; solicitor general's report, vol. 12, 22; William Baker to D. Daly, Dunham, 14 Sept. 1841, 2 Apr. 1842, vol. 6, 2364–3, 2434, RG4 B36.

38 Missisquoi District Minutes, vol. 6, 2400–1, 2416, 2424, 2426. RG4 B36.

39 William Baker to D. Daly, Dunham, 2 Apr. 1842, vol. 6, 2434–6, RG4 B36.

40 Missisquoi District Minutes, vol. 6, 2431–2; William Baker to D. Daly, Dunham, 2 Apr. 1842, vol. 6, 2435, RG4 B36.

41 On the popularity of these special assessments in Upper Canada, see Aitchison, "The Development of Local Government," 286–7.

42 Ibid., 293, 296–303.

43 E. Hale to Eliza, Kingston, 12 and 15 July 1841, HP; E. Hale to D. Daly, Kingston, 27 Aug. 1841, vol. 6, 2473, RG4 B36.

44 J.S. Walton to D. Daly, Sherbrooke, 16 Nov. 1841, vol. 6, 2494; E. Hale to
D. Daly, Sherbrooke, 20 Nov. 1841, vol. 6, 2498; E. Hale to D. Daly, Sherbrooke, 10 Sept. 1841, vol. 6, 2475, RG4 B36; Marie-Paule LaBrèque, "Jesse
Pennoyer," *DCB*, vol. 6; Bernard Epps, *The Eastern Townships Adventure, Volume 1: A History to 1837* (Ayer's Cliff, Que.: Pigwidgeon Press, 1992), 84–7,
138–4,152–7, 205–6.

45 Leonard S. Channell, *History of Compton County* (Cookshire, Que.: L.S. Channel, 1896; reprint Belleville, Ont.: Mika, 1975), 172–3; Thibault, *Samuel
Brooks.*

46 Instructions for the use of Chairmen, 1841, HP.

47 George Slack to E. Hale, Eaton (Woodcote Place), 27 Aug. and 15 Nov.
1841; Daniel Webster to E. Hale, Barnston, 13 Jan. 1842, HP.

48 Sherbrooke District Minutes, 8 Sept. 1841, 2477, 2481–4, RG4 B36.

49 E. Hale to Sir, Sherbrooke, 15 Nov. 1841, vol. 6, 2484, RG4 B36.

50 E. Hale to D. Daly, Sherbrooke, 15 Dec. 1841, vol. 6, 2500–1; Sherbooke District Council to Governor-General, 11 Dec. 1841, vol. 6, 2505; E. Hale to Sir,
Sherbrooke, 18 Dec. 1841, vol. 6, 2507–9, RG4 B36.

51 P. McGill to My Dear Sir, Montreal, 29 Dec. 1841, vol. 6, 2511–12, RG4 B36;
George Moffat [*sic*] to E. Hale, Montreal, 4 Jan. 1842, HP. For an analysis of
the British American Land Company's colonization activities, see J.I. Little,
*Nationalism, Capitalism, and Colonization in Nineteenth-Century Quebec: The
Upper St Francis District* (Kingston and Montreal: McGill-Queen's University
Press, 1989), chapter 2.

52 Memorial of undersigned inhabitants of township of Shipton, etc., Richmond, 18 Mar. 1840, 6904, no. 1785, 1839–40, RG4 C1. Drummond
County's MLA, R.N. Watts, later wrote that he supported the petitioners'
views. R.N. Watts to Secretary Daly, Kingston, 7 July 1841, 4618, no. 190,
1840–1, RG4 A1; G. Moffat, P. M'Gill and John Shuter of London to D. Daly,
Montreal, 29 Dec. 1841, vol. 6, 2513–17, RG4 B36.

53 S. Brooks to H. Black, Sherbrooke, 19 Feb. 1842, 10845–6; H. Black to
S. Brooks, Quebec, 28 Feb. 1842, 10847–8, no. 2079, 1846, RG4 C1.

54 Municipal Letter Books, vol. 12, 20–1; E. Hale to D. Daly, Sherbrooke,
5 Mar. 1842, vol. 6, 2528; Sherbrooke Council Minutes, vol. 6, 2533–5, RG4
B36; Petition of District Council of District of Sherbrooke to Sir Charles
Bagot, 1 Mar. 1842, vol. 9, 3618–25, RG7 G14, NA.

55 Sherbrooke Council Minutes, 8 June 1842, vol. 6, 2541–2, RG4 B36.

56 John Fraser to Metcalfe, Sherbrooke, 21 Sept. 1843, 6961, no. 1897, 1843,
RG4 C1; Leo A. Johnson, "Land Policy, Population Growth and Economic
Structure in the Home District, 1793–1851," in *Historical Essays on Upper
Canada*, edited by J.K. Johnson (Toronto: McClelland and Stewart, 1975),
48.

57 E. Hale to D. Daly, Kingston, 15 Sept. 1842, vol. 6, 2550; Thomas Tait to
D. Daly, Melbourne, 7 Dec. 1842, vol. 6, 2552, RG4 B36; Minutes of

Sherbrooke Council, 6 Dec. 1842, 7397–401, 1842, no. 1971; 6 June 1843, 7406–9, 1843, RG4 C1.

58 Memorandum on the District Council made by Edward Hale; Municipal Elections, 1844. Both documents are filed in the 1841 section of HP.

59 Seth Huntington to E. Hale, Hatley, 9 Jan. 1844; Asher Jones to E. Hale, Bury, 11 Jan. 1844, HP.

60 Ascot Township Records, p. 12, Bureau de municipalité d'Ascot; Hollis Smith to E. Hale, Lennoxville, 13 Jan. 1844; Asher Jones to E. Hale, Robinson, 13 Feb. 1844; Petition to E. Hale, Eaton, 15 Jan. 1845; P. Hubbard to E. Hale, Stanstead, 21 Jan. 1845, HP.

61 Petition by James Laing to Attorney-General East, Danville, 18 July 1844, 9904; James Laing to Metcalfe, Danville, 8 Aug. 1844, 9896–9, no. 2716, 1844, RG4 C1.

62 Alexander T. Galt to Metcalfe, Kingston, 20 Nov. 1843, vol. 1, RG4 C4, NA.

63 Aitchison, "The Development of Local Government," 293.

64 Quoted in Oscar Douglas Skelton, *The Life and Times of Sir Alexander Tilloch Galt* (Toronto: Oxford University Press, 1920), 132.

65 J.S. Walton to E. Hale, Sherbrooke, 16 Dec. 1844, HP (emphasis in original).

66 Edward Hale to C. Dunkin, Sherbrooke, 7 Feb. 1846, 1702, no. 394, 1846, RG4 C1; *JLAC*, vol. 5 (1846), appendix K, no. 15. Secretary J.S. Walton was still attempting to collect a claim of $790.03 nearly twenty years later, in 1862, and he added that Joseph Pennoyer was owed $200 as the district surveyor. J.S. Walton to A.T. Galt, Sherbrooke, 9 May 1862, 598, vol. 17, RG1 E5, NA.

67 E. Hale to Eliza Hale, Kingston, 15 Oct. 1843, HP.

68 A similar dynamic unfolded in the Quebec City Council. See McCulloch, "The Defeat of Imperial Urbanism," 17–29. On Sydenham's institution of a free-grants system along a colonization road south of Quebec and into the still vacant northeastern townships, see Little, *Nationalism, Capitalism*, 74–7.

69 Ernestine Charland-Rajotte, *Drummondville 150 ans de vie quotidienne au coeur du Québec* (Drummondville: Éditions des Cantons, 1972), 42–3.

70 C.F.J. Whebell, "Why Pembroke? The Politics of Selecting a County Capital in the Mid-Nineteenth Century," *Ontario History* 78, no. 2 (1986): 128.

71 James F. Brady to Col. Rowen, Durham, 23 Mar. 1838, 126, vol. 532; J.F. Brady to C. Buller, Durham, 16 Sept. 1838, 1, vol. 549, RG4 A1; R.N. Watts to Secretary Daly, Kingston, 17 June 1841, 3730, no. 966, 1840–41; Mrs E. Bready to D. Daly, Wickham Falls, 8 June 1843, 4171, no. 1263, 1843, RG4 C1. (Brady is also spelled Bready in some of these documents.)

72 James Brady to Civil Secretary, Drummondville, 31 Aug. 1841, 2028, vol. 6, Nicolet County, RG4 B36.

73 J. Brady to D. Daly, Drummondville, 9 Sept. 1841, 2042–3; Minutes of the Council Meeting, 7 and 9 Sept. 1841, 2072–4, 2043–5, vol. 6, RG4 B36.

74 K.C. Chandler to D. Daly, Nicolet, 17 Sept. 1841, 2050–7; Statistical information from the last census, 2122, vol. 6, RG4 B36.

75 Petition of A.N. Morin, MLA, and other members of the legislature, Quebec, 15 Nov. 1841, 2113–17, vol. 6, RG4 B36; J.I. Little, "Colonization and Municipal Reform in Canada East," *Histoire sociale/Social History* 14 (1981): 115–17; J.C. Langelier, *Lands Granted by the Crown, 1763–1890* (Quebec, 1891), 62, 75, 81–2, 101, 571, 602, 609–10; Petition from the City of Quebec to Bagot, Nov. 1841, 2119–37; T. Trigge to J. Neilson, Que., 19 Jan. 1842, 2143–4, vol. 6, RG4 B36.

76 J. Brady to C. Dunkin, Drummondville, 20 Nov. 1841, 2081, vol. 6, RG4 B36.

77 Quarterly meeting of District Council, Nicolet, 7 Dec. 1841, 2086–90, 2094; J. Brady to D. Daly, Drummondville, 11 Dec. 1841, 2098–01, vol. 6, RG4 B36.

78 R.N. Watts to D. Daly, Montreal, 7 Apr. 1841, 921–7, no. 232, 1840–41, RG4 C1; Petition of inhabitants of various places entered in margin within the District of Nicolet, 2109–10; J.B. David, Wm Robins, and James Miller to Secretary Daly, Drummondville, 7 Jan. 1842, 2111, vol. 6, RG4 B36.

79 Petition from divers citoyens de Montréal, 27 Jan. 1842, 2212; J.G. Barthe to Daly, Montreal, 24 Feb. 1842, 2215; K.C. Chandler to Bagot, Manor House, Nicolet, 4 Feb. 1842, 2193–04; printed circular signed by J. Jutras, Secretary of the Committee [n.d.], 2210, vol. 6, RG4 B36.

80 Brady's warrant, 28 Dec. 1841, 2171; W. Demers to J. Brady, St Pierre les Becquets, 19 Jan. 1842, 2168–9; J.B. Legendre to J. Brady, Gentilly, 20 Jan. 1841, 2160–1; J. Brady to D. Daly, Drummondville, 25 Jan. 1842, 2173–5; F. Ployart to M.T. Legendre, 2164–6; Testimonial of L. Genest, 26 Feb. 1842, 2243–5; J. Brady to Daly, Drummondville, 4 Mar. 1842, 2241–3; Report of J.G. Legendre, président, 2 Feb. 1842, 2247–8, vol. 6, RG4 B36.

81 Nicolet District Minutes, 1 Mar. 1842, 2227–33; Resolutions passed at third trimester meeting of Nicolet Council, 2218–19; G. Crépeau to D. Daly, Drummondville, 2 Mar. 1842, 2222, vol. 6, RG4 B36.

82 J. Brady to D. Daly, Drummondville, 4 Mar. 1842, 2237–9, vol. 6; Circular to Wardens of Saguenay, Berthier, Leinster, Nicolet, and Chaudière, 91–2, vol. 12, RG4 B36.

83 Resolutions passed at a session of the municipal council held at Drummondville, 7 June 1842, 2287–94, vol. 6, RG4 B36.

84 J. Brady to C. Dunkin, Drummondville, 10 Sept. 1842, 2297; J. Brady to D. Daly, Drummondville, 9 Dec. 1842, 2299, vol. 6, RG4 B36.

85 James Brady to D. Daly, Wickham Falls, 18 Jan. 1843, 488, no. 176; Mrs E. Brady to D. Daly, Wickham Falls, 8 June 1843, 4169, no. 1263, 1843, RG4 C1.

86 Report of Committee of Executive Council, 17 July, 3226; memo, 3224; William Pitt to D. Daly, St François, 9 Sept. 1844, 3225, 1844, RG4 C1.

87 *JLAC*, vol. 5 (1846), appendix K, no. 14.

88 *Quebec Gazette*, 1 Sept. 1841.

89 Quoted in Michael E. McCulloch, "English-Speaking Liberals in Canada East, 1840–1854" (PH.D. thesis, University of Ottawa, 1986), 150–1.

90 Petition of habitants and proprietors from Chaudière and Etchemin Rivers and Frampton Township, Beauce, Aug. 1841, 2971–4, vol. 7, Chaudière District, RG4 B36.

91 *JLAC*, vol. 1 (1841), appendix SS.

92 Francis Percy et al. to Gentlemen, Inverness, 30 July 1838, 1911–19, vol. 543; John Smith et al. to Sir, Inverness, 15 Dec. 1838, 236, vol. 559; John Smith et al. to George Futvoye, Inverness, 20 Jan. 1839, 129, vol. 566, RG4 A1.

93 Lambly would move to Leeds in 1844 where he would serve as county registrar until his death in 1863. For a brief biography, see Marion L. Phelps, "John Robert Lambly," *DCB*, vol. 9.

94 Arch.'d McKillop and nine others to D. Daly, Hamilton, Inverness, 23 Aug. 1841, vol. 7, 2979–80, RG4 B36.

95 Robert Cobban to Honourable Sir, Inverness, 28 Aug. 1841, vol. 7, 2986–93, RG4 B36.

96 A. McKillop to D. Daly, Hamilton, Inverness, 26 Aug. 1841, vol. 7, 2893–4, RG4 B36.

97 John Campbell to Sir, Inverness, the 11th Range, 24 Aug. 1841, 2995, vol. 7, RG4 B36.

98 Robert Cobban to D. Daly, Inverness Township, 13 Sept. 1841, 3014; John R. Lambly to D. Daly, Halifax, 30 Aug., 11 Sept. 1841, 3001–2, 3018–20, vol. 7, RG4 B36.

99 Robert Cobban to D. Daly, Inverness Township, 13 Sept. 1841, 3014–15, vol. 7, RG4 B36.

100 D. Daly to J. Lambly, confidential, 5 Oct. 1841, 30–1, vol. 11, RG4 B36.

101 Meeting of the District Council of Chaudière, 7 Sept. 1841, 3006–8; John R. Lambly to D. Daly, Halifax, 11 Sept. 1841, 3009, vol. 7, RG4 B36.

102 J. Lambly to D. Daly, Halifax, 27 Dec. 1841, 3045–8, vol. 7, RG4 B36.

103 See Aidan D. McQuillan, "Beaurivage: The Development of an Irish Ethnic Identity in Rural Quebec, 1820–1860," in *The Untold Story*, edited by Robert O'Driscoll and Lorna Reynolds (Toronto: Celtic Arts, 1988).

104 George Edwards to Murdoch, St Sylvester, 24 Jan. 1842, 3053–5, vol. 7, RG4 B36.

105 Edward Hayes Lindsay to D. Daly, St Mary's, Beauce, 28 Jan. 1842, 3060–3, vol. 7, RG4 B36.

106 J. Lambly to D. Daly, Halifax, 12 Mar. 1842, 3083–3, vol. 7, RG4 B36. The solicitor-general (p. 3084) informed Lambly that being a squatter was not among the disqualifications and exemptions named in the municipal act.

107 J. Lambly to D. Daly, Halifax, 5 Mar. 1842, 3067–8, vol. 7, RG4 B36.

108 Meeting of Council for the District of Chaudière, 7 June 1842, 3089–91, vol. 7, RG4 B36.
109 J. Lambly to D. Daly, Halifax, 25 July 1842, 3085–6, vol. 7, RG4 B36.

CHAPTER FIVE

1 D. Thomas to E. Hale, Melbourne, 3 June 1843; J.M. Taylor to E. Hale, Melbourne, 25 March 1845, HP, McCord Museum.
2 E. Hale to Eliza, Kingston, 21 Oct. 1843, HP; *SPC*, 8 Vict., cap. 40.
3 J. Anderson to E. Hale, Richmond, 25 Nov. 1843, J.S. Walton to E. Hale, Sherbrooke, 16 Dec. 1844; Samuel Brooks to E. Hale, Sherbrooke, 30 April 1845; Thomas Tait to E. Hale, Melbourne, 1 Nov. 1843; B. Pomroy to E. Hale, Compton, 19 March 1845, HP.
4 The minutes are located in the Ascot municipal office and the other records are in the ETRC archives. Both collections extend beyond the 1840s.
5 Edward Hale to D. Daly, Sherbrooke, 19 Sept. 1845, 12827–9; J.S. Walton to D. Daly, Sherbrooke, 16 Sept. 1845, 12824–6, no. 2642, 1845, RG4 C1, NA.
6 First session, 21 and 24 July 1845, 17–21, Township Record – Ascot, Bureau de municipalité d'Ascot [hereafter Ascot minutes].
7 Ascot minutes, 1 Sept. 1845, 37–9; 24 July 1845, 22; 28 July 1845, 25–8.
8 Ibid., 8 Aug. 1845, 29; 14 Aug. 1845, 32; 1 Sept. 1845, 35.
9 Ibid., 12 Sept. 1845, 41–2; 15 Sept. 1845, 46. The councillors still did not resolve the problem of what exact path the road would take without a good deal more debate. See minutes for 17 Oct. 1845, 51; 18 Oct. 1845, 53–4; 21 Oct. 1845, 54; 15 Nov. 1845, 57; 1 Dec. 1845, 58; 16 Mar. 1846, 67.
10 Ibid., 12 Sept. 1845, 48; 27 Oct. 1845, 54–5; 26 and 27 Dec. 1845, 58–60.
11 Ibid., 12 and 15 Sept. 1845, 44–7.
12 J.S. Walton to E. Hale, Sherbrooke, 12 Apr. 1846; 12 May 1846, HP.
13 Road Surveyor's Report, Dist. No. 2, June 1846, Municipality of Ascot Fonds, P095/001/002, ETRC.
14 Ascot minutes, 15 Sept. 1845, 47; 1 Dec. 1845, 59.
15 At least two councils, Eaton and Shipton, would pass a number of the same resolutions, in addition to making some additions of their own. Memorial of Members of Eaton Council and others of Eaton municipality [n.d.], 5077–8, no. 921; Petition of Municipal Council of Shipton, 6 Apr. 1846, 6670–3, no. 1233, 1846, RG4 C1.
16 *Stanstead Journal*, 22 Jan. 1846.
17 Ascot minutes, 7 Sept. 1846, 75; 1 March 1847, 79.
18 Ibid., 27 Sept. 1845, 48–9; 24 Jan. 1846, 64; 15 May 1847, 80; 17 June 1847, 81; 26 Aug. 1847, 86.
19 *Stanstead Journal*, 4, 11 and 25 Dec. 1845, 22 Jan. 1846.

20 Ibid., 5 and 12 Feb. 1846.

21 E. Clark to C. Dunkin, Sherbrooke, 6 Apr. 1846, 6913–14; Avery Greene to E. Clark, Compton, 4 Apr. 1846, 6915, no. 1269; E. Clark to C. Dunkin, Sherbrooke, 13 Apr. 1846, 7291; E. Clark to C. Dunkin, Sherbrooke, 8 June 1846, no. 1378, 1846, RG4 C1; *Stanstead Journal*, 11 June 1846, 25 Feb. 1847.

22 See, for examples, the complaint by "One of the People" in *Stanstead Journal*, 8 June 1848; and R.N. Watts to Secretary of Province, Drummondville, 6 Mar. 1847, no. 506, 1847, RG4 C1.

23 Petition to D. Daly, Tingwick, 26 Aug. 1845, 12242, no. 2492, 1845, RG4 C1.

24 School commissioners of Bury Township to Dr Meilleur, Bury, 17 July 1845, 14422, no. 3012; Memorial of inhabitants of Bury to Metcalfe, Bury, 30 July 1845, 14463–4, no. 3012; Nathaniel Ebbs to D. Daly, Bury, 9 Sept. 1845, 14470–1, no. 3012, 1845, RG4 C1.

25 H. McClintock to D. Daly, Robinson, 2 Sept. 1845, 14465–9; government memo, 16 Oct. 1845, 14461–2, no. 3012, 1845, RG4 C1.

26 Petition of inhabitants of Lingwick, 2 June 1845, 8605–9, no. 1737, 1845, RG4 C1.

27 John Ingram to Metcalfe, rec'd 23 July 1845, 9988, no. 2143, 1845, RG4 C1.

28 S.S. Foster to D. Daly, 17 July 1845, 9811; Petition of freeholders inhabitants of Milton, 16 July 1845, 9813–14, no. 2104, 1845, RG4 C1.

29 Petition of electors of Milton Township, Milton, 20 Aug. 1846, 15017–18; S.S. Foster to D. Daly, Aug. 1846, 15016; memo to S.S. Foster, 3 Sept. 1846, no. 2913, 1846, RG4 C1.

30 Daniel McMillan to D. Daly, Milton, 19 May 1847, no. 1475, 1847, RG4 C1, NA.

31 Nathan Parker and Abijah Willard to D. Daly, Stukely, 19 Mar. 1847; Petition of inhabitants of five southern ranges, lots 1–5, Stukely, 13 Mar. 1847; Petition of inhabitants of Stukely, Stukely, 16 Mar. 1847; S.S. Foster to D. Daly, Frost Village, 1847 [only date given]; S.S. Foster to D. Daly, 20 Apr. 1847, no. 704, 1847, RG4 C1.

32 Louis Richard to C. Dunkin (private), Stanfold, 31 July 1845, 11027–30, no. 2242, 1845. An earlier letter penned by Richard stated that only one of the councilors was a squatter, but only two were qualified. Louis Richard, Jos. Girouard, and F.X. Pratte to D. Daly, Stanfold, 24 July 1845, 11024–6, no. 2242, 1845, RG4 C1.

33 Petition of Somerset landowners, 5 July 1845, 9736–7, no. 2091, 1845, RG4 C1.

34 Chas. E. Bélanger to Monsieur, Somerset, 15 July 1845, 9738–9, no. 2091, 1845, RG4 C1.

35 Charles E. Bélanger to Civil Secretary, Somerset, 10 Aug. 1845, 9742–3, no. 2091; Petition of curé, marguillers, commissaires, etc., 9 Aug. 1845, 9744–5, 1845, RG4 C1.

36 Petition of Joseph Juneau, St Norbert, 8 May 1847; Joseph Juneau, j.p., et al. to Civil Secretary, St Norbert, 26 July 1847; Attorney-General Badgely to D. Daly, Montreal, 27 May 1847, no. 2555, 1847, RG4 C1.

37 Wm Hall to D. Daly, Broughton, 24 July, 4 Oct. 1845, 11943; Report of the Executive Council, 11 Nov. 1845, 11945–6; memo, Nov. 1845, 11941–2, no. 2417, 1845, RG4 C1.

38 Wm Hall to D. Daly, Broughton, 30 July 1846, 14018; 2 Sept. 1846, 14019; D. Daly to Hall, 17 Sept. 1846, 14021, no. 2737, 1846, RG4 C1.

39 Walter Hargrave to D. Daly, Inverness, 16 July 1845, 10124–5, no. 2173, 1845, RG4 C1.

40 Memorial of Donald McLean to Governor-General, n.d., no. 3260, 1847, RG4 C1.

41 *Stanstead Journal*, 22 Jan. 1846, 20 May, 3 June 1847.

42 Edward Tourneaux to E. Hale, Melbourne, 24 Nov. 1847, HP; *Stanstead Journal*, 18 Nov. 1847.

43 *SPC*, 10 & 11 Vict., cap. 7.

44 Stanstead Journal, 16 Sept., 7 Oct., 4 Nov. 1847; William Morris to D. Daly, Lennoxville, 15 Sept. 1847, no. 3189; John Bellows to D. Daly [n.d.], no. 3294; D. Thomas to D. Daly, Melbourne, 13 Sept. 1847; L. Ford to D. Daly, Philipsburg [n.d.], no. 3329; Patrick McCabe to D. Daly [n.p.], 18 Sept. 1847, no. 3333; Lemuel Pope to D. Daly, Bury, 16 Sept. 1847, no. 3333, 1847, RG4 C1.

45 John Bothwell to D. Daly, Durham, 15 Sept. 1847; B. Smith to D. Daly, Durham, 15 Sept. 1847; memo to J. Bothwell, 23 Sept. 1847, no. 3176, 1847, RG4 C1.

46 W. Badgley to D. Daly, Montreal, 19 Nov. 1847, no. 4296; Charles Prince et al. to D. Daly, Somerset, 18 Sept. 1847, no. 3370; Petition of J. Juneau and three others, 14 Sept. 1847, no. 3484; Petition from Chester, no. 3485, 1847; Thomas Sheridan to D. Daly, Halifax, 18 Sept. 1847, no. 3383; Peter C. Lord, Ireland, 13 Sept. 1847, no. 3384, 1847, RG4 C1.

47 *Stanstead Journal*, 30 Dec. 1847, 20 Jan. 1848, 14 Sept. 1848.

48 Petition of inhabitants of Town of Sherbrooke and vicinity [n.d.], no. 574; Presentment of Grand Jury, District of St Francis, Queen's Bench, 14 Jan. 1849, no. 151. Thirty inhabitants of Stanstead Township presented a petition to the same effect. Stanstead Township, 10 Jan. 1849, no. 768, 1849, RG4 C1.

49 Draft response to Galt, 2 Dec. 1848; A.T. Galt to J. Leslie, Sherbrooke, 18 Dec. 1848, no. 3298, 1848, RG4 C1; Oscar Douglas Skelton, *Life and Times of Sir Alexander Tilloch Galt* (Toronto: Oxford University Press, 1920), 47–8.

50 Petition of Alden Plumley of Hatley Township, 8 Feb. 1849, no. 601, 1849, RG4 C1; Stanstead Journal, 20 Dec. 1849, 21 Mar. 1850.

51 *Stanstead Journal*, 16 Mar., 13 Apr. 1848.

52 Ibid., 1 June 1848.

53 Ibid., 8 June, 21 Sept. 1848.

54 Ibid., 11 July, 26 Dec. 1850, 20 Mar., 27 Mar. 1851. Basically the same issue remained unsettled in Shefford County as late as 1851. H.L. Robinson, secretary-treasurer, Shefford, Mar. 1851, no. 604, 1851, RG4 C1.

55 *Stanstead Journal*, 21 Dec. 1848.

56 Ibid., *Stanstead Journal*, 27 June 1850. This incident is explored further in *The Georgeville Enterprise* 3, no. 2 (Winter 1995).

57 *Stanstead Journal*, 19 June, 16 Oct. 1851.

58 Returns of Elections, Municipal Councillors, 1849–50, no. 2227, 1849, RG4 C1.

59 William Vondenvelden and John Wadleigh to Provincial Secretary, Kingsey, 10 Jan. 1850, no. 112, 1850, RG4 C1.

60 Returns, Elections of Mayors and Secretary-Treasurers in Municipalities, no. 404, 1850; no. 1733, 1851; no. 1492, 1851; Petition from Halifax, New Ireland, Somerset, Inverness, and Wolfestown, Halifax, 29 May 1850, no. 1352, 1850; Petition of Lambton, Price, Forsyth, and Tring, St Vital de Lambton, 10 Jan. 1849, no. 1352, 1850, RG4 C1.

61 Dunbar Ross to J. Leslie, Que., 13 Apr. 1851, no. 1591; Dunbar Ross to editor, 20 May 1851, press clipping, *Quebec Gazette*, no. 1591, 1851; James Burray and James Aylwin to Dunbar Ross, Leeds, 22 Aug. 1851; endorsed by John R. Lambly, j.p., John Hume, j.p., et al., no. 1591, 1851, RG4 C1.

62 Etienne Pomerleau et al. to J. Leslie, Tring, 5 Sept. 1851; Proclamation re clause 34, 13 & 14 Vict., cap. 34, 7 Nov. 1851, no. 1591, 1851, RG4 C1.

63 Petition of inhabitants of Windsor, etc., received 27 Feb. 1849, no. 1352, 1850, RG4 C1; *SPC*, 13 & 14 Vict., cap. 34.

64 *Stanstead Journal*, 11 Sept. 1851.

65 *SPC*, 14 & 15 Vict., cap. 98.

66 Petition of Sherbrooke Municipal Council for continuation of present municipal system, *JLAC*, vol. 11 (1852–53), xcix.

67 Boutillier's proposal is printed in the appendix to the Special Report of the Special Committee, *JLAC*, vol. 10 (1851).

68 *Stanstead Journal*, 15 May, 19 June 1851; Memorial of inhabitants of Shipton, Melbourne, and vicinity, Sherbrooke County, 20 July 1851, no. 1272, 1851, RG4 C1.

69 *Stanstead Journal*, 19 June 1851. The post would re-emerge in a considerably diluted form in 1855 under the name of county superintendent, a position which would be abolished three years later. For details on the 1855 municipal act and the subsequent amendments, see J.I. Little, "Colonization and Municipal Reform in Canada East," *Histoire sociale/Social History* 14 (1981) 105–7.

70 *JLAC*, vol. 10 (1851), 320, 331; *Stanstead Journal*, 11 Sept. 1851.

71 There are a number of these petitions from the Bois-Francs and surrounding townships filed with no. 974 and no. 1352, 1850; and no. 871 and no. 872, 1851, RG4 C1.
72 Presentment of Grand Jury, District St Francis, 14 Feb. 1852, no. 381, 1852, RG4 C1.
73 *Stanstead Journal,* 30 Oct. 1851.
74 Ibid., 27 Nov. 1851.
75 Ibid., 12 Feb. 1852.
76 On the positive impact of the 1855 act on the Bois-Francs, see Little, "Colonization and Municipal Reform," 108–17.
77 *Stanstead Journal,* 16 Nov. 1848.

CHAPTER SIX

1 Wendie Nelson, "The 'Guerre des Éteignoirs': School Reform and Popular Resistance in Lower Canada, 1841–1850" (MA thesis, Simon Fraser University, 1989), 13–16.
2 This number was calculated from various pages throughout Réal G. Boulianne, "The Royal Institution for the Advancement of Learning: The Correspondence, 1820–1829, A Historical and Analytical Study" (PH.D. thesis, McGill University, 1970).
3 Andrée Dufour, "La scolarisation au Bas-Canada, 1826–1859: Une interaction état-communautés locales" (PH.D. thesis, Université du Québec à Montréal, 1992), 61–3.
4 Dufour, "La scolarisation," 70–2, 74–5, 97–9, 118.
5 Sir Charles Lucas, ed., *Lord Durham's Report on the Affairs of British North America,* 3 vols. (Oxford: Clarendon Press, 1912), vol. 3, 256, 262–4. For a detailed summary of Buller's report, see Louis-Phillippe Audet, *Le système scolaire de la Province de Québec,* vol. 6, *La situation scolaire à la veille de l'Union 1836–1840* (Québec: Les Éditions de l'Érable, 1956), chapter 4.
6 Lucas, ed., *Lord Durham's Report,* vol. 3, 254; Louis-Phillippe Audet and Armand Gauthier, *Le système scolaire du Québec: organisation et fonctionnement* (Montréal: Librairie Beauchemin, 1967), 10–11; André Laberrère-Paulé, *Les instituteurs laïques au Canada Français, 1836–1900* (Québec: Les Presses de l'Université Laval, 1965), 95–101.
7 Dufour, "La scolarisation," 72. The bishops remained adamantly opposed to the Assembly schools even after the clergy were permitted to be trustees without holding land, and to act as school visitors. Nelson, "'Guerre des Éteignoirs,'" 20; Richard Chabot, *Le curé de campagne et la contestation locale au Québec de 1791 aux troubles de 1837–38* (Montréal: Hurtubise HMH, 1975), 60–3.
8 Fifteenth Report, County of Sherbrooke, Robert Armour, Jr, School Visitor, Sherbrooke, 1 Apr. 1840, vol. 14, RG4 B30, NA [hereafter Armour Report], 2. Armour reported on schools thoughout Lower Canada in 1839–40.

9 Armine W. Mountain (comp.), *A Memoir of George Jehoshaphat Mountain, D.D., D.C.L.* (Montreal: John Lovell, 1866), 142.

10 Audet, *Le système scolaire*, 6:37; Labarrère-Paulé, *Les instituteurs*, 23.

11 Proposals for educational reform in Lower Canada, by Stephen Randall, pp. 712–20, MG24 A27, NA.

12 Serge Gagnon. "L'école élémentaire québécoise au XIXᵉ siècle," in *La culture inventée; Les stratégies culturelles aux 19ᵉ et 20ᵉ siècles*, edited by Pierre Lanthier and Guildo Rousseau (Québec: Institut Québécois de Recherche sur la Culture, 1990), 149.

13 Henry Leslie Rennie, "History of Education in the Eastern Townships" (MA thesis, Bishop's University, 1930), 28. The number of students in the province as a whole dropped from almost 42,000 in 1831 to approximately 30,000 in 1833. Andrée Dufour, "Financement des écoles et scolarisation au Bas-Canada: une interaction état-communautés locales (1826–1859)," *Historical Studies in Education* 6, no. 2 (1994): 231.

14 Allan Greer, "The Pattern of Literacy in Quebec, 1745–1899," *Histoire sociale/Social History* 11 (1978): 321; Dufour, "La scolarisation," 72.

15 Audet, *Le système scolaire*, 9–12; Labarrère-Paulé, *Les instituteurs*, 464–5.

16 Armour Report, 62; Dufour, "La scolarisation," 130. Based on Buller's report, Dufour estimates that half the schools in Lower Canada closed between 1836 and 1838 (129).

17 Lucas, ed., *Lord Durham's Report*, vol. 3, 287. According to Hunte, a pamphlet by lawyer Charles-Joseph Mondelet was "the real source of inspiration behind the Common School Act of 1841." K.D. Hunte, "The Development of the System of Education in Canada East, 1841–1867, an Historical Survey" (MA thesis, McGill University, 1962), 77. However, Mondelet's scheme provided for more clerical influence than Buller would have allowed.

18 The "assistant" would be dropped from Meilleur's title in 1845. Léon Lortie, "Jean-Baptiste Meilleur," *DCB*, vol. 10.

19 Nelson, "'Guerre des Éteignoirs,'" 47–8; Audet and Gauthier, *Le système scolaire*, 16–17; Labarrère-Paulé, *Les instituteurs*, 109. In the original draft of this bill, prepared by Solicitor General East Charles Dewey Day, most of the responsibilities lay with a government-appointed, five-member board of examiners for each municipal district. Reformers in committee ensured that this centralizing measure was dropped. Bruce Curtis, *Building the Educational State: Canada West, 1836–1871* (London, Ont.: Althouse Press, 1988), 52–5.

20 Petition of the District Council of the District of Sherbrooke to Sir Charles Bagot, 1 Mar. 1842, vol. 9, 3624, Governor General's Correspondence, RG7 G14, NA.

21 J.S. Sabins to Meilleur, Sherbrooke, 9 June 1843, no. 172, LR, E13, ANQQ.

22 J.S. Sabins to Meilleur, Sherbrooke, 19 Sept. 1843, no. 224, LR, E13.

23 Lucas, ed., *Lord Durham's Report*, vol. 3, 253, 256–9; Dufour, "Financement des écoles," 228; Gagnon, "L'école élémentaire,"149.

24 Lucas, ed., *Lord Durham's Report*, vol. 3, 278–9.

25 *JLAC*, vol. 3 (1843), appendix Z; Lucas, ed., *Lord Durham's Report*, vol. 3, 279–80; Labarrère-Paulé, *Les instituteurs*, 34–6; Dufour, "La scolarisation," 148.

26 Meilleur's Report, 10 July, 7 Nov. 1843, *JLAC*, vol. 3 (1843), appendix Z.

27 Ibid., 16 June 1847, *JLAC*, vol. 6 (1847), Appendix FF.

28 Outside the municipal districts of Missisquoi and Sherbrooke, only one other township in the region received a school grant. The eight schools in Durham Township (Nicolet District) each received £20, while nothing was granted to the six schools in Kingsey (also in Nicolet), four in Halifax, two in Leeds, and one in Inverness (all in the Chaudière District).

29 *JLAC*, vol. 3 (1843), appendix Z.

30 J. Bureau to Meilleur, Sherbrooke, 17 Apr. 1844, no. 666, LR, E13.

31 W. Wilson et al. to Meilleur, Ascot, 7 Oct. 1843, no. 289, LR, E13. See also W. Wilson to Edward Hale, Lennoxville, 8 Sept. 1843, HP, McCord Museum.

32 J.S. Sabins to Meilleur, Sherbrooke, 19 Sept. 1843, no. 224; J.S. Walton to Meilleur, Sherbrooke, 20 Sept. 1843, no. 226, LR, E13.

33 Meilleur to Sir Charles Metcalf [*sic*], 31 May 1844, no. 454, art. 136, LE, E13.

34 Donald McRay to Meilleur, Bury, 8 Mar. 1844, newspaper clipping in no. 758, LR, E13.

35 Rev. C.P. Reid to Meilleur, Compton, 1 Feb. 1843, no. 139; J.S. Sabins to Meilleur [no date], no. 163; Meilleur to J.S. Sabins, 5 July 1843, art. 136, no. 68, LE, E13. Meilleur also thanked Walton for the support offered by the *Sherbrooke Gazette*, and asked several times for copies of the newspaper. Meilleur to J.S. Walton, 7 Oct. 1843, no. 96; 30 Jan. 1844, no. 198, art. 136, LE, E13.

36 Rev. C.P. Reid to Meilleur, Compton, 1 Feb. 1843, no. 139, LR, E13; *SPC*, 9 Vict., cap. 27, s. 27.

37 J. Cook to Meilleur, 14 Dec. 1844, no. 1080, LR, E13; *SPC*, 12 Vict., cap. 50, s. 19.

38 *JLAC*, vol. 3 (1843), appendix Z; Petition of District Council of District of Sherbrooke to Sir Charles Bagot, 1 Mar. 1842, 3623, vol. 9, RG7 G14.

39 Dufour, "La scolarisation," 225, 228; Meilleur to J. Bureau, 24 Apr. 1844, no. 383, art. 136, LE, E13.

40 Minutes of the Missisquoi District Municipal Council, 5 Mar. 1842, 2431, vol. 6, RG4 B36, NA; petition of District Council of District of Sherbrooke to Sir Charles Bagot, 1 Mar. 1842, 3625, vol. 9, RG7 G14; Inhabitants of Compton Township to Metcalfe, 4 Oct. 1843, 8841, no. 2287, RG4 C1; *JLAC*, vol. 3 (1843), appendix Z.

41 Meilleur's Report, 10 July and 7 Nov. 1843, *JLAC*, vol. 3 (1843), appendix Z.

42 Ibid., 18 Nov. 1844, *JLAC*, vol. 4 (1844–5).

43 Minutes of the Missisquoi District Municipal Council, 5 Mar. 1842, 2429; 9 Sept. 1842, 2462–3, vol. 6, RG4 B36.

298 Notes to pages 182–8

44 The decline in Barnston and Barford was four, Compton four, Eaton and Newport four, Shipton seven, Melbourne three, and Westbury, Bury, and Lingwick two.

45 Annual Report to the Superintendent of Education by the Municipal Council of the Sherbrooke District, for the year ending 31st December 1842, no. 141, LR, E13.

46 George J. Mountain to Bishop Stewart, Quebec, 22 Mar. 1830, Eastern Townships Visitation, G.J. Mountain, case 2, folder 13, QDA, ETRC.

47 Andrew Balfour to Meilleur, Waterloo, 5 Aug. 1844, no. 287; Joshua Foss to Meilleur, Eaton, 8 July 1845, no. 1719, LR, E13.

48 On this issue, see Marta Danylewycz, Beth Light, and Alison Prentice, "The Evolution of the Sexual Division of Labour in Teaching: A Nineteenth-Century Ontario and Quebec Case Study," *Histoire sociale/Social History* 16 (1983): 89, 93–4, 97–8, 103.

49 The average for Canada East was higher than that for Canada West in 1846–47. Dufour, "La scolarisation," 207.

50 Dufour ("La scolarisation," 307–10) tends towards the former conclusion for Canada East based on the inspectors' reports of the 1850s, while Labarrère-Paulé (*Les instituteurs*, 133, 179) accepts the contemporary complaint that women were undermining teaching as a profession in the province.

51 27 Nov. 1845, 30 June 1846, School Commission Minute Book, Municipality Township of East Farnham, 1845–74, Brome County Historical Society Archives.

52 no. 142, no. 122, LR, E13.

53 Contract between John McGregor and Chester B. Cleveland, 10 Oct. 1835, Greffe Daniel Thomas, n.p., ANQS.

54 Jos. B. Smith to Meilleur, Eaton, 24 Apr. 1844, no. 676, LR, E13.

55 Labarrère-Paulé, *Les instituteurs*, 135. According to Meilleur, the boundaries of amalgamated school districts no longer had to conform to those of municipal unions. J.B. Meilleur to Edward Hale, Montreal, 9 Aug. 1845, HP.

56 Rather than being fixed at 1s. 3d. per student, this sum now became the maximum, with commissioners empowered to charge less for younger children, or according to the ability of parents to pay and the nature of the program offered. Dufour, "La scolarisation," 158–9.

57 Meilleur to Dr John E. Bangs of Stanbridge, 2 Oct. 1845, no. 1167; Meilleur to Dudswell school commissioners, 25 Sept. 1845, no. 1151; Meilleur to Compton school commissioners, 23 Oct. 1845, no. 2387, art. 137, LE, E13.

58 Minutes of the Ascot Municipal Council, 17–18 Oct. 1845, 51, 53, Township Records, Ascot, Bureau de municipalité d'Ascot.

59 M. Child to My Dear Wife, Leg. Ass., 24 Nov. 1843, from J.I. Little, *The Child Letters: Public and Private Life in a Canadian Merchant-Politician's Family, 1841–1845* (Montreal and Kingston: McGill-Queen's University Press, 1995), 119–20.

60 James Reid to Edward Hale, St Armand East, 13 Feb. 1845, HP.

61 Petition signed by D. Wood, chairman, and M. Dougherty, secretary, Shefford, December 1845, no. 2595, LR, E13; *Stanstead Journal,* 1 Jan. 1846.

62 Rev. J. Anderson to Meilleur, 30 July 1845, no. 2054, LR, E13.

63 *JLAC,* vol. 5 (1846), appendix P; vol. 3, (1843), appendix Z; J. Green et al. to District Council, Barnston, 30 Nov. 1842, no. 142, LR, E13.

64 G.J. Mountain to Bishop Stewart, Quebec, 22 Mar. 1830, Eastern Townships Visitation, G.J. Mountain, case 2, folder 13, QDA, ETRC; *The Christian Messenger,* 1844, p. 21, UCA, Victoria University. In 1837 another New Connexion missionary reported that local schools were open as "preaching houses" to "all denominations of the church." *Methodist New Connexion Magazine,* 3rd series, vol. 6 (1838), 74, UCA, Victoria University.

65 J. Donald Wilson, "The Ryerson Years in Canada West," in J. Donald Wilson, Robert M. Stamp, and Louis-Philippe Audet, *Canadian Education: A History* (Scarborough, Ont.: Prentice-Hall, 1970), 222; and Susan E. Houston and Alison Prentice, *Schooling and Scholars in Nineteenth-Century Ontario* (Toronto: University of Toronto Press, 1988), 121.

66 *JLAC,* vol. 4 (1844–5), appendix Z.

67 Meilleur to Shefford school commissioners, 5 July 1844, art. 136, no. 510, LE; C.P. Reid to Meilleur, Compton, 20 Feb. 1846, no. 166, LR, E13.

68 Jos. Scott to Meilleur, Brome, 16 Oct. 1847, no. 1303, LR, E13.

69 Meilleur to Rev. Reid, 24 Feb. 1846, no. 120, art. 105, LE, E13.

70 H. Robinson to Meilleur, Waterloo, 4 May 1844, no. 689, LR, E13.

71 Meilleur to gentlemen, 15 May 1844, no. 414, art. 136, LE; H. Robinson et al. to Meilleur, Shefford, 15 June 1844, no. 835, LR, E13.

72 Meilleur to Shefford school commissioners, 20 June 1844, no. 490, art. 136, LE, E13.

73 Labarrère-Paulé, *Les instituteurs,* 137; Dufour, "La scolarisation," 258–61, 167–70, 270–1, 273.

74 Nelson, "'Guerre des Éteignoirs'," 54–5; Labarrère-Paulé, *Les instituteurs,* 140–1; *SPC,* 9 Vict., cap. 27, s. 38. The correspondence to and from Meilleur includes a number of references to teachers' salaries being paid partly or wholly in produce. E.g. Meilleur to Philip N. Smith of Stanstead, 22 Aug. 1845, no. 137, art. 136, LE; J.S. Walton to Meilleur, Sherbrooke, no. 95, LR, E13.

75 Prior to 1856 teachers could choose instead to be examined by the local school commissioners. Nelson, "'Guerre des Éteignoirs'," 55; Dufour, "La scolarisation," 195–8.

76 The table published for the last six months of 1846 in the 1847 volume of the *JLAC* records more townships and parishes without schools than does the table for the same time period in the 1848 volume. Within the Eastern Townships all the later additions but one were for townships in Sherbrooke County.

77 Meilleur to Melbourne school commissioners, 25 Aug. 1846, no. 439, art. 105, LE; Melbourne school commissioners to Meilleur, 7 Nov. 1846, no. 1398, LR, E13.

78 Melbourne school commissioners to Meilleur, 18 Aug. 1847, no. 1064; 15 July 1847, no. 835; 20 Sept. 1847, no. 1192, LR; Meilleur to W.R. Doak, 23 Aug. 1847, no. 635; 25 Sept. 1847, no. 728, art. 107, LE; Melbourne school commissioners to Meilleur, 10 oct. 1848, no. 1271, LR, E13.

79 A. Wooler to Meilleur, 4 Feb. 1847, no. 311, LR; Meilleur to A. Wooler, 24 May 1847, no. 383, art. 108, LE, E13.

80 Meilleur to Samuel McCullogh, 4 Sept. 1846, no. 468, art. 105; Meilleur to W.J. Chapman, 5 Aug. 1848, no. 479, art. 110, LE, E13; *JLAC*, vol. 10 (1851), appendix KK.

81 M. Child to Meilleur, Stanstead, 17 Aug. 1846, no. 989, LR; Meilleur to Marcus Child, 21 Aug. 1846, no. 434, art. 105, LE, E13.

82 M. Child to Meilleur, Stanstead, 25 Aug. 1846, no. 1056, LR; Meilleur to Marcus Child, 3 Sept. 1846, no. 464, art. 105, LE, E13.

83 *Stanstead Journal*, 17 Sept., 29 Oct. 1846; D. Mack to Meilleur, Stanstead, 5 Dec. 1846, no. 1539, LR, E13.

84 M. Child to Meilleur, Stanstead, 12 Jan. 1847, no. 81; D.W. Mack to Meilleur, Stanstead, 30 June 1847, no. 727, LR, E13; Petition of Board of School Commissioners, Stanstead Township, 10 Sept. 1847; Report of J.B. Meilleur, Montreal, 9 Oct. 1847, no. 3629, RG4 C1; Meilleur to D.W. Mack, 12 July 1847, no. 478, art 108, LE, E13.

85 C. Bullock to Meilleur, Georgeville, 2 Feb. 1848, no. 94, LR; Meilleur to C. Bullock, 11 Feb. 1848, no. 86, art. 109, LE, E13.

86 See, for example, Meilleur to Dr S.S. Foster, 20 Feb. 1844, no. 256, art. 136; Meilleur to David Connell, Esq., 9 Dec. 1847, no. 899, art. 107, LE, E13.

87 Meilleur to D.W. Mack, 10 Dec. 1847, no. 900, art. 107, LE, E13.

88 D.W. Mack to Meilleur, Stanstead, 4 Dec. 1847, no. 1444; 19 June 1848, no. 577; 1 Sept. 1848, no. 131; 2 July 1849, no. 691, LR; Meilleur to D.W. Mack, 23 June 1848, no. 350, art. 109, LE; M. Child to Meilleur, 20 Jan. 1853, no. 158, LR, E13; *Stanstead Journal*, 28 Sept. 1848.

89 James Green to Meilleur, Barnston, 4 Apr. 1848, no. 287, LR; Meilleur to Barnston school commissioners, 10 Nov. 1846, no. 686, art. 106, LE, E13.

90 See J.I. Little, "The Short Life of a Local Protest Movement: The Annexation Crisis of 1849–50 in the Eastern Townships," *Journal of the Canadian Historical Association* (1992), 55.

91 James Green to Meilleur, Barnston, 7 Dec. 1846, no. 1624; 4 Apr. 1848, no. 287, LR, E13.

92 *Stanstead Journal*, 31 Dec. 1846.

93 Ibid., 21 Jan., 11 Mar. 1847.

94 Ibid., 18 Jan. 1849.

95 James Green to Meilleur, Barnston,10 Jan. 1848, no. 27, LR, E13; *JLAC*, vol. 6 (1847), 167.
96 James Green to Meilleur, Barnston, 4 Apr. 1848, no. 287, LR; Meilleur to James Green, 6 Apr. 1848, no. 206, art. 109, LE, E13.
97 James Green to Meilleur, Barnston, 1 Sept. 1849, no. 1272, LR; Meilleur to Barnston school commissioners, 15 Jan. 1850, no. 35, art. 138, LE, E13; *Stanstead Journal*, 20 June 1850.
98 Edward Hale to Meilleur, Sherbrooke, 7 Sept. 1846, no. 1097, LR, E13.
99 Meilleur to E. Hale, 10 Sept. 1846, no. 479, 22 Sept. 1846, no. 529, art. 105, LE, E13.
100 J.S. Walton to Meilleur, Sherbrooke, 14 Jan. 1847, no. 95; 28 Sept. 1848, no. 1220, LR, E13.
101 Hatley school commissioners to Meilleur, 24 Sept. 1846, no. 1206, LR, E13.
102 Eaton school commissioners to Meilleur, 10 July 1847, no. 757, LR, E13.
103 *Stanstead Journal*, 20 Jan. 1848.

CHAPTER SEVEN

1 K.D. Hunte, "The Development of the System of Education in Canada East, 1841–1867, an Historical Survey" (MA thesis, McGill University, 1962), 40–4. Founded in England in 1823, the Newfoundland Society broadened its name and mandate to British North America in 1834. J.W. Netten, "The Anglican Church: Its Influence on the Development of Education in the Province of Canada, from 1760–1900" (M Ed. thesis, Bishop's University, 1965), 151–3.
2 It appears that in the post-1836 interim only one school in the Megantic County area was kept open by local initiative. Francis Percy to Gentlemen, Inverness, 30 July 1838, 1911–19, vol. 543; John Smith et al., to Sir, Inverness, 15 Dec. 1838, 236, vol. 559; John Smith et al. to George Futvoye, Inverness, 20 Jan. 1839, 129, vol. 566, RG4 A1; vol. 16A, Statistical Reports on Schools, 1843, RG4 B30, NA.
3 Report by J. Lambly for Chaudière District, 1 May 1843, *JLAC*, vol. 3 (1843), appendix Z; 10 (1851), appendix KK; Meilleur to Messire L.E.A. Dupuis, 14 Dec. 1847, no. 906, art. 107, LE, E13, ANQQ.
4 Robert Layfield et al. to Meilleur, 8 May 1846, no. 359; Inverness school commissioners to Meilleur, 30 Nov. 1846, no. 1522, LR, E13.
5 Report of J.S. Clarke, inspector, 28 June 1852, *JLAC*, vol. 11 (1852–3), appendix JJ.
6 Ireland school commissioners to Meilleur, 4 Jan. 1847, no. 66, LR, E13.
7 John Hough to Meilleur, 9 Dec. 1847, no. 1459, LR, E13.
8 Meilleur to Rev. L.H. Simpson, 14 Oct. 1850, no. 308, art. 139, LE, E13; Report of J.S. Clarke, 28 June 1852, *JLAC*, vol. 11 (1852–3), appendix JJ.

9 See W.O. Rothney, "Schools in the Township of Leeds, County of Megantic, One Hundred Years Ago," *The Educational Record of the Province of Quebec* (Dec. 1941), 295–8.

10 John Corbett et al. to Meilleur, 17 Apr. 1850, no. 628; J. Hume to Meilleur, 20 Jan. 1851, no. 259, LR, E13.

11 *JLAC*, vol. 11 (1852–3), appendix JJ; J. Hume to Meilleur, 4 Sept. 1851, no. 1602; J. Hume to Meilleur, 17 Jan. 1852, no. 112, LR, E13.

12 Meilleur to Sir Charles Bagot, 2 Nov. 1842, no. 10; Meilleur to Sir Charles Metcalfe, 28 May 1844, no. 445, art. 136, LE, E13.

13 Donald McRay to Meilleur, Bury, 8 Mar. 1844, newsclipping, no. 758, LR, E13; Edward Hale to J.B. Meilleur, Sherbrooke, 27 Mar. 1844, HP, McCord Museum; Petition to Metcalfe, n.d., 14426–9, no. 3012, 1845, RG4 C1, NA.

14 Edward Hale to J.B. Meilleur, Sherbrooke, 22 Mar. 1844, HP; Meilleur to Hon. Edward Hale, 23 Mar. 1844, no. 332, art. 135, LE, E13; J.B. Meilleur to governor-general, Montreal, 28 May 1844, 14447–55, no. 3012, 1845, RG4 C1.

15 H. McLintock to Meilleur, Bury, 29 Apr. 1844, no. 684; Meilleur to Hon. D. Daly, 28 May 1844, no. 444, art. 136, Departmental note, 27/31 Oct. 1845, no. 2430, LR, E13; Lemuel Pope, Sr and John Martin to J.B. Meilleur, Bury, 27 Oct. 1845, 14409; Petition of school commissioners of Bury municipality to Metcalfe, Robinson, 12 Nov. 1845, 14412–14, no. 3012, 1845, RG4 C1.

16 United townships of Bury, Westbury, and Lingwick to Meilleur, May 1845, no. 1508; W. King et al. to Meilleur, Robinson, 9 June 1845, no. 1604; W. King and Henry W. Taylor to Meilleur, Robinson, 19 June 1845, no. 1605, LR, E13; Report of J.B. Meilleur, Montreal, 15 Aug. 1845, no. 3012, 1845, RG4 C1.

17 Nath. Ebbs to Meilleur, Robinson, 21 July 1846, no. 762, LR, E13. The school commisioners of Lingwick and Bury had operated independently of each other even though they had been in the same school district from the start. Meilleur to James Ross, 3 Oct. 1846, no. 563, art. 105, LE, E13.

18 James Ross to Meilleur, Lingwick, 17 Dec. 1846, no. 189, LR, E13.

19 F. Martin and Nath. Ebbs to Meilleur, Robinson, 23 Mar. 1847, no. 422, LR, E13.

20 Meilleur to school commissioners, 2 Apr. 1847, no. 257, art. 108, LE; J. Peabody and John Dorman to Meilleur, Bury, 1 July 1850, no. 1101, LR, E13.

21 Meilleur to school commissioners, 19 May 1850, no. 392, art. 139, LE, E13.

22 Meilleur to school commissioners, 23 Jan. 1851, no. 87; Meilleur to H. McLintock, 8 May 1851, no. 425; Meilleur to school commissioners, 6 June 1851, no. 492, art. 139, LE, E13.

23 Report of M. Child, inspector, 16 Apr. 1853, *JLAC*, vol. 11 (1853), appendix JJ.

24 Hunte, "The Development," 84–6, 110–11; *Statutes of the Province of Canada*, 9 Vict., cap. 27, s. 26.

25 Hunte, "The Development," 142; 12 Vict., cap. 50, s. 18.

26 Meilleur thereby earned the enmity of John Dougal's *Montreal Witness*, but Hunte ("The Development," 128–32, 161) to the contrary, there is little evidence in the school correspondence to suggest that the Eastern Townships resented Meilleur as a tool of the Catholic Church.

27 Meilleur to Amos Hall, jr. et al., 1 Apr. 1845, no. 766, art. 137, LE, E13.

28 John Hough to Meilleur, Ireland Township, 15 Dec. 1845, no. 2586, LR; Meilleur to Ireland school commissioners, 23 Dec. 1845, no. 1331, art. 137, LE, E13.

29 J.B. Vincent to Meilleur, Kingsey Township, 10 Feb. 1843, no. 149. LR, E13.

30 Meilleur to Rev. John Butler, 22 May 1844, no. 425; Meilleur to Rev. Robson, 23 May 1844, no. 429, art. 136, LE, E13.

31 Meilleur to Kingsey school commissioners, 1 June 1844, no. 456; Meilleur to Messire H. Robson, 1 June 1844, no. 458, art. 136, LE, E13.

32 Kingsey commissioners to Meilleur, 5 May 1845, no. 1515, LR, E13.

33 Meilleur to Rev. Charles Tardif et al., 27 Mar. 1845, no. 752, art. 136, LE, E13.

34 Meilleur to J.B. Blanchard and G.H. Browne, 19 Aug. 1845, nos. 1007 and 1008; Meilleur to Messire Tardif, 28 Aug. 1845, no. 1054; Meilleur to Rev. Butler, 28 Aug. 1845, no. 1056, art. 136, LE, E13.

35 Meilleur to Rev. John Butler, 17 Oct. 1845, no. 1208, art. 136, LE; Kingsey Protestants to Meilleur, 23 May 1846, no. 362, LR, E13.

36 Wendie Nelson, "The 'Guerre des Éteignoirs': School Reform and Popular Resistance in Lower Canada, 1841–1850" (MA thesis, Simon Fraser University, 1989), 73–85, 95.

37 Report of M. Child, inspector, 16 Apr. 1853; Report of the Select Committee appointed to inquire into the state of Education in Lower Canada, Rev. Paradis, St Félix de Kingsey, *JLAC*, vol. 11 (1852–3), appendix JJ.

38 Report of the Select Committee appointed to inquire into the state of Education in Lower Canada, Rev. Trahan, Shipton, *JLAC*, vol. 11 (1852–3), appendix JJ; Canada, *Census Reports*, 1851–2.

39 Meilleur to Damase Marcotte, 10 Sept. 1845, no. 1108, art. 137, LE, E13.

40 Meilleur to Milton school commissioners, 24 July 1846, no. 348, art. 105; Meilleur to M. Legendre, 10 Apr. 1851, no. 330, art. 139, Meilleur to C. Gillespie, 10 Mar. 1852, no.214, art. 140, LE, E13.

41 Sir Charles Lucas, ed., *Lord Durham's Report on the Affairs of British North America*, 3 vols. (Oxford: Clarendon Press, 1912),vol. 3, 277–9.

42 See the petitions listed in *JLAC*, vol. 1 (1841): e.g., p. 35, W. King and settlers of Bury and Lingwick; p. 69, clergymen and members of Church of England of St Armand; p. 95, inhabitants of Charleston, Hatley, and its neighbourhood; p. 164, clergymen and members of Church of England in

Melbourne; p. 165, Rev. A. Balfour and other residents of Shefford Township; p. 233, A.A. Adams and others, Stanstead Township; p. 365, Rev. S.C. Fraser and others, Inverness Township; p. 388, Rev. Jos. Anderson and others, members of Congregational Church of Melbourne and vicinity.

43 Nelson, "'Guerre des Éteignoirs'," 53, 56, 66; André Labarrère-Paulé, *Les instituteurs laïques au Canada Français, 1836–1900* (Québec: Les Presses de l'Université Laval, 1965), 136, 140.

44 Victor Chabot to Dominick Daly, Somerset, 30 Aug. 1843; Pierre Bruneau to Dominick Daly, Maddington, 1 Sept. 1843, vol. 1, RG4 C4, NA.

45 James Goodhue to Meilleur, Bulstrode, 17 July 1843, no. 179; Clovis Gagnon to Meilleur, St Norbert d'Arthabaska, 22 July 1846, no. 923, LR, E13.

46 P.N. Pacaud to Meilleur, 15 Mar. 1847, no. 378, LR, E13.

47 Pierre Dufour and Gérard Goyer, "Philippe-Napoléon Pacaud," *DCB*, vol. 11.

48 P.N. Pacaud and P.Z. Belliveau to Meilleur, St Norbert d'Arthabaska, 13 May 1847, art. 298, LR, E13; affidavits of François D. Baril, constable, 26 Dec. 1846, 5 Jan. 1847; affidavit of Zoël Belliveau et al., Arthabaska, 5 Jan. 1847; Petition of School Commissioners of Arthabaska, Arthabaska, 5 Jan. 1847; E.L. Pacaud to D. Daly, Trois-Rivières, 11 Jan. 1847, no. 103, 1847, RG4 C1.

49 E.L Pacaud to J. Smith, Trois-Rivières, 11 Jan. 1847, no. 103, 1847, RG4 C1.

50 Petition of proprietors and residents of Arthabaska Township, 24 Mar. 1847. The same petition was dated the same day in English by 204 inhabitants of Durham Township. nos. 742, 743, RG4 C1.

51 Petition of inhabitants of Arthabaska [n.d.], no. 1907, 1847, RG4 C1.

52 P.N. Pacaud to Meilleur, Trois-Rivières, 12 June 1847, no. 245, LR, E13.

53 P.N. Pacaud and P.Z Belliveau to Meilleur, St Norbert d'Arthabaska, 13 May 1847, no. 548, LR, E13. The curé was not necessarily attempting to remain aloof from the issue, since clerics had automatically become school visitors with the 1846 school bill.

54 Meilleur to certain inhabitants of St Norbert d'Arthabaska, 15 June 1847, art. 108, no. 420; 3 Aug. 1847, art. 108, no. 569; Alary Roi to Meilleur, Arthabaska, 12 Apr. 1849, no. 430, LR, E13; Meilleur to Clovis Gagnon, 28 Jan. 1848, no. 20, art. 108, LE, E13.

55 E. Bélanger et al. to Meilleur, Somerset, 19 July 1845, no. 2007, art. 291, LR, E13.

56 Charles Prince to D. Daly, Somerset, 4 Mar. 1847, no. 536, 1847, RG4 C1.

57 Louis Richard to Provincial Secretary, Stanfold, 10 Feb. 1851, no. 136, RG4 C1.

58 There were twenty-seven boys and twenty-eight girls in the two schools. Annual reports from Somerset Township for 1845, no. 61 and 100, LR, E13.

59 Petition of Somerset school commissioners, [1846], no. 1654, LR, E13.

60 Meilleur to Charles E. Bélanger, 20 Aug. 1845, no. 1033, art. 137, LR, E13.

61 O. Cormier to Meilleur, Somerset, 20 Apr. 1847, no. 509; F.L. Poudrier et al. to Meilleur, [June 1847], no. 615; Report of Somerset School Commission, 10 June 1847, no. 616, LR, E13.

62 Meilleur to O. Cormier, 5 May 1847, no. 344, art. 108, LE; F.L. Poudrier to Meilleur, Hotel de Québec [Montreal], 29 Sept. 1847, no. 1230, LR, E13.
63 F.L. Poudrier et al. to Meilleur, Somerset, 10 Nov. 1847, no. 1407; 16 July 1849, no. 922, LR, E13.
64 Report of the Select Committee appointed to inquire into the state of Education in Lower Canada, Rev. Dorion, Drummondville, *JLAC*, vol. 11 (1852–3), appendix JJ.
65 Report of J.S. Clarke, inspector, 10 Oct. 1852, *JLAC*, vol. 11 (1852–3), appendix JJ.
66 Affidavit, St Victor de Tring, 20 Oct. 1847, no. 1343; Z. Bertrand to Meilleur, St Victor de Tring, 11 July 1849, no. 832; 10 Nov. 1849, no. 1704, LR, E13.
67 Alexi Poulin to Meilleur, Tring, 13 July 1847, no. 1070; Z. Bertrand to Meilleur, St Victor de Tring, 29 June 1849, no. 700; Meilleur to Messire Provancher, 5 Feb. 1849, no. 83, art. 138, LE; Z. Bertrand to Meilleur, St Victor de Tring, no. 832, LR, E13. Such conflicts of interest were not unknown in the English-speaking districts as well. See Meilleur to S.S. Foster, 6 Feb. 1845, no. 717, art. 137, LE, E13.
68 Report of J.S. Clarke, inspector, 10 October 1852, *JLAC*, vol. 11 (1852–3), appendix JJ.
69 Nelson, "'Guerre des Éteignoirs'," chapter 5.
70 *SPC*, 12 Vict., cap. 50, ss. 24–5.
71 Ibid., sect. 4.
72 *Stanstead Journal*, 15 Feb. 1849.
73 Meilleur to S.A. Hurd, 17 Aug. 1849, no. 548, art. 138. LE, E13.
74 Circular no. 12, 4 June 1849, *JLAC*, vol. 9 (1850), appendix U; Meilleur to Alfred Rogers, 12 Jan. 1851, no. 32, art. 139, LE, E13.
75 A.M. Delisle to LaFontaine, 2 Nov. and 4 Nov. 1850, MG24 B14, NA.
76 Meilleur to LaFontaine, Montreal, 29 Nov. 1850, MG24 B14; *JLAC*, vol. 9 (1850), 156.
77 J. Harold Putman, *Egerton Ryerson and Education in Upper Canada* (Toronto: William Briggs, 1912), 153.
78 J. Donald Wilson, "The Ryerson Years in Canada West," in J. Donald Wilson, Robert M. Stamp, and Louis-Philippe Audet, *Canadian Education: a History* (Scarborough, Ont.: Prentice-Hall, 1970), 224.
79 Andrée Dufour, "Financement des écoles et scolarisation au Bas-Canada: une interpétation état-communautés locales (1826–1859)," *Historical Studies in Education* 6, no. 2 (1994): 246–51.
80 L. Giard to LaFontaine, Bureau de l'Éducation, 30 July 1850, MG24 B14; David Connell to Meilleur, 17 Oct. 1850, no. 1769; J. Green to Meilleur, 23 Sept. 1850, no. 610, LR, E13.
81 *Stanstead Journal*, 8 Aug. 1850.
82 Ibid., 15 May 1851.
83 Ibid., 3 July 1851.

84 Andrée Dufour, "La scolarisation au Bas-Canada, 1826–1859: Une inter-action état-communautés locales" (PH.D. thesis, Université du Québec à Montréal, 1992), 258, 267–9, 276–7.
85 Louise Lapicerella, "Le groupe anglophone du Québec et l'éducation, 1840–1870" (MA thesis, Université du Québec à Montréal, 1980), 112, 177.
86 *JLAC*, vol. 11 (1852–3), appendix JJ.
87 Circular no. 9 to school commissioners, 15 June 1846, *JLAC*, vol. 7 (1848), appendix P.
88 Meilleur to Edward Hale, 14 June 1844, no. 482, art. 136, LE, E13.
89 Meilleur to D.W. Mack, 19 Dec. 1847, no. 900, art. 107; Meilleur to James Green, 27 Sept. 1850, no. 820, art. 139, LE, E13.
90 Petition, Compton, 25 Jan. 1849, no. 377; Petition of Trustees of Compton Township Academy, 9 May 1850, no. 1238, RG4 C1.
91 Report of Rotus Parmelee, inspector, 21 July 1852, *JLAC*, vol. 11 (1852–3), appendix JJ.
92 Melbourne school commissioners to Meilleur, 30 June 1851, no. 986, LR, E13. See also the correspondence in nos. 1506, 1513, 1730 and 1790, 1851, RG4 C1.
93 Meilleur to C. French, 16 July 1851, no. 613, art. 139, LE, E13.
94 Memorial Complaint and Petition of a Majority of Freeholders of Mel-bourne, 12 July 1851, no. 1230, LR, E13.
95 Melbourne school commissioners to Meilleur, 9 Sept. 1851, no. 1642, LR, E13.
96 James R. Laing to J. Leslie, Melbourne, 10 Nov. 1851; draft reply, Que., 18 Nov. 1851, no. 1790, 1851, RG4 C1.
97 Meilleur to W. Lloyd, 19 Nov. 1851, no. 1050, art. 140, LE, E13; *JLAC*, vol. 11 (1852–3), appendix JJ.
98 Meilleur to James Green, 27 Sept. 1850, no. 820, art. 139, LE; J. Green to Meilleur, Barnston, 7 Oct. 1850, no. 1702, LR, E13.
99 J. Green to Meilleur, Barnston, 18 Nov. 1850, no. 1997; 29 Jan. 1851, no. 323; 6 Mar. 1851, no. 490.5; 17 May 1852, no. 670, LR, E13; *JLAC*, vol. 11 (1852–3), appendix JJ.
100 F. Poudrier et al. to Meilleur, Somerset, 10 Aug. 1849, no. 1115; 2 July 1850, no. 910, LR, E13; *JLAC*, vol. 10 (1851), appendix kk.
101 Wm Ritchie to Civil Secretary Murdoch, Stanstead Plain, 18 Apr. 1840, 13925, no. 6096, 1839–40, RG4 C1.
102 Petition of proprietors of a superior English School in Marlow District of S.W. quarter of Stanstead Township, Stanstead, 31 Mar. 1840, 6868, no. 1775, 1839–40, RG4 C1.
103 Louis-Philippe Audet, *Le système scolaire du Québec: organisation et fonctionne-ment* (Montréal: Librairie Beauchemin, 1967), vol. 6, 20–4; *JLAC*, vol. 1 (1841), 129, 174; vol. 2 (1842), 25, 33.

104 Petition of Andrew Balfour, Waterloo, 23 July 1841, 5300–1, no. 1370, 1840–41;14196–7, no. 3758, 1844, RG4 C1.

105 Anne Drummond, "From Autonomous Academy to Public 'High School': Quebec English Protestant Education, 1829–1889" (MA thesis, McGill University, 1986), 16; Wilson, "The Ryerson Years," 225.

106 Return of Rev. Jos. Anderson for Richmond Academy, 1841, RG4 B30, NA. According to Drummond, senior students' education reflected their masters' special interests and training ("From Autonomous Academy," 23).

107 Meilleur to Wm Lloyd, 30 Jan. 1844, no. 200, art. 136, LE, E13.

108 Stanstead Journal, 25 Feb. 1847.

109 Jacques Monet, The Last Cannon Shot: A Study of French-Canadian Nationalism, 1837–1850 (Toronto: University of Toronto Press, 1969), 246.

110 JLAC, vol. 6 (1847), appendix CC; vol. 9 (1850), appendix C, no. 20; Stanstead Journal, 19 Aug. 1847; D.C. Masters, "Jasper Nicolls and English Protestant Education in Canada East," in His Own Man. Essays in Honour of Arthur Reginald Marsden Lower, edited by W.H. Heick and Roger Graham (Montreal: McGill-Queen's University Press, 1974), 156.

111 Stanstead Journal, 19 Aug. 1847, 16 Nov. 1848, 29 Nov. 1849, 5 June 1851.

112 Ibid., 16 Nov. 1848, 22 Feb.,16 Aug., 6 Sept. 1849. In 1851 the principal reported that about fifteen of his students had become teachers. Ibid., 20 Feb. 1851.

113 Drummond, "From Autonomous Academy," 27–8, 34; JLAC, vol. 11 (1852–3), appendix JJ; J.I. Little, The Child Letters: Public and Private Life in a Canadian Merchant-Politician's Family, 1841–1845 (Montreal and Kingston: McGill-Queen's University Press, 1995), 34–5.

114 Stanstead Seminary grant application, 16 May 1850, no. 1163, 1850, RG4 C1; Report of M. Child, inspector, 16 Apr. 1853, JLAC, vol. 11 (1853), appendix JJ.

115 Report of R. Parmelee, inspector, 10 Mar. 1853, JLAC, vol. 11 (1852–3), appendix JJ.

116 Petition of Trustees of Charleston Academy to Metcalfe, Hatley, 28 Sept. 1843, 7524, no. 1946, 1843; Petition of Trustees of Stanstead Seminary, 4 Dec. 1844, 14093–4, no. 3729, 1844, RG4 C1; Henry Leslie Rennie, "History of Education in the Eastern Townships" (MA thesis, Bishop's University, 1930), 49–50.

117 Bruce Curtis, "Mapping the Social: Notes from Jacob Keefer's Educational Tours, 1845," Journal of Canadian Studies 28, no. 2 (1993): 65.

118 Arch'd McKillop to A. Buller, Hamilton Inverness, 19 Nov. 1838, 85, vol. 555, RG4 A1.

119 J.S. Sabins to Meilleur, Sherbrooke, 19 Sept. 1843, no. 224, LR, E13; JLAC, vol. 3 (1843), appendix Z.

120 J. Anderson to E. Hale, Melbourne, 23 July 1847, HP.

121 Circular no. 12, 4 June 1849, JLAC, vol. 9 (1850), appendix U.

122 T. Crémazie to Jos. Cauchon, 29 Apr. 1851, MG24 B14.

123 Dufour, "La scolarisation," 243, 247, 283–5, 295.

124 *JLAC*, vol. 11 (1852–3), appendix JJ; Labarrère-Paulé, *Les instituteurs*, 145–6.

125 R.D. Gidney and D.A. Lawr, "The Development of an Administrative System for the Public Schools: The First Stage, 1841–50," in *Egerton Ryerson and His Times*, edited by Neil McDonald and Alf Chaiton (Toronto: Macmillan, 1978), 173–4. For a conflicting interpretation, see Bruce Curtis, *True Government by Choice Men? Inspection, Education, and State Formation in Canada West* (Toronto: University of Toronto Press, 1992), 98–100.

126 Rennie, "History of Education," 97; Report of R. Parmelee, inspector, 10 Mar. 1853, *JLAC*, vol. 11 (1852–3), appendix JJ.

127 Dufour, "La scolarisation," 250–7.

128 M. Child to Meilleur, Stanstead, 15 June 1853, no. 788, LR, E13.

129 Report of M. Child, 31 July 1853, *JLAC*, vol. 11 (1852–3), appendix JJ. The deadline for appearing before the board of examiners had been moved back from 1856, as had originally been required by the 1846 school bill. *SPC*, 12 Vict., cap 50, s. 29.

130 Report of R. Parmelee, inspector, 10 Mar. 1853, *JLAC*, vol. 11 (1852–3), appendix JJ. Two months later, a new law provided for seven additional examining boards, including one in Stanstead and one in Sherbrooke. Dufour, "La scolarisation," 304.

131 In Farnham East the school commissioners appointed committees of three to manage schools which they as individuals were not in charge of. School Commission Minute Book, Municipality Township of East Farnham, 1845–74, Brome County Historical Society Archives.

132 Reports of R. Parmelee, inspector, 21 July 1852, 10 March 1853, *JLAC*, vol. 11 (1852–3), appendix JJ.

133 Labarrère-Paulé, *Les instituteurs*, 169–70; Rev. Dorion's testimony in the Report of the Select Committee appointed to inquire into the state of education in Lower Canada, L.V. Sicotte, chairman, *JLAC*, vol. 11 (1852–53), appendix JJ.

134 Report of J.S. Clarke, inspector, 28 June 1852, *JLAC*, vol. 11 (1852–3), appendix JJ.

135 Rev. Roe's testimony in the Report of the Select Committee appointed to inquire into the state of Education in Lower Canada, *JLAC*, vol. 11 (1852–3), appendix JJ.

136 Quoted in Hunte, "The Development," 159.

137 Inspector Parmelee noted in 1853 that even in his more prosperous district, the school commissions' lack of such a power "has seriously embarrassed several Municipalities in which there are large tracts of unoccupied lands, on which rates are due." *JLAC*, vol. 11 (1852–3), appendix JJ.

138 Meilleur to Rev. Reid, 1 Feb. 1843, art. 136, no 56, LE, E13.

139 The issue of American school texts was a heated one in Canada West. See James Love, "Cultural Survival and Social Control: The Development of a Curriculum for Upper Canada's Common Schools in 1846," *Histoire sociale/Social History* 15, no. 30 (1982): 357–82; and Bruce Curtis, "Schoolbooks and the Myth of Curricular Republicanism: The State and the Curriculum in Canada West, 1820–1850," ibid., 16, no. 32 (1983): 305–29.

140 See Anne Drummond, "Sydney Arthur Fisher and the Limits of School Consolidation in Brome County, 1901–1921," *Journal of Eastern Townships Studies*, 3 (1993): 31–47. Other factors which undermined rural community control of the schools in late nineteenth-century Ontario are discussed in R.D. Gidney and W.P.J. Millar, "Rural Schools and the Decline of Community Control in Nineteenth-Century Ontario," *Fourth Annual Agricultural History of Ontario Seminar Proceedings* (1979), 70–91.

CONCLUSION

1 See Jean-Pierre Charland, "Le reseau d'enseignment public Canadien, 1841–1867: Une institution de l'état libéral," *RHAF* 40 (1987): 505–35.

2 Greg Marquis, "Doing Justice to 'British Justice': Law, Ideology and Canadian Historiography," in *Canadian Perspectives on Law & Society: Issues in Legal History*, edited by W. Wesley Pue and Barry Wright (Ottawa: Carleton University Press, 1988), 44.

3 Rusty Bitterman, "Agrarian Alternatives: The Ideas of the Escheat Movement in Prince Edward Island, 1832–42" (paper presented to the annual meeting of the Canadian Historical Association, 1990), 29. Bitterman is referring particularly to Michael Cross's interpretation in "The Laws Are Like Cobwebs: Popular Resistance to Authority in Mid-Nineteenth Century British North America," in *Law in a Colonial Society: The Nova Scotia Experience*, edited by Peter Waite et al. (Toronto: Carswell, 1984).

Index